The Rolls of the 1281 Derbyshire Eyre

The Rolls of the

1281 Derbyshire Eyre

Edited by Aileen M. Hopkinson
with an Introduction by David Crook

Derbyshire Record Society
Volume XXVII, 2000

Published by the Derbyshire Record Society
57 New Road, Wingerworth, Chesterfield S42 6UJ

First published 2000

ISBN 0 946324 23 9

Printed by Dinfewr Press Ltd
Rawlings Road, Landybïe
Carmarthenshire SA18 1YD

CONTENTS

The Eyre

Appendices

ACKNOWLEDGEMENTS

I would like to express my thanks to Philip Riden and the Derbyshire Record Society for entrusting this work to me.

Particular thanks must go to the facilities offered at the Keele University summer schools in Latin and medieval palaeography instituted by Denis Stuart, now retired, who first encouraged me to step backwards from sixteenth- and seventeenth-century handwriting and to revive my Latin. Throughout I have been encouraged by Dr David Crook, the most friendly and approachable of mentors, who fed my growing interest in judicial history, first suggested a topic to focus that interest and set my feet on the way.

In the later stages of preparation thorny problems presented by incompatibilities between word-processing applications were expertly ironed out by Geoffrey Amos.

Nor must I forget my husband, who has given the constant behind the scenes support which only a sympathetic partner can afford and, *'nisi per quem'* (as the writ would say), I am 'of Derbyshire'.

June 2000   Aileen M. Hopkinson

INTRODUCTION

The general eyre

The expression 'general eyre' is a modern term coined as a convenient way of describing the occasional visits by royal justices to an English county to hear all the kinds of pleas which belonged to the jurisdiction of the king. The term is useful in distinguishing these sessions from those held by royal justices with a more limited jurisdiction, such as justices of assize, who held assizes to deal with disputes over the possession of land or other property, or justices of gaol delivery, who tried all the prisoners awaiting trial in the county gaol. These activities, as well as many others, were carried out by justices in eyre as a matter of course whenever they visited a particular county. Those responsible for organising an eyre or carrying it out, and who were living when the system of general eyres was at its height in the middle of the thirteenth century, knew it rather as the eyre 'for all pleas', or 'for common pleas', the latter to distinguish it from the sessions of the justices for forest pleas, who held forest eyres in counties, like Derbyshire, which included royal forests.

During the thirteenth century a general eyre in a particular county usually took place as part of a programme of visits to most of the counties in England, arranged in a number of geographical circuits and carried out in each circuit by a group of justices appointed for the purpose and under a recognised chief justice. Such programmes seem to have begun, as a regular event, during the reign of Henry II, and the decision to hold them was taken at the highest political level, by the king on the advice of his council. During the thirteenth century a decision to hold eyres over the country as a whole, or even occasionally in one or a few counties, was a matter of extreme political as well as legal significance.

Derbyshire eyres, 1194–1269

The king's justices who arrived in a county to hold a general eyre did so by holding what was in some senses simply a special session of the county court of that county. Derbyshire was unique among English counties in this period in that until 1256 it had no separate county court of its own, meeting on its own territory. It was in a position of subordination to neighbouring Nottinghamshire, with which it shared a sheriff, who was based at Nottingham castle, until 1567. Arrangements whereby neighbouring counties shared a sheriff were common in medieval England, but the arrangement by which Derbyshire shared a joint county court with Nottinghamshire, and which met at Nottingham, was unknown elsewhere. Between 1194, the date of the first surviving record of an eyre relating to Derbyshire, and 1256, when a separate Derbyshire county court was created, eleven general eyres were held jointly for the two counties. They were in October 1194, about November 1198, June to July 1202, November 1208, February to May 1219, September to October 1226, June to July 1232, September to October 1236, February 1240, June to July 1245, and April to May 1252. All of them were, as far as is known, held at Nottingham, with the single exception of that for 1208, which was held at Derby. After 1256 separate eyres for Derbyshire were held at Derby in January to February 1258, and April to May 1269.

Most of what little is known about them comes from final concords, formal agreements written in Latin on parchment, which recorded the settlement of civil cases in the eyre. They have survived mostly in the form of feet of fines, the court's own copy of the agreements, which were preserved in the Exchequer treasury at Westminster and survive in some numbers for all Derbyshire eyres from 1202 onwards. For the 1258 Derbyshire eyre, for example, there are 33, of which 23 relate to Derbyshire properties. The eyres of 1252 and 1258 were noticed by the monastic chronicler of Dunstable priory in Bedfordshire, whose house held Derbyshire property at Bradbourne and Ballidon, but were not described in detail. A single plea roll recording, in entries written in Latin, the proceedings in civil pleas brought to the court, following the issue of royal writs, has survived for the eyre of 1269. It was made for the chief justice of that eyre, Gilbert de Preston, and it is now in two parts (JUST 1/144, 145). An English calendar of it was privately printed by C. E. Lugard in *Calendar of the cases for Derbyshire from eyre and assize rolls* (Ashover, 1938), but copies of the book are very rare. The roll gives no information about the crown pleas of the eyre. They resulted from the answers given by juries, representing each of the local government units within the county, to written questions about crown rights and matters of governmental concern, given to them by the justices and called the articles of the eyre. The next Derbyshire eyre, held at Derby between 21 April and about 11 May 1281, is the first for which we have full sets of plea rolls, and consequently the first for which were are able to learn something of the crown and other pleas for the county.

The eyre circuits of 1278–1289

Between the Derbyshire eyre of 1269 and that of 1281 the general eyre was remodelled, at the Gloucester parliament of 1278. It then achieved what proved to be its most fully developed form, which remained unaltered until the eyre suddenly ceased to be a regular part of the local administration of royal justice in England, on the outbreak of war with France in June 1294, and which it retained during its brief revival between 1329 and 1331 and in occasional eyres held in individual counties during the fourteenth century. The changes of 1278 gave the justices in eyre the regular duty of hearing pleas of quo warranto, which involved the trial of the rights to franchises claimed at the beginning of the eyre, and for the first time specific provision for them to hear plaints, cases brought by bill rather than by writ.

The new arrangements also meant that eyres tended to take longer to hold, and two groups of justices, one broadly dealing with the north of England and one with the south, whose composition changed from time to time, worked continuously in their allotted counties from 1278 to 1289, apart from the interruption resulting from the war of conquest in Wales in 1282 and 1283. During their eyres in particular counties, each group of eyre justices dealt with some civil pleas from other counties in their circuit. During that period, with the Common Bench also sitting at Westminster during regular terms, England in effect had three regular benches to deal with common pleas, in addition to the court coram rege (later King's Bench), which followed the king when he was not overseas, and itself dealt with many cases falling into the same categories as those heard by the other courts.

The Derbyshire eyre of 1281 and its records

Derbyshire fell within the 'northern' eyre circuit, headed by John de Vaux as chief justice, which began work in Cumberland at Carlisle in November 1278 and moved on successively to Westmorland, Northumberland, Yorkshire and Nottinghamshire before the end of 1280. Vaux received an annual fee of 50 marks (£33 13s. 4d.), and his team of puisne (junior) justices for the eyre each received an annual fee of 40 marks (£26 13s. 4d.). They were, in the order of precedence in which their names appeared in the feet of fines, William de Saham, Roger Loveday, John de Mettingham and Master Thomas de Siddington. Mettingham in particular had a distinguished later career, but there is no need to give details about them here because much is written elsewhere. The keeper of the writs and rolls of the circuit, in effect its chief clerk and record keeper, was Elias de Sutton, who had been appointed in the spring of 1279. The king's interests in the eyre were represented by his attorneys, who at Derby were Gilbert de Thornton,[1] who was later to become the most senior judge in England as chief justice of the Court of King's Bench, and William de Beverley (see **688, 709, 712, 714, 734**).[2] Thornton seems to have been paid £10 for his service in this eyre.[3] Evidence of the presence of the lesser eyre officials appears from the records of their taking their accustomed share of damages in civil cases, including the clerks (e.g. **6, 23, 88, 105**) and the court crier (**50**).

For most eyres there is a record, on the close rolls of the king's Chancery, of the date on which it was summoned, but no such record was enrolled for the Derbyshire eyre. It is likely to have been planned some months before it took place, probably some time before the preceding Nottinghamshire eyre, which began on 3 November 1280. The succeeding Lincolnshire eyre, which began on 9 or 15 June 1281, was certainly being planned by 18 January that year, over three months before the Derbyshire eyre began. Those who did not appear for the eyre on the appointed day for its opening were, in this eyre as in others, liable to a penalty for not doing so (**428, 464, 487, 518, 545**); some were men of considerable consequence not resident in the county.

The eyre opened at Derby on the morrow of the close of Easter in the ninth year of Edward's reign (21 April 1281), as the headings in both rolls show (**1, 401**), precisely where in the town is not known, and continued until about Easter four weeks, 11 May, the date of the latest five feet of fines (CP 25/1/37/16, nos. 49–50; 17, nos. 51–53). The latest adjournment of civil cases within the eyre were to Friday after Easter three weeks, 9 May (**75, 223, 244, 263**); after that the next adjournments were to the Lincolnshire eyre on the quindene of Trinity, 22 June (**64, 76, 87,** etc.) Its surviving records amount to 38 feet of fines, 37 relating to Derbyshire and one to Yorkshire, and a set of plea rolls for each of the five justices, plus a 'Rex' roll kept by the keeper of writs and rolls. The authoritative rolls were those of Vaux, the chief justice, made up as one roll of civil pleas (JUST 1/151) and one of crown and other pleas (JUST 1/152). Saham's record of the eyre was in a single roll (JUST 1/154), as were Loveday's (JUST 1/147) and Mettingham's (JUST 1/153); Loveday's roll included the amercements and fines for the crown pleas, while Mettingham's included them for both civil

---

[1] For Thornton's career, see *The Earliest English Law Reports*, II, ed. P.A. Brand (Selden Society, cxii, 1996), pp. cviii–cxviii.

[2] Numbers in bold type refer to entries in the calendar below.

[3] PRO, E 159/56, rot. 1.

and crown pleas. Siddington's record consisted of separate civil and crown pleas rolls (JUST 1/149, 150), both of them very short and incomplete, but the 'Rex' roll kept by Elias de Sutton is apparently a full record, including both amercements sections (JUST 1/148).

For the purposes of this calendar, Vaux's rolls (JUST 1/151, text **1–400**; JUST 1/152, text **401–757**) have been used. They are, as normal with chief justices' rolls, estreated; that is, with the notes of the amounts of amercements and fines, in the margin alongside the relevant entries, struck through as the sums were written in the estreat, the name given to the list of amercements and fines sent to the Exchequer so that the sums due could be put into the sheriff's summons for collection. Also as usual with chief justices' rolls, Vaux's rolls do not include a copy of the estreat, so the copy in Sutton's Rex roll has been used instead (JUST 1/148, text **758–881**).

These rolls survive because, in common with most of the other plea rolls of the courts at that period, they were handed in to the royal treasury at the Exchequer, following a general order to that effect made in 1257. They were kept there until their transfer to the new Public Record Office, which was created in 1838. It is known that Vaux was ordered to hand over his eyre rolls to Walter of Wimborne in October 1283, when he was on the point of departing for Gascony, while Saham, Loveday, Mettingham and Siddington, as well as Sutton, were ordered to hand in their rolls in September 1284.[1] The references in the Chancery rolls to these transactions between them account for the survival of all the rolls created as a result of the Derbyshire eyre of 1281 until the present day.

The wapentake and town juries

Medieval Derbyshire was sub-divided into a number of local districts for administrative and legal purposes, while some of the towns had varying degrees of independence within that structure. In most English counties the sub-divisions were called hundreds, but in Derbyshire, like a number of other counties in the north and east where there had been significant settlement or political domination by Vikings from Scandinavia, the equivalent units were called wapentakes. By 1281 some of these wapentakes and their courts were said to be under the control of lords other than the king. The king's brother Edmund earl of Lancaster held the wapentakes of Wirksworth, Appletree and Gresley, five-eighths of the wapentake of Repton and nearly half of that of

---

[1] *Calendar of Patent Rolls 1281–92*, pp. 86, 131.

Litchurch, while the other half of Repton wapentake was held by the heirs to the earldom of Chester, which had been divided between them in 1237 on the death of the last non-royal earl, John the Scot. High Peak, Morleyston and the other half of Litchurch remained in the king's hands (**720**). No reference was made to Scarsdale wapentake in the entry.

At the eyre each administrative subdivision was represented by a jury, selected after the eyre opened, which was required to take an oath before the justices and then to make written answers to a series of written questions about crime and royal rights given to them at the beginning of the eyre by a senior clerk, who received a fee of 6s. 8d. for supplying the copy. The questions were called the 'articles of the eyre', and the answers to them were referred to as the jurors' verdict (*veredictum*). The number of articles had steadily lengthened throughout the century, and since 1278 there had been a total of 143 questions to be answered, 69 of which had been used by the end of the reign of Henry III in 1272, 39 more having been added as a result of the Hundred Rolls enquiry into liberties in 1274–5, and a further 35 as a result of statutes made in the first years of the reign of Edward I. Original *veredicta* survive for some other counties as far back as 1235, but none at all has survived for any Derbyshire eyre. What we know of their answers is what is recorded in the crown pleas roll (see below), but our present concern is the lists of jurors themselves, which appear at the end of that roll (**747–757**).

Seven wapentakes (High Peak, Wirksworth, Appletree, Scarsdale, Morleyston, Litchurch and Repton), and four towns (Derby, Chesterfield, Ashbourne and Bakewell) were represented in the eyre by a jury of twelve, the normal number, including two identified as 'electors'. They were two of the more senior men of the locality, often knights, who were responsible for choosing the others. William of Stainsby, for example, one of the electors for Scarsdale wapentake (**750**), and also known as William of Hardwick (**275, 385**), was the first known resident of the old Hardwick Hall and a distant ancestor of Bess of Hardwick. He was a knight active in local government both in Scarsdale and in the county as a whole, and became one of the county coroners at some point between the date of the eyre and his death in 1289.[1] Adam de Harthill and Giles de Meynill, electors of the High Peak and Litchurch juries respectively (**747, 752**), were also knights. Henry

---

[1] D. Crook, 'Hardwick before Bess: the origins and early history of the Hardwick family and therir estate', *Derbyshire Archaeological Journal*, cvii (1987), pp. 41–54, esp. 45–7; *Derbyshire Charters* (ed. I.H. Jeayes) (1906), nos. 191, 1461, 1564, 1567, 1568.

FitzHerbert of Norbury, an elector of the Appletree wapentake jury (**748**), had also served as a coroner since the last eyre in 1269 (**402**), and was important enough to serve twice as an elector of a grand assize jury, which was supposed to consist only of knights, to deal with major civil cases over rights to land (**3, 243**); one of the men he chose for the grand assize jury on each occasion, Hugh de Strelley, was also an ordinary member of the High Peak wapentake jury (**747**). Also sworn were the bailiffs of the wapentakes and towns, who were present ex officio, and were also prominent men. Among them were Simon de Clifton, bailiff of Ashbourne (**755**), leading witness of a minor grant of property in Clifton, near Ashbourne, perhaps his native village; and Robert of Nottingham, bailiff of Derby (**757**), who in that capacity witnessed a lease of land in the territory of Derby.[1]

The majority of the jurors who are not known to have been knights were probably substantial freeholders, many of whom may be also be identified in charters; a few of them were also litigants in civil cases, which may give information about their interests. Some, like William Foljambe of High Peak (**747**), were only just below knightly level and immediately followed the knights in charter witness lists.[2] There is sometimes detailed information in charters about the lesser freeholders, such as Henry son of Thomas of Alsop, a Wirksworth wapentake juror (**748**), who was able to give land and buildings in Alsop both to an Ashbourne man and to lord Walter of Lichfield, chaplain, who was apparently bringing up two of his younger daughters, Avice and Margery, in his own household.[3] Others, like Simon of Glapwell (**750**), who appear only as witnesses, are more obscure.[4] Four towns were represented by separate juries of their own: Bakewell, Ashbourne, Chesterfield and Derby, the latter the only one described as a borough. Derby's first borough charter was granted by Henry II between 1155 and 1160; Chesterfield was a seignorial borough, granted by King John to his senior official William Brewer in 1204. During the eyre Queen Eleanor's bailiff of Bakewell, Ralph le Wyne, claimed that the town was a free borough in which the writ of mort d'ancestor could not run, but the knights and stewards of the shire affirmed that it was not a borough and did not have borough liberties (**91**). According to the High Peak jury, she had only a life interest in the manor of Bakewell, it having been demised to her

---

[1] *Derbyshire Charters*, nos. 880, 971.

[2] Ibid., nos. 1211, 1427, 1794–5, 2340–43, 2427, 2706.

[3] Ibid., nos. 30, 31.

[4] Ibid., nos. 1317–19.

by an ancestor of William Gernun (**725**). Ashbourne was a major royal demesne manor, where the current bailiff was Simon de Clifton (**755**). Bakewell and Ashbourne were also represented by separate juries in the Derbyshire eyre of 1330–31, the only other Derbyshire eyre for which we have any information.

Crown pleas

The crown pleas begin with a series of general notes customary in eyre rolls. First there is a list of the names of the sheriffs of Nottinghamshire and Derbyshire who had held office since the last eyre in 1269, ending with the current sheriff, Gervase de Clifton (**401**). Next there is a note of who had served as coroners during the same period, six men in all, two of whom had since died and therefore could not appear to answer for their actions (**402**). Finally there is a note of how Englishry was presented in Derbyshire and Nottinghamshire (**403**). The meaning of the term is explained in the note to this entry.

There then follow the answers made by the local juries to the articles of the eyre under the oath which they had sworn in the presence of the justices (**404–675**). The answers were made in a written document, the *veredictum*. The word means 'verdict', but in the sense of facts truly presented, not conclusions reached after trial. Trial juries were quite separate from those which presented the answers to the articles. None of the original veredicta survive for this eyre, but one of the best surviving examples, and the only one so far to be printed, comes from the Wiltshire eyre which began in the southern eyre circuit at Wilton on the same day as the 1281 Derbyshire eyre began at Derby, and which provides a valuable insight into the nature and contents of the lost Derbyshire veredicta.[1] It relates to Chippenham hundred, and shows that the jurors of that hundred made presentments in response to only 5 of the pre-1272 eyre articles and 16 of the new post-1278 ones, that is only 21 articles in all out of the total of 143. It also shows that the veredicta contained precise information about the dates of crimes within the period since the last eyre, information which was omitted when the case was entered in the plea roll.

The crown pleas roll records the substance of the entries the veredicta contained, and any action taken upon them, under headings for each of the

---

[1] JUST 1/1017A, printed in *Collectanea* (Wiltshire Archaeological and Natural History Society, Records Branch, xii, 1956), pp. 50–128.

presenting districts. Some of the entries begin with a short phrase represent-ing the eyre article to which the answer was being made (e.g. **428**, 'concerning defaults'; **466**, 'concerning warrens'; **651**, 'concerning purprest-ures'), but most do not. The entries appear in the plea roll in the order in which they were written in the veredictum. We know from the Chippenham veredictum that a clerk annotated the entries with information about proceedings in the eyre so that the plea roll could later be written up from them, and that not every entry in the veredictum resulted in a corresponding entry in the roll.

A great many of the entries at the beginning of each verdictum concerned violent or sudden death, which was of interest to the crown because it was entitled to the chattels of the deceased and amercements from any procedural defaults made by individuals or communities as part of the process of investigation and notification of the death. The court could decide to classify those deaths in one of several ways.

Murder

Murder had a precise technical meaning in thirteenth-century eyre rolls: it was 'the name of a fine, not of a crime', a judgment given against a local district, like a Derbyshire wapentake, as a result of which all individuals owing suit to the wapentake court would have to pay the common fine known as 'murdrum' when a person who could not be proved to have been English had been killed. It was believed that Cnut, the Scandinavian king who ruled England from 1016 to 1035, had introduced it into the kingdom to protect his Danish followers, and that it had been adopted by William the Conqueror after 1066 to protect Frenchmen. The dead person was assumed to be French, and the wapentake could only avoid paying the resultant murder fine if it could produce relations of the deceased to prove that he or she was English, known as proof of Englishry. The method of doing this varied from county to county: in Derbyshire and in Nottinghamshire it had to be done by one male from the father's side and one from the mother's side (**403**).

There are 18 judgments of murder among the Derbyshire crown pleas in 1281 (**404–5**, **413**, **415**, **436**, **445**, **473**, **478**, **497–8**, **512**, **527**, **532–3**, **541**, **557**, **570**, **572**), at least one against each wapentake but none against any of the towns which presented their crown pleas separately. The greatest numbers relate to High Peak and Litchurch wapentakes, which had to pay for four each (**758–9**, **764–5**; **809**, **813**, **815**). In all but three cases (**413**, **473**, **527**) the victims were identified, but in ten (**413**, **415**, **473**, **478**, **498**, **527**,

532–3, **541**, **557**, **570**) it was stated that the names of the killers were not known. In no case where the killer's identity was known had he been arrested; he was outlawed, and his frankpledge was amerced (e.g. **404**, **497**). Some vills were amerced for not arresting murderers who had committed their crimes during daylight (**512**, **532**). If the suspect had not been pursued by the men of the four neighbouring vills, or they had made a false evaluation of his chattels, they too were amerced (e.g. **404–5**, **758–9**). The vills could also be amerced for not attending an inquest on the victims, known or unknown (e.g. **413**, **415**, **764–5**), or for burying one without the coroner seeing him (**570**). The coroner himself could be amerced for omitting to value property in his inquest (**445**).

In no case was the person who found the body, the 'first finder', suspected of the crime, although in some entries no first finder is mentioned. The first finders were supposed to appear at the eyre, but in a number of cases they had died before it took place. Only two are named, in one case when the jury was amerced for not mentioning him in its presentment (**473**, **788**), and in another when her sureties failed to produce her at the eyre and so were also amerced (**497**). Another jury was amerced simply for not naming the first finder's sureties in its presentment (**527**, **809**). One jury was amerced for falsely giving the name of a finder in its presentment (**557**).

Homicides other than murder

The vast majority of the presentments relate to the main general articles recording deaths by homicide, accident or in suspicious circumstances, which had been mentioned in the eyre articles ever since they began in the twelfth century. A total of 73 homicides was presented, other than those in which murder was adjudged, and mentioned in this roll. In one case the jurors thought that a killing in a brawl outside a tavern in Hazlebadge resulted from self-defence, so the matter was to be referred to the king (**430**), but most cases appear to have been easily settled. The entries usually record the names of both the perpetrators and the victims, the place and the weapon, and what happened subsequently. Death was not always immediate, but could follow days or weeks later (e.g. **407**, **434**, **647**). Suspects who were not arrested usually fled or took sanctuary in a church (see below). The chattels of those who fled were seized, and if they held freehold land the king was entitled to year and waste of it (e.g. **435**, **506**). Their frankpledge (or their lord if in his mainpast) was usually amerced, and the vill frequently punished for not pursuing them, while the jurors were often amerced for undervaluing or sometimes concealing the chattels.

The circumstantial details given in these entries, and of those where murder was adjudged, are of general interest. The most common implements used were knives (**405, 412, 430, 436, 442, 445, 474, 484, 503, 513, 576, 587, 604, 662**), axes (**417, 435, 448–9, 477, 506, 510, 540, 592, 635, 654, 663–4**), staffs (**497, 530, 589, 591**) and arrows (**434, 598, 655**); less common were swords (**407, 502**), a gimlet (**528**), a stick (**558**), a stake (**560**), and a spade (**647**). A murdered child and a woman resisting rape were thought to have been strangled (**541, 602**).

Places where killings occurred are also usually mentioned. Often what is given is the name of a village or town, or the names of more than one between which a killing occurred (e.g **416**), but sometimes the information is more specific. Urban killings include those which took place in the market places at Chesterfield and Derby (**442, 654**). Others whose location is mentioned occurred in a sheepfold in a park (**473**), a mill (**485**) and a parson's hall (**572**), but more often they are said to have taken place in remote places like Hathersage moor or Haddon wood (**413, 415**). Many took place in the fields of a particular village (**417, 453, 497, 500, 507, 511, 527, 532, 541, 555, 647**). The reasons why they occurred are rarely even hinted at. One may have resulted from a drunken brawl following a visit to a tavern (**430**), and another arose from a dispute mentioned but not specified (**598**).

Sanctuary and abjuration

A frequent resort of those who had committed homicide or theft was to flee to the sanctuary of a church and then abjure the realm in the presence of a coroner; that is, they agreed to leave England for ever in return for their lives. The coroner recorded the abjuration in his roll (**435, 540**); if he failed in his duties he was punished (**566**). They were assigned the port from which they had to leave, but no indication of the ports in question is given in the records of this eyre. When an abjuration occurred, the chattels of the person making it were of course forfeit to the crown; as with homicide, there were often penalties for falsely valuing them. The frankpledge in which the abjurer had been was invariably amerced; in one case a thief who was being taken to Nottingham gaol escaped into Shardlow church, so the villagers of Repton who were responsible for his custody were amerced for the escape (**520, 806**). In another a man was arrested after leaving Langley church voluntarily and then escaped (**546**). Vills could be amerced for not being represented at an abjuration (**441, 779**).

The churches or chapels in which abjurations occurred during the years since the last eyre in 1269 included Darley, Harthill, Hope, Bowden,

Alfreton (twice), Eckington, Staveley, Hognaston, Willersley, Shardlow, Mickleover, Alvaston (twice), Langley, Potlock, Doveridge, Sutton on the Hill, Horsley, Wilsthorpe, Ashbourne, Bakewell (thrice, once by a woman), Chesterfield, All Saints Derby, St Alkmund's Derby (twice), the nunnery of Derby, and St Peter's Derby (**406, 409, 412, 425, 440–1, 450–1, 482, 508, 520, 536, 539, 542, 546, 554, 563, 579, 594, 603, 619, 633, 636–7, 646, 653, 656-7, 661, 666**).

Misadventure and suicide

Accidents were a frequent cause of death and had to be reported to the justices by the coroners who held inquests upon the victims, because the object causing the death, or at least its monetary value, was due to the crown. It was 'given to God', and thus called a 'deodand'.[1] Such objects causing accidental deaths in Derbyshire in the years before 1281 included horses from which people fell (**421**), wild or domestic animals, especially responsible for the deaths of children, such as a boar, a tame stag or a horse (**423, 564, 638**); collapsing buildings (**426, 452**); a beam or tree from which someone fell (**439, 447**); a vat of hot water into which someone fell (**443**); carts (**446, 531, 573–5**); between the wheel and spindle of a watermill, while greasing the former (**501**); by the wheel of a watermill after falling under it from a plank (**505**); a collapsing haystack (**559**); crushed by a collapsing marl pit (**562**); frozen to death (**567**).

Many people also died by drowning in rivers such as the Derwent (**418, 660**), the Dove (**476**) and the Trent (**496, 499**), or smaller named watercourses such as the 'Bradelepte' (unidentified), Bradbourne stream or Holbrook or Scow Brook (Henmore Brook) (**419, 569, 620**), or unnamed streams (**556**), or wells (**438, 509**). Even in some of these cases a deodand was due; such as the horse from which the victim fell (**418–19, 475–6**), or the boat (**496**). Not all drownings were, however, thought to be accidental (**570**). As with chattels of felons and suicides, false valuations of deodands often led to financial penalties (e.g. **448, 781**), and a bailiff who took a deodand horse without warrant was also amerced (**421, 768**). The abbot of Tutbury was even punished for taking the hay that had crushed a man to death (**559, 823**). Also, the first finder of someone who died accidentally was expected to appear at the eyre (e.g. **452**), although they were only occasionally named in the roll (**574, 620**) and were often dead by the time it was

---

[1] For an analysis see Appendix E.

held. If they did not appear, their sureties could be amerced (**620, 842**). Villages had to take care that someone who had died in an accident was seen by the coroner before he or she was buried (**556, 569–70, 820, 829**).

Suicide was also a felony, and when suicide was adjudged the deceased's chattels were forfeit to the crown.[1] Methods of suicide mentioned in the roll include hanging in places as varied as a wood, a pigsty, from an oak tree in a park (**411, 437, 494**), and stabbing oneself in the stomach (**537**). Penalties could result if the four neighbouring vills did not attend the coroner's inquest (**437–8, 776–7**), and any failing by the coroner in his duties led to him also being punished, as in a case dealt with by John Grim (**537, 814**).

Presentments for burglary, larceny and theft

From about 1194 to 1232 burglary had been the subject of a separate eyre article, 'De malefactoribus et burgatoribus', but since then it seems to have been presented under the general article concerning crown pleas since the last eyre, along with all the entries relating to sudden death. This roll contains only two entries relating to burglary alone. A couple and their son who burgled a house in Morleyston wapentake were immediately arrested, taken to Nottingham gaol, tried by the justices of gaol delivery and hanged (**588**). In Derby, the other gang of burglars, three men, were more successful, killing their victim and escaping (**665**). In a third case, burglary of a sheepfold at Cronkston was followed by the murder of the shepherd (**478**).

Larceny was not always the subject of presentments, more often of indictments, but several apparent presentments for larceny in this roll resulted in the sentence of hanging upon some of the thieves who had been arrested before the eyre; one of them was a woman, but a widow accused of stealing lead from the chapel at Alderwasley was found not guilty (**431, 471, 492, 525**). Two of these entries may have resulted from indictments rather than presentments (see below). The son of a chaplain of Markeaton had absconded on being suspected of larceny, and was living at Hanbury in Staffordshire; the sheriff was ordered to bring him before the justices two weeks after the opening of the eyre. Another man, arrested on suspicion of larceny, pleaded his clergy and was handed over to the dean of the court Christian at Derby, representing the bishop of Coventry, for trial in the church courts (**584**).

Many of those who took sanctuary in a church and abjured the realm

---

[1] Financial details of suicides' and others' chattels are given in Appendix F.

admitted to being thieves (**482, 520, 579, 603, 619, 633, 636, 646, 653, 656–7, 661, 666**). The Ashbourne jury made a presentment about two thieves who had brought seven stolen oxen into the town, which they abandoned and fled; the result was the significant sum of 46s. 8d. due to the crown as the value of the oxen, regarded as chattels (**618, 842**). A man in Chesterfield was suspected of stealing 20 ewes (**673**).

Indictments

The jurors were also obliged to make indictments by '*privata*', further written documents, of people suspected of ill-doing or of generally dubious reputation, but not connected with any specific criminal acts, a duty which apparently began with the assize of Clarendon in 1166. In the thirteenth century the procedure was, according to a contemporary legal treatise, that before they withdrew to prepare their *veredicta*, the justices told the jurors privately that if there was anyone in their wapentake who was suspected of evil-doing they were to arrest him if they could; but if they could not, they must give to the justices, privately in a schedule, the names of those they suspected, who could then be arrested by the sheriff and brought before the justices to be dealt with.

Entries derived from privata usually appear at the end of a jury's section of the roll, after the answers to the eyre articles, and begin with the phrase 'concerning those indicted' (**432, 472, 493, 524, 553, 586, 632, 645, 652, 675**). All the entries in this roll consist of grouped lists of individuals said to have absconded and to be suspected of larceny; the men among them were outlawed, and the women waived, and their chattels confiscated. They were nearly always outside frankpledge and were sometimes described as vagabonds. Some of these groups may have been organised criminal gangs, but the entries are not phrased in such a way as to make it clear whether the individuals mentioned were working together or not. A man who had been indicted and imprisoned some time before the eyre and then bailed to appear before it did so and was acquitted by a jury (**519**). Another man arrested on suspicion of larceny in Scarsdale wapentake, found guilty and hanged (**471**), may have been the subject of an indictment rather than a presentment; the entry immediately precedes the indictments entry for that wapentake. Other entries which may be similar are **431, 492, 525–6, 551**, which all involve larceny or the harbouring of thieves, and either precede or follow indictments entries. One of those indicted in Ashbourne, Richard son of Richard le Clerk, was noteworthy in that he had once been a lay clerk in the king's Chancery, but had stolen 30s. from Robert le Thorp of Clifton (**632**), while one of

those who fled in High Peak wapentake was a former shepherd of the
countess of Derby (**432**). The most important of all was a knight, William
de Langford, who obtained a pardon for his indictment for larceny at request
of the queen in 1282 (**472** and note).

Appeals of felony

Appeals of felony were still made in some numbers in Derbyshire in 1281
(**453, 458–62, 489–90, 514–15, 547, 549, 577–8, 580, 582, 605-13, 627–8,
668–70**). This was the procedure whereby one individual made a specific
accusation of felony or breach of the king's peace against another or others
at five successive meetings of the county court, where the coroner made a
record of proceedings in his roll (**453, 458**), but the resolution of which was
held over until the next eyre in the county. If an appeal had been prosecuted
in four county courts, it was nevertheless allowed to proceed during the eyre
(**607**), but if it proceeded for only two or three county courts it could not go
ahead (**613, 627–8**). In one case the county was reprimanded for mistakenly
allowing the appeal to go forward (**458**). Failure to proceed with the appeal
at the required number of county courts could result in arrest (**461–2, 489,
547**), and failure to attend the eyre court after making an appeal or failure
to prosecute there brought the arrest of the appellor and financial penalties
upon his or her sureties (**459, 462, 489–90, 514–15, 577, 582, 607–8,
610–13, 668–70, 783, 796, 803–4, 817, 833, 840–1, 853-4**). Nevertheless, in
such cases the jury could still be asked to pronounce on the guilt or
otherwise of the accused 'so that the king's peace may be maintained' (**460,
490, 547, 582, 606, 608, 610**). Failure by the appellee to appear also resulted
in an order for his arrest, even if he was known to be residing in another
county, like Jordan de Darley; the sheriff was censured for not ensuring his
appearance after he had been granted bail (**578**).

Appeals had to be presented by the jurors in their *veredicta*, but by the
1280s they were not given in so much detail there as they had been earlier,
which suggests that the justices were depending mainly on the coroners' rolls
for their information.[1] Since there are no coroners' rolls for this eyre, we are
entirely dependent on the information given in the *veredicta* and summarised
on the plea roll, which lacks some of the detail formerly given in plea rolls,
such as the dates of incidents. In the roll the entries relating to appeals tend
to be grouped after the main sequence of criminal presentments and before

---

[1] Meekings, *Wiltshire Crown Pleas*, p. 35.

the returns to lesser eyre articles and the indictments.

Formerly trial in appeals had been by judicial duel, but by 1281 jury trial had long been the normal method, except in the case of appeals by approvers, self-confessed criminals who fought against their alleged accomplices in an attempt to avoid or at least postpone hanging. There were apparently some approvers' appeals in the 1281 Derbyshire eyre, because William Lether, an approver from Cheshire, withdrew his charges and was to be hanged (**470**), but a man and a woman accused of harbouring him were found not guilty (**469**). There is no other evidence for the activities of approvers in this eyre. Of ordinary appeals there were as usual some appeals of homicide (e.g. **458**) or rape (**606–8, 611**). Examples of appeals for lesser offences include mayhem (**549, 610, 612, 668**), robbery (**627**), wounding and battery (**460–1, 514, 547**), mayhem and wounding (**515**), burning houses (**462**); in all these cases breach of the king's peace was also alleged, as a matter of form. Agreements could be involved where the alleged offence was not a felony; in one case the parties came to an agreement about alleged mayhem, but the appellee was found guilty of wounding (**515**). In many cases (**459–62, 490, 577–8, 606, 608, 610, 612–13**) the parties were specifically said not to have come to an agreement. A fine was also an acceptable way of settling an appeal. John Penicod paid 4 marks because five men in his mainpast beat a shepherd, even though he himself was not involved (**580, 832**), while in another case a fine of one mark was paid (**582, 833**).

Appeals by women, other than for rape (**606–8, 611**), included for the death of a husband (**490, 553, 578, 613**), a son (**558**), one or two brothers (**577, 609**) or a daughter (**670**). It appears from one entry that the county court was aware of the clause of Magna Carta (1225, c. 34) which said that no-one could be arrested or imprisoned by a woman's appeal for the death of a man other than her husband killed in her arms (**558**). It did not, however, prevent women from appealing in the cases noted, although if the rule were followed it must have meant that the accused was not held in custody before trial. A woman held to have made a false appeal against one of a number of men was waived when he appeared in court, and was found not guilty by a jury; she was, however, pardoned by the justices (**453**; see also **607**). Others found not guilty in the same case nevertheless forfeited their chattels because they absconded. Exactly the same happened to a male appellant after the man whom he had appealed of mayhem was found not guilty, except that he was of course outlawed, not waived (**549**).

Trial juries in criminal cases

Little is said about trial juries in crown pleas, brought by presentment, indictment or appeal of felony, in this roll, referring to them simply as 'the jurors', but we know from earlier rolls that in the 1240s at least that such a jury normally consisted of the 12 jurors of the presenting jury plus the representatives of the four neighbouring townships. Here the only reference to a specific jury is to that of the borough of Derby (**670**). These eyre juries represent the earliest form of the petty jury, but it is known that the classic form of the petty jury was a development of the gaol delivery system, and we know from early gaol delivery files from other counties that jurors from the hundreds were summoned to gaol delivery sessions by the later 1270s at the latest.

The roll gives little information about jurors' opinions, although in one case they were unable to be certain that one man who killed another would have been killed himself had he not done so (**430**).

Prisoners, gaol and gaol delivery

The roll shows that Derbyshire prisoners were normally taken to the sheriff's prison in Nottingham (**424**, **499**, **520**, **561**, **588**, **622**, **634**). Prisoners not infrequently escaped. When this happened, the person or community held to blame was charged with an standard amercement of £8, a very severe punishment indeed. A former sergeant imprisoned in Peak castle by its constable, Llewellyn, presumably a Welshman, later escaped, but it was Roger Lestrange, the keeper of the castle and a prominent royal servant, who was held responsible (**408**, **761**). A woman had escaped from the custody of Queen Eleanor's former bailiff in Bakewell, for which he also had to pay £8 (**644**, **847**). The man imprisoned in a house at Langley after leaving sanctuary in the church was presumably only put there as a temporary measure pending a more secure custody, and indeed escaped, leaving the village with a heavy financial penalty (**546**, **816**); so did another man held in Eckington before being taken to Nottingham to await trial, this time the culprit being the current sheriff, Hugh de Babington (**454**, **782**). In this case William de Stainsby, a prominent local man described in royal letters as a king's squire, was a direct beneficiary of the sum levied (note to **454**). Another prisoner arrested in Ashbourne by the king's bailiff escaped when being taken to Nottingham by the men of the four neighbouring vills; the vills were held responsible and the five men from them named as escorts were also amerced (**622**, **843**).

Men could be released on bail to await trial by royal order (**453**, **552**), but if they absconded those who had stood bail for them were punished. A Taddington man was released on the surety of 12 of his neighbours in Taddington and Priestcliffe, who suffered accordingly (**424, 769**). Bail was available to some of those imprisoned for larceny (**519**), while a cleric accused of larceny claimed benefit of clergy and was handed over to the bishop of Coventry for trial (**584**).

Derbyshire prisoners were delivered from Nottingham gaol by the regular sessions of the justices of gaol delivery, and occasional references are made to action taken by them prior to the eyre (**453, 500, 588, 602**). Only in two cases from Bakewell are the justices identified by a reference to their senior justice, William de Meynill (**633–4**). In another case their action in releasing a man whom they considered had committed an accidental homicide was set aside by the eyre justices because the release had not been certified to them by the justices of gaol delivery, whose identity was not known (**534**). Eyre justices also regularly delivered gaols when they made their far less frequent visits to the county, since their rolls contain gaol delivery sections, regularly from 1279 onwards and occasionally since 1249. The records of the Derbyshire eyre of 1281, however, contain no special gaol delivery sections; the gaol delivery material is divided between the appropriate presenting districts almost at the end of their crown pleas sections, for Wirksworth and Repton wapentakes (before **492, 525**), immediately before the indictments. This unusual arrangement occurs in the rolls of only two other eyres, both in the same circuit, the Nottinghamshire eyre of 1280–1 and the Leicester-shire eyre of 1284, which were probably written by the same clerks. The single entries which follow these two headings each involve groups of people arrested for larceny; in the first case one and in the second case three of the accused were sentenced to be hanged. They were presumably brought from Nottingham to Derby for their trial at the eyre.

Punishments

Those who were not present to be dealt with in person had their chattels forfeited and were ordered to be exacted and oulawed in the county court. In this eyre this fate befell a total of 149 men involved in crown pleas, while six women suffered the female equivalent, being exacted and waived. Temporary confinement in gaol, followed by a pardon from the justices, was the normal punishment for those found to have made a false appeal (e.g. **549**).

At least nine people tried and found guilty in the eyre of various offences were sentenced to be hanged (**431, 453, 471, 492, 525, 581**), including one woman (**431**) and one approver (**470**), while there are also references to people, including women, who had been hanged earlier after sentence by gaol delivery justices (**453, 500, 588**). Thieves captured in flight with their stolen goods could be and were summarily beheaded (**444, 454** and note, **457, 486, 523**). The sheriff accounted for the chattels of many people hanged or beheaded before the eyre (**457, 467, 548, 782, 785, 818**).

Infringements of royal rights and regulations

The main crown pleas articles under which the vast majority of all presentments were made were followed by a group of even more ancient articles, some of which dated back as far as the assize of Northampton (1176), and related to infringements or possible infringements of royal rights. In Derbyshire in 1281 only a handful of returns were made to them. Two articles relating to royal rights, which had both been included in the list since 1194, occur once only in this eyre: 'Concerning ladies [in the king's gift, whether they are marriagable or married (and if married who gave them in marriage and to whom) and how much their land is worth]'; and 'Concerning churches [in the king's gift, who holds them, by whom was he presented and how much they are worth]'. The lady mentioned was Joan de Montalt, who had lands worth 20 marks (£13 13s. 4d.) in the county and was said to be marriageable; what was to be done was a matter for further discussion (**517**). The church in question was Melbourne, which had earlier been in the king's gift, but was now held by the bishop of Carlisle. His authority for doing so was not known, so the sheriff was to investigate (**516** and note). 'Concerning purprestures [or encroachments made on the king, whether in land or water or in liberties or otherwise, wherever it be]' was an article which originated in 1198. The entries resulting from it record encroachment on highways, especially in towns like Derby, by raising obstructions of various sorts, such as walls and embankments (**671**). Even buildings could be erected there; one man built 20 shops on the king's highway in Bakewell (**640**). In Chesterfield Henry Clerk obstructed a lane leading to the river Hipper, and was charged with the cost of having it removed by the sheriff (**651**).

Evasion of knighthood

There are some returns to an article added in 1246 as part of a royal campaign to try to ensure that those who were liable to become knights did so, or at least paid for the privilege of exemption from that duty. The process was known as distraint of knighthood.[1] The article is sometimes introduced by the words 'concerning squires' [who hold full knights' fees and are of full age and not knighted]. In Scarsdale Roger le Bret had royal letters patent exempting him for seven years, of which only two had yet elapsed, while John de Ayncurt had not yet received his lands (**458**). Ralph de Shirley also had letters patent, valid for five years (**585**), but Robert de Dethick, Roger de Bradbourne and John de Balliol had no such excuses and were subject to amercement (**488, 521** and note).

Rights of free warren

Another article, 'concerning warrens', checked whether those who held warrens had royal sanction in the form of a charter of free warren (**466** and note, **522, 614**). Such charters were granted in large numbers to important members of local society during the thirteenth century. They gave to the grantee control over hunting of the beasts of the warren (principally the hare and fox) in the demesne lands of his manor or manors.[2] All the warrens mentioned in Derbyshire were in the eastern and southern parts of the county, where most of the gentry lived. The majority were in Scarsdale wapentake, where there were 11: at Pleasley (the bishop of St Davids); Langwith (Henry de Pierrepont); Barlborough (Annora de Hathersage); Scarcliffe (Anquer de Freschville); Ashover (Ralph de Reresby); Shirland (Reynold de Grey); Alfreton and Norton (Thomas de Chaworth); Stainsby (William de Stainsby); and Elmton and Holmesfield (Edmund de Ayncurt). Of them, only Grey and Ayncurt were able to produce charters when they were asked to (**466** and note). In Morleyston there were seven: at Crich, Kirk Hallam and Sandiacre (Richard de Grey); Shipley (Robert de Strelley junior); Ilkeston (William de Ros); Sawley (the bishop of Chester); and Codnor (Henry de Grey). All were asked to produce their charters, but were not recorded as having done so (**614**). In Repton wapentake neither Roger de Montalt, who had a warren in Walton, nor Geoffrey de Gresley, who had one in Drakelow, are said to have done so either (**522**). No warrens were reported in the other wapentakes of the county. Further information about warrens appears among the ragman pleas, for which see below.

---

[1] On distraint of knighthood in this period see M. Powicke, *Military Obligation in Medieval England* (1962).

[2] On Derbyshire warrens see D. Crook, 'The development of private hunting rights in Derbyshire, 1189–1258', *Derbyshire Archaeological Journal* (forthcoming).

Misconduct of officials

Corruption by officials could be presented by the local juries under various eyre articles, and there are a small number of examples in this eyre. Robert of Buxton, bailiff of High Peak, was liable to amercement for taking bribes from those wishing to avoid jury service, an article probably introduced in 1239 (**429**). Another official accused was a private one, Walter de Cantia, the queen's bailiff in Bakewell, who was apparently taking prises on her behalf every year at Bakewell fair, for which he was punished with a £5 penalty (**643**). He was presumably presented under the article 'concerning prises or goods commandeered by sheriffs, constables or other bailiffs, against the will of the owners', introduced in 1208.

Economic and coinage offences

'Concerning the king's exchange' was an article designed to discover anyone who held a mint or exchange without the permission of the king, which was introduced in 1226 but for which no returns are known before 1249. The only return to it in this eyre concerned the sale by four merchants of goods for old coin after its use had been prohibited; this is a reference to the recoinage of 1278 (**625** and note). 'Concerning cloth sold against the assize' (**630, 641, 650, 844, 846, 849**) and 'concerning wines sold against the assize' (**463, 631, 642, 649, 674, 784, 849, 855**) refer to articles dating back to 1194 as to whether vintners observed the assizes of wine and cloth. The former prescribed the maximum prices of different kinds of wine, but in the latter the government was concerned to regulate the measurement of cloth, fixed at two ells (45 to 46 inches) in 1197. By 1281 these regulations had long been enshrined in a clause of Magna Carta (1225, c. 25). The entries in this roll give only the information that particular people in Ashbourne, Bakewell, Chesterfield and Derby, and in one case (**463**) apparently in Alfreton, broke these assizes and were amerced.

Forgery of the king's coinage was a serious offence, included as an eyre article 'concerning forgers and clippers of coin' since 1194, but those accused of it in Derby, but who apparently came respectively from Chapel en le Frith and Chesterfield, in this eyre were found not guilty (**672**).

The 'new chapters' of the eyre

The newer questions in the eyre articles which were put to the jurors involved enquiries into royal rights, which had become particularly prominent after the quo warranto enquiry of 1274–5, and offences against royal regulations, which became more numerous as the thirteenth century went on.[1] There seem to be no returns at all to them in this eyre; there are certainly no short versions of their terms at the beginning of any of the presentments.

Failure to attend the eyre

Failure to answer the summons of the eyre was dealt with under the brief heading 'concerning defaults'. The full article, which went back to 1194, was 'concerning those who were summoned to come before the justices on the first day of the eyre and did not come'. Defaulters who owed attendance at the court were liable to an automatic penalty if they did not do so. In Derbyshire in 1281 a good many people, and one community, defaulted: 23 in High Peak; nine in Scarsdale, including the bishops of St Davids and Dunblane, and the prior of Thurgarton in Nottinghamshire; 18 in Wirksworth, including the prior of Felley in Nottinghamshire; seven in Repton, including the vill of Edingale; seven in Litchurch, including the earl of Lincoln, Henry de Lacy; but none in Appletree or Morleyston, or any of the towns (**428** and note, **464**, **487** and note, **518**, **545** and note, **617**, **771**, **784**, **795**, **805**, **817**). A few people were listed as having defaulted in more than one wapentake, but even so over 50 people defaulted in all. Quittances from attending were obtained from the government for this eyre by ten important people, mostly men not normally resident in the county but with interests there: the abbot of Basingwerk in Flintshire, Edmund earl of Lancaster, the king's brother, Roger bishop of Coventry and Lichfield, Master Nicholas de Hegham, dean of Lincoln, Ralph Pipard, William de Audley, the abbot of Combermere in Cheshire, Robert de Halsted, the master of the Templars in England and Geoffrey de Picheford.[2] Of these, Audley, Halsted and Pichford alone appeared in the default entries (**428**, **487**).

Plaints and recognisances

A very short section of pleas by plaint (complaints made by bill rather than by writ) follows the crown pleas (**676–81**); in the 1280s it was normal for plaints to appear in the crown pleas roll, but in the 1290s they are always

---

[1] For their text, taken from a Gloucestershire eyre veredictum of 1287, see H.M. Cam, 'Studies in the Hundred Rolls: some aspects of thirteenth-century administration', in *Oxford Studies in Social and Legal History*, VI (1921), pp. 94–100.

[2] *Calendar of Close Rolls 1279–88*, p. 117.

filed with the civil pleas. Of the plaints, the most interesting is that brought by the executors of William de Handesacre against the sheriff, Gervase de Wilford, and Miles de Melton for taking two of William's oxen from them in October 1280 and detaining them at Nottingham; their case fell when they had to admit that William had still been alive on the day they were taken (**676**). The other cases concerned a mare wrongfully detained after possession of it had been adjudged in the county court, and allegedly unpaid debts by three men which was to be settled by a Nottingham jury (**677, 681**).

The heading for this section is 'plaints and trespasses', but three of the entries are in fact recognisances, financial agreements voluntarily entered into before the justices and recorded in their rolls (**678-80**). They record the terms for the repayment of loans, and in two cases the names of sureties for the debt; if the payments were not made, the sheriff could levy them from the lands and chattels of the defaulters. Much the largest sum involved was the £20 lent to Richard de Stapleford by Geoffrey son of Ralph Bugge of Nottingham; Ralph is well known as the merchant ancestor of the notable Willoughby family.[1] Recognisances are in fact far more numerous among the civil pleas, the first being for a sack and 20 stones of wool, the sack deemed to be worth 10 marks and the 20 stones 5 marks (**47, 121, 125, 138, 236, 291**), while other cases were settled by what the clerks described as recognisances (**59, 66, 75, 92, 95, 158, 199, 248**).

Ragman and quo warranto pleas

The Ragman inquest of 1274–5

The first half of the reign of Edward I is notable for what has often been described as a 'campaign' to investigate both the legitimacy of franchises held by individuals from the crown, and whether any of them had been abused; and also whether any royal or franchisal officials had oppressed anyone with their powers. The information on which the campaign was based was among that collected by commissioners throughout England from sworn juries during the winter of 1274–5 and recorded in returns sealed with jurors' seals. The seals gave them a ragged appearance which led to their contemporary nickname 'ragman rolls'. They later became known as the 'hundred rolls', since most of the juries represented hundreds, the main subdivision of English counties, which were not, as Derbyshire was, in the

---

[1] J.C. Holt, 'Willoughby Deeds', in *A Medieval Miscellany for Doris Mary Stenton*, ed. P.M. Barnes and C.F. Slade (Pipe Roll Society, new ser. xxxvi, 1962 for 1960), pp. 167–87.

Danelaw area, where they were called wapentakes. Six original rolls for Derbyshire have survived (SC 5/DERB/TOWER/1–6), for High Peak, Appletree, Ashbourne, Derby borough, Repton and Litchurch, and the first four of them are printed in *Rotuli Hundredorum*, vol. II (Record Commission, 1818), pp. 287–99. A roll of extracts from the rolls includes a Derbyshire section (SC 5/8/3, mm. 24–5), printed in the first volume of *Rotuli Hundredorum* (1812), pp. 58–62.

The beginning of the quo warranto enquiries

For a few years attempts were made to examine the rights to franchises of some important individuals, especially the heads of major monastic houses, in parliaments, but that did not work particularly well, and it was decided in 1278 to continue the investigations through the justices in eyre in individual counties. The new eyre programme began in that year, when the articles of the inquest of 1274–5 were added to the existing eyre articles, with some others, so that the judges could deal with the abuses of officials. It was also ordered that in each eyre those who claimed any franchises were to appear and describe them and show their warrants for holding them; if any could show that his ancestor held them at his death, it was necessary for the king's representative to sue out a writ of *quo warranto* ('by what warrant') against him.

From 1278 quo warranto pleas were held in many of the eyres in both eyre circuits. In the northern circuit there was little effective action in the first three eyres, in Cumberland, Westmorland and Northumberland (1278–9), but then there were a number of quo warranto cases in the long Yorkshire eyre of 1279 to 1281, and some in the Nottinghamshire eyre of 1280–1. That Nottinghamshire eyre, our Derbyshire eyre which followed it, and the subsequent Lincolnshire eyre which began in June 1281, are the only three eyres in which it is clear that all cases arising from the ragman rolls, both those concerning royal rights and those concerning abuses of power by officials, are dealt with together in a separate section of the rolls.

Derbyshire ragman and quo warranto pleas

The Derbyshire indictments against officials and its quo warranto pleas appear in this calendar as **682–743**, following the heading 'Rolls of ragman and quo warranto', and take the form of presentments by the jurors for the county or the appropriate division 'in the Ragman Pleas', using that form of words to refer to the ragman rolls of 1275 themselves, which were sent to the eyre for use and returned afterwards. The inquisitions concerning the king and relating to Nottinghamshire, Derbyshire and Lincolnshire which were handed in to Chancery by Gilbert de Thornton at Chester on 9 October 1284 to be kept in the treasury were probably the ragman rolls being returned after the completion of the eyres in those three counties.[1] Franchise holders were obliged to claim them at the begining of the eyre, and failure to do so could result in an order to the sheriff to take them into his hand, as the dean and chapter of Lichfield and the bishop of Chester found to their cost in this eyre (**732, 736**). The quo warranto pleas of most eyres were printed in *Placita de Quo Warranto* (Record Commission, 1818) but those of this eyre were not, perhaps because of the admixture of the presentments against officials with the quo warranto pleas themselves.

Quo warranto pleas

Actions for the king, by his attorneys William de Beverley or Gilbert de Thornton, occur in a few entries (**688, 709, 710, 712, 714, 734, 743**). Some pleading took place in all but the first of these cases, but no judgments were given in this eyre. They were all adjourned to various dates early in the Lincolnshire eyre beginning at Lincoln in June 1281, except one in which the defendants made fines (**743**), and another where the case was partly resolved and required the issue of a writ of quo warranto before any subsequent proceedings (**734**). All the ragman pleas concerning Edmund earl of Lancaster, the king's brother, were adjourned without pleading to the Lincolnshire eyre, when he was to appear with his charters; he was given the same date concerning his liberties in Nottinghamshire and the honour of Lancaster (**713**). A case involving warren which concerned Queen Eleanor's interest in the manor of Bakewell could not proceed at all because it was not known whether she wished to claim the manor in fee or merely a life interest in it (**725**). The king's advocates could not bring a writ of quo warranto against a minor (**684**).

Derbyshire quo warranto cases not continued subsequently

Some Derbyshire cases which do not appear to have continued later are of especial interest. In High Peak Ralph le Wyne was said to have encroached on royal land in Taddington and Priestcliffe in making a lead mine from which the crown had received a levy of a thirteenth (*le lot minere*), but a jury disagreed, agreeing with Ralph that he had only mined

---

[1] *Calendar of Close Rolls 1279–88*, p. 306.

on his own land at Monyash (**686** and note). Thomas le Archer was less fortunate, since he was found to have appropriated 6s. rent from two bovates of land in Hucklow and associated forest rights, formerly payable to the crown at Peak castle, for 18 years, and was liable for substantial arrears (**687** and note). In a similar case at Taddington and Priestcliffe, Richard de Morley and his wife had withdrawn 10s. rent nine years before (**695**).

The Scarsdale jury in 1274–5 had said that Roger Savage claimed free warren in his manor of Stainsby. When Roger appeared, he claimed not only warren but the rights to deal with breaches of the assize of ale, to a gallows (with the right to hang criminals), and waif (the right to take wandering or unclaimed animals). He argued that his ancestors held them by ancient prescriptive right, and that he could not be made to answer for them without the issue of a royal writ. Thornton for the king claimed that Roger had usurped the franchises, and asked for an enquiry. The jurors recalled that under Henry III Stainsby had been within the royal forest, and that the village became a warren because of the forest law; and that Roger and all his ancestors had exercised all the privileges mentioned. As a result Roger was quit as far as the assize of ale, gallows and waif were concerned, but the king's representative intended to bring a writ of quo warranto to test his title to the warren (**734**).

The inhabitants of Derby had several grievances. Navigation of the Derwent to Derby, which had allowed ships and boats to bring wood, food and other merchandise to the town during the reign of King John at the beginning of the century, was said by the town jury to have been blocked by weirs erected by the abbot of Dale at Borrowash and the bishop of Chester at Wilne. Because the burgesses had held of the king in fee-farm, they were entitled to proceed against both the abbot and the bishop in the king's court (**735**). The men of Derby also complained about encroachments on the king's highway in Derby by a house and a drain, the perpetrators of both of which were punished (**738, 739**). The vicar of St Werburgh's had also built a privy over the 'Oddbrook', which had polluted it for three years; he was ordered to remove it at his own charge (**741**).

Quo warranto cases adjourned to the Lincolnshire eyre

A number of Derbyshire proceedings in pleas of quo warranto were adjourned to the Lincolnshire eyre, and are printed in *Placita de Quo Warranto*, pp. 431–44, interspersed with many similar pleas held over from the Yorkshire and Nottinghamshire eyres of 1279–81, from JUST 1/498. The corresponding calendar entries are here annotated with the page numbers of

Placita de Quo Warranto on which the continuation entries appear. Cases involving Edmund earl of Lancaster, including one concerning his tenure of the wapentakes of Litchurch, Wirksworth, Appletree and Repton, are on pp. 433 and 435. However, most of the cases which were adjourned to Lincoln do not appear in *Placita de Quo Warranto*; only four (**709, 724, 736, 740**) were certainly continued there because the pleas are printed. One of them (**724**), was a case of official misconduct. Some other Derbyshire cases which proceeded there are not mentioned in our roll at all. They include proceedings against Stephen de Miners about £4 unpaid crown rents in Cromford (p. 431); against Thomas Bardolf for allowing his villeins of Ockbrook to make suit at the king's wapentake court of Morleyston (pp. 434, 439); against William le Bret and his wife Maria about their right to possess the manors of Whittington and Brimington (p. 436); against the abbot of Dale concerning his right to five bovates of land in Sandiacre (pp. 436, 443); against the dean and chapter of Lincoln concerning the manors of Eaton, Little Chester and a third of the manor of Chesterfield (p. 440); and against the abbot of Welbeck about the manor of Crookhill (p. 440). Four of these cases later continued in the Court of King's Bench (see below).

The first case continued at Lincoln concerned the alleged right of Simon de Gousel and Oliver de Langford to free chase in Hathersage from time out of mind. Both claimed it in right of their common ancestor Matthew de Hathersage, and Oliver, his direct heir, produced a charter of Henry III granting Matthew free warren there. For the king, William de Beverley pleaded that in doing so he gave up the greater privilege of free chase (**709**). On the adjournment to Lincoln, Oliver at first failed to appear, and on the second occasion the sheriff had done nothing to ensure his appearance, nor summoned a jury. On the third neither the defendants nor the jury appeared and it was again adjourned, this time to the Court of King's Bench on 27 April 1282, a few days after the eyre was suspended because of the Welsh war.

Another franchise case which continued at Lincoln was about the bishop of Chester's claim to regalian franchises at Sawley, which excluded only the rights to hear crown pleas, have a gallows and deal with the assize of bread and ale. He had not come, even though summoned, and had not brought his charters to show to the court, so the sheriff was ordered to seize his land and cause him to appear at Lincoln on 1 July (**736**). At Lincoln he appeared by attorney, claiming his market and fair by virtue of a charter of Henry III, dated 2 July 1259,[1] pillory and tumbrill because of the market and fair, and all the other liberties by use of his predecessors from time out of mind. He also claimed free warren in Sawley and all its members (Long Eaton, Draycott, Wilsthorpe, Wilne, Hopewell and Langford) except in the latter, a hamlet where he had no demesne. Thornton, for the king, alleged that he had enlarged his warren outside his demesne lands, and that the hamlets mentioned were not part of the manor of Sawley; he only had the other liberties de facto since the reign of Henry III. The matter went to an enquiry, with the jury to be summoned for 27 October, unless the matter came before the local assize justices in the meantime. The case was still continuing in the Court of King's Bench in Easter term 1283, when a royal order was given to the court through the prominent official John de Kirkby for the bishop to be given respite.[2]

Thornton also sued for the king against the prior or master of the Hospital of St John of Jerusalem over tenements in Derby. Four named tenants who held of the king had let their tenements to the master, giving him annual levies which served to allow him to appropriate lordship over them. He was also alleged, ten years previously, to have placed the hospital's sign over another tenement there, said to have been held of the king in chief by burgage tenure. Its current tenant, Nicholas le Lorymer, appeared and claimed that he held the latter tenement of the king in chief for 22½d. rent, while the town jury said that twenty years before a previous tenant had granted the hospital an annual rent of 12d. from it. The master was considered to have used that grant as a basis for appropriating lordship over it, to the disinheritance of the king, and the master was ordered to appear at Lincoln on 22 June, while Lorymer was to appear in the Bench at Westminster at the same date (**740**). At Lincoln the master failed to appear, and was distrained to appear again later in the Lincolnshire eyre, when he again failed to do so. He was to be further distrained to appear again on 20 January 1282, and, when he again failed to appear, to 27 April 1282, by which time the eyre had been suspended because of the Welsh revolt, not to be resumed for two years. The other case arising in that entry was settled at Derby. The four tenants of the other tenements appeared in the eyre, and stated that they paid their master annual levies as alms, not as a token of lordship, but Thornton for the king alleged that they had paid chevage (in this context probably a levy made by the lord on a man as a token of

[1] *Cal. Charter Rolls 1257–1300*, pp. 18–19.
[2] PRO, KB 27/75, rot. 2.

lordship over him) to be under the protection of the master, not as alms, and had sued their neighbouring royal tenants before a court of the Hospitallers, the 'Conservators of Privilege', in London and elsewhere in England. The tenants could not deny that they had paid chevage, so they were detained, but later made fines with the king, and were prohibited by the court from encumbering their crown tenements with charges which put his lordship over them in jeopardy (**743**).

A number of cases said by entries in the roll to have been adjourned to Lincoln find no mention in the plea roll of proceedings there. One indicates how King John had come to possess Horston castle, previously a private castle, during his reign in exchange for 13 bovates of land (**708** and note). Beverley sought to recover allegedly lost royal rights of wardship and escheat from the demesne at Boythorpe (**710**). The grant of the manor of Hanley to Beauchief abbey by Ralph Musard was queried by Thornton for the king on the grounds that the charter itself should not be valid without royal confirmation, reflecting current concern about alienation of land to the church in mortmain (**712**). A similar view seems to have been taken in connection with the old grant of Newbold to the abbot of Welbeck by William Brewer early in the century (**722**). Both cases were set for discussion with the king, as was the politically difficult question of the justices' stay of proceedings concerning lands held by feoffees of the former earl of Derby, dispossessed after the battle of Chesterfield in 1266 and now in the hands of the king's brother Edmund (**716**; see also **705, 707**). William son of Thomas Bardolf's possession of half of Ockbrook was also to be discussed with the king (**726**). Thornton also questioned the abbot of Chester's claim in Aston-on-Trent, based on a charter of King John, to plaints involving the shedding of blood and the raising of the hue, on the grounds that they belonged entirely to the king (**714** and note).

The claim of John Daniel to administer the assize of bread and ale at Tideswell, derived from a market and fair charter of 1251,[1] was referred to the king and his council because it was found that Daniel was the assignee, not the heir, of the charter grantee, Master Paulinus de Brampton (**683** and note). Master Thomas Bek, bishop of St Davids, held the manor of Pleasley, alienated to him by Robert de Willoughby, to whom it had earlier been demised by Ralph de Reresby; this situation was also to be referred to the king before the case was continued at Lincoln in June, and the bishop was also to answer for his right of free warren (**699** and note). Reresby's widow

---

[1] *Cal. Charter Rolls 1226–57*, p. 353.

Margery was in another case prevented from exercising free warren at Ashover (**721**).

One entry gives an interesting account of how the franchise known as return of writs operated in High Peak wapentake. This was the procedure whereby royal instructions were carried out in a liberty by the sheriff giving it to the bailiff of the liberty to execute rather than executing it himself.[1] In High Peak the sheriff stated that the practice was for the bailiff to make summons and attachments in his bailiwick without making mention of the king's writ in his return, but if he did not do so within eight days of the sheriff's order, the sheriff himself entered the wapentake to distrain the bailiff without the king's order by a writ of *non omittas propter libertatem.* The bailiff asserted that for the previous seven years the sheriffs of Derbyshire had used to mention the king's writ, and they were not accustomed to enter the wapentake to distrain a bailiff with the writ of *non omittas* being issued. The court considered that because the distraint was a royal right, the matter should be considered at the next parliament (**682**). Master Thomas de Louth's claim to liberties at Mapperley was also given a day in the parliament (**727** and note), but no parliament roll has survived to show what the outcome of either of the cases was.

Cases in King's Bench, 1282–85

Four cases which progressed at Lincoln were later continued in the Court of King's Bench. That concerning the land in Sandiacre eventually went in favour of the abbot of Dale after a jury verdict, in Easter term 1282.[2] That concerning the dean and chapter of Lincoln property in Chesterfield and elsewhere continued for some time. The defendants claimed on the basis of seisin from King Richard I, and went to a jury in the form of the grand assize. The jury eventually came a month after Easter in 1285, but the case was then adjourned without day until the king was informed about the inquisition, and has not been traced any further.[3] That concerning Whittington and Brimington, which the defendants claimed on the basis of seisin by King John, also went to a jury, in Easter term 1283, but the outcome has

---

[1] For a detailed account see M.T. Clanchy, 'The franchise of return of writs', *Transactions of the Royal Historical Society*, 5th ser. xvii (1967), pp. 59–82.

[2] PRO, KB 27/67, rot. 30d.

[3] PRO, KB 27/67, rot. 7; KB 27/90, rot. 25d.

not been traced.[1] The fourth, against the abbot of Welbeck in Nottingham-shire, concerning the manor of Crookhill, also eventually disappeared from the rolls. In Easter term 1282 the abbot claimed Crookhill on the basis of charters of King John when he was count of Mortain, and a confirmation dated 8 May 1214 when he was king, and another of Henry III dated 29 December 1250, all of which recited the topographical boundaries of the manor. The king's counsel, John le Fauconer, claimed that the abbot held lands other than those mentioned in the charter, and the case was postponed until the following Michaelmas term.[2]

At least two Derbyshire quo warranto cases which probably resulted from the eyre but which did not give rise to plea roll entries in it or even during the Lincolnshire eyre have been found in the rolls of the Court of King's Bench. The first is in the roll for Easter term 1282 and concerned the right of the dean and chapter of Lincoln to the advowson of Darley, judgment on which was adjourned; it continued in Easter term 1285 when the record of proceedings at Lincoln, which had been sent in and filed on the court's recorda file for Michaelmas 1284, was enrolled on the plea roll, with a list of subsequent adjournments. The dean came and based his right on seisin by Henry II, putting himself on a jury in the form of a grand assize; the jury was to come in Michaelmas term 1285, but no subsequent entry has been found.[3] The second first appears in Michaelmas term 1282, when Nicholas Wake's tenure of Scarsdale wapentake and a third of Chesterfield was questioned. John son of Baldwin Wake was vouched to warrant; he was in the king's wardship and under age, so the case was adjourned until he came of age.[4]

Offences by officials

A large group of entries deal with general misdemeanors by wapentake bailiffs, shrieval and franchisal officials, coroners' clerks, various others and two sheriffs themselves, taking advantage of the powers conveyed by their office (**689–94, 696–8, 700–4, 706, 711, 717–19, 728–30, 738**). They lack detail, but details of many of them can be obtained from the extract ragman roll (see the related notes). The most interesting are those where the bailiff

---

[1] PRO, KB 27/75, rot. 17.
[2] PRO, KB 27/67, rot. 3.
[3] PRO, KB 27/67, rot. 7; KB 27/90, rot. 25d.
[4] PRO, KB 27/71, rot. 14.

of Roger Lestrange, constable of Peak castle, took a large sum from Richard de Buxton for concealment of unspecified treasure found at Winshill, and where a bailiff of Edmund earl of Lancaster took 26s. from Matthew de Kniveton for respite from distraint of knighthood (**693, 718**).

Proceedings against a sub-escheator who was alleged to have wasted the king's woods at Horston for 11 years had to be adjourned to Lincoln, because he had not appeared and had to be distrained in Leicestershire (**731**). Nothing appears in the Lincolnshire roll, and only one of the cases of official misconduct is known to have continued at Lincoln. It involved the king's escheator, William de Boyville, and his sub-bailiff, Nigel Duredent, who seized the manor of Langford after the death of Nigel de Langford, who actually held it of the bishop of Chester, not the king, and levied 100s. of its issues in 1274. Duredent came to the eyre, and alleged that Boyville and not himself had taken the money. He asked for jury trial, but then paid a fine of a mark (13s. 4d.) instead (**724**). Boyville appeared at Lincoln about 22 June and stated that he had received only 74s., as his Exchequer account would show, and asked for a jury. He fined a mark, and the case was postponed until 18 November for the Exchequer rolls to be checked, but no further entry in the case appears.

Civil pleas: Derbyshire litigants

Attorneys

The largest body of material concerns civil pleas cases involving Derbyshire litigants (**1–400**), although over a quarter of the entries (**293-400**) are appointments by parties of attorneys to represent their interests in the conduct of a case. Each entry gives the name of the litigant, the name or names of the attorney or attorneys, the name of the opponent, and a brief indication of the nature of the case. The relationships between party and attorney can be revealing, but it can often only be known from other sources. Abbots of monastic houses frequently appointed men who were apparently members of their community to represent them (e.g. **298, 304, 328, 355**), while married female litigants usually appointed their husband or son (e.g. **300**), or widows their son (**303**). The connection between a party and his or her attorney is rarely stated in other cases, but men or women sometimes appointed their groom (**391, 392**). Some attorneys in Bench cases were appointed during the eyre (**346**). A handful of professional attorneys appear to have been at work. Richard de Stapleford was appointed in 14 cases, Richard Huberd in seven, Richard de Marnham in five.

Right of land

Actions for right of land were the oldest category of civil plea litigated in royal courts, often originally settled by judicial duel, until the institution of the grand assize jury of local knights about 1179 provided an alternative means of resolution. When a defendant put himself on the grand assize, the sheriff summoned four knights to the next eyre in the county to elect 12 knights from a panel of 16 to give their verdict on the issue put to them. Lists of grand assize electors and jurors are now frequently used to indicate who were the leading knights in the county at the time of an eyre, but there are only two grand assize panels named in the civil pleas roll of this eyre (**3, 243**), so the amount of information provided in this instance is rather limited. Henry FitzHerbert was the only man serving as an elector in both cases, and was also on both panels, although he was not marked as having been sworn in the first, while both panels included Hugh de Strelley, John Fannel, Simon de Gousil, Roger de Marston, Geoffrey de Gresley, Alfred de Sulney and Robert de Sacheverell. Because of the need to trace the development of rights to a particular estate, some of the actions for right of land themselves give information about the descent of prominent local families and their manors in recent generations, such as the Greys of Shirland, the Staveleys of Whitwell and the Cromwells of West Hallam (**3, 92, 120, 243**), while others give details about several families with property in the same village, like Breadsall (**66, 71–2, 129–30, 255**). None of the pedigrees go back further than the reign of Richard I, the beginning of that reign in 1189 being now firmly established as the limit of legal memory. Cases relating to minor freeholder families can also give valuable family data, such as that concerning the family of Henry son of Richard of Normanton near Derby (**132**), and light is shed by some entries on the descent of urban properties within families (**203**).

Cases where the disputed land was not held in chief were begun by the writ of right to the lord; it was frequently removed from his court to the county court, and from there to a royal court under a writ of pone. Where the land in question was held of the crown in chief the initiating writ was the *precipe in capite*, which is mentioned by name in two cases involving the abbot of Burton in Coton (**117, 134**) and the grand assize case over the manor of Shirland between John Bek and Reynold de Grey (**3**).

The occasions for delay in right cases were such that some of them proceeded very slowly. Nevertheless, in this eyre seventeen (**3, 17, 66, 72, 92, 111, 113, 117, 132, 134, 152, 161, 171, 203, 218, 237, 241**) were concluded during it. Six of them (**3, 66, 72, 92, 111, 218**) ended by agreement, either enrolled or by final concord; the largest consideration involved was the £100 paid by Henry de Grey to settle John Bek's claim to Shirland, while Reynold de Grey was one of five who agreed to pay 100 silver marks to Henry de Ireton and his wife and sister-in-law as part of the settlement of a dispute over a carucate of land in Breadsall (**66, 134**). The dispute between the abbot of Burton and Nicholas de Segrave over the manor of Coton was postponed sine die because Nicholas's ancestor Stephen de Segrave (who was justiciar of England between 1232 and 1234) had received a grant of the manor from Henry III in 1228, which meant that Nicholas could not answer without the king; the charter is given in full in the roll (**134**). The abbot's other writ over smaller properties in Coton against Adam le Keu was withdrawn because his wife Mabel, joint holder of the property, was not mentioned in it (**117**).

Most of the other cases were adjourned to the Lincolnshire eyre or the Bench (**87, 129, 219, 243, 250, 251, 255, 268, 271**). Subsequent process has been traced for many of them in Appendix A, but usually not as far as the judgment, with one exception (**A7**). A claim for a quarter of the manor of Repton, by Richard son of Ralph Bugge against John son of Nicholas of St Maur, was delayed for discussion with the king, because the defendant was only four years of age, before being adjourned to Lincoln (**219, A19**). Many of the disputes were over holdings of a relatively minor nature between people of no great significance in the county, except for the important Shirland, Whitwell and Breadsall cases, and three involved urban properties in Derby (**17, 161, 203**). One involved a tenancy held of Edmund earl of Lancaster in Hognaston (**237**). In a dispute over minor properties in Whittington, the plaintiff Ralph de Handley was allowed to wage his law, a method of proof which involved the production of twelve oath helpers prepared to swear as to truth of his own statement (**97**), but there is no record that it actually took place at the appointed time. The second grand assize case, which was adjourned to Lincoln, was an interesting dispute between Ralph de Cromwell and seven men claiming common of pasture in West Hallam (**243**). The claim was for common in 160 acres of wood and moor for all their beasts throughout the year, and for pigs between 29 September and 11 November, based on tenure from time out of mind; Ralph claimed that his ancestor, another Ralph, had held the 160 acres in fee in the time of King John, and the common by the defendants was usurped. At Lincoln the jurors did not appear (**A27**), and the ultimate outcome, if there was one, has not been traced. A case against the bishop of Lichfield and a tenant of his concerning property in Stanton by Dale was further delayed when it reached Lincoln because of the villein status of the tenant, Julia widow of William Tornepeny (**250, A24**). A dispute between the abbot of Burton and the prior of Tutbury over the manor of Osmaston was delayed by disputes as to whether other properties in the village should have been mentioned in the writ; it had still not been settled by early 1283, when a jury failed to appear in the Bench, then at Shrewsbury (**252, A35**). Similar delays took place in a case over 1½ carucates in Breadsall because of an allegation of bastardy against Joan, wife of the plaintiff Henry de Curzon (**255, A48**).

Assizes of novel disseisin

The assize of novel disseisin, instituted by Henry II in 1166 and very popular ever since then, had long been the routine remedy for anyone who was disseised (dispossessed) of freehold property unjustly and without a court judgment. The procedure was the classic 'possessory assize' for many generations of litigants, the key element in which was a decision of a jury of neighbouring freeholders able to view the tenement in question and assumed to have detailed knowledge of local affairs. Every civil pleas roll in this period contains significant numbers of assizes of novel disseisin, and the one for this eyre is no exception. The period during which complaint about an allegedly unlawful disseisin was permissible was limited by time, but by the late thirteenth century this was such a long period that it had very little restrictive effective. By 1281 the limit of legal memory for assizes had been fixed at the date of Henry III's first expedition to Gascony in 1230 (e.g. **2**).

The types of property covered by the assizes in this roll encompass rents, shops, tofts, messuages and tenements in towns, as well as rural landholdings. The property specified was often apparently relatively small in value, and much of it was in towns, clearly indicating the wide social reach of royal justice by the reign of Edward I. A number of the entries are limited to the information that an assize has been brought and withdrawn or not prosecuted, leaving the plaintiffs and their sureties facing amercement (e.g. **24–6, 28, 52, 61, 80, 183–8**). None of the people involved in such cases was apparently of great note, and one was pardoned any amercement because he was poor (**186**). One writ, concerning a toft in Ashbourne, was agreed to be invalid because of that town's ancient demesne status (**144**); presumably a little writ of right close was required. In another Ashbourne assize the defendant produced a lease issued by the king's steward, Thomas de Normanvill, in 1277 as his warrant; because of the crown interest, the case was adjourned to the Lincoln eyre and settled there after consultation, the result being recorded as a postea in the Derbyshire roll (**35** and note).

More prominent men were involved in a few cases as defendants, such as Matthew de Kniveton, Thomas de Chaworth and the abbot of Burton (**24, 61, 207**), while there are retrospective references to the activities of Ralph de Frescheville in the eyre of 1269 (**128**). There is little of significant procedural interest in many of the assizes of novel disseisin in this eyre. Of the completed cases, one plaintiff won by jury verdict after the defendant's default (**2**), another when the defendant admitted the disseisin before the jury gave its verdict (**154**), while in two others the jury decided that the alleged diseissin had indeed taken place (**2, 6**). Verdicts for the defendants took place when the jurors judged that the plaintiffs had never been seised (**18, 55, 78, 143**), when they considered that the defendants held the property (two shops in Bakewell) by the goodwill of the plaintiffs (**124**), or when the plaintiff withdrew (**37**). In one case the plaintiff, Thomas le Curzon, wasted his writ, because the defendant, Robert de Mountjoy, was able to point out that the land in question was in Stenson, not in Twyford as the writ stated (**163**).

The details of three particular cases are of more than average interest. In one concerning the seisin of a messuage in Derby (**78**), there are allegations which, if true, indicate the lengths to which people were prepared to go to gain a legally defensible possession of the property. The plaintiff apparently intruded into the messuage on the very night of the death of the original enfeoffor, after one of the defendants had intruded while the enfeoffor was still alive, and the defendant immediately ejected the plaintiff on the following day. A complicated case between the prominent Frescheville and Dethick families over the rent from a tenement in Locko involved reference to the rolls of Gilbert de Preston's Derbyshire eyre of 1269 for information about a case brought on a writ of entry in that eyre; the rolls were checked by early May, before the case was postponed to the Lincolnshire eyre for judgment (**128**). Preston's civil pleas roll for that eyre is the only Derbyshire eyre roll to survive before 1281, and the entry can still be found in it.[1]

Finally, when the abbot of Burton was accused of disseising William son of William of Mickleover of a messuage and four bovates in Mickleover, the abbot claimed that earlier William had sued him before a royal court for demanding customs and services other than those owed to the kings of England when they held the manor; on that occasion, he said William had not been able to verify his claim to ancient demesne status either by

---

[1] *Calendar of the cases for Derbyshire from eyre and assize rolls*, ed. C.E. Lugard (privately printed, 1938), pp. 129–30.

reference to Domesday Book or by royal charter (**207**).[1] The case was adjourned to the Lincolnshire eyre, when judgment was postponed to 20 October 1281 (**A18**). It seems to represent part of the consequences of a series of disputes which arose early in 1280 and which are narrated at great length and in fascinating detail in the Burton cartulary.[2] The abbey's view of the events is clearly indicated by a rubric in red ink, *Malicia Villanorum*, 'the malice of the villeins'. The abbot was sued on a writ issued on 10 February 1280 by ten of his tenements in Mickleover, the tenants claiming ancient demesne, while ten days later the abbot himself obtained a writ to the sheriff ordering him to assist the abbot in distraining the tenants.

The case was conducted in the Bench at Westminster during the following months, and during it Domesday Book was indeed consulted. Judgment for the abbot on 3 June was followed three days later by a massive distraint on the tenants (including no less than 506 sheep) by the abbot, whose agents lodged some of the beasts in Derbyshire and some in Staffordshire. Another writ against this new distraint was issued for the tenants on 8 June and brought to the abbot at Burton on 22 June by six of their number. According to the cartulary, the abbot decided to resist the writ because no mention had been made when it was obtained that he had won his case, and because when his steward had removed the reeve of Mickleover from office in a session of his court at Findern, the other tenants all refused to accept the office because of the distraint. His view was that, as his villeins, they owned nothing except their own bellies. Another writ obtained by the tenants directed to the sheriff of Staffordshire included the stipulation that anyone who resisted the order was to appear in parliament in October to answer for their contempt. Resistance by the bailiff at Abbot's Bromley led to the tenants appearing before the chancellor and others accompanying the king at Selborne in Hampshire on 9 July to complain about the abbot's refusal; a monk representing the abbot, after discussing the matter with Ralph de Hengham, presumably the abbot's legal advisor, appeared before the chancellor and agreed that the abbot would abide by the Bench judgment until another was made. He then ejected the ten tenants from their homes, leaving the women and children in place, but then ejected them too on 13

---

[1] The case had been heard in the Bench at Westminster in Easter term 1280: PRO, CP 40/33, rot. 81d.

[2] For a full account of the dispute see D. Crook, 'Freedom, villeinage and legal process: the dispute between the abbot of Burton and his tenants of Mickleover, 1280', *Nottingham Medieval Studies*, xliv (2000), 123–40.

July, 'in order that they might sue out a writ of novel disseisin'. The tenants then followed the king for several days before they obtained, at Langley in Hertfordshire on 21 July, a writ to the sheriff of Derbyshire for the replevin of the cattle of 39 named tenants, one of them being a William son of William. This and a similar writ to the sheriff of Staffordshire were not entirely successful, so the tenants, with their wives and children, went to the king at Nottingham, complaining of robbery and expulsion from their houses, obtaining new writs to replevy their cattle. The narrative then recounts in some detail the submission of some of the tenants and acknowledgment of their villeinage during August. On 13 September two of the other tenants were punished by spending a day in the stocks at Burton, and the cartulary narrative comes to an end.[1] The eyre case at Derby and Lincoln indicates that the matter was not settled in all respects, but the abbot's victory over his tenants was effectively complete eight months before the Derbyshire eyre began.

Novel disseisin of common of pasture

Rights of pasture associated with free-holdings were an important part of the rural economy and were a frequent subject of litigation, by a variant of the assize of novel disseisin which seems to have been as old as the assize itself. Of the cases which occur in this eyre, four, in Marston,[2] Snelston, Quorndon and Radbourne (**48, 49, 82, 199**), did not proceed very far, the writs being withdrawn, the first because the defendant's wife, co-holder of heathland in Marston, was not named in the writ, which was therefore invalid. In the first two cases and the last, the tenement to which the pasture was attached lay in another parish, respectively Barton Blount, Yeaveley and Kirk Langley. In the first, the plaintiff was given leave by the court to withdraw, but in the others the plaintiff and his sureties were in mercy, as also was the plaintiff in another case in Doveridge who simply failed to prosecute (**162**); two plaintiffs paid fines to compound for their offence (**82, 199, 865, 876**). In the Radbourne case, the plaintiff's withdrawal was followed by an agreement in the form of a recognisance before the court, whereby the plaintiff remitted his claim to the 100 acres of common of pasture in the assarts for all kinds of beasts during the whole year in return

---

[1] *Collections for a History of Staffordshire* (William Salt Archaeological Society, Pt I, Vol. V, 1884), pp. 81–6.

[2] Probably Marston Montgomery, rather than Marston on Dove.

for being allowed to pasture them there in the open season only and a payment of 5 silver marks from Robert de Stafford, one of the defendants and a prominent county knight (**199**).

Assize juries settled two cases, although the findings of one of them was questioned. Robert de Dethick and his wife Ellen claimed that John de Newbold had no rights to pasture in 100 acres of Whittington moor, Ellen as a co-heiress claiming it in severalty and exercised by her guardian before she came of age, but the jury decided in favour of John (**77**). William de Coddington sued the prior of Tutbury for both common of pasture in 20 acres of moor and pasture in Edlaston belonging to a holding in (Great) Clifton, and for the tenement itself, consisting of 12 acres. The prior's bailiff, John Fucher, claimed that the two villages were in different wapentakes and that neither had commons in the other, and was upheld by the jury on that issue and his denial that William ever had seisin of the tenement (**143** and note). William immediately fined 20s. for an assize to attaint the jury in respect of both verdicts, but then failed to appear, but on both counts he was pardoned any amercement at the request of Ralph de Hengham, chief justice of the King's Bench and the most senior judge in England (**147, 148, 389, 870**).

Assizes of nuisance

The assize of nuisance was apparently created at the same time as novel disseisin in 1166, and made it possible for a man to challenge an action taken by a neighbour which would result in damage or nuisance to himself. Only three cases occurred in this eyre, involving respectively the destruction of a bank in Langford put up between common and arable land to prevent beasts straying into the crops, replacing a defective hedge (**50**); a fence raised in Shirley, probably to mark a boundary (**79**); and the gutters of a house in Derby, excessive water from which allegedly swamped and spoiled a neighbour's vegetables and prevented anything else being grown; and the creation of two doors in the same house, facing the neighbour's land and often left open to the detriment of the privacy of his garden (**116**).

Assizes of mort d'ancestor

This assise, just over a century old in 1281, was the one available to an heir when a deceased relative, whether father, mother, brother, sister, aunt or uncle, died seized of an estate of which he was now being denied seisin to which he considered himself entitled. In this eyre assizes of novel disseisin are in fact outnumbered by assizes of mort d'ancestor.

By 1281 the same legal limit applied as in novel disseisin (e.g. **1**). In 13 cases the plaintiff failed to prosecute the writ, so they and their pledges were liable to amercement (**27, 30, 31, 33, 39, 40, 86, 145, 155, 174, 196, 211, 212, 248**); in the last case the amercement was pardoned because he was under age. In three other cases the plaintiff had to withdraw because of an omission or mistake in the writ, such as the non-inclusion of the name of the defendant's wife, who was enfeoffed at the same time as her husband (**1**), or an incorrect description of a tenure as being in common (**29**), or the incorrect naming of a plaintiff's uncle (**91**). In one case (**131**) the defendant claimed that he did not hold the entire property at the time the writ was obtained, but did not thereby prevent the holding of the assize. In another a defendant sought judgment on the writ because he was a brother of the ancestor and held the tenements through the same descent as the plaintiff (**164**). A defendant against whom the assize was brought by Nicholas de Segrave did not appear, but the assize proceeded by default and Segrave was successful (**105**).

Successful defences by defendants included claims that he did not hold the property on the day the writ was obtained, when it was held by someone else (**13**), or the ancestor did not hold it at the time of his death (**32**), or the ancestor demised the land to the defendant for a term still unexpired (**96**). Interesting details include a decision in an assize over property in Horsley in favour of a sister of the ancestor by both parents over a half-brother by a different wife (**164**); and the claim in a Bakewell case by Queen Eleanor's bailiff for the town that the writ did not run there because it was a free borough (**91**), but he was unsuccessful and the assize proceeded.

In one case the entry in the roll ends suddenly with a postponement until the following day, and was not resumed (**170**), and others were adjourned to the Lincolnshire eyre to allow for the summoning of a vouchee to warrant who was thought to be resident in Lancashire (**206**), or to hear judgment (**149, 239**). Assizes could be held over because the current holder of the property or a vouchee to warrant was under age (**36, 98, 149**). As so often with this particular assize, five cases were settled by agreement, before or after pleading, and after paying a fine to obtain leave from the court to do so (**90, 95, 136, 166, 248**).

Writs of aiel and besaiel

The assize of mort d'ancestor was available only when the person whose seisin at death was in question was the father, mother, brother, sister, uncle or aunt of the plaintiff. Under Henry III, about 1237, new actions of aiel (grandfather), besaiel (grandmother) and cosinage (cousin) were added to mort d'ancestor to cover claims for seisin based on the seisin of those three more distant relatives; they were not assizes. An early tradition attributed the invention of the writ of aiel to Walter de Merton when he was a Chancery clerk, which he may have been in 1237; he was subsequently chancellor under both Henry III and Edward I.[1] There are no cosinage cases in this eyre, but there are a number begun on writs of aiel, the claim being based on the seisin of the grandfather. Of them, four were not prosecuted, so little detail is given in the enrolment (**9, 14, 209, 214**). Three others were concluded by agreements (**126, 158, 281**); the defendant in the first was the abbot of Chester. Three others were adjourned to the Lincolnshire eyre and then to the Bench (**142, 221, 257, A8, A9, A30**). One (**103**) was referred to a jury in the Derbyshire eyre, but there is no record of the verdict. Another, relating to a messuage attached to the vicarage of Tideswell, was delayed because the vicar would not answer without the dean and chapter of Lichfield, who had presented him (**65**). The only case to be concluded during the eyre related to a bovate of land in Morley, where the jury chosen by the parties decided in favour of the plaintiff (**43**).

A single writ of besaiel, based on the seisin of the grandmother, relates to Milnhay, and was postponed to the Lincoln eyre (**270, A45**).

Assizes of darrein presentment

Much less frequent in occurrence than the other assizes was the assize of darrein presentment, 'last presentation', which deals with possessory actions relating to advowsons, the right of presentations to churches. If a church was vacant the person who last presented to it, or his heir, did so again, but if anyone wished to dispute the possession of that right he could bring this assize. This eyre included only a single case, an important one between the king and the dean and chapter of Lichfield over the church of Bakewell. The king's case, argued by Gilbert de Thornton, was based on the presentation of a clerk called Levenoth by Henry II, after which it appears from subsequent pleading that the church had been handed down from father to son until March 1281. The treasurer and canons of Lichfield argued that when the writ was issued, on 18 April 1281, there was no dean, although Master John of Derby had been elected but not confirmed, and the assize

---

[1] *Early Registers of Writs*, ed. E. de Haas and G.D.G. Hall (Selden Society, lxxxvii, 1970), pp. xv*n.*, 91.

should not be held until he was. The case was adjourned to the Lincolnshire eyre, where there was further pleading in October 1281. Eventually, the clergy requested the king to inspect relevant charters of John and Henry III, and on 12 November 1282, at Rhuddlan during his Welsh campaign, Edward quitclaimed his right to the advowson in return for a fine of 1,000 marks (**247, A52**).

Dower

Widows of deceased men were entitled to claim a third of the property which their husband had held on the day of their marriage in dower to sustain them in their old age, and dower cases are common in late thirteenth-century civil pleas rolls. If they were not in a hurry, widows seeking dower might wait until the next eyre in their county before bringing their writ, but if they had an immediate need they would be obliged to proceed in the Bench at Westminster. Two writs brought by the same widow had both been begun in the Bench and had reached the stage where the issue was to be put to a jury in the eyre, which in both cases decided in favour of the defendants (**141, 189**). Most of those widows whose writs were heard in the Derbyshire eyre had not obtained them earlier, and indeed the husbands of a few must have died some time before, since their former wives sued jointly with new husbands (**16, 215, 228**). Some of the dower cases related to urban property: a burgage in Bakewell (**12**); two stalls and a shop in Derby (**141, 189**); and a messuage in Chesterfield (**254**). More often, however, they concerned rural landed holdings, usually small (**15, 51, 172, 198, 215, 240**). The most significant amount of property in which dower was claimed consisted of 200 acres of wood, agistment rights in 1,000 acres of pasture and 3 bovates of land in Tissington (**228**). The most important case in terms of the status of the litigants was brought by the widow of Roger Deincourt against the abbot of Welbeck in North Wingfield (**264**). In both this case and one brought by the widow of William de Saundby against Richard de Grey in Sandiacre (**285**), dower was claimed in a watermill.

In three cases the defendant accepted the widow's claim without any defence (**12, 15, 51**), but in others denied it on the grounds that the former husband of the claimant was not seised of the property in question either at the time of the marriage or indeed at any subsequent time (**16, 141, 172, 189, 285, A44**); two of these cases went to a jury but no verdicts appear in the roll. In the Tissington case some of the defendants claimed that the widow, Lucy de Audley, had secured her agistment rights as a result of an earlier case in the Bench against an earlier lord of the manor, and had had rights of equivalent value elsewhere which nullified her claim to dower in a wood, so the dispute went to a jury; her other claims against a different defendant were settled by a detailed agreement, which was enrolled (**228**). Two widows failed to prosecute their writs and were liable to amercement (**215**, **235**), while another withdrew from hers, with the agreement of the court, after the defendant made six vouchers to warrant, including five daughters of her former husband (**240**). In one case the defendant exercised the right to view the property from which dower was being sought, resulting in a postponement to the Lincolnshire eyre, where the defendant disputed the claim, and the case was still unresolved early in 1283, mainly because of the failure of a jury to appear (**285**, **343**, **380**, **A44**). In the Deincourt v. Welbeck case the abbot vouched John Deincourt to warrant, and Roger Deincourt's widow Alice claimed that he had assigned her dower in tenements in Norton and Boythorpe, of which she was only a feoffee, and nothing from her husband's other lands. The issue went to a jury, which was summoned to appear at Lincoln, but there John Deincourt was allowed to go without day because of Alice's default (**264**, **311**, **315**, **A16**). In another case the defendant failed to appear, so the dower third was taken into the king's hand until his appearance at Lincoln (**254**); another group of defendants who had already failed to appear lost by default and the widow received her dower (**198**). Finally, an ultimately unsuccessful claim for dower at Oxcroft in Bolsover made after the failure of a writ of entry in the eyre led to a lengthy dispute over the relevance to the case of the abjuration of the realm by the former husband at the church of Newton in Kesteven in Lincolnshire; the husband's father had given his lands to his son before his own death on taking the religious habit, but the son had died first (**179**, **A5**).

Warranty of charter

By the late thirteenth century it was customary for grants of land or the income from it to include warranty clauses, which were intended by the grantor to guarantee the property to the grantee against other parties, and which bound the grantor's wife and heirs as well as himself. If the property subsequently became the subject of litigation, as was not infrequently the case, the grantee or his heir could summon the grantor or his heir to court to confirm the obligation, so that if the estate were lost he would have to provide another equivalent estate to the grantee on the same terms. A writ of warranty of charter could be obtained to try to ensure that such warranty was carried out.

Two plaintiffs who brought writs of warranty of charter in the eyre failed to prosecute them, so they and their sureties were liable to be amerced (**5, 182**). In the great majority of the other cases they were settled by a final concord, for which a fine, normally of half a mark but occasionally 10s. or 20s., was payable (**22, 34, 38, 53, 54, 62, 70, 84, 85, 110, 122, 210, 220, 222, 224, 231, 238, 253, 262, 269, 282, 859–64, 866, 868, 869, 877, 879–881**). These entries are very short, only six (**85, 220, 224, 234, 238, 269**), giving any details about the size and nature of the estate for which warranty was required. It is probable that most or all of these cases were collusive, the writ having been brought with the deliberate intention of levying a final concord in the court, a function in which it was entirely replaced by the writ of covenant about half a century after this eyre, largely as a result of Edward I's legislation against subinfeudation. One of the concorded cases (**224**) concerned Matthew of Kniveton, but the fine was not, as might have been expected, entered in the family cartulary.[1]

There are only a handful of warranty cases which appear to have been genuinely contentious, not because there was any substantive pleading but because the defendants failed to appear, and all but one of them are recorded close together in the roll (**242, 245, 246, 249, 289**). In three cases land of the appropriate value was to be taken into the king's hand pending their appearance at Lincoln, with the plaintiffs given the same day to appear in the Bench by attorney (**242, 245, 289**). At Lincoln and subsequently in the Bench two of the cases continued, but were not resolved until at least Hilary term 1283 (**A53, A20**). In two initially similar cases, the plaintiffs in one eventually appeared and concorded (**246**), while in the other the sheriff was also to appear at Lincoln to hear judgment on himself for not summoning the defendant (**249**). In one case which resulted from an assize of novel disseisin brought by Hubert de Frescheville in the eyre (possibly **128**), the defendant simply acknowledged his obligation to warrant, and did so (**252**).

Covenant

Writs of covenant began to be used in about 1200, as a means of enforcing agreements, particularly leases of land. From the 1330s onwards, for five subsequent centuries, writs of covenant became virtually the only writs on which collusive actions initiated to levy a final concord could be grounded. In this eyre four resulted in a concord with no pleading (**146, 229,**

---

[1] It is, however, printed in an appendix of the modern edition from the original foot, PRO, CP 25/1/37/17, no. 61: *The Kniveton Leiger*, ed. A. Saltman (Derbyshire Archaeological Society Record Series, vii, 1977 for 1972–3), pp. 275–6.

234, 880). Others were not prosecuted or were withdrawn and resulted in amercements (**156, 160, 871**). The only other covenant case, between the abbot of Croxden and Richard de Pres, had to be postponed to Lincoln because Richard could not be distrained to appear because he had no property in Derbyshire; the sheriff of Staffordshire was ordered to distrain him to appear at Lincoln, where there was a further adjournment because the sheriff had failed to make the distraint (**106, 304, A11**).

Writs of entry

Writs of entry developed in the late twelfth century as a means of dealing with cases relating to the possession of land where none of the possessory assizes or actions of right could be used. They became very popular during the thirteenth century and are numerous in this eyre. There were several forms, but many of the entries in the roll are too short to reveal the nature of a particular case, such as when a writ of entry was not prosecuted (**8, 11, 45, 69, 73, 93, 167, 190, 192, 193, 217**); postponed to Lincoln because of vouchers to warranty of parties resident in foreign counties (**58, 64, 101, 169**); or because the defendants claimed a view of the property (**274, A23**), accepted without pleading by the defendant (**89**), proceeded to a final concord without pleading (**19, 119, 168**), or a combination of two of these (**165**). One case was concorded at Lincoln (**A6**), and another described at Derby as being about the right to a marriage portion claimed by writ of entry (**169**) was later described as a plea of dower (**A10**). What was described as a writ of entry brought to establish a woman's right to holdings at Oxcroft in Bolsover failed when the defendants claimed that her rights there depended entirely on her former husband (**179**), but she continued her litigation by a writ of dower which eventually failed after disputes about the abjuration of the realm for larceny in Lincolnshire by her former husband (**A5**).

Cases which were recorded more fully provide a great deal of information of interest to local historians, about families and their pedigrees, sometimes over several generations, and about leases and conveyances of estates. Entry *ad terminum qui preteriit* (to a term which has expired), was an action which a plaintiff could bring against a lessee, or someone who had obtained an estate from a lessee, who was still in possession after a lease had expired. One case was won by the defendant when a jury agreed with him that an aunt of the plaintiff who he had denied had an heir did in fact have one (**44**). One plaintiff failed to prosecute his writ (**102**), while another withdrew his because the defendant showed that he had obtained entry by a person other than the one named in it (**104**). Also withdrawn was a claim against the vicar of Doveridge, after the dispute had gone to a jury; the plaintiff paid a fine (**153, 871**). Two former vicars were mentioned by name during pleading. A case brought against the abbot of Dale by the husbands of two sisters with their wives failed because their writ claimed their right in common, whereas they could only claim through their wives; the plaintiffs were given leave by the court to withdraw (**286**). Another was concorded after an assertion by the defendants that they held the property in question, in Egginton, in fee under the terms of a charter rather than on a lease, after which the plaintiff disputed the authorship of the charter (**109**). Another dispute over the terms of a charter relating to property in Hartington, between Walter de Ridware and the abbot of Cumbermere, also turned on whether the charter conveyed in fee or was a lease for, in this case, 14 years. The charter had already been acknowledged by Walter's predecessor William in the Staffordshire eyre of 1255, but judgment was reserved to the Lincolnshire eyre, where Walter defaulted and the abbot went without day (**151, A32**). Another plaintiff lost his case when a jury decided that the alleged lease made by his grandfather had never taken place (**176**). The only successful plaintiff among the cases completed at Derby was a man who sued for only half an acre in Scropton, and whose opponent vouched the abbot of Rocester to warrant (**200**). One of the cases whose type of writ is unidentifiable in the Derby roll (**151**) proves to relate to an allegedly expired lease, and in further pleading in the Bench at Westminster in Hilary term 1282 an alleged act of homage performed at Simon Basset's house at Nether Haddon in 1273 was referred to as justifying a disputed voucher to warranty, and the case went to a jury (**A12**).

A writ of entry *cui in vita sua contradicere non potuit* (who in his life could not be contradicted) was a remedy for a widow whose own land had been alienated by her husband against her will during his lifetime, when she could not prevent him from doing so (**284**). One plaintiff's writ failed because the defendant showed that in it the means by which she had secured her possession was inaccurately defined (**123**). In another case a jury agreed with the defendant that her former husband had held the property in question by tenancy and in his own right (**114**). In another the defendant vouched to warranty two men but should, according to the plaintiff, also have vouched a third, but he was in turn said to have been outlawed for a felony and to have lost his share of an inheritance to his two brothers; she did however eventually obtain seisin (**140, 272**). One plaintiff's right to two sums of rent was acknowledged by the defendants, but subject to their lease for two years (**197**), while another defendant returned the disputed messuage in Derby

(**272**). In another case the defendant was an under-age girl, who was allowed by the justices to be represented by Richard de Marnham, who seems to have been a professional attorney (**284**). The case was adjourned to Lincoln following a voucher to warranty, and it continued into 1283 without being resolved (**A31**).

In two other cases the writs alleged intrusion after the death of the previous holder, a lessee for life in one case and a dowager in the other (**226, 227**). In both cases the plaintiffs were Richard de Draycott and his wife Agnes and the defendant was Henry Fitzherbert of Norbury. In the first, Henry denied that he held the property, and in the second case that he held all of it, in Norbury and Roston, on the day the writ was obtained, when it was held by someone else; the jury agreed. There were also a number of cases of entry *sur disseisin*, brought by an ejected possessor of an estate or his or her heir against someone who held it as a result of a earlier disseisin. In a Mercaston case, after an earlier attempt with a writ which failed because the defendant did not hold all of the estate (**67**), the defendant denied that any disseisin had taken place and a jury was summoned, but before it gave its verdict the parties came to an agreement in which some additional land 'lying ... towards the sun' (i.e. to the south) of the disputed property was included (**75**). For other cases which went to a jury after similar denials no outcome is recorded either in the eyre or subsequently after further process (**94, 159, 223, A36, A42**). One case about Wirksworth, in which one of those vouched to warrant was the abbot of Darley, was won by the defendant Hugh de Staunton, but the plaintiffs had their amercement pardoned because they were poor (**208**). Richard de Grey won a case against two sons of Hugh of Morley over quite a sizeable estate in Kirk Hallam after the jury agreed with him that they had never been seised and so could not have been disseised (**133**). The brothers however attempted to attaint the jury, so the dispute went on for some time after the eyre closed (**A43**). Finally, a Hollington case which turned on a quitclaim allegedly made in Robert de Lexington's 1252 Nottinghamshire eyre was eventually won by the plaintiff in the Bench at Shrewsbury in Michaelmas term 1282 because the alleged disseisor, who had been vouched to warrant by the defendant, could not produce any evidence of the transaction (**118, A58**). Lexington's roll was clearly not available for consultation, and was probably never handed in. Later in 1281, on 24 July and again on 10 December, writs were sent to the Exchequer from the Lincolnshire eyre asking for a search to be made in Lexington's rolls for an earlier Lincolnshire case which it was expected would be recorded in them. The treasurer and chamberlains replied that they had found nothing 'because the said rolls remained in the custody of Robert de Lexington, whose son and heir, who ought to answer for them, is under age and in the king's keeping, and cannot be distrained to answer for those rolls until he becomes of legal age.[1]

In two cases it was alleged that entry had been obtained as a result of an estate being demised while the holder was of unsound mind (**108**). The first was against the abbot of Rocester, who successfully claimed that his possession had been obtained through his predecessor in the office. In the other the defendants agreed that their claims derived from the plaintiff's father, but denied that he had been of unsound mind. The case went to a jury, the verdict of which is not recorded (**127**). In three cases it was alleged that the person through whom entry had been obtained was a minor at the time. In one, over a tenement in Derby, the defendants claimed that according to the custom of the town someone who could count 20s., measure cloth, and weigh merchandise was deemed to be of full age. The jury in the case stated that the age at which a man was of full enough age to sell or grant a tenement was 15, and that in any case the plaintiff, Simon of Nottingham, was 18 at the time of the transaction, and so his claim failed (**63**). In another Derby case, in which the plaintiff was a woman, a similar statement was made, except that on this occasion it was merely stated that the custom of the borough was that 'any woman is of full age ... (and may sell her tenements in the borough), when she knows how to trade'; the verdict of the jury is not recorded (**115**). The third case of this kind, in which the abbot of Croxden was the defendant, turned on whether the one of the plaintiffs, who was sueing jointly with her husband, had been under age when she made a quitclaim concerning some land earlier granted by her father. A jury was asked to decide, but the case was concorded before it gave its verdict (**100**).

Customs and services

There are a few disputes over the services owed to a tenant by a lord in the eyre, which could be brought by a writ of right of customs and services. Because it was an action of right procedure could be slow. Edmund son of

---

[1] British Library, Harl. MS 742 (Spalding priory cartulary), ff. 20r–21r. In fact Lexington, as an unmarried clerk, had died without a son in 1250, and his heirs had been his brothers, who had all themselves died without heirs by 1258: *Rufford Charters*, I, ed. C.J. Holdsworth (Thoroton Society Record Series, xxix, 1972 for 1970–1), pp. xcv–xcviii. Lexington's last Nottingham and Lincoln eyres were in 1240. The 1252 Nottingham eyre was held by Roger de Thirkleby.

Hugh del Hull of Aston on Trent, summoned as mesne lord to acquit two tenants of his of services owed to the abbot of Chester, was able to avoid answering the writs altogether until he came of age (**7, 21**). A case brought by the abbot of Welbeck against his mesne lord John de Mentham for the service due from a tenement he held from William de Stuteville in Duckmanton was delayed because the defendant could only be distrained in Nottinghamshire; John was still defaulting when the case was being dealt with in the Bench at Shrewsbury early in 1283 (**10, A15**). A similar delay occurred in a case brought by the abbot of Croxden against Richard de Pres over customs and services due from a tenement in Ashbourne, because Richard had to be distrained in Staffordshire (**107, A11**). In another case the defendant failed to appear (**258, A60**), and one writ was not prosecuted (**137**). The only two cases to be concluded were one concerning Wirksworth where judgment went against the plaintiff because his opponent objected that he was claiming his alleged right through his father's seisin (**83**). The second was brought by Richard de Chatsworth against Ralph le Wyne over 300 acres of moor and pasture and 40 acres of heath in Chatsworth, for which he alleged that he was due 20s. a year, which had not been paid for eight years. Ralph denied this and a jury was summoned, but before it gave its verdict they concorded, Ralph agreeing to render the service to Richard in future in return for remission of the 100s. damages he had claimed (**201**).

Debt and detinue

Debts could be sued for by civil writ, but there is only one such case in this eyre, for the sum of 24 marks, which was settled by an enrolled recognisance (**59**). Detinue was an action which derived from that for debt, and was used to recover items allegedly illegally detained by another party. The plea roll entries of the few such cases in the roll are disappointing in the amount of detail that they give about the circumstances of the dispute. Some users of the writ of detinue simply wished to recover unspecified chattels of significant monetary value, but the cases still often dragged on for years (**56, 57, A26, A33**); others were trying to recover a charter (**139**), or cattle (**178**).

Waste

There is only a single and apparently unconcluded action for waste of lands in the roll, but an interesting one. Nicholas son of Ellis de Breaston sued Henry de Aston and his wife Alice over their treatment of an estate in Breaston, which he alleged had been leased to Alice for a term of 20 years. They had apparently demolished and sold a hall, kitchen and barn, and he claimed damages of £40. The defendants claimed that they were not lessees but freeeholders holding by a grant of a certain Master Nicholas; the entry gives no further information (**60**).

Formedon

The protection of reversionary interests in land was a major concern in legislation of 1285, the *De donis conditionalibus* chapter of the Statute of Westminster II, but long ago Maitland noted that writs of formedon in the reverter were quite common a few years before the statute, and that he had come across five in the records of an unspecified eyre of 1280-81.[1] More recently, Paul Brand has shown that formedon in the reverter was in existence by 1257, and that another formedon writ, formedon in the remainder, had been perfected by 1279, when it was used in the Yorkshire eyre in this circuit.[2] The Derbyshire eyre roll contains but one brief entry concerning an unprosecuted writ of formedon of unspecified type brought by Henry de Curzon and his wife against John de Ferrers over an unspecified tenement in Breadsall (**81**). Henry was pardoned any amercement resulting from his withdrawal by a pardon from William de Saham, the most senior justice on the eyre bench after chief justice Vaux himself.

Naifty

A writ of naifty was available to lords wishing to assert their ownership of men alleged to be unfree. Only three cases of naifty are found in the roll, and only one of them was settled, when Richard son of Ralph Wygot accepted that he was a villein of Henry de Brailsford, a senior knight (**256**). Another writ, by Ralph de Mountjoy, was withdrawn, and a third, by Henry de Chandos, not prosecuted (**204, 205**).

Estovers

Estovers were rights to take materials from woods for fuel, fencing and building purposes attached to a tenement; in one case concerning Shirley wood the defendant, accused of preventing the collection of estovers for two years to the damage of 200s., won by denying that the plaintiff had any free

---

[1] Pollock and Maitland, *History of English Law* (1895), II, p. 28.

[2] P.A. Brand, 'Formedon in the remainder before *De Donis*', *Irish Jurist*, new ser. x (1975), pp. 318–23; reprinted in his *The Making of the Common Law* (1992), pp. 227–32.

tenement which would give him the right to them, the tenement belonging to his mother (74). Henry FitzHerbert of Norbury was alleged to have withdrawn husbote and haybote from 40 acres in Norbury wood for nine years, but the case was settled by a final concord (202); so was the one between Thomas de Mapleton and Matthew de Kniveton (4), but this time there was no pleading so no details are given. The most interesting case was between Roger Duredent and Oliver de Langford and involved estovers in the latter's woods in Langford, Brandwood (or Brentwood) and Le Parrock (263, 279). A final concord about the matter had been made in the Derbyshire eyre of 1258 between Roger and Oliver's father Nigel, but waste had been made contrary to the agreement, and there was a dispute as to who had caused it. Roger later withdrew his writ, and a new agreement was made before the court and enrolled. Chirographs of the agreement were also exchanged, one of which has survived.[1]

Civil trespass

There are entries concerning two unprosecuted writs of trespass among the civil pleas (20, 213), but no details to suggest what these civil trespasses might have been.

Concorded cases

A number of civil cases in this eyre were settled by agreements, and many references to them have been made in this section of the Introduction. A number were still enrolled in the record of the plea on the plea roll (e.g. 100, 168, 199, 201, 281) but by the later thirteenth century they were outnumbered by those recorded in final concords, a tripartite indenture of which one copy, the 'foot', had been kept by the king's court since the procedure was initiated in the king's court at Westminster by Archbishop Hubert Walter in 1195. The Derbyshire feet of fines for the period down to 1323 are to be the subject of a future volume in this series, so there is no need to deal with them in detail as a group here. All 37 of the Derbyshire fines made in the eyre are given below as footnotes to the civil pleas, using the versions printed in the *Journal of the Derbyshire Archaeological and Natural History Society*, xii (1890), pp. 31–42. In a few cases (e.g. 109, 110) the parties were said to have a chirograph, but no foot of fine survives. In one case (99) an agreement was simply enrolled by the court with no

---

[1] Jeayes, *Derbyshire Charters*, no. 1564.

indication that it resulted from the issue of a writ. Another entry (**135**) recorded the handing over of both final concords and charters by the abbot of Darley to William de Balliol.

Civil pleas: foreign pleas

'Foreign pleas' were civil pleas relating to counties other than that in which the eyre was being held. They were probably at their most numerous during the 1280s, when the Common Bench at Westminster and the two eyre circuits were in effect three royal regular courts dealing with civil pleas, one at the centre and two in the regions, one broadly serving the south of England and one the north. During the period of the Derbyshire eyre, the court at Derby was thus a centre of civil pleas for a number of northern counties, although the overwhelming number came from Derbyshire's two neighbours on the north and east, Yorkshire and Nottinghamshire, which had been visited by the justices before they came to Derby. They presumably represent for the most part the continuation of cases begun in those eyres, just as many Derbyshire cases begun at Derby were continued in the Lincolnshire eyre which followed. A large section of foreign pleas occurs in Vaux's civil pleas roll (JUST 1/151, rots. 14–34). They are not included in this calendar, but no account of the eyre would be complete without some reference to them. Excluding vacated entries, there are 448 entries in the roll relating to foreign counties, as follows:

Yorkshire	224
Nottinghamshire	112
Westmorland	27
Northumberland	21
Cumberland	15
Lincolnshire	11
Staffordshire	6
Miscellaneous	22

The last group includes entries where the county name in the margin is illegible, or the county is not identified.

Foreign pleas not concluded at Derby were continued in the succeeding eyre held at Lincoln, and their progress may be followed in the main foreign pleas roll of the Lincolnshire eyre (JUST 1/499). Only one final concord for a foreign county, for a Yorkshire case, was made in the Derbyshire eyre.[1]

Amercements and fines

Penalties for crown pleas

The penalties for crown pleas are arranged in sections for the differing presenting districts, as indicated in Appendix B. The differences in the amounts imposed are striking, with Scarsdale having to pay nearly three and a half times the amount paid by neighbouring Wirksworth. The surprisingly large sum due from Ashbourne, nearly double that for Derby, is accounted for by three large sums of £8 each for the escape of named prisoners. Each of the wapentakes paid a fixed common fine for murder, which appeared first in its list, and which may have been customary. It probably roughly indicated the relative ability of each district to pay. High Peak paid £10; Scarsdale, Wirksworth, Appletree and Morleyston £4 each; Repton and Litchurch £3 6s. 8d. (5 marks) each. All seven wapentake juries, each consisting of the two electors and 12 jurors, were heavily fined for concealment and other trespasses (**772, 787, 796, 808, 819, 833, 841**), while for the towns there was a similar fine on the jurors for breaches of the assizes of cloth and wine, and for other trespasses (**844, 846, 849, 855**). These again appear to be graduated, with High Peak wapentake paying £4 while the rest paid £2, and the borough of Derby's £10 contrasting with the £5 of Ashbourne and Bakewell and the £3 6s. 8d. (5 marks) of Chesterfield. A handful of amercements were imposed on individuals from neighbouring counties (**804, 807, 843**), while a number of Scarsdale entries, mostly for chattels, were deleted (**784–6**).

The main objective seems to have been to ensure that the crown received its monetary dues, such as the chattels of fugitives, hanged or beheaded convicts and suicides; deodands, the articles deemed to have caused the deaths of those killed in accidents, and the penalties imposed on communities for falsely valuing them; failure of communities to pursue fleeing suspects or to attend inquests; the concealments made by the hundred juries and already referred to; on frankpledge tithings for the flight of members; and the penalties paid by communities or bailiffs for the escapes of prisoners. Apart from the largest murder fine, most of the largest sums due were those of £8 for escapes of prisoners, due from important men such as

---

[1] PRO, CP 25/1/267/61, no. 6, calendared in *Yorkshire Fines 1272–1300*, ed. F.H. Slingsby (Yorkshire Archaeological Society, Record Series, cxxi, 1956), p. 61.

Roger Lestrange, keeper of Peak castle, and Hugh Babington, a sheriff. A handful of mostly prominent individuals, including Henry de Lacy, earl of Lincoln (against whose name the word 'baron' was written), Thomas Bek, bishop of St Davids and Geoffrey de Pichford (against both of whose names a small cross was drawn), Peter de Chester and William de Walton, the bailiff of Repton wapentake, but also including two pairs of obscure sureties, apparently escaped, because no sums were entered against their names (**771, 784, 814, 817, 820, 829**). The largest imposition on one individual was £20 on Thomas de Furnival simply for a respite to the Lincoln eyre (**433, 772**).

Amercements imposed on different communities for the same offence seem to have borne some relation to their size and importance. For example, Bolsover paid £3 6s. 8d. for not attending a coroner's inquest, but other places paid much less, Killamarsh and several others only a tenth of that (**776–8**). The effect of the communal penalties on possibly small and lightly populated vills can only be guessed at, but they are likely to have been severe. A murder in Shatton (**404**), for example, resulted in a murder fine on High Peak wapentake, because Englishry was not presented; an amercement on the wapentake jury for not mentioning the name of the first finder of the body in their presentment; the frankpledge in which the suspected killer was suffered another amercement for not producing him; and the vills of Shatton, Bradwell, Hope and Aston did not pursue him, so they were subject to yet another amercement (**758**). Many similar examples could be cited from all parts of the county.

Not all men were in frankpledge, but amercements could sometimes still be levied when those who were not committed crimes. Prominent men could suffer for offences committed by members of their households (those said to be in their mainpast), like Sir Henry de Pierrepont, an important knight, because one of his men committed a murder in Langwith (**436, 775**), or the abbot of Lilleshall, a house in Shropshire, and Engelard de Curzon, because in each case one of their sergeants killed a man (**507, 528, 801, 810**), or Urian de St Peter or Hugh de Gurney (**568, 587, 828, 835**). In the case of strangers from outside Derbyshire, frankpledges could not be amerced: mention is made of men from Staffordshire (**405, 622**), Wales (**414**) and Yorkshire (**609**), as well as strangers or vagabonds from unknown places (**425, 441, 456, 524, 536, 544, 546, 553–4, 563, 578, 590, 600, 619, 628, 632, 636, 645, 656, 666**). Women (**637**) and clerks (**652**) were outside the frankpledge system. One man was not in frankpledge because he was of free status (**540**). Local inhabitants could even suffer financially as a result of a suicide, like Nether Haddon, where the vill was amerced for falsely valuing the chattels of a man who had hanged himself in Nether Haddon wood

(**411**); or because of an abjuration of the realm made in a local church, as when the vills of Ashford, Shatton, Hope and Bradwell falsely valued the chattels of a self-confessed homicide who took refuge in Hope church (**412**); or because of an accident, as when the vill of Hathersage falsely valued a horse from which a sergeant of the royal clerk William de Hamelton fell into the Derwent and was drowned (**418**), or when the four neighbouring vills failed to attend the inquest on a man who drowned in a well in the field of Killamarsh (**438**). The county court was put in mercy because a self-confessed killer who had been outlawed following the 1269 eyre had not been arrested (**440**), but no amercement appears in the roll.

Penalties for civil pleas

The total amount of amercements and fines imposed as a result of civil pleas amounted to £49 5s., less than a tenth of the much larger sum resulting from crown pleas. 120 of the 132 penalties were of one mark, a half or a quarter of a mark (13s. 4d, 6s. 8d. or 3s. 4d.), with two of 10s., three of 1s. 8d. (one eighth of a mark), six of £1, and just one, on a sheriff for the issues of Oliver de Longford's lands, of £2 (**875**). The entries are arranged in the order in which the related pleas had been recorded in the chief justice's roll, and are not of any particular interest except when related to the main plea roll entries for the individual cases. They consisted overwhelmingly of small penalties for not prosecuting writs, leave to make final concords, and by unsuccessful plaintiffs for false claims and defeated defendants for disseisin, unjust detention and the like.

The financial results of the eyre

It is also worthwhile to look at the financial penalties as a whole, and their effect on the county and its people. The financial aspect of eyres had for over a century been one which the king's government had closely in mind, particularly that of the more lucrative crown pleas. A few years later, government financial managers made specific allowance for the income from each eyre circuit in their calculations of annual royal income, a figure of £333 6s. 8d. being allowed for each circuit.[1]

At the end of the eyre a session was held to deal with the fiscal issues, the sums imposed as amercements, accepted as fines, and forfeited chattels.

---

[1] M.H. Mills, 'Exchequer agenda and estimate of revenue, Easter term, 1284', *English Historical Review*, xl (1925), p. 233.

An amercements roll was drawn up and became part of one of the plea rolls, in this eyre that of Ellis de Sutton, keeper of the writs and rolls. When it had been completed a copy of it, known as an estreat, was sent to the Exchequer so that the debts it contained could be put in the next summons sent to the sheriff of the county; he was then responsible for collecting them and accounting for them, along with many other debts, at his annual audit session at the Exchequer.

The sheriff's account was recorded, along with those of the other sheriffs and other officials, in a large annual account roll, the great roll of the Exchequer or, as it came to be called, the pipe roll. The financial issues for the Derbyshire eyre of 1281 first appeared in the pipe roll for the tenth year of Edward I, in the account of the sheriff of Nottinghamshire and Derbyshire, and continued to appear in them in successive years until cleared, but the amount accounted for each year usually diminished greatly after the second account in which the issues of a particular eyre appeared. The lump sums accounted for in the sheriff's accounts in the pipe rolls for the first three years after the eyre took place were as follows, with those of the Nottinghamshire eyre of 1281, which formed part of the same account and follow the same pattern, placed alongside for comparison:

Pipe roll year	Derbyshire			Nottinghamshire		
	£	s.	d.	£	s.	d.
10 Edward I[1]	360	12	6½	460	11	6½
11 Edward I[2]	147	12	11	106	10	8½
12 Edward I[3]	12	5	10	9	2	0

The greater amount collected from Nottinghamshire in the first year can be explained by the earlier date of the eyre there, giving the sheriff more time to collect the issues; in the second and third years less was collected there than in Derbyshire. To cover the accounting process to its conclusion would involve looking at many more rolls to discover the payment of quite small sums, and this has not been undertaken. A few of the debts may have remained unaccounted for until the systematic removal of old debts from the rolls which took place in the reign of Edward II.

The amount accounted for after three years amounted to £576 4s. 3d.,

Notts

---

[1] PRO, E 372/126, rot. 8d.

[2] PRO, E 372/127, rot. 17d.

[3] PRO, E 372/128, rot. 23.

which exceeds by nearly £4 the total sums imposed, £572 0s. 7d. Virtually the whole amount was collected and accounted for in two years, which is an impressive tribute to the efficiency of the administrative machinery. The accounting for individual debts cannot be followed for this eyre, because their details were not recorded in the pipe rolls. Following a precedure which began to be used in the later years of Henry II and became firmly established in the 1220s, to prevent the pipe roll being burdened with the enrolment of many small judicial debts, the entries in the eyre estreat were annotated by a system of letters and marks to indicate when they had been paid, and a lump sum covering those cleared during each year was entered into the sheriff's account for formal clearance.[1] These are the figures quoted above for the first three years; few estreats have survived because when all the debts in them had been cleared there was little point in preserving them.

The accounting for the last small sums due to the crown must have helped to maintain memories of the eyre in Derbyshire into the 1290s at least. During that decade, following the commencement of war with France in 1294, the general eyre ceased to be a regular means of administering royal justice in the counties.[2] The great majority of the counties never had another eyre after 1294, but Derbyshire was one of the few that did, as part of a short-lived revival of the institution by the regime of Queen Isabella and Roger Mortimer in 1329 and 1330. A short session for outlawries held at Derby on 27 May 1331 to complete the business of that eyre proved to be of great symbolic significance in the history of English legal administration.[3] It was the final session of the last general eyre ever to be completed in any county.

---

[1] For the details of the development of this proceedure and its operation, see C.A.F. Meekings, 'The Pipe Roll Order of 12 February 1270', in *Studies Presented to Sir Hilary Jenkinson*, ed. J. Conway Davies (1957); reprinted in C.A.F.Meekings, *Studies in Thirteenth-Century Justice and Administration* (1981).

[2] On the decline and cessation of eyres, see D. Crook, 'The later eyres', *English Historical Review*, xcvii (1982), pp. 241–68.

[3] PRO, JUST 1/169, rot. 55.

BIBLIOGRAPHICAL NOTE

Detailed information about eyres and their records is taken from D. Crook, *Records of the General Eyre* (Public Record Office Handbooks, 20, 1982). Details of the activities carried out by eyres are best described in C.A.F. Meekings (ed.), *Crown Pleas of the Wiltshire Eyre, 1249* (Wiltshire Archaeological and Natural History Society, Records Branch, xvi, 1961), and C.A.F. Meekings and D. Crook, *The 1235 Surrey Eyre*, I (Surrey Record Society, xxxi, 1979); some other useful works on the subject are mentioned in the latter, especially in the eyre bibliography on pp. 156–61. Of particular value for the articles of the eyre and crown pleas is C.A.F. Meekings, 'The Veredictum of Chippenham Hundred, 1281', in *Collectanea* (Wiltshire Archaeological and Natural History Society, Records Branch, xii, 1956), pp. 50–128. Still valuable for the articles of the eyre is H.M. Cam, 'Studies in the Hundred Rolls: some aspects of thirteenth-century administration', in *Oxford Studies in Social and Legal History*, vi (1921). On quo warranto the indispensible work is D.W. Sutherland, *Quo Warranto Proceedings in the Reign of Edward I, 1278–1294* (1963), while the first English version of those pleas for any county has recently been published in *Yorkshire Hundred and Quo Warranto Rolls*, ed. B. English (Yorkshire Archaeological Society, Record Series, cli, 1996 for 1993–4). On the origins of the Derbyshire county court, see D. Crook, 'The establishment of the Derbyshire county court, 1256', *Derbyshire Archaeological Journal*, ciii (1983), pp. 99–106. The references to Derbyshire eyres in the Dunstable annals are in *Annales Monastici*, iii, ed. H.R. Luard (Rolls Series, 1866), pp. 184, 206, 286; see also p. 199. Biographical material on some of the justices and officials of 1281 is in *Select Cases in the Court of King's Bench under Edward I*, vol. I, ed. G.O. Sayles (Selden Society, lv, 1936), pp. li–lii (Saham), lvi–lviii (Sutton and Thornton); a much fuller biography of Thornton is in *The Earliest English Law Reports*, II, ed. P.A. Brand (Selden Society, cxii, 1996), pp. cviii–cxvii.

EDITORIAL METHOD

This is an English version of the Civil and Crown Plea Rolls of the 1281 General Eyre for Derbyshire held at Derby between 21 April and 11 May 1281. It is a composite edition drawing on the following rolls:

JUST 1/151   Civil Pleas and
JUST 1/152   Crown Pleas, the rolls of the chief justice John de Vaux.
JUST 1/148   Rex Roll for Estreats of Fines and Amercements.

Cases adjourned from Derby (see Appendix A) were followed up first to Lincoln, where the justices next sat, through Trinity and Michaelmas terms 1281 and Hilary 1282, using the Foreign Pleas rolls of the Lincolnshire Eyre, JUST 1/499 (Rex Roll) and JUST 1/500A (Siddington's Roll). A few *quo warranto* cases adjourned *coram rege* were in JUST 1/125. Further adjournments from Lincoln to Westminster were followed to the Bench, or Court of Common Pleas, CP 40/45 (Easter 1282) and CP 40/46 (Trinity 1282). Cases still remaining were then followed to that court at Shrewsbury, CP 40/47 (Martinmas 1282) and CP 40/48 (Hilary 1283). Adjournment entries have been much abbreviated except where extra information has been presented.

The aim has been to present a comprehensible, consistent version which reads easily while preserving the legal structure. Translation is fairly literal, abbreviated by cutting out or shortening repetitious words, phrases or lists of names where not prejudicial to meaning. Each entry has been given a serial number, printed in **bold**.

Marginations

Words or phrases in the text which are repeated as marginations are italicised. Marginations additional to or differing from wording in the text are printed within angle brackets, italicised and put in the appropriate place in the text.

Editorial additions

Explanatory datings, reference numbers etc. are in square brackets.

Clerical additions

Clerical insertions other than odd words are in round brackets.

Treatment of 'etc.'

The clerks who wrote the original Latin text made constant use of 'etc.', particularly in omitting or shortening formulaic terms. To keep 'etc.' to a minimum, on the first occurrence of each main type of civil action the text is given with the 'etc.' replaced by the appropriate phrases. Thereafter a shortened form is used. For Mort d'Ancestor see **1**, Novel Disseisin **2**, Right **3**, Quittance of Service **7**, Dower **16**, Entry **44**.

Estreats of Fines and Amercements

The almost 670 separate entries, many of only one line, have been printed in groups of four to six taking account of the text entries to which they refer. Where this number is exceeded the entries refer to the same case. All are cross-referenced to the main text.

Personal and Place-names

Latin Christian and occupational surnames have been translated. Occupational surnames in French are printed as in the text. Place-names and toponymics are printed as in the original text. All place-name variants appear in the index and are cross-referenced to the modern spelling, where the name has been identified. All place-names in the index are grouped under parish names as used in K. Cameron, *The Place-Names of Derbyshire* (English Place Name Society, xxvii–xxix, 1959).

ABBREVIATIONS
USED IN THE FOOTNOTES

Cal.Ch.R.	*Calendar of Charter Rolls*
Cal.Cl.R.	*Calendar of Close Rolls*
Cal.Inq.	*Calendar of Inquisitions*
Cal.Inq. p.m.	*Calendar of Inquisitions Post Mortem*
Cal.Pat.R.	*Calendar of Patent Rolls*
CP	PRO, Court of Common Pleas records
DAJ	*Journal of the Derbyshire Archaeological [and Natural History] Society*
JUST	PRO, Records of Justices Itinerant
PRO	Public Record Office
Rot. Hun.	*Rotuli Hundredorum* (Record Commission, 1812–18)

PLEAS OF JURIES AND ASSIZES BEFORE JOHN DE VAUX, WILLIAM DE SAHAM AND THEIR FELLOWS, JUSTICES IN EYRE IN THE COUNTY OF DERBY, ON THE MORROW OF THE CLOSE OF EASTER IN THE NINTH YEAR OF THE LORD KING EDWARD [*21 APRIL 1281*][1]

1   An assize comes to recognise if Geoffrey de Tydeswell, father of Thomas de Tydeswell, was seised in his demesne as of fee of a messuage and 8 acres of land with appurtenances in Tydeswell on the day he died and if Thomas is his next heir, and if he died after the first voyage of king Henry father of the present king to Gascony, which messuage and land Hugh son of Roger de Tydeswell holds, who comes and says that he cannot answer him on his writ because Agnes his wife was enfeoffed of the tenement at the same time as he. Because she is not named in the writ, he seeks judgment thereon. Thomas cannot deny this and seeks leave to withdraw. He has it.

2   An assize comes to recognise if Henry de Aston and Alice his wife unjustly and without judgment disseised Nicholas son of Ellis de Breydeston of his free tenement in Breydeston after the first voyage of king Henry father of the present king to Gascony. He complains that they have disseised him of 2s. rent with appurtenances. They have not come nor were they attached because they were not found. So let the assize be taken by default.

The jurors say on oath that Henry and Alice unjustly disseised Nicholas of the rent as the writ says, so it was adjudged that Nicholas recover seisin by view of the recognitors and that Henry and Alice are in *mercy*. Damages: half a mark, all to the clerks.

[ref. 856]

---

[1] The opening date of the eyre is confirmed from the Dunstable Annals: 'In the year of grace MCCLxxxj immediately after the octave of Easter the itinerant justices sat at Derby, and the prior appeared before them ... ' (*Annales Monastici* (Rolls Series), iii. 286).

3   John Bek (before the justices of the Bench) claimed by *precipe in capite* against Reynold de Grey the manor of Schirlound with appurtenances as his right and inheritance, whereof he says that a certain Hugh his ancestor was seised as of fee and right in the time of peace in the reign of king Richard, kinsman of the present king, by taking therefrom profits to the value of [*blank*]. From that Hugh, who died without heir of his body, the right descended to Henry his brother and heir, and from him to Walter his son and heir. From Walter it descended to this John who now claims as son and heir. That such is his right he offers to prove.

Reynold has come and elsewhere vouched to warranty Henry de Grey who now comes by summons, warrants him and denies the right of John's ancestor Hugh as of fee and right. He puts himself on the king's grand assize and claims recognition be made as to whether he has greater right in the aforesaid tenements than John. He offers the king *half a mark* for the fixing of a time and it is received.

John and Henry have now come and Ralph de Monjoye, John Fannel, Henry FitzHerbert and Henry de Appelby, four knights summoned to elect 12 knights, have come and elect these: Richard de Grey (sworn), Simon de Gousyl (sworn), Robert de Saucheverell (sworn), Ranulph de Wendeslegh (sworn), Hugh de Stredeley (sworn), Simon Basset (sworn), Alfred Suleney (sworn), Geoffrey de Greseleye (sworn), John Grym, Roger de Merchyngton (sworn), John Fannel (sworn), Henry FitzHerbert, Henry de Appelby (sworn), John de Hecham (sworn) and Richard de Stratton.

Afterwards they concorded and John gives [*blank*] for leave to concord and they have a chirograph. Henry agreed that he owes John £100 whereof he will pay him at Michaelmas in the 9th beginning 10th year of the present king, 50 marks, at Easter following 50 marks and at Michaelmas following 50 marks[1] [*29 Sept. 1281, 29 March and 29 Sept. 1282*]. If he does not do so he grants that the sheriff may levy it from his lands and chattels. Moreover he finds these sureties, Reynold de Grey and Robert de Tatersale, who grant both as principal debtors and sureties each to be bound in that amount. They acknowledge that if Henry does not pay at the said terms, the sheriff of Derbyshire may levy it of Reynold's lands and chattels and the sheriff of Lincolnshire of Robert's. <*recognizance*> [ref. 856]

---

[1] At Derby, within two weeks of Easter 1281. Grant on recognizance of great assize and in consideration of £100 by the plaintiff John Bek to Henry de Grey and his heirs for ever, of the manor of Schirland with appurtenances (*DAJ*, xii. 32).

4   Thomas de Mapelton gives *half a mark* for leave to concord with Matthew de Knyveton in a plea of reasonable estovers and they have a chirograph.
   [ref. 856]

5   Robert son of William de Barleye who brought a writ of warranty of charter against Jordan de Barley has not prosecuted, so he and his sureties for prosecuting are in *mercy*, namely Adam de Catteclive and Hugh de Holmesfeud.
   [ref. 856]

6   Assize of novel disseisin to recognise if Nicholas Theobaud and Roger Trillock unjustly disseised William Dormy jun. of half a messuage in Derby.
   Nicholas and Roger have come and Roger says that William brought this assize against him unjustly because he entered the tenement by Nicholas and if there has been any disseisin, it has been by Nicholas and not by him.
   Nicholas says that William brought this assize against him unjustly because he entered by William's enfeoffment and not by any disseisin. On this both put themselves on the assize, so let it be taken.
   The jurors say that Roger did enter by Nicholas who had disseised William as the writ says. So it was adjudged that William recover seisin by view of the recognitors and that Nicholas is in *mercy*.
   Damages 20s., all to the clerks.
   [ref. 856]

7   Edmund son of Hugh del Hull of Aston has been summoned to answer Emma daughter of Richard del Hull in a plea that he acquit her of the service which the abbot of Cestre exacts from her for her free tenement which she holds of Edmund in Aston upon Trent which Edmund as mesne lord ought to do.
   Edmund comes, says he is under age and need not answer her writ as touching right until he is of age. Because this is clear from his appearance the action is to stay until he is of *age*.

8   William son of Walter de Wylne who brought a writ of entry against the abbot of Cestre concerning tenements in Wylne has not prosecuted, so he and his sureties for prosecuting are in *mercy*, namely John de Aspervile

and William de Gyppesmere.[1]
   [refs. 295, 857, A51]

9   John de Tadenton and Petronilla his wife who brought a writ of aiel against Richard de Morley and others concerning a tenement in Toftes have not prosecuted, so they and their sureties for prosecuting are in *mercy*, William son of William son of Walter de Tonenstides and John Smith of Tokeston.
   [ref. 857]

[*rot. 1d*]   Still Juries and Assizes at Derby   J. de Vaux

10   The abbot of Wellebeck appeared on the fourth day against John de Mentham in a plea that John should acquit him of the service which William de Stotevill demands from him for the free tenement which he holds from John in Dukmanton which John who is mesne lord ought to do. John has not come and the sheriff was ordered to summon him for this day and did nothing, but he testifies that John has no lands or tenements in this county whereby he can be summoned but that he has sufficient in the county of Notyngham. So the sheriff of *Notyngham* is ordered to summon him for Monday next after the quindene of Easter [*28 April 1281*]. This the sheriff attests.
   The abbot appoints Hugh de Grenley or [*blank*] as his attorney. *<process mark>*
   [refs. 287, A15]

11   Agnes widow of William de Audewerk who brought a writ of entry against Robert son of William le Wyne concerning tenements in Overhaddon has not prosecuted, so she and her sureties for prosecuting are in *mercy*, namely William de Bonteshall and Robert de Kesteven.
   [ref. 857]

12   Agnes widow of Richard Achard claims against Reynold le Brun a

---

[1] This action, which was not prosecuted, may have been revived later. At Shrewsbury on the morrow of Martinmas (12 Nov.) 1282 the jury between William son of Walter de Wylne and the abbot of Chester concerning a plea of land was respited until Easter three weeks for default of jury (CP 40/47 rot. 101).

third of a burgage in Bathekewell as dower. Reynold comes and says nothing against her having it, so she is to have seisin and Reynold is in *mercy*.
[ref. 857]

13 Assize of mort d'ancestor to recognise if Robert le Mouner father of Robert le Mouner of Parva Roysle died seised in his demesne as of fee of a toft and a bovate of land in Parva Roysley which Adam son of Peter de Roysle holds, who comes and says that he need not answer because he does not and did not hold the tenements on the day of the sueing out of the writ, namely on 30 July in the present king's 8th year [*30 July 1280*]. Nor does he claim anything in them. He says moreover that a certain Richard de Byngham holds and held them on the aforesaid date and if it is found by the assize that he held them on that date, Adam says nothing to stay the assize. So let it be taken.

The jurors say that Adam did not hold the tenements on that day, so it is adjudged that he is without day and that Robert should take nothing but be in *mercy* for a false claim.
[ref. 359, 857]

14 William de Catteclyve, Alice his wife and Nicholas de Wakebrugge who brought a writ of aiel against Richard de Byngham concerning a tenement in Edenesovere have not prosecuted, so they and their sureties for prosecuting are in *mercy*, namely Henry de Codyngton and John de Lytelchyrche.
[ref. 858]

15 Emma widow of Peter de Skyrebrok claims against Hervey son of Henry Attegrene a third of 15 acres of land in Styrston as her dower. Hervey comes and by licence renders her dower, so she is to have her seisin.

16 Reynold del Medewe and Emma his wife claim against Reynold le Marscal of Burge a third of a messuage and of 2 bovates of land in Burge near Hope as Emma's dower by the endowment of William del Morhaw her first husband.

Reynold le Marscall comes and says that Emma ought not to have her dower because William her first husband was not, on the day he married her nor ever after, seised of the aforesaid tenements so that he could have dowered her. On this he puts himself on the country, Reynold likewise. So let there be a jury. <*quindene of Easter*> [*27 April 1281*]

17   John Swyft claims against Henry Swyft half of 7 messuages, of 7s. 6d. rent and of 1½ roods of land in Derby as his right and reasonable share of their inheritance from Peter de Derby in Derby their father, whose heirs they are and who recently died.

Henry comes and readily acknowledges all the articles in the writ and by licence renders him half of the aforesaid tenements. So John is to have his seisin.

18   An assize of novel disseisin to recognise if Peter son of Peter de la Marche, Richard de Karlio and Thomas Sillecok unjustly disseised Walter le Mercer and Edith his wife and Roger de Cestre and Maud his wife of a messuage in Derby, (the free tenement of Edith and Maud).

Peter, Richard and Thomas come and say nothing to stay the assize except that Edith and Maud were never in seisin so that they could be disseised. Thereon they put themselves on the assize, Walter and the others likewise. So let the assize be taken.

The jurors say that Edith and Maud were never in seisin so that they could be disseised, so it is adjudged that Peter, Richard and Thomas are without day and that Walter and the others are to take nothing but are to be in *mercy* for a false claim.

[ref. 858]

19   Robert le Escreveyn, said to be of full age, claims against Henry abbot of Derley three mills with appurtenances in Derby as his by writ of entry.

The abbot comes and they concorded. Robert gives *a mark* for leave to concord and they have a chirograph.[1]

[ref. 858]

20   Hugh son of Simon de Twyford who brought a writ of trespass against William de Waleton and Richard de Waleton has not prosecuted, so he and his sureties for prosecuting are in *mercy,* namely Ralph Feyrbra and Fucher de Marketon. [ref. 858]

---

[1] At Derby, within two weeks of Easter 1281. Acknowledgment by plaintiff that three mills in Derby with appurtenances are the right of the tenant and his church of St Mary of Derleye and grant by tenant to plaintiff of the aforesaid mills to hold of the tenant and his successors and church all the life of the plaintiff at yearly rent of £4 sterling payable at the feasts of the Nativity of St John the Baptist, St Michael, the Nativity of our Lord and Easter. Clause as to distraint in case of plaintiff being in arrears. After decease of plaintiff the mills to revert wholly to tenant and his successors. (*DAJ*, xii. 33).

21   Edmund son of Hugh del Hull of Aston was summoned to answer Agatha daughter of Richard del Hull in a plea that he acquit her of the service which the abbot of Cestre demands of her for her free tenement held of Edmund in Aston upon Trent, which Edmund who is mesne lord ought to do.

Edmund comes, says he is under age and need not answer on this writ as touching right until he is of age. Because this is clear from his appearance the action is to stay until he is of *age*.

22   Roger le Whyte and Felicity his wife give *half a mark* for leave to concord with Ranulph de Hassopp and Mabel his wife in a plea of warranty of charter. They have a chirograph. Roger and Felicity appoint Richard Huberd and Ranulph and Mabel appoint Richard de Marnham as their attorneys for the taking of the chirograph.[1]
[ref. 859]

[*rot. 2*]   Still Juries and Assizes at Derby   Vaux

23   Assize of mort d'ancestor to recognise if Ralph Bolle father of Isabella Bolle died seised in his demesne as of fee of a messuage and a bovate of land in Ekinton which Alan de Wychinford and William his son hold. They come and William says that he holds the entire tenement and he vouches Alan to warranty who warrants him. He further vouches Matthew de Sancto Claro.

Isabella says that Alan ought not to vouch Matthew because he was never seised of the tenements after Ralph's death and she seeks inquiry by an assize, Alan likewise.

The jurors say that Matthew was seised after Ralph's death, so it was adjudged that the voucher should stand and Matthew be summoned in this county to be present on Thursday after the close of Easter [*24 April 1281*]. Summoned for that day he did not come. Judgment: he is to be resummoned to be present on Monday next after the quindene of Easter [*28 April 1281*], when he again defaulted. So it was adjudged that the assize be taken against

---

[1] At Derby, 21 April 1281. Grant and in consideration of a sparrowhawk by the defendants Ranulph de Hassop and Mabel his wife to the plaintiffs and heirs of Felicity for ever, of the moiety of a messuage and a bovate etc, in Bobenhull. To hold of the defendants and heirs of Mabel at the yearly rent of one clove gilly flower at Easter for all service. (*DAJ*, xii. 42).

him by default.

The jurors say that Ralph did die seised of the tenements and that Isabella is his next heir, so it was adjudged that she recover seisin against William. He is to have land from Alan and Alan is to have land to the value from Matthew in a suitable place. Matthew is in *mercy*.

Damages 20s., all to the clerks.

[ref. 859]

24   Robert son of Robert de Watenhou who brought an assize of novel disseisin against Thomas de Chaworth and others in a writ concerning a tenement in Auferton has not prosecuted, so he and his sureties for prosecuting are in *mercy,* namely William Reeve of Watenhowe and Nicholas his brother.

[ref. 859]

25   John son of Robert le Clerke who brought an assize of novel disseisin against Brichtiva de Cestrefeud concerning a tenement in Cestrefeud has not prosecuted, so he and his sureties for prosecuting are in mercy. Nothing concerning sureties because he has pledged his faith.

26   Robert son of Robert de Scheldeford who brought an assize of novel disseisin against John son of Walter de Munkarston concerning a tenement in Munkarston has not prosecuted, so he and his sureties for prosecuting are in *mercy,* namely Robert le Champion of Munkarston and William le Burgon.

[ref. 859]

27   Richard Whiteknave and Eleanor his wife who brought an assize of mort d'ancestor against Alota de Derley have not prosecuted, so they and their sureties for prosecuting are in *mercy,* namely Nicholas de Clifton and Matthew Mareballock.

28   Emma daughter of Payne le Fevere of Derby who brought an assize of novel disseisin against Thomas son of Ellis de Osmundeston, has not prosecuted, so she and her sureties for prosecuting are in *mercy,* namely Robert de Notingham in Derby and Walter le Roer of the same.

[ref. 859]

29   An assize of mort d'ancestor to recognise if Agnes daughter of Adam Bek, mother of Avice de Siwardeston, and Margery her sister died seised in her demesne as of fee of a messuage and 15 acres of land in Wyardeston, which Thomas Winter, Margery his wife and her son William hold. They come and say that they need not answer this writ because they do not hold the tenements in common as claimed, but that Thomas and Margery hold the messuage and a moiety of the land in severalty and William holds the other moiety. On this they seek judgment.

30 Robert son of Richard de Wistan(ton) who brought an assize of mort d'ancestor against Mabel widow of Robert le Forester concerning tenements in Weston and Mugenton, has not prosecuted, so he and his sureties for prosecuting are in *mercy,* namely Hugh le Mareschall of Irton and Henry son of Richard de Weston.

[ref. 860]

31 Giles son of Robert le Wis who brought an assize of mort d'ancestor against Henry Russell and John Scot concerning a tenement in Kirkelangeley has not prosecuted, so he and his sureties for prosecuting are in *mercy,* namely Robert son of Ives de Langel' and William his brother.

[ref. 860]

32 An assize of mort d'ancestor to recognise if Adam atte Cros, uncle of Robert son of Henry de Wyneleye, died seised in his demesne as of fee of a messuage, 6 acres of land and half of 7s. 6d. rent in Wirkesworth, which William son of Henry le Heyr holds, deforcing him of the rent.

William comes and says nothing to stay the assize except that Adam did not die seised of those tenements and that a long time before his death had enfeoffed him and put him in seisin. On this he puts himself on the assize. So let the assize be taken.

The jurors say that Adam did not die seised, because one month before his death he had enfeoffed William and put him in seisin. So it was adjudged that William is without day and Robert is to take nothing but is to be in *mercy* for a false claim.

[ref. 860]

33 Isabella daughter of Adam Blundy who brought an assize of mort d'ancestor against Philip de Cestrefeld concerning a tenement in Cestrefeld has not prosecuted, so she and her sureties for prosecuting are in *mercy,* namely William de Hampton and Roger de Grangia both of Cesterfeld.

34 William son of Peter de Brenyngton gives *a mark* for leave to concord with Richard son of Roger de Newhahe and Agnes his wife in a plea of warranty of charter by surety of Richard and they have a chirograph.[1]

[ref. 860]

35 An assize of novel disseisin to recognise if Ralph Sparewatre, Richard le Mareschal and Thomas le Coteler unjustly disseised Stephen Fizburge and Mazelina his wife of a messuage in Esseburne. Ralph comes and, answering for himself and the others, says that he holds the messuage by demise of Thomas de Normanvill the king's steward at an annual rental paid to the king. He proffers a charter of the present king testifying this in these words:

'Edward by the grace of God etc. To all etc. to whom these presents shall come, greeting. Whereas our beloved and faithful Thomas de Normanvill has demised in fee-farm to Robert de Houby, Henry le Clerk, John son of Hugh, Robert de Bredlawe, William de Bukston, Thomas le Coteler, Robert son of Orm, Ralph Sperwatre and Hugh le Pescur, our men of that town, certain places in our town of Esseburn for building upon, paying to us and our heirs by the hands of our bailiffs there, 52s. 4d. annually, we accept this our demise according to the tenor of these presents. In testimony of which we have caused these our letters to be made patent. Given by the hand of the venerable father R. Bishop of Bath and Wells, chancellor, at Shrewsbury on the 28th day of October in the 5th year of our reign [*28 October 1277*].'[2]

Thus they say that they cannot answer without the king. So a day is given before the justices in eyre at Lincoln at the quindene of Trinity [*22 June*]. Meanwhile there is to be *discussion with the king*. Afterwards at the octave of St John the Baptist [*1 July 1281*] Stephen and Mazelina by his attorney came to Lincoln and withdrew, so they and their sureties are in mercy. They are pardoned at the request of Thomas de Normanvill.

[ref. 370]

---

[1] At Derby, 21 April 1281. Grant etc. and in consideration of one soar hawk by the defendants Richard son of Roger de Newehahe and Agnes his wife to the plaintiff and his heirs for ever of one toft and 40 acres of land in Staveleye, to hold of the defendants and heirs of Agnes at yearly rent of a rose at the feast of the Nativity of St John the Baptist and performing all other services to the chief lords of that fee for the defendants and the heirs of Agnes. (*DAJ*, xii. 41).

[2] 28 Oct. 1277. Acceptance of a demise in fee-farm made by Thomas de Normanville of divers places in the town of Essheburn to Robert de Houby, Henry le Clerc, John son of Hugh, Robert de Bredlawe, William de Bukston, Thomas le Cotiller, Robert son of Orm, Ralph Sparewater and Hugh le Pescur, men of that town, for them to build upon, at a rent of 52s. 4d by the hands of the bailiff of that town. (*Cal. Pat. R. 1272–81*, p. 234).

36   An assize of mort d'ancestor to recognise if Richard son of William Herbert, brother of Ellen wife of Robert le Hore died seised in his demesne as of fee of a messuage, 5 acres of land and half an acre of meadow in Baukewell, which messuage, land and meadow Robert son of Richard de Baukewell holds. He comes and says that he has those tenements by descent from Richard his father who died seised thereof and that he is under age. Because this is apparent to the court the action is to stay until he comes of *age.*

37   William Swyft who brought a writ of novel disseisin against Henry le Joevene of Derby concerning a tenement in Derby comes and withdraws. So Henry is without day and William and his sureties for prosecuting are in mercy. Afterwards William comes and makes fine by *half a mark* for himself and his sureties which is received by surety of Robert de Notingham of Derby.
    [ref. 860]

38   John de Kingeston gives *half a mark* for leave to concord with Walter son of Godfrey le Rour and Cecilia his wife concerning warranty of charter. They have a chirograph by surety of Walter.[1]
    [ref. 861]

[rot. 2d]   Still Juries and Assizes of the same Eyre

39   Thomas de Tyddeswell who brought an assize of mort d'ancestor against Richard Redman concerning a tenement in Tiddeswell has not prosecuted, so he and his sureties for prosecuting are in *mercy,* namely Robert de Tiddeswell and Robert de Mapelton.
    [ref. 861]

40   Gregory son of William le Fevre of Alcmenton who brought an assize of mort d'ancestor against Richard Shyne of Alcmenton concerning a tenement in Alkmenton has not prosecuted, so he and his sureties for

---

[1]   At Derby, 21 April 1281. Grant etc. and in consideration of 40s. sterling by the defendants Walter son of Godfrey le Roer and Cecilia his wife to the plaintiff and his heirs for ever of a toft in Derby. To hold of the defendants and heirs of Cecilia at a yearly rent of a peppercorn and performing all other services to the chief lords of that fee for the defendants and heirs of Cecilia. (*DAJ*, xii. 42).

prosecuting are in *mercy,* namely John de Kingeston and Peter de Hatton.
[ref. 861]

41   An assize of mort d'ancestor to recognise if William Wyne father of
Ralph Wyne died seised in his demesne as of fee of half an acre of land in
Baukewell which Roger de Asseburne holds, who comes. He elsewhere
vouched to warranty Ralph son of Roger de Scheladon who now comes by
summons, warrants him and readily acknowledges that William died seised
of the aforesaid land after the term limited by the writ and that Ralph is
William's next heir.

So it is adjudged that Ralph recover seisin against Roger and that Roger
is to have land to the value from Ralph son of Roger.

42   An assize of mort d'ancestor to recognise if Adam le Blundy father of
Isabella died seised in his demesne as of fee of 2 acres of land in Brampton
which land Henry de Cestrefeld holds. He comes and says nothing to stay
the assize, so let it be taken.

The jurors say that Adam did not die seised of the tenement because it
was given him in free marriage with a certain Maud, Isabella's mother. So
it is adjudged that Henry is without day and Isabella is to take nothing but
is to be in *mercy.* Afterwards the amercement is pardoned because she is
poor.

43   Nicholas son of Richard de Morley claims against Hugh son of Roger
de Morley a bovate of land in Morley whereof Roger de Morley, Nicholas's
grandfather, died seised in his demesne as of fee. Hugh comes, denies force
and injury and maintains that Roger did not die thus seised because a long
time before his death Roger enfeoffed him and put him in seisin. On this
Hugh puts himself on the country, likewise Nicholas. So let there be a jury.
<*quindene of Easter*>

The jurors elected by assent of the parties say that Roger did die seised
of the tenements, so it was adjudged that Nicholas recover seisin and that
Hugh be in *mercy.*

(No) damages because the land has been sown.
[ref. 861]

44   Nicholas son of Ellis de Braydeston claims against Henry son of Henry
de Braydeston 1½ acres of land in Breydeston in which Henry has no entry
except by William son of Henry de Breydeston to whom John le Escot,
uncle of Nicholas whose heir he is, demised them for a term which has

expired and whereof he says that John his uncle was seised as of fee and right in the peacetime of king Henry, father of the present king, taking therefrom profits. From that John, who died without direct heir, the right descended to a certain Robert as brother and heir, and from Robert, who died without direct heir, it descended to Cecilia and Sybil as sisters and heirs. From Cecilia, who died without direct heir, her right in purparty descended to Sybil as sister and heir and from Sybil it descended in entirety to this Nicholas who now claims as son and heir. On this he brings suit.

Henry comes, denies Nicholas's right and says that Cecilia did not die without direct heir but did indeed have a daughter and heir, Maud, who is still alive. He seeks judgment as to whether Nicholas or Maud can claim any right in the tenement. Nicholas cannot deny this, so Henry is without day and Nicholas is to take nothing but is to be in *mercy* for a false claim.

[ref. 861]

45   Giles de Bobinhull who is said to be of full age and who brought a writ of entry against Osbert de Catesworth concerning a tenement in Grene has not prosecuted, so he and his sureties for prosecuting are in *mercy*, Roger de Bukstanes and William son of Walter de Tunstedes.

[ref. 862]

46   William de Folegaumbe of Wormhill and Henry de Mapilton of Esseburne, executors of the will of Henry de Mapelton, acknowledge that they owe to Reginald de Monacheto, Bonus Johannes de Phelippo, William son of Agady and their other fellow-merchants of Plestencia of the Society of the Scotti, three sacks and 10 stones of wool or 20 marks of silver which they will pay as follows: at the Nativity of St John the Baptist next, a sack and 10 stones or 10 marks, and at the same feast next following a sack and 10 stones or 10 marks, and at the same feast next again following 20 stones or 10 marks[1] [*24 June 1281, 1282, 1283*]. If they do not do so, they grant that the sheriff may cause the aforesaid amounts to be levied of their lands and chattels. <*recognizance*>

47   Thomas le Ragged acknowledges that he owes the same Reginald and the others a sack and 20 stones of wool or 15 marks, of which he will pay

---

[1] These merchants of the Society of Bernardus Scotus of Piacenza (described as merchants of the Pope (*Cal.Pat.R. 1272–81*, p. 85), along with five other named colleagues, had protection and safe conduct for three years' trading in England (*Cal.Pat.R. 1281–91*, p. 74).

them a sack or 10 marks at the feast of the Nativity of St John the Baptist
and at the same feast next following 20 stones or 5 marks [*24 June 1281,
1282*]. If he does not do so he grants that the sheriff may cause the amounts
to be levied of his lands and chattels. *<recognizance>*

48   An assize of novel disseisin to recognise if Roger de Merchington
unjustly disseised John son of Peter de Baggepuz of his common of pasture
in an acre of heath in Marchinton belonging to his free tenement in Barton.
    Roger comes and says that he need not answer him on this writ because
he was conjointly enfeoffed of the heath with Eleanor his wife who is not
named in the writ and without her he cannot answer. John cannot deny this
and seeks leave to withdraw and he has it.

49   William de Meynill who brought an assize of novel disseisin against
Nicholas vicar of Machelfeld church and others in a writ concerning a
tenement in the common pasture in Snelston which belongs to his free
tenement in Yveley, comes and withdraws. So he and his sureties for
prosecuting are in *mercy,* namely Matthew de Yveley and Richard son of
Alan de Yveley.
    [ref. 862]

50   An assize to recognise if Roger de Marchenton unjustly overthrew a
certain dike in Langeford to the nuisance of Oliver de Langeford's free
tenement there. Oliver complains that when the dike was raised between his
arable land in Langeford and the common pasture in that vill, Roger
overthrew it so that the beasts in the common pasture graze in Oliver's
arable land trampling the growing corn and grazing it down.
    Roger says that in the place where Oliver complains of the dike having
been overthrown, there used to be a hedge through which men and beasts
could pass and that Oliver wished it blocked up. Roger did not allow this
and that he has done no injury he puts himself on the assize.
    Oliver denies that he wished the hedge to be blocked up but says that it
was Roger who overthrew part of the dike next to it. On this he puts himself
on the assize, so let it be taken.
    The jurors say that Roger did overthrow the dike to Oliver's nuisance so
it is adjudged that since it is a nuisance, it should be levelled at Roger's
costs by view of the recognitors. Roger is in *mercy.*
Damages: 12d. to William le Cryur.
    [ref. 862]

51   Edith, widow of Adam son of Warin de Hokenaston, claims against Richard son of Roger Spenecurteys a third of half a bovate of land in Hokenaston as her dower. Richard comes and by licence renders Edith her dower so she is to have seisin.

52   Robert de Estthwayt who brought an assize of novel disseisin against Eudes le Kerkemon of Henovere and others in a writ concerning a tenement in Ylkuston, has not prosecuted, so he and his sureties for prosecuting are in *mercy*, namely Hugh de Neuthorp and Robert de Chillewell.
   [ref. 862]

53   Thomas son of Ralph atte Brigge and Alice his wife give *half a mark* for leave to concord with Henry Scherewynd and Scolastica his wife in a plea of warranty of charter by surety of Henry. They have a chirograph.[1]
   [ref. 862]

54   Nicholas Martel gives *half a mark* for leave to concord with Robert Bozun and Philippa his wife in a plea of warranty of charter by surety of Robert. They have a chirograph.[2]
   [ref. 863]

55   An assize of novel disseisin to recognise if Simon de Notingham and William Foyle unjustly disseised Emma daughter of Simon le Paumer of a messuage and 1½ acres of land in Derby.
   Simon comes and answering for himself and William says nothing to stay the assize except that Emma never was in seisin so that she could have been disseised. On this he puts himself on the assize, so let it be taken.

---

[1] At Derby, within two weeks of Easter 1281 between Thomas son of Ralph de Thurleston and Alice his wife, plaintiffs, and Henry Scherewynd and Scolastica his wife, defendants. Grant on a plea etc. and in consideration of a sparrowhawk by the defendants to the plaintiffs and the heirs of Alice for ever, of 10 acres of land, 1 acre of meadow and a fourth part of a messuage etc. in Thurleston. To hold of the defendants and the heirs of Scolastica at the yearly rent of one rose at the Nativity of St John the Baptist and performing all other services to the chief lords of that fee, for the defendants and the heirs of Scolastica. (*DAJ*, xii. 32).

[2] At Derby, within three weeks of Easter 1281. Grant etc. and in consideration of one sparrowhawk by the defendants Robert Bozun and Philippa to plaintiff Nicholas Martel and his heirs of a messuage and 2 bovates of land in Tyssington. To hold of the defendants and their heirs for ever at the yearly rent of one rose payable at the feast of the Nativity of St John the Baptist for ever and performing all other services to the chief lords of that fee for the defendants and their heirs. (*DAJ*, xii. 35).

The jurors say that Emma never was in seisin so it is adjudged that Simon and William are without day and Emma is to be in *mercy* for a false claim. The amercement is pardoned because she is poor.

56 Roger Scot of Notingham appeared on the fourth day against Robert de Mylnaus of Wyrkeworth and John Laufol in a plea that they return to him chattels to the value of 12 marks which they unjustly detain. They have not come and were summoned. Judgment: they are to be attached to be at *Lincoln* at the octave of St John the Baptist [*1 July 1281*].

[ref. A26]

57 The same Roger appeared on the fourth day against Ala widow of William de Handesacre, John de Handesacre chaplain, and Thomas le Harpur, executors of the will of William de Handesacre, in a plea that they return to him chattels to the value of 12 marks which they unjustly detain. They have not come and were summoned. Judgment: they are to be attached to be at *Lincoln* at the aforesaid term.

[ref. A33]

58 Henry son of Robert Portejoye, who is of full age, claims against Robert Schiret and Aline his wife 2½ acres of land in Scropton as his by writ of entry. Robert and Aline come and vouch Thomas Morel to warranty. They are to have him at *Lincoln* at the quindene of St John the Baptist [*8 July 1281*].

He is to be summoned in *Staffordshire*.[1]

[refs. 323, 368]

[*rot. 3*]   Still Juries and Assizes at Derby   J. de Vaux

59 John de Marketon of Wynley, Henry de Guordon, Henry de Schone of Wynley and Robert le Archer of Weston were summoned to answer Henry

---

[1] At Shrewsbury, quindene and three weeks of Michaelmas 1282. Henry son of Robert Portejoy presented himself on the 4th day against Robert Shyret and Aline his wife in a plea of 2 acres of land in Scropton which he claimed as his right. They did not come and had a day by their essoiner. Judgment: the land was to be taken into the king's hand and they were to be ᐧsummoned to be present at Hilary three weeks [cancelled because they came]. They vouched Thomas Morel whom they were to have at Hilary three weeks. He was to be summoned in Staffs. (CP 40/47 rot. 45).

de Burgoylon in a plea that they return to him 24 marks which they owe and unjustly detain. John and the others come and they concorded. Henry de Burgoylon gives *a mark* for leave to concord. The agreement is this: Henry and the others acknowledge that they owe Henry the aforesaid sum and that they will pay him at the feast of St James in the present king's 9th year [*25 July 1281*] and if they do not, that the sheriff may cause it to be levied of their lands and chattels. *<recognizance>*
   [ref. 863]

60   Henry de Aston and Alice his wife were summoned to answer Nicholas son of Ellis de Breydeston in a plea as to why, when it is stipulated that no one is allowed to make waste, sale or destruction of lands, houses, woods or gardens demised to them for a term of years, they did so in lands, house and gardens in Breydeston which Nicholas had demised to Alice for a term of years, to his disinheritance. He says that though he had demised a messuage and 20 acres of land with appurtenances in Braydeston to Alice to hold of him for a term of years not yet expired, Henry and Alice demolished and sold a hall, kitchen and barn situated in that messuage, wherefore he has suffered damage amounting to £40. Thereon he brings suit.
   Henry and Alice come, deny force and injury and say that they do not claim to hold those tenements for any term but rather as Alice's free tenement by demise of a certain Master Nicholas.

61   Norman de Bygeham and Cecilia his wife, who brought an assize of novel disseisin against Matthew de Knyveton and others in a writ concerning a tenement in Braddelegh, have not prosecuted. So they and their sureties for prosecuting are in *mercy,* William Balle of Skyrlegh and William de Bentlay.
   [ref. 863]

62   Gervase de la Corner gives *10s.* for leave to concord with Henry le Gaunter and Eustacia his wife in a plea of warranty of charter and they have a chirograph.[1]
   [ref. 863]

---

[1] At Derby, within two weeks of Easter 1281. Grant on a plea etc. and in consideration of one soar hawk by the defendants, Henry le Gaunter and his wife Eustachia to the plaintiff Gervase de la Cornere and his heirs for ever, of 14 acres of land, 4s. rent and two parts of a messuage etc. in Derby and Normanton near Derby. To hold to the defendants and the heirs of Eustachia at the yearly rent of one penny at Easter for all service and performing all other services to the chief lords of that fee for the defendants and heirs of Eustachia. (*DAJ*, xii. 32).

63   Simon de Notyngham claims against Thomas de Thorleston and Maud his wife a moiety of half a messuage in Derby which Simon and Robert his brother (who does not prosecute for his part) demised to him while they were under age. Thomas and Maud come and readily acknowledge that they entered through Simon and Robert, but at the time of the demise Simon was of full age according to the custom of the town of Derby which is that anyone there is held to be of full age when he knows how to count 20s., measure cloth and weigh merchandise. They say that at the time of the demise Simon was old enough to do those things properly. On this they put themselves on the country, likewise Simon. So let there be a jury.

The jurors say that in Derby according to customary usage from time out of mind anyone of 15 years is held to be a man of full age and can sell and grant his tenements there. Questioned as to Simon's age on the day of the demise, they say that he was 18 years old. So it was adjudged that Thomas and Maud are without day. Simon is to take nothing but is to be in *mercy* for a false claim.

[ref. 863]

64   Richard de Byngham claims against Adam Basset two messuages and a virgate of land, half an acre excepted, in Stanton Leyes as his right by writ of entry. Adam comes and vouches John Asser to warranty. He is to have him at *Lincoln* at the quindene of Trinity [*22 June 1281*] by aid of the court and is to be summoned in the county of *Cambridge.* <process mark>

[refs. 318, 320, A12]

65   Thomas son of Adam de Herdewykwalle claims against Roger vicar of Tiddeswell a messuage in Tyddeswelle of which Wulvet de Litton, Thomas's grandfather whose heir he is, died seised. Roger comes and says that the tenements were attached to his vicarage of Tyddeswelle which he holds by presentation of the dean and chapter of Lychefeud. On the day of his institution he found the vicarage so seised, so cannot answer without the dean and chapter. They are to be summoned to be present at Easter three weeks.

[refs. 209, 335]

66   Henry de Irton, Philippa his wife and Isabella her sister claim against John de Ferrars a carucate of land in Braydesale which Robert de Dun, great-grandfather of Philippa and Isabella whose heirs they are, gave to Sampson de Dun and the heirs of his body and which after Sampson's death ought to revert to Philippa and Isabella according to the form of the grant because Sampson died without direct heir.

John has come. They concorded and he gives *half a mark* for leave to concord. The agreement is this: Henry, Philippa and Isabella acknowledge the tenement along with all the tenements and lands which John held in that vill on that day, namely the morrow of the close of Easter in the present king's 9th year [*21 April 1281*], to be John's by right and they remised and quitclaimed them for themselves and the heirs of Philippa and Isabella to John and his heirs for ever. And for this Reynold de Grey, Thomas de Bray, Thomas Meverel, Thomas Foleiambe and Ralph Monioy for John acknowledge themselves bound to Henry, Philippa and Isabella in 100 marks of silver of which they will pay them half at the quindene of Michaelmas in the king's 9th year and the other half at the quindene of Easter next following [*13 October 1281, 12 April 1282*]. If they default they grant that the sheriff may levy it of their lands and chattels. They also have a chirograph.[1]

<*recognizance*>

[ref. 864]

67   John de Weston and Millicent his wife claim against Robert son of Geoffrey de Seldeford a messuage, a toft and a bovate of land in Murkaston as their right by writ of entry.

Robert comes and says that he cannot answer on their writ because he does not hold those tenements in entirety. Moreover, a certain Robert son of Robert de Murkeston holds 1½ acres of land thereof. John and Millicent cannot deny this and seek leave to withdraw and they have it.

[ref. 75]

68   Robert de Saucheverell claims right of advowson of the church of Boleton by writ against the abbot of Derley.

The abbot has come and they concorded. He gives *half a mark* for leave to concord and they have a chirograph.[2]

[refs. 225, 864]

69   Robert le Taylur of Quenesburgh and Agnes his wife who brought a

---

[1]   At Derby, within two weeks of Easter 1281. (*DAJ*, xii. 36; no further details beyond those given in this entry).

[2]   At Derby, within two weeks of Easter 1281. Acknowledgment in consideration of 10 marks silver by the plaintiff Robert de Saucheverell that the advowson of the church of Bolton with appurtenances is the right of the tenant Henry, abbot of Derleye, and his church of St Mary. (*DAJ*, xii. 33).

writ of entry against the abbot of Crokesden concerning a tenement in Herteshorn have not prosecuted, so they and their sureties for prosecuting are in mercy, namely Hugh de Haregreve and William de Melton. [cancelled]
[ref. 100]

70 Stephen de Ireton gives *20s.* for leave to concord with Joan daughter of Stephen de Irton in a plea of warranty of charter. They have a chirograph. Joan appoints Richard de Colsill as her attorney for the taking of the chirograph.[1]
[ref. 864]

[*rot. 3d*] Still Juries and Assizes at Derby J. de Vaux

71 Henry de Irton, Philippa his wife and Isabella her sister claim the following tenements in Bridesale against the following: against Henry de Curzon and Joan his wife 1½ carucates; against Geoffrey le Provost of Brydesale a messuage and a virgate; against Agnes de Cravene a messuage and 18 acres; against Robert le Pope and Alice his wife 6 acres; against Geoffrey de Devek a messuage and 40 acres; against Geoffrey son of Geoffrey de Dethek and Juliana his wife a messuage and a virgate; against Stephen de Donesmor a messuage and a bovate; against Henry son of Gilbert de Chaddesden a messuage and half a virgate; against Alan le Clerk of Breydesale a messuage and 16 acres; against Richard de Dun a messuage and 30 acres; and against John son of Geoffrey de Skeftlyngton 5 tofts, 4 virgates, 60 acres of wood[2] and 13s. 4d. rent with appurtenances, which

---

[1] At Derby, within two weeks of Easter 1281. Grant on a plea etc. and in consideration of one soar hawk by the defendant Stephen de Irton to the plaintiff Joan daughter of Stephen de Irton and the heirs of her body, of the manor of Hatton with appurtenances and two messuages, 21 acres of land etc. in Lee *iuxta* Bradeburn and 1 acre of meadow and 5s. rent etc. in Peverwych, Snelleston and Murcaneston. To hold of the defendant and his heirs at the yearly rent of 1d. at Easter for all services. In default of heirs of the plaintiff's body, the premises shall wholly revert to the defendant and his heirs quit of the other heirs of the plaintiff. The plaintiff granted for herself and her heirs that from henceforth they will render every year to the defendant 30 quarters of corn, 12 quarters of mixed corn and 60 quarters of oats all the life of the defendant at the four terms, viz. at the feast of the Nativity of St John the Baptist 7½ quarters of corn, 3 quarters of mixed corn and 15 quarters of oats, at the feasts of Michaelmas, the Nativity of the Lord and Easter, similar quantities. And after the decease of the defendant, the plaintiff and her heirs shall be quit of the aforesaid payments for ever. (*DAJ*, xii. 32).

[2] On the tail of rot. 3 is a note: 'the wood is in Morley and not in Breydesale'. This may refer to the claim against John son of Geoffrey de Skeffington.

Robert de Dun, great-grandfather of Philippa and Isabella whose heirs they are, gave to Sampson de Dun and the heirs of his body and which after his death should revert to Philippa and Isabella according to the form of the grant because Sampson died without direct heir. Thus they say that Robert their great-grandfather was seised in his demesne as of fee and right in the peacetime of king Henry father of the present king, taking profits therefrom. Robert gave the tenements to Sampson and the heirs of his body, who dying without such heirs, the right reverted ...

[cancelled][1]

72 Henry de Irton, Philippa his wife and Isabella her sister claim the following tenements in Braydesale against the following: against Henry son of Gilbert de Chaddesden a messuage and half a virgate; against Alan le Clerke of Braydesale a messuage and 16 acres; against Richard de Dun a messuage and 30 acres; and against John son of Geoffrey de Skeftington 5 tofts, 4 virgates, 60 acres of wood[2] and 13s. 4d. rent, which Robert de Dun, great-grandfather of Philippa and Isabella whose heirs they are, granted to Sampson de Dun and the heirs of his body and which should revert to Philippa and Isabella after his death according to the form of the grant because Sampson died without direct heir. They say that Robert de Dun was seised thereof in the peacetime of king Henry father of the present king, taking profits therefrom. Robert granted the tenements to Sampson and the heirs of his body and Sampson, dying without direct heir, for that reason the right reverted to Robert as feoffor according to the form of the grant. From Robert descended the right of reversion to his son and heir Roger and from him to his son and heir Roger, from him to his daughter Margery and from her to Philippa and Isabella as daughters and heirs.[3] On this they bring suit.

Henry and the others have come and he says that he need not answer them because the tenements which they claim are Maud his wife's by right. He found her seised of them on the day of their marriage and without her he cannot bring the matter to judgment as she is not named in the writ. On this he seeks judgment. Henry de Irton, Philippa and Isabella cannot deny this and seek leave to withdraw from their writ and they have it.

Alan vouched to warranty John, son and heir of Robert de Ferrars former

---

[1] The whole entry is marked 'cancelled' [*vacat*]. Most of the eleven claims made are covered in later entries, the last four in **72**, four others in **129** and one in **130**.

[2] See note 2 on the previous page.

[3] For the succession referred to here see *DAJ*, xvi. 157–60, 167–9; xxxvii. 38–42.

earl of Derby, who is under age. By a charter of that Robert, which he proffers, it is attested that Robert Ferrars granted and confirmed the aforesaid tenements to Alan with warranty. Because Henry, Philippa and Isabella acknowledge that John is under age, the action is to stay until he is of *age*.

Richard asks that it be shown him whether the demandants have anything in the form of a grant. They say that such a charter was in Sampson's possession until his death, after which it was removed so that they could not obtain it. But they say that they are ready to verify the form of the grant in any other way which the court decides.

Richard acknowledges that Robert enfeoffed Sampson of the tenements by a form of grant but not in the aforesaid form. He says that the form was such that Robert granted the tenements to Sampson and the heirs of his body and that if Sampson died without direct heir, the tenements should remain to Sampson's brother Hugh and the heirs of his body.

Afterwards Richard de Dun comes and they concorded. Henry, Philippa and Isabella give *a mark* for leave to concord by surety of Giles de Meynill.

The agreement is this: Richard acknowledged the said messuages and land to be the right of Philippa and Isabella and he surrendered, demised and quitclaimed them for himself and his heirs to Henry, Philippa and Isabella and the heirs of Philippa and Isabella for ever.

[ref. 864]

73　Adam son of Adam le Blund of Cesterfeld who brought a writ of entry against Geoffrey de Beghton and others (concerning a tenement in Cesterfeld) has not prosecuted, so he and his sureties for prosecuting are in *mercy,* namely William de Barleburgh and Gilbert de Marcheham of the same.

[ref. 864]

74　Ralph de Shyrlegh was summoned to answer William son of Simon de Shyrlegh in a plea that he allow him reasonable estovers in Ralph's wood in Skirlegh which he ought and is accustomed to have. He says that in 200 acres of Ralph's wood in his manor of Schirlegh he had seisin of estovers such as were necessary for fuel, fencing and building as of fee and right in the time of the present king, taking profits therefrom. For the past two years Ralph has not allowed him to take estovers. Thus he says that he has suffered damage to the value of 100s.

Ralph has come, denies force and injury and says that William has no free tenement in Shyrlegh for which he can or ought to have estovers and that in fact, on the day of the sueing out of the writ on 17 March this year, the tenement was his mother Sarra's. Thereon Ralph puts himself on the

country, William likewise. So let there be a jury. *<Friday next after Easter
3 weeks>* [*9 May 1281*]

The jurors say that William had no such free tenement in Schirleye nor
estovers because at that time the tenement was Sarra's and still is. So it is
adjudged that Ralph is without day and William is to take nothing but is to
be in *mercy* for a false claim.

75 John de Weston and Millicent his wife claim against Robert son of
Geoffrey de Skelford a messuage, a toft and a bovate of land, 2 acres
excepted, in Murkaston in which Robert has no entry except by Mabel
widow of Robert de Shelford who unjustly disseised Millicent thereof.
Robert has come, denies their right and readily acknowledges that he has
entry by Mabel, but he strongly maintains that she did not disseise Millicent
because Millicent never had any seisin whereby she could be disseised.
Thereon he puts himself on the country, John and Millicent likewise. So let
there be a jury.

<Friday next after Easter 3 weeks> [*9 May 1281*]

Afterwards by leave they concorded. The agreement is this: Robert
acknowledged half of the bovate to be the right of Millicent and he rendered
it to them. Moreover he granted them 1½ acres of land lying near the bovate
towards the sun, to hold to them and the heirs of Millicent along with the
half bovate for ever. John and Millicent granted to Robert the remainder of
the land to hold to himself and his heirs, of John and Millicent and her heirs
for ever. *<recognizance>*[1]

[ref. 67]

[*rot. 4*]   Still Juries and Assizes of the same Eyre   J. de Vaux

76 An assize of mort d'ancestor to recognise if William son of Gregory,
father of William de Lek, died seised in his demesne as of fee of a messuage
and 2 bovates of land in Athelastre, which land and messuage John de Luk
holds. He has come and vouches to warranty Robert de Braydesale whom
he is to have before the justices in eyre at Lincoln at the quindene of Trinity
by aid of the court. [*22 June 1281*] He is to be summoned in the county of
Stafford. <process mark>

[ref. A49]

---

[1] The postea which forms this paragraph was written in a later and larger hand.

77   An assize to recognise if Robert de Dethek and Ellen his wife unjustly disseised John de Neubode of common of pasture in 100 acres of moor in Wytinton belonging to his free tenement in Neubode in which he was accustomed to have commons for all his beasts throughout the year. Robert and Ellen have come and Robert denies injury or disseisin because he found Ellen seised in severalty of the aforesaid pasture on terms such that John never had any right of common in it. Ellen denies disseisin, saying that Simon her father died seised in severalty of the pasture and that because at the time of his death she was under age, her guardian throughout her minority held that pasture in severalty and she herself has held it so hitherto. Thus John never had any right of common in it. Thereon she puts herself on the assize.

John says that he was in seisin of commons such as belonged to his free tenement in Neubode until Robert and Ellen distrained him there, prevented him having those rights and thus disseised him. He seeks inquiry by assize, likewise Robert and Ellen. So let an assize be taken. *<Scarthdale>*

The jurors say that Robert and Ellen did disseise John as he complains. So it was adjudged that John recover seisin by view of the recognitors and Robert and Ellen be in *mercy*.

Damages: 40s. to the clerks.

78   An assize to recognise if Geoffrey son of Hugh de Repindon, Hugh de Repindon and John le Bercher unjustly disseised Hugh son of Simon de Barwe of a messuage in Derby. Geoffrey has come and answers for himself as tenant and for the others, saying that he made no disseisin because a certain Geoffrey de Derby had enfeoffed him of the messuage, so that Hugh never had seisin after that enfeoffment whereof he could have been disseised. On this he puts himself on the assize.

The jurors say that Geoffrey de Derby did enfeoff Geoffrey son of Hugh and put him in seisin for one whole month. Afterwards, by the grace and permission of Geoffrey son of Hugh, he re-entered that messuage, remaining in it until his death. They also say that before Geoffrey's death, Geoffrey son of Hugh intruded himself into the messuage, remaining in it after Geoffrey's death, and that Hugh the complainant intruded into the messuage by night, the very night of Geoffrey's death, and that Geoffrey son of Hugh and the others ejected him on the following day. Thus they say that Hugh never was seised so that he could have been disseised. So it is adjudged that Geoffrey and the others are without day and that Hugh is to take nothing and is to be in *mercy* for a false claim.

[ref. 865]

79   An assize to recognise if John son of John unjustly raised a fence in Shirley to the nuisance of Thomas le Curcun's free tenement there. John says that he need not answer because the ground where the fence is situated is the rightful boundary of Alice his wife who is not named in the writ. Without her he cannot answer. Thomas cannot deny this, so John is without day and Thomas is to be in *mercy* for a false claim.
   [ref. 865]

80   Peter Pollard and William his brother who brought a writ of novel disseisin against Peter son of Eustace and William his son concerning a tenement in Derby, have not prosecuted, so they and their sureties for prosecuting are in *mercy,* John de Chaddesden and Henry le Gaunter.
   [ref. 865]

81   Henry de Curzun and Joan his wife who brought a writ of formedon against John de Ferrars concerning a tenement in Braydesale have not prosecuted, so they and their sureties for prosecuting are in *mercy,* namely Peter Pope of Breidesale and Geoffrey son of Alan of the same.
   Afterwards he is pardoned by William de Saham.

82   Robert Sauncheverell, who brought a writ of novel disseisin against the bishop of Lincoln and others concerning common of pasture in an acre of land in Quorendon, comes and withdraws. So he and his sureties for prosecuting are in mercy. Afterwards Robert comes and makes fine by *half a mark* for himself and his sureties and it is received.
   [ref. 865]

83   Robert Hervy was summoned to answer Ralph son of Robert de Butterley in a plea that he render him the customs and services which he ought for his free tenement held of Ralph in Wirkesworth in rents, arrears and other things. Ralph says that although Robert holds and should hold a bovate of land in Wirkesworth by homage and service of 12d. annual rent, a certain Robert, Ralph's ancestor, was seised thereof in the peacetime of king Henry father of the present king, taking profits therefrom. From that Robert descended right in the aforesaid services to his son and heir Ralph who now complains. That such is his right he offers to prove.
   Robert has come and says that he need not answer because this is a writ of possession assuming personal seisin. Ralph, in stating his case, claims through his father's seisin. Thereon he seeks judgment. Ralph cannot deny this, so Robert is without day and Ralph is to take nothing but is to be in

mercy for a false claim.
[ref. 865]

84   Simon de Notingham and Joan his wife give *half a mark* for leave to concord with Alan Gos and Hawise his wife in a plea of warranty of charter by surety of Alan. They have a chirograph.[1]
[ref. 866]

85   Ralph de Saucheverell was summoned to answer Alice de Staunton in a plea that he warrant her 6 messuages, 4 virgates of land and 10 acres of meadow in Aston upon Trent which she holds and claims to hold of him, whereof she has his charter. Ralph comes, by leave they concord and have a chirograph.
[ref. 293]

86   Robert son of Robert Payn, who brought an assize of mort d'ancestor against William son of Roger Folegaumbe concerning a tenement in Crudekote, has not prosecuted. So he and his sureties for prosecuting are in *mercy,* namely William son of Walter de Tunstedes and William his son.
[ref. 866]

87   Sewall le Fowene of Holington claims against Letitia widow of Alexander le Mercer a messuage and a bovate of land in Schirleye as his by writ of right concerning which the chief lord of the fee granted his court to the king. Letitia has come and elsewhere vouched to warranty John le Fowene who now comes by summons and warrants her. He furthermore vouches Richard le Fowen whom he is to have before the justices in eyre at Lincoln at the quindene of Trinity by aid of the court [*22 June 1281*]. He is to be summoned in the county of *Suthantun.* <process mark>
[refs. 303, 387, A7]

88   Robert son of Ralph de Rerisby was summoned to answer Robert de Perton in a plea that he acquit him of the service which Constance widow of Henry de Aleman demands of him for his free tenement which he holds

---

[1] At Derby, within three weeks of Easter 1281. Grant etc. and in consideration of one sparrowhawk by Alan Gos and Hawise, defendants, to the plaintiffs of a messuage etc. in Derby, to hold to the plaintiffs and heirs of Simon, of the defendants and heirs of Hawise for ever at the rent of one rose at the feast of the Nativity of St John the Baptist and performing all other services to the chief lords of that fee, for the defendants and the heirs of Hawise. (*DAJ*, xii. 36).

of Robert son of Ralph in Schirebrok, which Robert, who is mesne lord, ought to do. Robert complains that since he holds of Robert 7 bovates of land in Schirebrok by service of 2d. rent annually, 17d. for guarding Tykehill Castle and by service of 3s. 9d. towards scutage of 40s. be it more or less, when required, Robert ought to acquit him of those services. Constance demands from Robert de Perton 100s. for Robert's relief. She also demands suit of her court at Tikehill every three weeks and she distrained Robert de Perton for the above services. Thus he says that through Robert son of Ralph withholding quittance, he suffers loss to the value of 100s. and thereon he brings suit.

Robert son of Ralph comes, denies force and injury, readily acknowledging that he ought to acquit Robert de Perton of those services but denying that he was ever distrained for default of quittance. On this he puts himself on the country, likewise Robert de Perton. So let there be a jury.

The jury says that Robert de Perton was distrained for default of Robert son of Ralph's quittance, so he is in *mercy* and Robert de Perton is to recover damages assessed by verdict of the jurors at 40s.[1]

Damages: 40s. to the clerks.

89 Henry son of Robert Portegoye of Scropton claims against Robert son of Hamo de Saperton and Amice his wife half an acre of land in Scropton as his by writ of entry. Robert and Amice come by her attorney and by leave render it to Henry. So he is to have seisin.

[ref. 324]

90 An assize of mort d'ancestor to recognise if William Hildebrond, uncle of Robert son of Ellis Hildebrond, died seised in his demesne as of fee of a messuage and a bovate of land in Bradeburne which are held by Stephen de Irton and Margery his wife. Elsewhere they vouched to warranty Roger de Bradeburne who now comes by summons and warrants them. They

---

[1] Henry of Almain was the son of Richard Earl of Cornwall and Isabel daughter of William Earl of Pembroke, widow of Gilbert de Clare. He was thus cousin to Edward I and to the de Montforts. He was with Edward at Lewes and was imprisoned. In 1271 he was murdered by Guy, son of Simon de Montfort in Viterbo. (*Complete Peerage*, iii. 432).

3 May 1274. Mandate to Roger le Estrange, keeper of the castle and land of the Peak, to deliver to Constance the widow of Henry de Alemannia or to Raymond de Nolverio her clerk and attorney, £100 of rent in the Peak long since assigned to her in dower but lately taken into the king's hands for certain causes together with the receipts since their caption. The like to John de Sandiacre, constable of the castle of Tykeshull, to deliver to her the castle of Tykeshull and the manor of Gringele and £100 rent in the Peak. (*Cal.Pat.R. 1272–81*, p. 49).

concorded and Robert gives *half a mark* for leave to agree by surety of
Roger. The agreement is this: Roger acknowledges the tenement to be
Robert's by right and he surrendered, remised and quitclaimed it for himself
and his heirs to Robert and his heirs for ever. Robert is to have seisin and
Stephen is to have land to the value from Roger in a suitable place.
   [refs. 306, 866]

[*rot. 4d*]   Still Juries and Assizes

91   An assize of mort d'ancestor to recognise if Nicholas, son of Ralph
Kay, uncle of Richard son of Henry de Middelton, died seised in his
demesne as of fee of half a messuage in Baukeswell which Maud widow of
William de Esseburne holds, who comes. On this a certain Ralph le Wyne,
the queen's bailiff in Baukewell, comes and says that Baukewell is a free
borough and that tenements in it may be bequeathed, since no such writ runs
in that vill. He seeks that this writ, prejudicial to the liberty, should not
proceed. Because the knights and stewards of the shire affirm definitely that
the vill is not a borough, nor has it burghal liberties, the assize proceeds and
Maud is told that she may answer if she wishes.
   Elsewhere she vouched to warranty Roger de Asseburne who now comes
by summons and warrants her, saying that he should not have to answer
because Richard had no uncle called Nicholas. Thereon he puts himself on
the assize.
   The jury says likewise, so Maud is without day and Richard is to take
nothing, but is to be in *mercy* for a false claim.
   [refs. 379, 866]

92   Adam de Staveley and Cassandra his wife claim against Geoffrey de
Beghton a messuage, 2 carucates of land and 6s. rent in Whytewell whereof
William de Funteneye, kinsman of Cassandra whose heir she is, died seised.
   Geoffrey comes and says that he cannot answer on this writ without his
wife Joan who was enfeoffed of the tenements along with him by a certain
Annora de Haversegge whose charter he proffers confirming this. Since Joan
is not named in the writ, he seeks judgment.
   Adam and Cassandra say that the omission should not allow Geoffrey to
quash their writ because recently, after the death of their kinsman William,
he intruded into the tenement before he married Joan, and has until now
continued his intrusion. He obtained the aforesaid charter for himself and
Joan later. They seek judgment as to whether or not he should answer

without her concerning his own intrusion. Moreover they say that Annora never had anything in the tenements so that she could have enfeoffed Geoffrey and Joan.

Geoffrey says that Annora was in seisin and enfeoffed him and Joan jointly. Thereon he puts himself on the country, likewise Adam and Cassandra. So let there be a jury. *<Wednesday next after quindene of Easter>* [*30 April 1281*]

Afterwards they agreed and Adam and Cassandra give *a mark* for leave to concord by surety of Stephen de Jarum and they have a chirograph.[1] Adam and Cassandra acknowledge that they owe Geoffrey 20 marks, whereof they have paid him 10 marks down and will pay the remainder at the feast of St John the Baptist next [*24 June 1281*.] On this they find Gilbert de Thorneton, Walter de Repinghale and Stephen de Jarum who grant that if Adam and Cassandra default in payment of the 10 marks, the sheriff may cause the amount to be levied of their lands and chattels. *<recognizance>*

[refs. 120, 866]

93 Joan, widow of Walter de Shyrleye, who brought a writ of entry against Alan le Bercher of Rossenton concerning a tenement in Rossenton, has not prosecuted, so she and her sureties are in *mercy,* namely Thomas de Whytechelf in Sturston and Henry Baret of the same.

[ref. 867]

94 Henry son of William le Warener claims against Hugh de Stapelford a messuage, 12 acres of land and 3 roods of meadow in Sandyacre in which Hugh has no entry except by William le Warener who unjustly disseised Henry thereof. Hugh comes, defends his right, readily acknowledging that he has entry by William, whom he maintains did not disseise Henry, whom he says was never in seisin, so that he could have been disseised. Thereon he puts himself on the country, Henry likewise. So let there be a jury. *<Wednesday next after quindene of Easter>* [*30 April 1281*]

95 An assize to recognise if Alice de Birsicote, mother of John de

---

[1] At Derby, within two weeks of Easter 1281. Grant in consideration of 20 marks of silver by the tenants to Cassandra of a messuage, 2 carucates of land and 6s. rent etc. in Whitwell and Pebley, except the site of the mill of Pebley and 7 acres in the same vill. Endorsed: Oliver de Langeford and Simon de Gousel put in their claim. Walter de Gousel puts in his claim. (*DAJ*, xii. 34).

Birsicote, died seised in her demesne as of fee of a messuage, 6 bovates of land, 7 acres of meadow and 16s. rent in Berewardecote, Brennaston and Pilcot, which messuage and land Richard de Dun holds, withholding the rent from John.

Richard comes and they are agreed. John gives *a mark* for leave to concord by surety of Henry de Notingham of the county of *Leycestre* and they have a chirograph.[1] John acknowledges that he owes Richard 9 marks of which he will pay him 4½ marks at the quindene of St John the Baptist next and at Michaelmas next following 4½ marks [*8 July, 29 Sept. 1281*]. If he does not do so, he grants that the sheriff may levy it of his lands and chattels.

<recognizance>
[ref. 867]

96   An assize to recognise if Roger de Seladon, father of Ralph de Seladon, died seised in his demesne as of fee of 8½ acres of land and 1½ acres of meadow in Baukewell whereof John son of Hugh Martyn of Tideswell holds 6 acres of land and 1½ acres of meadow and Henry Hyne of Baukewell 2½ acres of land. They come and Henry says that he has nothing nor claims anything in that tenement. John readily acknowledges all the articles in the writ but says that he has the land by demise of Ralph for a term not yet expired. Ralph cannot deny this so Henry and John are without day and Ralph is to take nothing but is to be in *mercy* for a false claim.

[refs. 325, 867, A47]

97   Ralph de Haneley claimed against William Bret and Maria his wife 4 acres and 3 roods of land in Wytyngton as his right, so the sheriff was ordered to summon William and Maria to be here on Thursday next after the close of Easter [*24 April 1281*] to answer Ralph in that plea. Summoned for that day, they defaulted, on account of which the sheriff was ordered to take the tenements into the king's hands, notify the day of the confiscation to the justices and summon them to be here on this day to answer Ralph concerning both the default and the capital plea. William, Ralph and Maria now come.

Ralph draws particular attention to the default. William and Maria readily

---

[1] At Derby, within two weeks of Easter 1281. The consideration was 10 marks of silver. (*DAJ*, xii. 31).

deny that they were ever summoned to be present on the aforesaid Thursday to answer Ralph and say they are ready to defend against him and his suit as the court decides.

So it was adjudged that Ralph bind himself 12-handed. He is to come with his law on the Thursday next after the quindene of Easter [*1 May 1281*]. Sureties for the *law,* William Pyte and Robert de Wytington.[1]

98   An assize to recognise if Robert Borard, father of Rose Borard, died seised in his demesne as of fee of a rood of land in Ravenstone, which land William Walkelyn holds, who comes and vouches to warranty Robert son of Simon who is under age. Rose readily acknowledges this, so the action is to stay until he is of *age.*

[ref. 149]

99   John son of Anketill de Bentleye acknowledges that he has granted, remised and wholly quitclaimed and by his deed confirmed for himself and his heirs for ever to God and the church of St Mary of Derley and the abbot and canons there serving God, a messuage, a carucate of land and 9 acres of meadow with appurtenances in Normanton near Derby which he demised to Roger de Draycot and which he claims against them as his right. He remised and wholly quitclaimed for himself and his heirs to the abbot, the convent, their successors and their church for ever, all the right and claim which he had or could have in all other lands and tenements, rents and properties which the abbot and convent held, both in demesne and in service in the aforesaid vill of Normanton on the day of the making of his deed, with the homage and service of free men, wards, reliefs, escheats and all other things which might fall due or pertain to him or to his heirs through any right or in any way. To have and to hold to the abbot, convent and church in free, quiet and perpetual alms with all their appurtenances, liberties and ease-ments. So that neither John nor his heirs nor anyone in their name can demand or lay legal claim to any right in the aforesaid tenements in Normanton or to any part of them or their appurtenances, John and his heirs will warrant all the aforesaid lands, tenements, rents and properties with homage, wards, services, reliefs, escheats and all their appurtenances to the abbot and convent and their church as free, quiet and perpetual alms against

---

[1] Easter 11 Edward I [1283]. Between the king, plaintiff, and William Brett and Maria his wife, defendants, for the manors of Whittington and Brimington. Judgment for the defendants. (*Abbreviatio Placitorum (Coram rege),* Easter 11 Edw. I rot. 17).

all people for ever. And for this acknowledgment, grant, quitclaim and warranty, the abbot and convent have given John a mark of silver over the sum which he received from them before, as is more fully contained in a certain deed from John to the abbot and convent.

[ref. 328]

[*rot. 5*]   Still Juries and Assizes   Vaux

100 Robert de Quenesburgh and Agnes his wife, who is said to be of full age, claim against Henry abbot of Crockesden 9 acres of land in Herteshorn as her right and in which the abbot has no entry except after the demise made to Walter, the former abbot, by William son of Bertram de Herteshorn who only had custody while Agnes was under age.[1]

The abbot comes and vouches Roger son of William Bartram to warranty. He is present and warrants the abbot, readily acknowledging that he has entry after the demise made to the former abbot by William, but he says that Agnes, after that demise, remised and quitclaimed for herself and her heirs to William his father, whose heir he is, all right and claim which she had in that land for ever. Roger seeks judgment as to whether he can bring action to claim the land and he proffers a certain deed under Agnes's name (attesting the quitclaim.)

Robert and Agnes readily acknowledge that it is her deed but they say that she was under age at the time of its making. That this is so, they seek inquiry by the country, likewise Roger. So let there be a jury. <*Tuesday after quindene of Easter*> [*29 April 1281*]

Afterwards they concorded and Robert and Agnes give *half a mark* for leave to concord by surety of Roger. The agreement is this: Robert and Agnes acknowledge the land to be Roger's by right and they remised and quitclaimed it for themselves and Agnes's heirs to Roger and his heirs for ever. Roger gives half a mark.

[refs. 304, 867]

101 William le Fevre of Sandiacre and Cecilia his wife claim against William Danvers 2 acres of land and 4 acres of meadow in Staunton by Sandiacre as Cecilia's right by writ of entry. William Danvers has come and

---

[1] Walter was Walter de London, abbot 1242–68; Henry was Henry de Meysham, abbot 1274–84.

vouches William Cressy to warranty. He is to have him at *Lincoln* at the quindene of Trinity by aid of the court. *[22 June 1281]* He is to be summoned in the county of *Bokynham.*[1] *<process mark>*
  [ref. A6]

102 Roger le Lorymer claims against Hugh le Lorymer half an acre of land in Cestrefeld in which Hugh has no entry except by Ralph le Lorymer, father of Roger whose heir he is. Ralph demised it to him for a term of three years which has expired. Afterwards Roger did not prosecute so Hugh is without day and Roger and his sureties for prosecuting are in *mercy.* He found no sureties because he had pledged his faith. Afterwards his amercement was pardoned by the justices because he is poor.

103 Roger de la Graunge and Alice his wife claim against Hugh Trout of Derley a messuage and half a bovate of land in Merlache whereof Thomas del Wode, Alice's grandfather whose heir she is, died seised in his demesne as of fee. Hugh comes, denies force and injury and that Thomas died seised of the tenements. On this he puts himself on the country, Roger and Alice likewise. So let there be a jury. *<Tuesday after quindene of Easter>* *[29 April 1281]*

104 Roger son of Robert de Hylton claims against Roger de Tok a messuage and 8 acres of land in Hylton as his right, in which Roger has no entry except by Margery widow of John de Etewalle, to whom Roger son of Robert demised them for a term now expired. Roger de Tock has come, defends his right, strongly maintaining that he has entry not by Margery but rather by a certain Henry de Tock. Roger son of Robert cannot deny this and seeks leave to withdraw and he has it.

105 An assize comes to recognise if Gilbert de Segrave, father of Nicholas de Segrave, died seised in his demesne as of fee of half a virgate, 4 acres excepted, in Roxlaston, which land Adam Harlewyn holds. Adam has not come and was resummoned. Judgment: Let the assize be taken against him by default.
  The jurors say that Gilbert did die seised of the tenements, so it is

---

[1] At Derby, within three weeks of Trinity 1281. Grant etc. and in consideration of 5 marks of silver by the plaintiffs to the tenant and his heirs for ever of the premises named. (*DAJ*, xii. 42).

adjudged that Nicholas recover seisin by view of the recognitors and Adam is in *mercy*.

Damages after the Statute of Gloucester,[1] half a mark, all to the clerks. Repyndon.[2] [ref. 314]

106   The abbot of Crokesden appeared on the fourth day against Richard de Pres in a plea that he keep the covenant made between Walter the former abbot, his predecessor, and Richard concerning a messuage in Esseburn.

Richard has not come and the sheriff, ordered to distrain him to be present on this day, did nothing but he attests that Richard has nothing in his bailiwick by which he can be distrained but has sufficient in the county of *Stafford*. So the sheriff there is ordered to distrain him to be present at *Lincoln* at the quindene of Trinity. [*22 June 1281*] This the sheriff attests. <process mark>

[refs. 304, A11]

107   The same abbot appeared on the fourth day against Richard de Pres in a plea that he render him the customs and services which he ought by right to do for his free tenement held of him in Esseburn.

Richard has not come and the sheriff, ordered to distrain him to be present on this day, did nothing but attests that he has nothing in his bailiwick by which he can be distrained but has sufficient in the county of *Stafford*. So the sheriff there is ordered to distrain him to be present at *Lincoln* at the quindene of Trinity. [*22 June 1281*] This the sheriff attests. <process mark>

[refs. 304, A11]

108   Robert de Acovere of Denston and Margery his wife claim against the abbot of Roucestre a messuage and 40 acres of land in Nether Somersale in which the abbot has no entry except by Henry de Denston, Margery's father whose heir she is, who while of unsound mind, demised them to the abbot.

The abbot has come, defends his right, maintaining that he does not enter by Henry but rather by Walter the former abbot, his predecessor. Robert and

---

[1] Cf. the Statute: 'Whereas heretofore damages were not awarded ... It is provided also that where before this time damages were not awarded in a plea of Mort d'ancestor but in one case where land was recovered against the chief lord, that from henceforth damages shall be awarded in all cases where a man recovereth by assize of Mort d'ancestor ... (*Statutes of the Realm*, i. 47).

[2] The significance of this word is unclear.

Margery cannot deny this, so it is adjudged that the abbot is without day and that Robert and Margery are to be in *mercy* for a false claim.
[refs. 297, 298, 867]

109 Robert de Stafford claims against Richard le Seriaunt and Ermintrude his wife a messuage and 9 acres of land in Eginton near Tuttebyr' in which they have no entry except by Agnes, daughter of William son of Walkelin, to whom Ermintrude de Stafford, Robert's mother whose heir he is, demised them for a term which has expired, that is, the lifetime of Agnes.

Richard and Ermintrude have come, defend their right and readily acknowledge that they have entry by Agnes, but they maintain that Ermintrude de Stafford did not demise the tenements to Agnes for any term but rather in fee, by a charter which they proffer attesting that Ermintrude gave and granted them to Agnes to have and to hold in fee and inheritance and that she and her heirs would warrant Agnes.

Robert says that the charter ought not to go against him because it is not Ermintrude's deed. On this he puts himself on the country and on the witnesses named in the charter, John de Weston and Robert son of Walkelin. The other witnesses have died. So let there be a jury.

<Thursday after quindene of Easter> [*1 May 1281*] Ermintrude appoints her husband Richard as her attorney.

Afterwards they agreed and Robert gives *half a mark* for leave to concord by surety of Richard. They have a chirograph and the aforesaid charter is handed over to Richard and Ermintrude.
[ref. 868]

110 Ranulph de Wandesley and Millicent his wife give *half a mark* for leave to concord with John de Wenesley and Margery his wife in a plea of warranty of charter by surety of John. They have a chirograph.
[ref. 868]

111 Richard son of Richard de Litton gives *half a mark* for leave to concord with Richard de Seyniorge of Barleborwe and Margery his wife concerning half of a toft and 30 acres of land in Barleborwe, by surety of Richard. They have a chirograph.[1] [ref. 868]

---

[1] At Derby, within three weeks of Easter 1281. Acknowledgment by tenants Richard de Seynierge of Barleburg and Margery his wife that a toft and 30 acres of land etc. in Barleburgh are the right of the plaintiff Richard son of Richard de Litton, and they quitclaimed a moiety

112 The king by his writ commanded his justices in these words.

'Edward by the grace of God king of England etc. to all his bailiffs and faithful, greeting. Know that the prior of Lenton, who by our permission is on business overseas, has appointed as his attorneys before us Brother Humphrey de Rysseden and Roger son of Richard de Lenton, to gain or lose in all pleas and plaints moved or moving, for the said prior or against him in any court in England whatsoever. At the request of the prior we have granted that Humphrey and Roger or either of them who happens to represent the prior, may appoint as attorneys or attorney those whom they or he wish, in our court before us, for prosecuting and defending all the aforesaid pleas and plaints and for gain or loss aforesaid. In testimony of which we have made these our letters patent. The validity of these presents is to extend until St Peter's Chains next to come [*1 August 1281*], whether or not the prior has returned by then from overseas parts. Witnessed by me at Wodestok, 14 April in the 9th year of our reign [*Monday 14 April 1281*].'[1]

113 Richard Meylur and Petronilla his wife appeared on the fourth day against William Attewall in a plea concerning a bovate of land in Oxcroft which they claim as Petronilla's right.

He has not come and defaulted previously on the morrow of the close of Easter so that the sheriff was ordered to take the land into the king's hands, to notify the day of confiscation and to summon him to be here on this day, the Monday next after the quindene of Easter [*28 April 1281*]. The sheriff now attests the day of confiscation and the summons. On this a certain Lecia de Attewalle comes and says that she holds and held the land on the day of the sueing out of the writ, namely 7 April in the 9th year of the king [*1281*]. She claims that through collusion between Richard, Petronilla and William she should not lose her seisin of the land when she is ready to answer them.

---

of themselves and the heirs of Margery to the plaintiff and his heirs for ever. Grant thereupon by plaintiff to tenant, of the other moiety of the premises which lie towards the shade to hold of the plaintiff and his heirs during the lifetime of both tenants at the yearly rent of 2s. 6d. payable at Pentecost and St Martin in winter. After the decease of both tenants, the moiety to remain to the plaintiff and his heirs for ever. (*DAJ*, xii. 35).

[1] 14 April 1281. Letters for the prior of Lenton going beyond the seas, with protection, nominating Humphrey de Rissheden and Roger son of Richard de Lenton until Aug. 1. [*Cal.Pat.R. 1272–81*, p.430].

She asks that they accept this.

Richard and Petronilla say that Lecia's defence of the land ought not to be accepted because she did not hold it on the aforesaid date, but rather William. That this is so, they seek inquiry by the country, Lecia likewise. So let there be a jury. <Thursday after quindene of Easter> [1 May 1281]

The jurors elected by consent of the parties say that Lecia did not hold the tenements on the aforesaid date but rather William Attewalle. So it is adjudged that Richard and Petronilla recover seisin against William by default and William and Lecia are in *mercy*. [refs. 343, 868]

114 The same Richard and Petronilla claim against Agnes de Percy a messuage and 8 bovates of land in the same vill as Petronilla's right by the gift of Richard Ingeram, who enfeoffed her thereof, and in which Agnes has no entry except by a demise made to her by Robert Ingeram, former husband of Petronilla, whom she in his lifetime could not gainsay.

Agnes comes and defends her right, maintaining that Petronilla was never seised of the tenements by Richard Ingeram nor had she anything in them except a tenancy with Robert, her former husband, whose right those tenements were. On this she puts herself on the country, likewise Richard and Petronilla. So let there be a jury.

The jurors elected by consent of the parties say that Petronilla never had anything in the tenements except with Robert, her former husband, so it is adjudged that Agnes is without day and that Richard and Petronilla are to be in *mercy* for a false claim.

[refs. 294, 868, A5]

115 Henry le Macy and Julia his wife, who is said to be of full age, claims against Ralph le Frounceys a messuage in Derby which Julia demised to him when she was under age.

Ralph has come, defends his right and says that he claims nothing except a free tenement demised by Julia, who at the time was of full age according to the custom of the borough of Derby, which is that any woman is of full age (and may sell her tenements in the borough) when she knows how to trade. Julia was of such age. On this he puts himself on the country, likewise Henry and Julia. So let there be a jury. <Tuesday after quindene of Easter> [29 April 1281]

116 Hugh Alybun was summoned to answer Roger Gery in a plea as to why he unjustly raised a certain house in Derby to the nuisance of Roger's free tenement in that vill. Roger says that he has land next to Hugh's house where he used to plant vegetables. Hugh raised the house so that rainwater falling from it swamps his vegetables which grow less well than formerly, nor is anything else able to grow there because of excessive dripping from the gutters. He also says that Hugh made two doors facing his land and very often keeps them open so that he has no privacy in his garden adjacent. He says that through the raising of the house, he has suffered loss to the value of 100s. and thus brings suit.

Hugh has come, denies force and injury, and says that Roger has brought this writ against him unjustly because if there has been injury, it has been by his father Hugh and not by him. His father raised the house, which afterwards suffered ruin and later he himself restored it to its former state. As to the doors, there are no more facing Roger's land than in his father's time. On this he puts himself on the country, likewise Roger. So let there be a jury.

Afterwards Roger comes and seeks leave to withdraw from his writ and he has it.

117   The abbot of Burton on Trent claims against Adam le Keu of Cotes 2 virgates of land and 7 acres of meadow in Cotes as the right of his church by writ of *precipe in capite*.

Adam has come and says that he cannot answer him on his writ because Mabel his wife was conjointly seised of a virgate in those tenements and without her he cannot take that virgate to judgment. The abbot cannot deny this and seeks leave to withdraw from his writ. He has it.

[*rot. 6*]   Still Juries and Assizes

118   Oliver son of Oliver le Foun claims against Roger de Merchynton 15 acres of land and an acre of meadow in Holyton as his right in which Roger has no entry except by John le Fowen, who unjustly disseised Juliana de Holynton, Oliver's mother, whose heir he is.

Roger comes and elsewhere vouched John le Fowen who now comes by summons, warrants him and defends his right. He says that Oliver can claim no right in the tenements because at another time in the court of king Henry before John de Lexinton, the justice assigned to it at Notingham [*April–May 1252*], Oliver brought a writ of attaint concerning other lands and tenements which John had at another time deraigned against him. Before that justice John surrendered to Oliver part of the tenements which were then in pledge. As to the other part, Oliver remised to John all right which he had in it and in all other lands which John then held. John says that he himself then held those tenements which Oliver now claims and seeks judgment as to whether an action on them can now be brought after the aforesaid remise and quitclaim. Questioned as to whether he had anything by that remise and quitclaim, he says he is but ready to verify by a jury.

So that by this action he may be able to refute him, Oliver seeks judgment as to whether such a remise and quitclaim can be ascertained except by an instrument made between them or by the record of the rolls of the aforesaid justice at that time. <to judgment>

A day was given them at the octave of St John the Baptist at Lincoln [*1 July 1281*].

[ref. A58]

119   Ralph le Bretton and Emma his wife claim against the abbot of Derley a messuage in Derby as Emma's right by writ of entry. The abbot comes and they are agreed. Ralph gives *half a mark* for leave to concord and they have a chirograph.[1]

[ref. 869]

120   Adam de Staveley and Cassandra his wife claim against Geoffrey de Beghton a messuage, 2 bovates of land and 6s. rent in Wythewell whereof William de Funteneye, kinsman of Cassandra whose heir she is, died seised, taking profits therefrom. From William who died without direct heir the fee reverted to Robert his uncle and heir who was brother to Alice, mother of Cassandra. From Robert who died without direct heir the fee descended to his brother and heir Jordan and from Jordan to his son and heir William. From William, who died without direct heir, the fee descended to his brother and heir John and from John, who died without direct heir, to Cristiana and Cassandra as sisters and right heirs. From Cristiana, who died without direct heir, the right in her share descended to this Cassandra who now claims as sister and heir. Thus they bring suit.[2]

[ref. 92]

---

[1]   At Derby, within two weeks of Easter 1281. Grant in consideration of 4 marks of silver by plaintiffs Ralph le Bretton and Emma his wife, to tenant the abbot of Darley and his church of St Mary of a messuage etc. in Derby for ever. (*DAJ*, xii. 33).

[2]   This entry refers to the adjournment for jury verdict (see **92**). The parties, however, concorded, the terms being recorded on that entry.

121 Nicholas de Penkriz, master of the hospital of St Helen of Derby, acknowledges that he owes Henry Columbel, Payne de la Riddinge, Eudes de Henovere and Cecilia widow of Robert de Loseskou, executors of the will of Robert de Lostskou, 46s. whereof he will pay half at the quindene of Michaelmas and the other half at Christmas next following [*13 Oct., 25 Dec.*].

If he does not, he grants that the sheriff may cause it to be levied of his lands and chattels. On this he finds these sureties, John de la Cornere and Nicholas le Lorimer of Derby, who grant that if Nicholas does not pay, the sheriff may cause it to be levied of theirs. <*recognizance*>

122 William de Bateleye and Joan his wife give *a mark* for leave to concord with Roger de Munpinzun and Cristiana his wife in a plea of warranty by surety of Roger. They have a chirograph.[1]
[ref. 869]

123 Sarra widow of William de Thurleston claims against Natalia daughter of Michael de Breydeston a messuage and 2 bovates of land in Aylwaston in which Natalia has no entry except after a demise made to Michael and Elizabeth his wife by William de Thurleston, Sarra's former husband, whom she could not gainsay in his lifetime.

Natalia comes and says she need not answer her on this writ because she has entry by Michael and he by William, Sarra's former husband. She claims judgment on this writ inasmuch as Sarra should have requested it in the form that Natalia has no entry except by Michael de Breydeston to whom William de Thurleston Sarra's former husband whom she etc. demised it.

After this Sarra cannot deny it, so Natalia is without day and Sarra is to take nothing but is to be in *mercy* for a false claim.
[ref. 284]

124 An assize to recognise if William le Tayllur and Geoffrey Hulme unjustly disseised Henry del Heithe and Emma his wife of two shops in Bathekewell. Geoffrey and William come and William for himself and

---

[1] At Derby, within three weeks of Easter 1281. Grant etc. and in consideration of 100s. silver by the defendants to the plaintiffs William de Batel' and Joan his wife, of a third part of the manor of Hurst iuxta Caldelowe etc. To hold of the defendants Roger de Munpinzun and Cristina his wife and her heirs for ever at yearly rent of a rose at the feast of St John the Baptist and performing all other services to the chief lords of that fee for the defendants and heirs of Cristina. (*DAJ*, xii. 35).

Geoffrey says that they have done no injury or disseisin because he has the shops by grant of Emma and Henry who enfeoffed him. On this he puts himself on the assize. So let it be taken.

The jurors say that William and Geoffrey did not disseise because they held the shops by the goodwill of Henry and Emma, so it is adjudged that William and Geoffrey are without day and Henry and Emma are to take nothing but are to be in *mercy* for a false claim.

[ref. 869]

125 Ranulph de Wandesleye acknowledges that he owes Hugh de Stapelford £20 sterling which he will pay him at the octave of Martinmas in the 9th beginning 10th year of the present king [*18 Nov. 1281*], and if he does not, he grants that the sheriff may cause it to be levied of his lands and chattels. *<recognizance>*

[*rot. 6d*]   Still Juries and Assizes   J. de Vaux

126 William de Bredon claims against the abbot of Cestre 5s. rent in Magna Wilne as his right whereof Ralph de Bredon, his grandfather whose heir he is, died seised in his demesne as of fee.

The abbot has come, denies force and injury, maintaining that Ralph did not die seised of the aforesaid rent. On this he puts himself on the country, likewise William. So let there be a jury.

<Saturday after SS. Philip and James> [*3 May 1281*]

Afterwards they agreed and William gives *half a mark* for leave to concord by surety of Geoffrey de Burgo and they have a chirograph. The abbot acknowledges that he owes William 40s. which he will pay him on the Saturday after Ascension Day [*24 May 1281*] and if he defaults, he grants that the sheriff may levy it of his lands and chattels.

[ref. 869]

127 William Thrippell of Spinkill claims against Michael le Tayllur 12 acres in Ekenton and against Robert de Bultham 10 acres in the same vill as his right, in which Michael and Robert have no entry except by William Tripell, William's father whose heir he is, who demised to them while of unsound mind.

Michael and Robert have come, deny his right and readily acknowledge that they have entry by William but they say that at the time of the demise he was of good and sound memory. On this they put themselves on the country, likewise William. So let there be a jury. *<the same Saturday>*

128 An assize comes to recognise if Robert de Karliolo, Geoffrey Dethek and William de Chaddesden unjustly disseised Hubert de Frechenvill of 20s. rent from his free tenement in Lochawe. Hubert, when asked, says he claims to receive the rent from Robert's hand.

Robert and William have come and Geoffrey has not. William for himself says that he has done no injury or disseisin because he has the rent by assignment of Geoffrey de Dethek who enfeoffed him. Therefore he says that if there has been any disseisin, it has been by Geoffrey and not by him. Robert as bailiff answers for himself and Geoffrey. He acknowledges that Hubert was seised at some time of the rent by his hand, but says that they did no injury or disseisin, because Geoffrey at another time, before Gilbert de Preston and his fellow justices in the last eyre in this county [*7 April–8 May 1269*], brought a writ of entry against Robert concerning the tenement whence this rent issued, as being that into which Robert had no entry except by Henry de Karliolo to whom Ralph de Frechenvill demised it, having unjustly disseised Ralph de Dethek, brother of Geoffrey whose heir he is. He recovered that tenement by a jury taken between them which found that Ralph de Frechenville had disseised Ralph Dethek. Thus he seeks judgment whether Hubert may now be able to claim or recover the aforesaid rent assessed for the intervening period at 20s., since Ralph de Frechenvill was the disseisor.

Hubert readily acknowledges that Geoffrey brought the aforesaid writ of entry against Robert, but he says that there was never any jury taken thereon, but rather that Robert, in deceit and to the disinheritance of Hubert, acknowledged that Ralph de Frechenvill had disseised Ralph Dethek. Thus it was that Geoffrey recovered the tenement and not by the aforesaid jury as Robert says. That this is so, he puts himself on the record of the rolls of the aforesaid eyre, likewise Robert. So Thursday next after Easter three3 weeks was given them [*8 May 1281*]. Meanwhile the rolls are to be searched.

Later, the rolls of that eyre having been searched, it was found that Geoffrey had claimed the tenement against Robert de Cardoil in the aforesaid form and that Robert had put himself on a jury that Ralph de Frechenvill had not disseised Ralph de Dethek, Geoffrey's brother whose heir he is, of that tenement. After he had put himself on that jury, Robert de Cardoil came before the justices and could not deny that Ralph de Freskenville had disseised Ralph de Dethek. So it was adjudged in that court that Geoffrey should recover his seisin of the tenement.

They were given a day to hear their *judgment* on the octave of St John

the Baptist at Lincoln [*1 July 1281*].
  [refs. 252, 393, A34]

129 Henry de Irton, Philippa his wife and Isabella her sister claim the
following tenements in Breydesale: against Agnes de Cravene a messuage
and 18 acres; against Robert Pope and Alice his wife 6 acres; against
Geoffrey de Dethek a messuage and 40 acres; and against Stephen de
Dunesmor a messuage and a bovate, which Robert de Dun, great-grandfather
of Philippa and Isabella whose heirs they are, granted in the form of a gift
to Hugh de Dun and the heirs of his body and which after Hugh's death
ought to revert to them because Hugh died without direct heir. They say that
Robert de Dun was seised of those tenements as of fee and right in the
peacetime of king Henry father of the present king by taking profits, and that
Robert granted the tenements to Hugh and the heirs of his body, who, dying
without such heirs, the right reverted to Robert as feoffor through the form
of the grant. From Robert the right of reversion descended to a certain Roger
as son and heir, and from him to Margery as daughter and heir. From her it
descended to Philippa and Isabella who now claim as daughters and heirs.
Thereon they bring suit.

Agnes and the others have come and elsewhere vouched to warranty
Henry de Curzun and Joan his wife who now come by summons, warrant
them and deny the right of Henry, Philippa and Isabella. They readily
acknowledge the form of the grant but say that by it Philippa and Isabella
can have no right in the tenements because Hugh de Dun did not die without
direct heir. They say in fact that Joan herself is Hugh's legitimate daughter
and heir and as such is in seisin of the tenements. They seek judgment as to
whether, Joan being still alive, action through the aforesaid reversion can be
competent for them.

Henry, Philippa and Isabella say ... [*unfinished*][1]

They were given a day to hear their judgment on the morrow of St John
the Baptist at Lincoln. [*25 June 1281*]
  [refs. 300, 345, 360, 361, A48]

130 The same Henry, Philippa and Isabella, by the attorney of Philippa and
Isabella, claim against Geoffrey son of Geoffrey de Dethek and Juliana his
wife a messuage and a virgate in Braydesale which Robert de Dun,
great-grandfather of Philippa and Isabella, gave to Hugh de Dun and the

----

[1] See **255**.

heirs of his body and which after Hugh's death should revert to them
according to the form of the grant because he died without direct heir.
Geoffrey and Juliana have come and say that they cannot answer them in
this because they do not hold the tenements, nor did they on the day of the
sueing out of the writ, namely on 16 April in the king's 9th year [*1281*].
Rather ... [*unfinished*]
  [refs. 71, 302]

[*rot. 7*]   Still Juries and Assizes at Derby   J. de Vaux

131   An assize comes to recognise if Richard de Morley father of Nicholas
de Morley died seised in his demesne as of fee of 2 acres of land in Morley
which Hugh son of Roger de Morley holds, who comes and says he cannot
answer on Nicholas's writ because he does not hold the entire land (and did
not on the day of the sueing out of the writ on 16 March in the present
king's 9th year) [*1281*].
  Hugh says in fact that a certain John le Lu holds half an acre and if the
assize finds that he himself holds the entire land, he replies moreover that
Richard de Morley did not die seised of the tenements because a long time
before his death he had enfeoffed him of them. On this he puts himself on
the country, likewise Nicholas. So let the assize be taken. <*Thursday next
after quindene of Easter*> [*1 May 1281*]
  The jurors say ... [*unfinished*]

132   Henry son of Richard de Normanton claims against William Grym and
Peter Cappe a third of two messuages and 3 bovates of land, half a bovate
and 12 acres excepted, in Normanton near Derby as his right and reasonable
share of the inheritance of Roger son of William who has lately died,
kinsman of Henry, William and Peter whose heirs they are.
  Henry says that Roger was seised of the tenements in entirety as of fee
and right in the peacetime of king Henry, taking profits therefrom. From that
Roger, who died without direct heir, the right descended to Isolda, Letitia
and Emma as sisters and heirs. From Isolda right in her share descended to
her son and heir William who now holds with Peter. From Letitia right in
her share descended to her son and heir William and from him to Peter who
now holds as son and heir along with the first-mentioned William. From
Emma right in her share descended to her son and heir Richard and from
him to this Henry who now claims as son and heir. He says that William and
Peter hold the entire tenements, deforcing him of his reasonable share.

Thereon he brings suit.

William and Peter come, deny his right and readily acknowledge that Roger died seised of the tenements, but not after the term limited in a writ of this kind, namely after the first voyage of king Henry father of the present king to Gascony. Concerning this they put themselves on the country, likewise Henry. So let there be a jury. *<Friday after quindene of Easter>* [2 *May 1281*]

The jurors elected by consent of the parties say that Roger their ancestor did not die after the time limited in such a writ, so it was adjudged that William and Peter are without day and that Henry is to take nothing but is to be in *mercy* for a false claim.

[ref. 869]

133 Richard son of Hugh de Morley and Walter his brother claim against Richard de Grey a messuage, a mill, 10 tofts, 13½ bovates and 45 acres of land and 40 acres of wood in Kirkehalum in which Richard de Grey has no entry except by William de Grey to whom Hugh de Morley demised them and who unjustly disseised Richard son of Hugh and Walter.

Richard comes, denies their right and strongly maintains that Richard son of Hugh and Walter his brother were never seised so that they could be disseised. Concerning this he puts himself on the coumtry, Richard and Walter likewise. So let there be a jury.

<Saturday after quindene of Easter> [*3 May 1281*]

The jurors elected by consent of the parties say that Richard and Walter his brother were never in seisin so that they could be disseised, so it was adjudged that Richard de Grey is without day and Richard and Walter are to take nothing but are to be in *mercy* for a false claim.

[ref. A25]

134 The abbot of Burton on Trent claims against Nicholas de Segrave the manor of Cotes, except 9 virgates of land, 7 acres of meadow and three parts of a messuage in the same manor, as the right of his church by the writ *precipe in capite*, whereof he says that a certain Nicholas, former abbot of Burton, his predecessor, was seised as of fee and right of his church of St Mary and St Modewenna of Burton in the peacetime of king John grandfather of the present king. That such is the right of his church he offers to prove.

Nicholas comes, denies the right of the abbot and his church, saying that king Henry the present king's father gave, granted and by his charter confirmed to a certain Stephen de Segrave, his ancestor whose heir he is, the aforesaid manor, to have and to hold to him and his heirs in fee and inheritance for ever. Thus he says he cannot answer without the king and he proffers a charter of king Henry attesting this in these words:

'Henry, by the grace of God etc. to his etc. greeting. Know that we, by the will and assent of Isolda de Bello Campo, Maud her sister, Ralph de Ardern, Aline his wife and Idonea widow of Henry de Alneto who came before us in our court at Westminster and quitclaimed and surrendered into our hand all right and claim which they had or could have in all the land with appurtenances in Cotes which belonged to Stephen de Bello Campo, brother of Isolda, Maud, Aline and Idonea whose heirs they are, have given, granted and by this our charter confirmed to our beloved and faithful Stephen de Segrave and his heirs for his homage and service, all the aforesaid lands with all their appurtenances and with all lands which may have fallen due to the heirs of Stephen de Bello Campo in the same vill, to have and to hold to the same Stephen and his heirs of us and our heirs in fee and inheritance, freely, quietly and completely with all liberties and free customs pertaining, by service of one brachet hound rendered to us yearly at Easter for all services and demands. Wherefore we desire and firmly ordain that Stephen and his heirs should have etc. These being witness: Richard Dunelm', Jocelin Bath', Walter Karlio', bishops, Hubert de Burgo Earl of Kent, justiciar in England, R. Earl of Cestre and Lincoln, Hugh de Nevill, Ralph de Trublevill, Hugh le Dispenser, Robert de Lexinton, Henry de Braybroc, Nicholas de Osol, Bartholomew Petch, William de London and others. Given by the hand of the venerable father Ralph Cycestr', bishop, our chancellor at Westminster 21 November in our 13th year.' [*1228*]

<*next day*> Because the aforesaid charter witnesses that king Henry gave and granted to Stephen and his heirs the aforesaid manor to hold of the king and his heirs forever, Nicholas cannot answer without the king, so the parties are told that they may go without day.[1] [refs. 314, 331]

---

[1] For the descent of this manor and the interest of Burton Abbey, see *The Burton Cartulary* (William Salt Arch. Soc. v (1), pp. 8–10, 14).

20 Nov. 1228. Gift of Stephen de Segrave and his heirs etc. following quitclaim and surrender by the sisters of Stephen de Bello Campo. [*Cal. Ch. R. 1226–57*, p. 84]

12 Dec. 1228. Grant to Margaret wife of Hubert de Burgo of the service of Stephen de Segrave etc. [ibid., p. 81]

13 Dec. 1228. Gift to Hubert de Burgo earl of Kent, his heirs etc. of the manor of Saham (Cambs.), also the homage and service of Stephen de Segrave and his heirs for the land of Kotes (Derbys.), late of Stephen de Bello Campo, whereof the said Stephen and his ancestors were wont to render a brachet to the king's ancestors to hold with its market, liberties and privileges by service of half a knight's fee. [ibid., p. 81]

[rot. 7d]

135 Memorandum that on Wednesday next after the quindene of Easter the abbot of Derley in the king's court here handed over 15 chirographs and charters to William de Balliol and the three parts of fines made in the court of king Henry. *[30 April 1281]*

136 An assize to recognise if Roger Balon uncle of Geoffrey Balon died seised in his demesne of a messuage and a bovate of land in Magna Irton which messuage and land William son of Matthew holds. He comes and they concorded. William gives *half a mark* for leave to concord by surety of Geoffrey. The agreement is this: William recognised the tenement to be Geoffrey's by right and he surrendered, remised and quitclaimed it to him for himself and his heirs for ever.
[ref. 870]

137 Oliver de Langeford who brought a writ of customs and services against Ralph son of James de Schirle has not prosecuted, so he and his sureties are in *mercy,* Robert son of Henry Reeve and Richard Reeve both of Langeford.
[ref. 870]

138 Walter de Radewar acknowledges that he owes John de Pateshull £4 which he will pay him at the quindene of Michaelmas next *[13 October 1281]*, and if he does not, he grants that the sheriff may levy it of his lands and chattels. *<recognizance>*

139 Ralph de Hanley who brought a writ against Adam son of Roger concerning the handing over of a charter, has not prosecuted, so he and his sureties are in *mercy,* namely William Tripell and Robert de Bromley.
[ref. 870]

140 Agnes widow of William de Chaddesden claims against William son of Richard Kempeknave a messuage in Derby as her right and inheritance in which William has no entry except by Richard to whom William de Chadesden, her former husband, demised it when she could not gainsay him in his lifetime.

William has come and elsewhere vouched to warranty Ralph and John, sons of William de Chaddesden, who now come by summons and say that they have a surviving brother Hugh, who shares in William's inheritance and who ought to be answerable for this warranty with them. Inasmuch as William Kempeknave did not vouch Hugh at the same time, they seek judgment on the voucher.

William says that Hugh was outlawed for a felony and that Ralph and John are tenants of the entire inheritance of their father William. <*to judgment*>

[ref. 272]

141 The jury on which Eda widow of Peter le Jovene, demandant, and Simon le Keu and Emma his wife put themselves before the justices of the Bench, comes to recognise whether or not Peter on the day he married Eda or ever after, was seised of two stalls with appurtenances in Derby so that he could have dowered her.

The jurors say that Peter was not in seisin of those tenements on that day or ever after so that he could have dowered her, so it is adjudged that Simon and Emma are without day and that Eda is to take nothing but is to be in *mercy* for a false claim. She is pardoned the amercement by the justices.

142 Henry son of Roger de Mapelton claims against John Hendeman of Eyton a messuage and a quarter virgate of land in Cold Eyton as his by writ of aiel. John has come and elsewhere vouched to warranty Roger de Mersington who now comes by summons and warrants him. He further vouches Henry son of William de Stansop whom he is to have at *Lincoln* at the quindene of Trinity by aid of the court [*22 June 1281*]. He is to be summoned in the county of Stafford.

[refs. 399, A9]

143 An assize to recognise if the prior of Tutebur' unjustly disseised William de Codyngton of his common of pasture in 20 acres of moor and pasture in Edulveston belonging to his free tenement in Magna Clifton where he used to common all his beasts throughout the whole year, likewise if the prior diseised him of 12 acres of land in Magna Clifton. The prior has not come but a certain John Fucher, his bailiff, has come and answers for him. As to the first assize, he says that William claims unjustly to have been disseised of commons because the vills of Clifton and Edulveston are in different wapentakes and neither communicates with the other.[1] Thus he

---

[1] Clifton, although adjacent to Edlaston in Appletree wapentake, lay within Morleyston wapentake, of which it was a detached portion.

says that William never was in seisin of commons belonging to his free tenement in Magna Clifton. On this he puts himself on the assize. As to the second assize, he says that the land which he has put in their view is in Clifton, not in Edulveston and if it is proved by the assize to be in Edulveston, then he says that William never was in seisin so that he could have been disseised. <process mark>

On the first assize the jurors say that no common of pasture in Edulveston belongs to any tenement in Magna Clifton, on the second that William never was seised of the aforesaid tenement. So it was adjudged that the prior is without day and William is to take nothing but is to be in *mercy* for a false claim.

Afterwards William makes fine by *20s.* for having a jury of 24 to attaint the jury of 12 and it is received by surety of William Cradok and Hugh Destecote

[refs. 147, 148, 389, 870]

144 An assize to recognise if William Gilbert of Melburne unjustly disseised Robert Wayn and Margery his wife of a toft in Meleburne. William has come and says that there ought not to be an assize because the toft is of the ancient demesne of the Crown wherein no such writ runs. Robert and Margery cannot deny this and seek leave to withdraw from their writ and they have it.

145 Hugh son of John de Schirebrok, who brought an assize of mort d'ancestor against Ralph Gylemyn and Beatrice his wife, has not prosecuted so he and his sureties are in *mercy,* Thomas de Thorp and John Sampson both of Bleselee.

146 Eudes de Henovere gives *half a mark* for leave to concord with Robert de Estweit in a plea of covenant and they have a chirograph.[1] He is pardoned at the request of William de Henovere.

147 The prior of Tutebyr' by his attorney appeared on the fourth day against William de Goldington in a plea concerning a jury of 24 to attaint

---

[1] At Derby, within three weeks of Easter 1281. Grant etc. and in consideration of 9 marks of silver by Robert de Estwayt deforciant, to the plaintiff Eudes de Henover and his heirs for ever, of a third part of a messuage and 2 bovates etc. in Ilkesdon and quitclaim by plaintiff to deforciant and his heirs of all right which he had in 2 parts of the premises etc. (*DAJ*, xii. 35).

12 which William arraigned against him in the king's court before the justices in eyre at Derby, concerning common of pasture in Edulveston belonging to his free tenement in Magna Clifton. William has not come and was the plaintiff, so the prior, the 24 and likewise the 12 are without day and William and his sureties are in *mercy*, Hugh de Gurney and Thomas Fucher. Afterwards he is pardoned at the request of Ralph de Hengham.[1]

  [ref. 143]

148 The same prior by his attorney appeared on the fourth day against the same William in a similar plea concerning 12 acres of land in Magna Clifton. William has not come and was the plaintiff, so the prior, the 24 and likewise the 12 are without day and William and his sureties are in *mercy*. Nothing concerning the amercement because he is pardoned at the request of Ralph de Hengham.

  [ref. 143]

[*rot. 8*]   Still Juries and Assizes

149 An assize to recognise if Robert Borard, father of Rose Borard, died seised in his demesne as of fee of 3 acres of land in Raveneston whereof Agnes Borard holds an acre, Robert le Chapeleyn half an acre, William son of Agnes half an acre, William Walkelyn a rood and Robert son of Simon le Charpenter 3 roods. They come and by leave Agnes and William her son surrender the tenements claimed to Rose, so she is to have her seisin.

  William Walkelyn says that he has the tenement by descent and that he is under age which the court can see. So this action is to stay without day until he comes of *age*. Robert son of Simon says likewise, so the action is to stay until he comes of *age*.

  Robert le Chapeleyn vouches to warranty Richard Walkelyn who comes, warrants him and says that there ought not to be an assize because a certain John Borard, Rose's grandfather whose heir she is, enfeoffed him of the tenement, put him in seisin and bound him and his heirs to warranty. By John's charter attesting this, which he proffers, if he were to be impleaded by another, Rose would have been bound to have warranted him. So he seeks judgment if the action may be competent for him.

---

[1] Ralph de Hengham was then chief justice of King's Bench, and seems also to have been a legal adviser to the abbot of Burton.

Rose says that after the death of Robert her father who died in seisin, her grandfather intruded himself into the tenement and alienated it. She seeks judgment as to whether she ought to be excluded from action by John's seisin from whose inheritance she has nothing. *<to judgment>*
A day was given them to hear judgment on the morrow of St John the Baptist [*25 June 1281*].
[refs. 98, 390, A17]

150 William de Morteyn by his attorney appeared on the fourth day against Robert de Pavely in a plea that he should be here on this day to hear a jury on which he put himself before the king's justices of the Bench, that Robert should acquit him of the service which Roger bishop of Coventre and Lichfeld demands from him for his free tenement held of him in Risseleye which Robert who is mesne lord ought to do.

Robert has not come and had a day given him. Afterwards he appeared in court and put himself on the jury. Judgment: Robert is to be distrained by all his lands. The sheriff is to answer for all the issues and is to have him in person at *Lincoln* at the quindene of Trinity [*22 June 1281*]. Because the sheriff of Derby attests that Robert has nothing in his county by which he can be distrained but has sufficient in the county of *Northampton*, the sheriff there is ordered to distrain him, answer for the issues and have him at the aforesaid term. The sheriff of Derby attests this.
[ref. A14]

151 Walter de Rydware claims against Richard abbot of Cumbermere 24 acres of land and 20 acres of meadow in Hertendon as his right, in which Richard has no entry except after a demise made to William the former abbot, Richard's predecessor, by William de Ridware uncle of Walter whose heir he is, for a term of 14 years which has expired and after which they ought to revert to Walter.

Richard the abbot comes by his attorney, denies Walter's right and readily acknowledges that he has entry after the demise made by William de Ridware to his predecessor, but not for a term, rather in fee, because William de Ridware gave, granted and by his charter confirmed to God and to the church of St Mary of Cumbermere and the monks there serving God, the aforesaid tenements with appurtenances to have and to hold to them and their successors in free and perpetual alms and he bound himself and his heirs to warranty. He proffers a charter in William's name attesting this. If he had been impleaded by any other than William over these tenements, Walter would have been bound by this charter to warrant them to him, so he seeks judgment as to whether action is competent for him now.

Walter readily acknowledges the charter but says that William the former abbot never had entry by it, but rather for a term as stated, nor was William de Rydware ever restored to that tenement after the demise, for a term by which he could have given it to William the abbot or improved his estate.

The abbot says that at another time William the abbot, before the abbot of Burgo St Peter and Master Simon de Waulton, justices in eyre at Lichefeld in the county of Stafford [*Jan. 1255*],[1] brought a writ of quittance against William de Ridware at whose petition the charter was shown before the justices and which William de Ridware there recognised and according to the tenor of that charter acknowledged himself to be acquitted. Since the abbot is now in seisin of the same tenement and William had acknowledged the charter previously, he seeks judgment just as Walter now does. <*to judgment*>

They were given a day to hear judgment at *Lincoln* at the octave of St John the Baptist. [*1 July 1281*]

[refs. 339, 378, A32]

152 Nicholas Herygo and Margery his wife claim against Avice widow of Henry de Calvore a bovate and 9 acres of land in Calvore and Basselawe whereof Henry de Calvore, kinsman of Margery whose heir she is, died seised.

Avice comes, denies force and injury and says that as to 6 acres in Basselawe she cannot answer, having only a term of years in them by demise of a certain Robert Baude, and as to the remainder, Henry de Calvore did not die seised of those tenements as of fee, but as of the right and marriage portion of Alice his wife. That this is so, she puts herself on the country.

Nicholas and Margery say that Henry did die seised of the tenements because they were his by right of purchase from a certain Richard de Threpewode to hold to him and his heirs, and that Avice immediately after Henry's death intruded herself into both the 6 acres and the remainder, so that Robert Baude never had anything in the 6 acres which he could have demised to Avice. On this they put themselves on the country, likewise Avice. So let there be a jury. <*Easter 3 weeks*> [*4 May 1281*]

The jurors elected by consent of the parties say that Henry did not die

---

[1] The eyre at Lichfield was held 14–27 Jan. 1255 (D. Crook, *Records of the General Eyre*, pp. 119–20).

seised of the bovate and 3 acres, and as to the 6 acres, Avice has only a term of years in them by demise of Robert Baude. So it was adjudged that Avice is without day and Nicholas and Margery are to take nothing but are to be in *mercy* for a false claim.

[refs. 334, 342, 870]

153 Ralph de Bosco claims against Robert vicar of Doubrigg church a messuage and 2½ acres of land in which Robert has no entry except after a demise which Ralph de Bosco, his grandfather whose heir he is, made to Ellis Shyret, former vicar of Doubrigg, for a term which has expired and after which it ought to revert to Ralph.

Robert comes, denies Ralph's right and readily maintains that Ralph the grandfather did not demise those tenements to Ellis, but rather that Ellis entered them through a certain Richard, former vicar of the church, his predecessor. On this he puts himself on the country, likewise Ralph. So let there be a jury. *<Tuesday after quindene of Easter>* [*29 April 1281*]

Afterwards Ralph comes and withdraws, so he and his sureties are in mercy. Their names are to be enquired. Afterwards he made fine for himself and his sureties by *half a mark*.

[ref. 871]

[*rot. 8d*]   Still Juries and Assizes

154 An assize to recognise if John de Hungry Bentaley unjustly disseised William le Herbergeur of Chaddesden of half an acre of land in various places, his free tenement in Hungry Benteley. John has come and says nothing to stay the assize except that William was never in seisin so that he could have been disseised. On this he puts himself on the assize. So let it be taken.

Afterwards John comes and acknowledges having disseised William of that tenement which he put in view. So William is to recover seisin and John is to be committed to *gaol*, but has remission at the request of Thomas de Bray.

155 Henry de Chaddesden, clerk, who brought an assize of mort d'ancestor against Nicholas le Wyne concerning a tenement in Chaddesden, has not prosecuted, so he and his sureties are in *mercy*, Richard de Maunnecestre of Chaddesden and Ralph son of Peter of the same.

[ref. 871]

156 Nicholas Keys, who brought a writ of covenant against Geoffrey de Skeftinton concerning a tenement in Breydesale, has not prosecuted, so he and his sureties are in *mercy*, John Dawe and John de Eton.
[ref. 871]

157 William Basket, who brought an assize of novel disseisin against John son of Ellis de Langedon and others in a writ concerning a tenement in Yolegrave, has not prosecuted, so he and his sureties are in *mercy*, Robert de Yolgrave and Adam of the same.
[ref. 871]

158 William de Bredon claims against Syward de Hoylaund 8s. rent in Aston of which Ralph de Bredon, William's grandfather whose heir he is, died seised.

Siward has come, denies force and injury, readily maintaining that Ralph did not die seised of that rent. On this he puts himself on the country, William likewise. So let there be a jury.

Afterwards by leave they concorded. The agreement is this: William acknowledged the rent to be Siward's by right and he remised and quitclaimed it for himself and his heirs to Siward and his heirs for ever. And for this etc., Siward acknowledges that he owes William 4 marks of silver which he will pay him on the Sunday after Ascension Day this year [*25 May 1281*], and if he defaults, he grants that the sheriff may cause it to be levied of his lands and chattels. <*recognizance*>

159 Maud daughter of Peter le Persone claims against Agnes de Engelby a messuage, an acre and 3½ roods of land in Chelardeston in which Agnes has no entry except by Nicholas de Wermesworth who unjustly disseised Maud.

Agnes has come and says that she cannot answer her because she has nothing nor does she claim anything in those tenements. She says moreover that they are the hereditary right of Maud, daughter of John Blaumboyley who purchased them for himself and his heirs from Nicholas de Wermesworth. On this she seeks judgment.

Maud says that Agnes holds the tenements as her right and marriage portion of the gift of Nicholas who had unjustly disseised her. On this she puts herself on the country, Agnes likewise. So let there be a jury.
<*Easter 3 weeks*> [*4 May 1281*]
[ref. A42]

160 Emma de Narudale,[1] who brought a writ of covenant against Richard le Eyr, comes and withdraws, so she and her sureties are in *mercy,* William de Langeton and Henry de Hotoft.
[ref. 871]

161 Richard le Taverner of Dereby and Emma his wife claim against Robert Hervy of Dereby a third of a messuage in Derby, and against Simon le Keu of Dereby and Emma his wife a third of a messuage in the same vill as the hereditary right of Emma, of which Robert, Simon and his wife Emma disseised Roger le Jovene, brother of the first-mentioned Emma whose heir she is.

Robert, Simon and Emma his wife have come, deny Emma [le Taverner's] right, maintaining that they did not disseise Roger because he never was in seisin so that he could have been disseised. On this they put themselves on the country, Richard and Emma likewise. So let there be a jury

The jury elected by consent of the parties says that Roger never was in seisin, so it was adjudged that Robert, Simon and Emma are without day and Richard and Emma take nothing but are to be in *mercy* for a false claim.
[ref. 872]

162 Ralph de Bosco who brought an assize of novel disseisin against Thomas de Auddeley and Agnes his wife concerning common of pasture in Doubrigg has not prosecuted, so he and his sureties are in *mercy,* John Gaumbon of Doubrigg and John le Chaumberleyng of the same.
[ref. 872]

163 An assize comes to recognise if Robert de Mounioye and Margaret his wife, Walter le Orpid, Robert Horn, Richard Scol, Roger le Someter, Hugh le Messer and William Wegil unjustly disseised Thomas le Curzun of a rood of land in Twyford.

Robert de Mounioye comes, answers for himself and the others as tenant, saying that he need not answer on this writ because the rood is not in Twyford but in Stayneston.

Thomas cannot deny this, so Robert is without day and Thomas is to be in *mercy* for a false claim.

---

[1] The clerk had written Farndale with N superscribed. The name is clearly Narudale in the Roll of Amercementa. Narrowdale is on the Staffs. side of the Dove, west of Eaton and Alsop.

164   An assize to recognise if William le Chapeleyn of Killeburne, uncle of
Alice wife of Nicholas de Killeburne, died seised in his demesne as of fee,
of 3½ acres of land and 2 parts of a rood of meadow in Horseleye which
Roger son of Henry de Marketon holds. He comes and says that the assize
ought not to be taken because he is William's brother and is in seisin of
those tenements as brother and next heir. He says that he claims to hold
them through the same descent as Alice and seeks judgment on this writ.
<to judgment>
　　Nicholas and Alice say that Roger is William's brother on the father's
side only and that Alice is the daughter of Emma, sister of William by the
same parents, wherefore inasmuch as there is greater kinship through the
blood of both parents than through that of the father alone, she seeks
judgment as to whether Roger's entry or intrusion after the death of William,
his brother on the father's side only, should exclude her from recovering the
seisin of William, brother of her mother Emma by the same parents.
　　Roger readily acknowledges that he is William's brother on the father's
side only and that Emma was William's sister by both parents, but he says
that Emma died before William and that he entered the land immediately
after William's death as brother and heir. He claims by that descent and
seeks judgment as to whether the assize ought to proceed between them.
　　Because Roger acknowledged that William died after the term limited by
the writ and that he is William's brother on the father's side only, while
Alice is the daughter of William's sister Emma by both parents, it is
adjudged that she is the nearer heir of William and that the seisin which
Roger had hitherto is to be reckoned only as intrusion and that Nicholas and
Alice are to recover her seisin. Roger is to be in *mercy*.
　　[ref. 357]

165   Simon Maskary of Foston claims a toft in Foston against Roger
Wildegos as his right by writ of entry. Roger has come and elsewhere
vouched to warranty the abbot of Rowecestre who now comes by summons
and warrants him. He further vouches Thomas Morell who now comes by
summons and asks that he be shown by what he should warrant him. The
abbot proffers a charter in the name of William, father of Thomas whose
heir he is, which attests that he gave, granted and by his charter confirmed
to the abbot and his successors and to his church of Rowecestre the aforesaid
tenement for ever and that he bound himself and his heirs to warranty. Thus
he vouches Thomas.
　　Thomas readily acknowledges the charter and that he is bound to warrant
him, but he says that he has nothing by descent from William his father by

which he could warrant the abbot, but as only he can do so, by leave he surrenders to Simon. So Simon is to have his seisin, Roger is to have land from the abbot and the abbot land to the value from Thomas in a suitable place at his pleasure.
[ref. 355]

[*rot. 9*]   Still Juries and Assizes   Vaux

166 An assize to recognise if Simon Baret, brother of William Baret, died seised in his demesne as of fee of a toft and 26s. 8d. rent in Kirkehalum which Richard de Grey holds, who comes. They are agreed and William gives *a mark* for leave to concord by surety of Gilbert his brother. The agreement is this: Richard acknowledges the tenement to be the right of William and he surrendered, remised and quitclaimed the rent for himself and his heirs for ever. And for this William granted the toft to Richard to hold to himself and his heirs quietly of William and his heirs for ever.
[ref. 872]

167 Margery widow of Hugh de Chaddesden, who brought a writ of entry against Henry le Chapeleyn of Derby, has not prosecuted, so she and her sureties are in *mercy*, Henry le Macy of Derby and Hugh son of Hugh de Chaddesden.
[ref. 872]

168 Nicholas Herigaud and Margery his wife claim against Richard de Morley and Joan his wife a messuage and 30 acres of land in Tadinton and Prestclive as their right by writ of entry.
Richard and Joan come and they are agreed. Nicholas and Margery give *half a mark* for leave to concord by surety of Richard and Joan and they have a chirograph. Nicholas and Margery acknowledge that they owe Richard and Joan 16 marks of which they will pay them 4 marks down, half of the remainder at the Nativity of St John the Baptist next and the other half at the Annunciation [*24 June 1281, 25 Mar. 1282*]. If they do not, they grant that the sheriff may levy it of their lands and chattels. <*recognizance*> Moreover they found this surety, William de Ryther of the county of York, who grants that if Nicholas and Margery do not pay at the aforesaid terms,

then the sheriff of that county may levy it of his lands and chattels.[1]
[refs. 308, 872]

169 Letitia widow of Alexander le Mercer of Esseburn claims against
Richard de Morleye and Joan his wife a messuage, 50 acres of land and an
acre of meadow in Alsop as her right and marriage portion by writ of entry.

Richard and Joan come and concerning one half, vouch Alan de
Waldechef and Lucy his wife to warranty. Concerning the other they vouch
John de la Plaunche and Ellen his wife. They are to have them at *Lincoln* at
the quindene of Trinity [*22 June 1281*]. Alan and Lucy are to be summoned
in this county and John and Ellen in the county of Lincoln.
[refs. 303, 308, 366, A10]

170 An assize to recognise if Eustace de Morteyn father of William de
Morteyn died seised in his demesne as of fee of 100 acres of wood in
Risselle which Robert Saudcheverell holds. He comes and says nothing to
stay the assize. <*next day*>
[refs. 354, A21]

171 Ralph de Hanleye appeared on the fourth day against Richard son of
Amice in a plea concerning a bovate of land in Whitynton: against Roger
son of Beatrice in a plea concerning 4 acres and 3 roods in the same vill:
also against Thomas de Wigele in a plea concerning right in 4s. rent in that
vill.

They have not come and defaulted at another time on the Monday after
the quindene of Easter [*28 April 1281*], so the sheriff was ordered to take the
tenements into the king's hand and to summon them to be here on this day,
namely the Friday after the quindene of Easter [*2 May 1281*]. The sheriff
now attests the day of the confiscation and that he had summoned them. So
it is adjudged that Ralph recover seisin against them by default and that

---

[1] Joan widow of Michael de Hockele was jointly enfeoffed with him of a messuage and
2 bovates in Taddington and Priestcliffe by Nicholas Herigaud and Margery his wife and
continued her seisin until the death of Michael and they pertain to her (*Cal. Inq. p.m.*, ii, no.
318, 1279).

At Derby, within three weeks of Easter 1281. Grant etc. by tenants and heirs of Joan to the
plaintiffs and heirs of Margery for ever etc. (*DAJ*, xii. 36).

Richard, Roger and Thomas are in *mercy*.[1]
  [ref. 873]

172 Joan widow of Nicholas de Wirmondesworth claims against William Nurry a third of a messuage and 6 acres of land in Maiseam as her dower.

William comes and says that she (should not have dower therein because Nicholas) was not in seisin of those tenements on the day he married her or ever afterwards so that he could have dowered her. On this he puts himself on the country, likewise Joan. So let there be a jury.

173 Robert de Estweit, clerk, who brought a writ of replevin concerning a horse against Eudes le Kirkeman of Henovere has not prosecuted. So he and his sureties are in *mercy,* Peter son of Thomas de Yssindon and Henry son of Min of the same.
  [ref. 873]

174 Orm son of Herbert de Burwes and Cristiana his wife who brought a writ of mort d'ancestor against Richard de Prys has not prosecuted. So he and his sureties are in *mercy,* Thomas de Burwys and William of the same.
  [ref. 873]

175 Richard de Makeney, who brought a writ of novel disseisin against Robert Bastard of Braydesal, has not prosecuted, so he and his sureties are in *mercy,* Henry le Rour and Robert Prince both of Etton.

176 Richard de Restweyt claims against William de Fletburgh of Maperley and Cecilia his wife a messuage and 1½ bovates of land in Maperley in which William and Cecilia have no entry except after a demise made by Roger Golde, grandfather of Richard whose heir he is, to Litholf Golde for a term which has expired and which should after that have reverted to Richard.

William and Cecilia come and vouch to warranty Richard Rachel who now comes by summons, warrants them and denies Richard's right and that Roger ever demised those tenements to Litholf. He says rather that a certain

---

[1] The following possibly refers to the premises which Ralph recovered by default of Richard: Grant from Ralph son of Richard de Hanley to Philip de Cesterfeld, son-in-law of Peter de Tappeton, of a bovate of land in Wytinton which the said Ralph acquired before the justices in eyre at Derby in Easter term 9 Edw. I (1281). Witnesses, John de Briminton, Peter de Dunston, Adam de Neubold etc. (I. Jeayes, *Derbyshire Charters*, no. 2557).

Henry father of Richard de Restweyt demised them to Litholf and on this he puts himself on the country, likewise Richard. So let there be a jury.

<Tuesday after Easter 3 weeks> [6 May 1281]

The jurors say that Roger never demised the tenements to Litholf. Therefore it is adjudged that Richard Rachel is without day and that Richard Restweyt is to take nothing but is to be in *mercy* for a false claim.

[ref. 873]

177 Richard son of Hugh de Morley was summoned to answer Eudes de Henovere in a plea that he restore 38s. 11d. which he owes him. <recognizance>

Richard comes and readily acknowledges that he owes the said debt which he will pay at the feast of St John the Baptist next [24 June 1281]. If he does not, he grants that the sheriff may levy it of his lands and chattels.

178 Thomas del Heved who brought a writ concerning detention of beasts against Hugh de Herice has not prosecuted, so he and his sureties are in *mercy*, Payne son of William de Schepel' and Matthew de Chaddesden.[1]

[ref. 873]

[*rot. 9d*]   Still Juries and Assizes   Vaux

179 Richard Meillur and Petronilla his wife claim against Roger de Crophull a bovate of land in Oxcroft, and against John le Palmer and Robert Levikeson each a bovate in the same vill as Petronilla's right by writ of entry.

Roger and the others have come, deny her right and say that she never had anything in those tenements except with a certain Richard her former husband. Richard and Petronilla cannot deny this, so Roger and the others are without day and Richard and Petronilla are to take nothing but are to be in *mercy* for a false claim.

[refs. 338, A5]

---

[1] The plea not prosecuted at Derby seems to have been revived later. At Shrewsbury, Octave of Michaelmas 1282. A day was given Thomas del Heved of Mapperley, querent and Hugh de Heriz, defendant in a plea of detinue of oxen, at the Octave of Hilary at prayer of the parties. (CP 40/47, rot. 2).

180 William le White and Roger his brother, who brought a writ concerning proof of liberty against Robert Dethek, have not prosecuted, so they and their sureties are in *mercy*, Henry Rosel and Nicholas de Kilburn.
[ref. 874]

181 Henry son of Richard de Mapelton, who brought a writ concerning attachment against Master Roger de Rothewell, has not prosecuted, so he and his sureties are in *mercy*, Henry de Wardinton and Walter de Ver.
[ref. 874]

182 Peter son of William Swift, who brought a writ of warranty of charter against Henry Dodde, has not prosecuted, so he and his sureties are in *mercy*, William Pollard and William de Okys both of Derby.
[ref. 874]

183 Ralph de Bosco, who brought a writ of novel disseisin against Robert vicar of Doubrug', has not prosecuted, so he and his sureties are in *mercy*, John Gaumbon and John le Chaumerleyn both of Duberigg.

184 William de Calton, who brought an assize of novel disseisin against Richard son of Richard de Kalton and Richard de Pillesley, has not prosecuted, so he and his sureties are in *mercy*, Ralph del Hull and Ralph his son. [ref. 874]

185 Payne le Fevere of Derby, who brought a writ of novel disseisin against Thomas son of Ellis de Osmundeston, has not prosecuted, so he and his sureties are in *mercy*, Robert de Notingham and Walter Wheelwright, both of Derby.

186 Robert son of William le Clerk of Mourstaldiston, who brought a writ of novel disseisin against John le Blund, Robert Chaumpion and Elizabeth his wife, has not prosecuted, so he and his sureties are in *mercy*, Walter son of Henry de Murdiston and Walter son of Walter de Riboef.
Afterwards Robert is pardoned because it was attested that he is poor.

187 Walter de Stepel and Margery his wife, who brought a writ of novel disseisin against Joan widow of Stephen de Miners, John her son and others, have not prosecuted, so they and their sureties are in *mercy*, Robert Hervy of Wyrk' and Roger son of Nicholas of the same.

188   Richard son of Robert de Thorp, chaplain, who brought a writ of novel disseisin against Roger son of Robert de Thorp and others, has not prosecuted so he and his sureties are in *mercy,* William son of Geoffrey de Bentil' and Robert de Esseburn.

189   The jury on which Eda, widow of Peter le Jovene, and Robert Hervy put themselves before the justices of the Bench comes to recognise if Peter, Eda's former husband, was seised of a shop in Derby on the day he married her or at any time after, so that he could have dowered her therewith, or not, as Robert says.

   The jurors say that Peter was not seised on the day he married her nor ever after so that he could have dowered her. So it is adjudged that Robert is without day and that Eda is to take nothing but is to be in *mercy* for a false claim.

190   Robert son of Philip, who brought a writ of entry against John de Mapilton and Maud his wife, concerning a tenement in Esseburn has not prosecuted, so he and his sureties are in *mercy,* Robert de Bokeston and Robert de Tisssington.
   [ref. 874]

191   William son of Simon de Schirlegh, who brought a writ of escheat against Letitia widow of Alexander le Mercer of Esseburn, has not prosecuted. so he and his sureties are in *mercy,* Ralph Ferbraz and John le Blound.
   [refs. 317, 874]

192   Richard son of Nicholas de Macworth, who brought a writ of entry against Ralph Sparewatre of Esseburn, has not prosecuted, so he and his sureties are in *mercy,* Herbert de Mora and Hugh Bugge, both of Macworth.
   [ref. 875]

193   Robert de Wodecote, who brought a writ of entry against John le Keu concerning 2 acres of land in Morley, has not prosecuted, so he and his sureties are in *mercy,* William son of Nigel de Morley and Ralph Smith of the same.
   [ref. 875]

194   Roger, parson of Snelleston chapel, who brought a writ of *utrum* against Robert de Acovere, has not prosecuted, so he and his sureties are in

mercy, William Hert and John Galyn both of Norbir'.[1]
[refs. 332, 875]

195 From Gervase de Clifton, sheriff, for issues of the lands of Oliver de Langeford, *<40s>*.
[ref. 875]

196 Robert le Blake of Brunnolveston, who brought an assize of mort d'ancestor against Nicholas Othehull, has not prosecuted, so he and his sureties are in *mercy,* Geoffrey de Stanley and Simon de Hopwell.
[ref. 875]

197 Agnes widow of William de Aldewerk claims against Robert, son of William le Wyne, 13s. 4d. rent in Overhaddon and against Robert, brother of the same Robert, 10s. rent in that vill in which Robert and Robert have no entry except by William le Wyne their father, to whom William de Aldewerk, Agnes's former husband, demised the rents and whom she could not gainsay in his lifetime.

Robert and Robert have come and say that they claim nothing in the tenements through William's demise except a term of two years. They readily acknowledge them to be Agnes's right, saving the aforesaid term to them.

Agnes holds herself content, so she is to have her seisin, saving the aforesaid term to Robert and Robert. They are without day.
[ref. 336]

198 Alice widow of Hugh de Sandiacre appeared on the fourth day against John Brunnelay in a plea of dower concerning a third of 3½ acres of land in Sandiacre, and against Agnes, widow of William son of William de Sandiacre, concerning a third of 1½ roods in the same vill, and against Hugh de Laundeford concerning a third of an acre in the same vill.

They have not come and defaulted at another time at the quindene of Easter [*27 April 1281*]. So the sheriff was ordered to take the thirds into the king's hands and to summon them to be here on this day, that is, Easter three weeks.

[*4 May 1281*] The sheriff attests the day of confiscation and the summons.

---

[1] What was to have been disputed was whether land, details not given, was a lay fee to which Robert de Acovere laid claim, or was held in free alms pertaining to Snelston chapel.

So it is adjudged that Alice should recover her seisin against them by default and that John, Agnes and Hugh are in *mercy*.
[ref. 876]

199 An assize to recognise if Robert de Stafford and Henry Chaundoys unjustly disseised William son of Alice de Kirkelangeley of his common of pasture in Reddeburn belonging to his free tenement in Kyrkelangeley, whereof he complains that they disseised him of 100 acres of common of pasture in the assarts on which he used to common all kinds of beasts throughout the year.

Robert and Henry have come and afterwards William withdraws, so he and his sureties are in mercy. He made fine for himself and his sureties by *a mark,* by surety of the aforesaid Robert.

Afterwards it was agreed between them that William remised and quitclaimed for himself and his heirs all right and claim which he had in the commons, saving to himself and his heirs commons in the 100 acres of assarts for all kinds of beasts in the open season. Robert acknowledges that he owes William 5 marks of silver which he will pay at Pentecost next [*5 June 1281*]. If he does not, he grants that the sheriff may cause it to be levied of his lands and chattels. <*recognizance*>
[ref. 876]

[*rot. 10*]   Still Juries and Assizes of the same eyre

200 Henry son of Robert Porteioye of Scropton claims against Adam son of Ralph Lingel of Somersale a moiety of an acre of land in Scropton in which Adam has no entry except after a demise which Henry's father Robert, whose heir he is, made to John son of William Morell for a term now expired and after which it ought to revert to Henry. Adam comes and elsewhere vouched to warranty the abbot of Rowecestre who now comes by summons and warrants him. He further vouches Thomas Morell who now comes by summons and warrants him but says that he has nothing at present whereby he is able to warrant him, therefore he warrants as he can. By licence he surrenders to Henry. So Henry is to have seisin, Adam is to have land from the abbot and the abbot land to the value from Thomas in a suitable place at his pleasure.
[ref. 355]

201 Ralph le Wine in *mercy* for many defaults is amerced at *20s.*

Ralph le Wyne was summoned to answer Richard de Chattesworth in a plea that he render him the customs and right services which he ought for his free tenement held of him in Chattesworth in rents, arrears and other things. He says that Ralph holds and ought to hold of him, (by homage) and service of 20s. yearly, 300 acres of moor and pasture and 40 acres of heath in Chattesworth whereof he himself was in seisin of rent and homage in his demesne as of fee and right in the peacetime of king Henry, until eight years ago Ralph refused and still refuses to render him the aforesaid services. He says he suffers loss to the value of 100s. and thus he brings suit.

Ralph comes, denies Richard's right and that he was ever seised of those services. On this he puts himself on the country, likewise Richard. So let there be a jury. <Tuesday after Easter 3 weeks> [6 May 1281]

Afterwards they are agreed and Richard gives 20s. for licence to concord with Ralph by surety of Ralph. The agreement is this: Ralph acknowledges that he should among other things render the aforesaid services to Richard and his heirs, namely, fealty and 20s. yearly forever. And for the licence etc. Richard remised his damages to Ralph.

[refs. 327, 876]

202 Henry FitzHerbert was summoned to answer Walter de Rideware and Ellen his wife in a plea that he allow them reasonable estovers in his wood at Northbyr' which they ought and are accustomed to have (in 40 acres of wood) for housebote and haybote for their houses in Northbyra and Rosseton, of which Ellen was seised in her demesne in the peacetime of king Henry. For the past nine years Henry has not allowed them to have estovers, whence they say that they suffer loss to the value of 100s. On this they bring suit.

Henry comes, denies their right and that Ellen was ever in seisin of those estovers and on this he puts himself on the country, likewise Walter and Ellen. So let there be a jury.

Afterwards they were agreed and Walter gives half a mark for licence to concord and they have a chirograph.[1]

[ref. 877]

203 Henry le Gaunter and Eustacia his wife claim against John de

---

[1] At Derby, within three weeks of Easter 1281. Grant in consideration of 40s. of silver by Henry FitzHerbert to the plaintiffs that they may have reasonable estovers in his wood in Northbyr' and Roscinton. (DAJ, xii. 34).

Bathekwell a messuage in Derby as her right, whereof John unjustly disseised John Theobaud, Eustacia's brother whose heir she is. John comes, says that he holds the messuage by the law of England of the inheritance of Robert and William, sons of a certain Cecilia his former wife and that he cannot answer without them.

Henry and Eustacia say that John ought not to enter by Robert and William because the messuage was not Cecilia's by right, that John entered as a result of her disseisin and that he had disseised John Theobaud. On this he puts himself on the country, likewise John. So let there be a jury.

The jurors elected by consent of the parties say that the messuage was purchased by a certain Roger father of John Theobaud and that Roger enfeoffed John of it, giving him a certain guardian [*blank*] because John was then under age. He put him in seisin so that John with his guardian was seised thereof for three days, taking profits such as he could, and always afterwards during his father's lifetime he took profits from it until his father's death, after which Cecilia had the messuage in custody with John as the next heir. She held it with John until John de Bathecwell married her. When John son of Theobaud came to inherit and wished to enter his messuage and Cecilia his mother wished to admit him, John de Bathekwell did not allow him. Therefore it is clear that John Bathekwell unjustly disseised John Theobaud as the writ states. So it is adjudged that Henry and Eustacia should recover seisin and that John is to be in *mercy*.

204 Ralph de Moungoye who brought a writ of naifty against Robert Sparwatre comes and withdraws, so he and his sureties are in mercy. Afterwards Ralph comes and makes fine for himself and his sureties by *half a mark* and it is received.
    [ref. 877]

205 Henry de Chaundos who brought a writ of naifty against Robert Smalrod has not prosecuted, so he and his sureties are in *mercy*, namely William son of Robert de Eginton and Roger le Provost of the same.
    [ref. 877]

206 An assize to recognise if Robert de Mapelton, father of Thomas de Mapelton, died seised in his demesne as of fee of 3s. 4d. rent in Underwode of which Matthew de Knyveton deforces Thomas.

Thomas de Mapelton comes and elsewhere vouched to warranty Roger de Merchinton who now comes by summons and warrants him. He further vouches Jordan son of Robert whom he is to have at *Lincoln* on the morrow

of St John the Baptist [*25 June 1281*], by aid of the court. He is to be summoned in Lancashire.
[refs. 260, 305, 399, A28]

207 An assize to recognise if the abbot of Burton on Trent, William de Thurleston, Roger Brayn and William de Tunstall unjustly disseised William son of William de Magna Overe of a messuage and 4 bovates of land in Magna Overe. The abbot comes and answering for himself and the others as tenants says that there ought not to be an assize between them because William at another time, claiming to be a free sokeman of the king and to hold the tenements in free socage, brought a writ before the king complaining that the abbot had demanded customs and other services from William which he was bound to do from the times when the manor of Overe was in the hands of the present king's predecessors. He says that William, neither by the king's book called le Domesday nor by a private charter of the king, could verify that he or his ancestors had been within the ancient demesne of the Crown. By this it was adjudged that the abbot was quit and that William should take nothing but should be in mercy for a false claim.[1]

A day was given them at Lincoln at the octave of St John the Baptist. [*1 July 1281*] [ref. A18]

208 Isolda de Wirkesworth, William son of Richard and Maud his wife claim against Hugh de Staunton and Clemence his wife a bovate of land in Wirkesworth in which Hugh and Clemence have no entry except after Robert de Esseburne unjustly disseised Isolda and Maud.

Hugh and Clemence come and vouch to warranty the abbot of Derley who comes and warrants them. He further vouches Ralph de Bradeburn (who comes, warrants him, defends his right and readily maintains that Robert did not) disseise Isolda and Maud because they were never in seisin. On this he puts himself on the country, likewise Isolda, William and Maud. So let there be a jury. <*Wednesday after Easter 3 weeks*>

The jurors elected by consent of the parties say that Isolda and Maud never were in seisin, so it was adjudged that Roger is without day and Isolda and the others are to take nothing but are to be in mercy for a false claim. Afterwards the amercement was pardoned by the justices because they were poor.

---

[1] In 1066 King Edward had 10 carucates of land in Mickleover. There was land for 15 ploughs. In 1086 Burton abbey had 5½ ploughs in demesne. (*V.C.H. Derbys.*, ii. 334).

209   Thomas son of Adam de Herdewykwall, who brought a writ of aiel against Roger vicar of the church of Tydeswell concerning a tenement in Tydeswell, has not prosecuted. So he and his sureties are in *mercy,* William son of William de Tunstides and Robert de Lullinton.
   [refs. 65, 335, 877]

[*rot. 10d*]   Still Juries and Assizes

210   Thomas de Curzun of Keteleston gives *half a mark* for licence to concord with Adam de Irton and Margery his wife in a plea of warranty of charter by surety of Adam. They have a chirograph. Margery appoints Adam her husband as her attorney for the taking of their part of the chirograph.[1]
   [ref. 877]

211   Robert son of Philip, who brought a writ of mort d'ancestor against Ralph Sparewatre concerning a tenement in Offedecote, has not prosecuted, so he and his sureties are in *mercy,* William de Bukeston and Robert de Tyssington.
   [ref. 878]

212   Henry de Chaddesden, who brought a writ of mort d'ancestor against Nicholas le Wyne concerning a tenement in Chaddesden, has not prosecuted, so he and his sureties are in *mercy,* Richard de Mamefeld in Chaddesden and Ralph son of Peter of the same.
   [ref. 878]

213   Roger son of Ralph de Weston, who brought a writ of trespass against Richard son of Hugh de Morlegh, has not prosecuted, so he and his sureties are in *mercy,* Richard de Weston and Walter atte Grene, both of Alewaxton.
   [ref. 878]

214   Thomas son of Adam de Herdewykwell, who brought a writ of aiel against the dean and chapter of Lychefeld concerning a tenement in

---

[1] At Derby, within three weeks of Easter 1281. Grant etc. and in consideration of 15 marks of silver by Adam de Irton and Margery his wife, defendants, to the plaintiff of a messuage and 2 bovates in Keteleston. To hold of the defendants and heirs of Margery for ever at yearly rent of a rose payable at the feast of St John the Baptist and performing all other services to the chief lord of that fee for the defendants and the heirs of Margery. (*DAJ*, xii. 37).

Lullinton, has not prosecuted, so he and his sureties are in *mercy*, Roger de Lyghtefote of Buckestanes and Richard son of Lucy del Frythe.
[ref. 878]

215 Thomas Abbot and Alice his wife, who brought a writ of dower against Ralph de la Haye concerning a tenement in Pakington next le Heth, has not prosecuted, so he and his sureties are in *mercy*, Simon Talbot of Wynesle and Thomas Abbot of Pakington.
[ref. 878]

216 Robert son of Thomas atte Kyrkeyerd, who brought a writ of cosinage against William Bonger concerning a tenement in Wylesthorp, has not prosecuted, so he and his sureties are in *mercy*, Richard Donger of Eyton and William atte Kirkeyerd of the same.
[ref. 879]

217 Robert son of John de Gildeford, who brought a writ of entry against John de Eyncurt, parson of the church of Halewynefeud, concerning a tenement in Estowe, has not prosecuted, so he and his sureties are in *mercy*, Thomas de Cacehors and William Manderell.
[ref. 879]

218 Thomas son of Swayn de Lytton gives *half a mark* for licence to concord with John son of Adam le Forester and Cecilia his wife concerning a messuage and a bovate of land in Lytton, by surety of John. They have a chirograph.[1]
[ref. 879]

219 Richard son of Ralph Bugge appeared on the fourth day against John son of Nicholas de Sancto Mauro in a plea concerning quarter of the manor of Repindon which he claims as his right. He has not come and defaulted at another time at the quindene of Easter [*27 April 1281*]. after he was summoned. The sheriff was ordered to take the tenement into the king's hands and to summon him. On this it was attested that John is under age,

---

[1] At Derby, within three weeks of Easter 1281. Grant in consideration of 4 marks of silver by the plaintiffs John son of Adam le Forester and Cicely his wife and heirs of Cicely, to the tenant Thomas son of Swayn de Litton of a messuage and a bovate etc. in Lytton. (*DAJ*, xii. 34).

namely four years old. So the justices stayed proceedings until they had discussed it with the king.

A day was given Richard at *Lincoln* at the octave of St John the Baptist [*1 July 1281*].

[ref. A19]

220   William Martin and Isabella his wife give *half a mark* for licence to concord with William de Stocton in a plea of warranty of charter concerning a messuage, 33 acres of land and 4s. rent in Tydeswell, by surety of William de Stocton. They have a chirograph.[1]

[ref. 879]

221   Peter de Rouland claims against William Bernak half of 9 acres of land and a third of 2 messuages and 2 bovates in Middelton as his right by writ of aiel. William has come and vouches Gervase de Bernak whom he is to have at Lincoln at the quindene of Trinity. [*22 June 1281*] He is to be summoned in the county of *Northampton* by aid of the court. *<process mark>*

[refs. 333, 396, A30]

222   William Fox gives *half a mark* for licence to concord with Robert le Raggede and Maud his wife in a plea of warranty of charter by surety of Robert. They have a chirograph. Robert and Maud appoint John Tempest as their attorney for the taking of the chirograph.[2]

[ref. 879]

223   Adam de Tapton claims against Robert Halewas and Alice his wife a

---

[1] At Derby, within three weeks of Easter 1281. Grant etc. and in consideration of a soar hawk by William de Stocton defendant, to the plaintiffs of the premises and rent named in Tydeswell. To hold to the plaintiffs and heirs of their bodies of the defendant during the life of the defendant at yearly rent of 4 marks of silver payable at the feasts of Michaelmas and Easter and performing all other services to the chief lords of that fee for the defendant. After the decease of the defendant, plaintiffs shall be quit of payment of rent and shall hold the tenements of the chief lords for ever. If the plaintiffs die without heirs of their bodies the tenement is to remain to the next heirs of William Martin. (*DAJ*, xii. 39).

[2] At Derby, within three weeks of Easter 1281. Grant etc. and in consideration of 6 marks of silver by Robert le Ragged and Maud, defendants, to the plaintiff William Fox of Offerton and his heirs for ever, of a messuage and 14 acres of land in Nether Offerton. To hold of the defendants and heirs of Maud at yearly rent of one penny at Easter and performing all other services to the chief lords of that fee for the defendants and heirs of Maud. (*DAJ*, xii. 38).

messuage in Magna Tapton in which Robert and Alice have no entry except after William de Tapton unjustly disseised Gilbert de Tapton, Adam's father whose heir he is.

Robert and Alice have come and vouched to warranty Ralph de Hanley who now comes by summons, warrants them and denies Adam's right. He maintains that William de Tapton did not disseise Gilbert after the time [limited by the writ] because Gilbert was not in seisin of that tenement so that he could have been disseised. On this he puts himself on the country, likewise Adam. So let there be a jury. <*Friday after Easter 3 weeks*> [*9 May 1281*]

[refs. 292, 309, A36]

224 Matthew de Knyveton and Elizabeth his wife were summoned to answer the prioress of Grace Dieu in a plea that they warrant her 10s. rent in Dalebyr' which she holds and claims to hold of them whereof she has her charter. Matthew and Elizabeth have come and they concorded by licence and have a chirograph.[1]

225 The abbot of Derley acknowledges an agreement between Robert Sauncheverel and himself at Easter three weeks this year when Robert, by fine made in the king's court, acknowledged the advowson of the church of Bolton to be the right of the abbot and his church of St Mary of Derley as a chapel belonging and subject to the mother church of St Peter of Derby.[2] The abbot and convent granted that in future Robert and his heirs should provide a suitable chaplain to serve the chapel and they will admit the chaplain at his request to minister in that chapel so long as the chaplain lives honestly and shows himself devoted and faithful in the above particulars. And if he is taken in any crime or public offence, by common counsel of the aforesaid parties, he will be removed without any other judgment required. The chaplain shall have and hold there, for his maintenance and for the

---

[1] At Derby, within three weeks of Easter 1281. Grant etc. by Matthew de Knyveton and Elizabeth his wife, defendants, to the plaintiff and her church of Holy Trinity of Grace Dieu of 10s. rent in Dalebury. To hold of the defendants and heirs of Matthew in free, pure and perpetual alms for ever. The plaintiff will receive the defendants and heirs of Matthew into all benefits and prayers which from henceforth shall be made in her church for ever. (*DAJ*, xii. 39).

[2] At Derby, within two weeks of Easter 1281. Acknowledgment in consideration of 10 marks of silver by Robert de Sauccheverell, plaintiff, that the advowson of the church of Bolton with appurtenances is the right of Henry abbot of Derley, tenant and his church of St Mary of Derley as a free chapel pertaining to his church of St Peter of Derby. (*DAJ*, xii. 33).

service of the chapel, 3 bovates and 9 selions of land and meadow in the vill
and territory of Bolton, not paying tithe thereon, and 12s. rent in the same
vill from the lands of William son of Richard of the same, previously
assigned by Ralph's ancestors to the chantry of the chapel, and moreover by
grant of the abbot and convent, all small tithes, mortuary dues and offerings
for the altar belonging to the chapel. For these they will pay to the abbot and
convent 4s. of silver yearly, half at Easter and half at Martinmas, with all
other tithes of sheaves and hay for the whole vill of Bolton, reserved wholly
for the abbot and convent for ever. The abbot, convent and their successors
granted that, on the death or removal of the chaplain, they will admit another
suitable chaplain at the request of Robert and his successors according to the
above written form.

    [refs. 68, 354]

[*rot. 11*]   Still Juries and Assizes of the same Eyre   Vaux

226 Richard de Draycote and Agnes his wife claim against Henry
FitzHerbert of Northbir' a messuage and 2 bovates of land in Northbur' and
Rossenton as Agnes's right in which Henry has no entry except by the
intrusion he made after the death of William de Botteslowe to whom
William FitzHerbert Agnes's grandfather whose heir she is, demised them
for the life of William de Botteslowe.

    Henry comes, denies Agnes's right and says that he need not answer her
because he does not, nor did he hold the tenements on the day of the sueing
out of the writ, namely 22 April in the 9th year of the present king [*1281*].
He also says that a certain Godfrey le Mouner held the tenements on that
day. Thus he seeks judgment.

    Richard and Agnes say that Henry did hold the tenements on that day. On
this they put themselves on the country, likewise Henry. So let there be a
jury.

    The jurors elected by consent of the parties say that Henry did not hold
the tenements on that day because Godfrey held them and still does. So it
was adjudged that Henry is without day and Richard and Agnes are to take
nothing but are to be in *mercy* for a false claim.

    [refs. 351, 880, A40]

227 The same Richard and Agnes claim against the same Henry 2
messuages, a carucate and 11 bovates of land, 6 acres of meadow, 3s. rent,
rent of a pound of pepper and a third of 40 acres of wood and of a mill in

Northbur' and Rossinton as Agnes's right in which Henry has no entry except by the intrusion which he made after the death of Margery, widow of John FitzHerbert of Northbur' who held them in dower of the gift of John her former husband, kinsman of Agnes whose heir she is.

Henry comes and says that he does not hold those tenements, but that a certain William Hert holds a bovate and held it on that day. As for the pepper rent he says that he holds nothing of that nor did he on that day. On this he seeks judgment.

Richard and Agnes say that Henry did hold on that day and on this they put themselves on the country, likewise Henry. So let there be a jury. <Wednesday after Easter 3 weeks> [7 May 1281]

The jurors elected by consent of the parties say that Henry did not hold the tenements entirely on that day because William Hert held a bovate and that Henry holds no pepper rent nor held it on that day. So it is adjudged that Henry is without day and that Richard and Agnes are to take nothing but are to be in *mercy* for a false claim.

[refs. 351, A41]

228 William de Rye and Lucy his wife claim against William de Audedeley a third of 200 acres of wood and a third of the agistment in 1000 acres of pasture in Tissington, also against Nicholas Martel a third of 3 bovates of land in the same vill as Lucy's dower of the gift of Henry de Audele her first husband. <next day>

William comes by his attorney and says that he need not answer because at another time before the justices of the Bench Lucy sued a certain Geoffrey de Skeftinton, who then held the manor of Tissington, over certain tenements, so that by counsel of the king's court she recovered in dower a third of the aforesaid tenements and she then had seisin of the agistment and still has, if she so wishes. As for the third of the wood, she had equivalent value elsewhere and therewith held herself content. As for that other part which she had elsewhere, she made her profit and still does so at her will.

William de Rya and Lucy say that she never had anything of the agistment nor in allowance for the wood. On this they put themselves on the country, likewise William de Audedeleye. So let there be a jury. <Friday after the quindene of Easter> [25 April 1281]

The same William and Lucy claim against Nicholas Martel a third of 26s. rent in the same vill as her dower.

Nicholas comes and elsewhere vouched to warranty William de Audedeley who now comes by summons and warrants him. Concerning both the tenement claimed against him and that which he warrants, they are agreed by licence. The agreement is this: William de Audelay granted to William and Lucy as dower a third of all profits of agistment in the entire waste of his manor of Tissington, in all issues and in all his part of the mill of Legh in allowance for the third of 26s. rent which they claimed against Nicholas Martel, to whom William de Audele granted it. Moreover, William de Audeley granted to William de Rie and Lucy a bovate of land in Tissington which Robert Loller and Richard Smith held of him. And for this William and Lucy remised to William all action for dower which they had in all the wood of the manor both within and without the park, saving to William and Lucy that previously given to her as dower and whereof she was seised on the day of this agreement.

229   Nicholas de Clifton gives *half a mark* for leave to concord with Simon de Clifton and Ellen his wife in a plea of covenant and they have a chirograph.[1]
   [ref. 880]

230   Geoffrey son of Nicholas de Blechel' who brought a writ of cosinage against William de Caverwell and others, has not prosecuted, so he and his sureties are in *mercy,* Robert son of Robert de Stanley and William son of John of the same.
   [refs. 365, 880]

231   Reynold le Vicarre of Derby gives *half a mark* for leave to concord with Avice daughter of Emma le Gaunter in a plea of warranty of charter by surety of Ralph son of Roger de Derby and they have a chirograph.[2]
   [ref. 880]

232   From Walter de Rideware, fine for trespasses, *20s.* by surety of

---

[1] At Derby, within three weeks of Easter 1281. Grant by Nicholas de Clyfton, plaintiff, to Simon de Clyfton and Elena his wife, deforciants, of a messuage and 25 acres of land etc. in Little Clyfton to hold of the plaintiff and his heirs for the lifetime of the deforciants at yearly rent of a rose payable at the feast of St John the Baptist. After the deaths of the deforciants the premises wholly to revert to the plaintiff and his heirs, to hold of the chief lords of that fee for ever. (*DAJ*, xii. 37).

[2] At Derby, within three weeks of Easter 1281. Grant etc. and in consideration of 6 marks of silver by Avice daughter of Ralph le Gaunter to plaintiff and his heirs for ever, of two parts of a messuage in Derby. To hold of the defendant and her heirs at yearly rent of a rose payable at the feast of St John the Baptist, performing all other services to the chief lord of that fee for the defendant and her heirs. (*DAJ*, xii. 39).

William Wyther.
  [ref. 880]

233 Robert de Stafford appeared on the fourth day against Robert le Megre
in a plea that he should be here on this day to warrant him a messuage, a
mill, 45 acres of land and 4 acres of meadow in Duffeld which William
Rocelin claims as his right. He has not come and was summoned. Judgment:
land to the value of Robert le Megre's is to be taken into the king's hand,
and he is to be summoned to be at *Lincoln* at the quindene of Trinity [*22
June*].
  <*process mark*> The same day was given to Robert de Stafford in the
Bench.
  [refs. 299, 367, A2]

234 John de Loyak was summoned to answer William de Henovere in a
plea that he keep the covenant made between them concerning 3s. rent in
Kidesley. John comes and they are agreed by licence and have a chirograph.[1]

235 Isabella widow of Ralph de la Rode, who brought a writ of dower
against Payne de Rodington, has not prosecuted, so she and her sureties are
in *mercy*, Richard de Reythwath and John his brother.
  [ref. 881]

236 The abbot of Derley acknowledges that he owes Robert de Saucheverell 5 marks which he will pay him at the Nativity of St John the Baptist next
to come [*24 June 1281*], and if he does not, he acknowledges that the sheriff
may levy it of his lands and chattels. <*recognizance*>

237 Isabella, daughter of Adam son of Warin de Hokenaston, and Isolda,
Juliana, Hawise and Agnes her sisters, by their attorney, claim against Henry
son of Swayn a moiety of a bovate of land in Hokenaston, also against
Isolda widow of Hugh de Combrigg a messuage in the same vill of which
Hugh de Combrigg, kinsman of Isabella, Isolda, Juliana and Agnes whose

---

[1] At Derby, within three weeks of Easter 1281. Grant on a plea of warranty of charter in
consideration of a sparrowhawk, by the defendant John de Loyak to the plaintiff William de
Henovere and his heirs of 3s. rent in Kydesley. To hold of the defendant and his heirs for ever
at rent of a rose at the feast of St John the Baptist for all services and exactions. (*DAJ*, xii. 34).

heirs they are, died seised in his demesne as of fee.

Henry and Isolda come and defend their right. Henry says that Hugh did not die seised of those tenements because he had enfeoffed him of them a long time before his death and put him in seisin. On this he puts himself on the country. Isabella and her sisters are to be summoned. So let there be a jury.

The jurors elected by consent of the parties say that Hugh, kinsman of Isabella, and the others did not die seised of the moiety claimed against Henry. So it is adjudged that Isabella and her sisters recover their seisin and Henry is to be in mercy. He is pardoned because he is poor.

Isolda, concerning the messuage claimed against her, says that she has nothing in it except at the will of Edmund the king's brother. Isabella and her sisters say that Isolda held the messuage in fee and concerning this they put themselves on the country, likewise Isolda. So let there be a jury.

The jurors elected by consent of the parties say that Isolda has nothing except at the will of the lord Edmund and so it is adjudged that she is without day and that Isabella and the others are to take nothing but are to be in *mercy* for a false claim. They are pardoned because they are poor.

238 Richard son of Henry le Seriant gives *half a mark* for leave to concord with John Morkoc of Esseburn in a plea concerning a messuage and 1½ acres of meadow in Fenni Benetley by surety of John. They have a chirograph.[1]
[ref. 881]

239 A day was given Robert de Bakepuz, demandant, and John de Luvenot, tenant, for hearing judgment in an assize of mort d'ancestor at the octave of St John the Baptist [*1 July 1281*], at request of the parties. <*Lincoln*>
[refs. 310, A37]

[*rot. 11d*]   Still Juries and Assizes   Vaux

240 Edith, widow of Adam son of Warin de Hokenaston, claims against

---

[1] At Derby, within three weeks of Easter 1281. Grant on a plea of warranty of charter and in consideration of 20s. of silver by Richard son of Henry le Sergaunt and Maud his wife, to the plaintiff, of premises named. To hold of the defendants and heirs of Maud for ever at yearly rent of a rose payable at the feast of St John the Baptist and performing all other services to the chief lords of that fee for the defendants and heirs of Maud. (*DAJ*, xii. 36).

Roger Godale of Peverwy a third of half a bovate of land in Hokenaston as her dower. Roger comes and vouches to warranty Henry son of Richard de Matton, who comes by summons and warrants him. He further vouches Isabella, Juliana, Hawise, Isolda and Agnes, daughters and heirs of Adam son of Warin.

Afterwards Edith seeks leave to withdraw from her writ and she has it.

241 Henry de Irton, Philippa his wife and Isabella her sister, by their attorney, claim against John Morel two parts of a messuage and of 2 bovates of land in Daleberie, and against Robert de Barton and Agnes his wife a third of a messuage and of 2 bovates in the same vill of which Robert de Dun, great-grandfather of Philippa and Isabella whose heirs they are, died seised.

John and Robert have come and John says that he holds the tenements claimed by the law of England, by inheritance from a certain Emma his former wife by whom he had a son William without whom he cannot bring this matter to judgment.

Robert and Agnes say that they hold the tenements as dower of Agnes by inheritance of the said William, of the endowment of a certain William de Macworth, Agnes's first husband. They vouch William who comes and warrants them. He likewise binds himself in answering John. Concerning the whole, he further vouches Matthew de Knyveton and Elycia his wife who come and warrant him, maintaining that Robert de Dun did not die seised of those tenements because a long time before his death, he enfeoffed a certain Hawise [*blank*] and she was in seisin during Robert's lifetime. Of her good seisin she enfeoffed Elycia. On this they put themselves on the country, likewise Henry, Philippa and Isabella. So let there be a jury.

The jurors elected by consent of the parties say that Robert de Dun did not die seised of the tenements, so it was adjudged that Matthew and Elycia are without day through their warranty and that Henry, Philippa and Isabella are to take nothing but are to be in *mercy* for a false claim.

[refs. 329, 369]

242 Maud daughter of Nicholas le Surreys appeared on the fourth day against Ralph le Wyne in a plea that he should be here on this day to warrant her two messuages and 11½ acres of land in Wyrkesworth which Margery daughter of William Kynne claims as her right against her.

He has not come and was summoned. Judgment: Ralph's land to the value is to be taken into the king's hand. He is to be summoned to be at Lincoln at the octave of St John the Baptist [*1 July 1281*]. The same day was given

Margery in the Bench. She appoints Walter de Okerton as her attorney.
[refs. 358, 400, A53]

243 William son of Stephen de Stanlegh, Geoffrey Wichman, Richard
Rachel, Geoffrey son of William, William Hawis, William le Waleis and
William son of Avota were summoned to answer Ralph de Crumwelle in a
plea concerning the right whereby they demand common of pasture in his
land in Westhalum for which they do not render the service they ought,
whereas he has no common in their land. He complains that they unjustly
demand common in 160 acres of wood and moor with all their beasts
throughout the year and with pigs between Michaelmas and Martinmas. He
says he suffers damage and loss to the value of £20 and thus brings suit.

  William and the others have come, saying that they rightly claim common
in that 160 acres because they and all their ancestors from time out of mind
were so seised in that wood and moor.

  Ralph says William and the others claim unjustly because a certain Ralph
his ancestor, in the peacetime of king John grandfather of the present king,
was seised in his demesne as of fee and right of those 160 acres of wood
and moor, holding them in his own severalty on such terms that William son
of Stephen and the others or their ancestors could not have had any common
therein. From that Ralph the right descended to this Ralph who now claims
as son and heir. That such is his right he offers to prove.

  William and the others deny Ralph's right and his ancestor Ralph's seisin
in severalty of those 160 acres as of fee and right. They put themselves on
the king's grand assize, asking for recognition as to whether they have
greater right to common in those 160 acres than Ralph has, holding in
severalty, such that they have no common as he claims.

  Henry de Brailesford, William de Caveriswelle, Henry FitzHerbert and
Oliver de Langeford, four knights summoned to elect twelve, come and elect
these: Robert de Mungomery, Geoffrey de Gresele, Robert de Saucheverell,
Simon de Gousil, Hugh de Stredle, Robert de Ockovere, John Fannel,
Nicholas de Verdun, William de Steynisby, Roger de Mersinton, Thomas
Tuschet, Oliver de Langeford, Henry de Braylesford, Henry FitzHerbert,
Alvred de Sulny and Ellis de Stanton.

  A day was given them at the octave of St John the Baptist at Lincoln.
[*1 July 1281*] Geoffrey and the others appoint as their attorney William son
of Stephen and William son of Avota.
[ref. A27]

244 Ralph de Crumwelle appeared on the fourth day against Robert son of

Pawe, Robert le Saer and William de Chedle in a plea concerning the right whereby they demand common of pasture in 160 acres of wood in his land in Westhalum with all their beasts throughout the year and with pigs between Michaelmas and Martinmas.

They have not come and had a day, namely this day, the Friday after Easter three weeks [*9 May 1281*]. Afterwards they appeared in court and claimed a view. Judgment: the commons are to be taken into the king's hand and they are to be summoned to be at *Lincoln* at the octave of St John the Baptist to hear their judgment [*1 July 1281*].

[ref. A39]

245 Geoffrey de Sceftinton, whom John de Sceftinton vouches and who warrants him, by his attorney appeared on the fourth day against William de Audedeley in a plea that he should be here on this day to warrant him 5 tofts, 4 virgates of land, 60 acres of wood and 13s. 4d. rent in Breidesale which Henry de Hirton, Philippa his wife and Isabella her sister claim as Philippa's and Isabella's right against him.

He has not come and was summoned. Judgment: land of William's to the value is to be taken into the king's hand and he is to be summoned to be at *Lincoln* at the octave of St John the Baptist [*1 July 1281*]. The same day was given Henry, Philippa and Isabella by their attorney in the Bench.

<process mark>

[ref. A20]

246 Robert son of Robert Dethek appeared on the fourth day against Robert son of Robert de Stredley and Elizabeth his wife in a plea that they warrant him six messuages, a bovate and a quarter bovate of land in Peverwik which he holds and claims to hold of them and in respect of which he has their charter.

They have not come and were summoned. Judgment: they are to be attached to be at *Lincoln* at the octave of St John the Baptist. [*1 July 1281*] Afterwards Robert and Elizabeth came. They concorded by licence, Robert giving *half a mark* and they have a chirograph.[1]

[ref. 881]

---

[1] At Derby, within a month of Easter 1281. Grant etc. and in consideration of a soar hawk by Robert son of Robert de Stretley and Elizabeth, defendants, to plaintiff and his heirs for ever of named premises in Peverwych. To hold of the defendants and heirs of Elizabeth at yearly rent of a peppercorn at the Lord's Nativity for all other services to the chief lords of that fee for the defendants and heirs of Elizabeth. (*DAJ*, xii. 40).

247 An assize to recognise who in time of peace presented the last parson, who has died, to the church of Baukewelle, which is vacant, which presentation the king claims against the dean and chapter of Lichesfeld. The king, by Gilbert de Thornton who sues for him, says that king Henry, great-grandfather of the present king, presented a certain Levenot his clerk to that church, who on his presentation was admitted and instituted by the bishop. The parson through whose death the church is vacant has lately died.

The dean has not come, but the treasurer and certain other canons of the church of Lichesfeld for the chapter have come, saying that they cannot answer on this writ because, on the day of its sueing out on 18 April this year, they had no dean. They say truly that a certain Master John de Derby has been elected to the deanery but has not yet been confirmed. They ask that the assize is not proceeded with to the prejudice of their church until the election is confirmed.

Afterwards on Thursday next after Easter three weeks [*8 May*], by writ of the king given at Quenington on 5 May this year, the dean came by his attorney. He and the chapter say that on that day the dean had not been confirmed.

A day was given them at the quindene of Trinity at Lincoln. [*22 June 1281*] The sheriff is ordered to have the jury at that time.[1]

[refs. 373, A52]

---

[1] When the estates of the Peverels were escheated in the reign of Henry II, both the manor and church of Bakewell reverted to the Crown and were bestowed by Henry on his son John count of Mortain. Henceforth manor and church were separated, the church (both advowson and property) being granted by John in 1192 to the cathedral church of Lichfield. (*J.C.Cox, Churches of Derbyshire*, ii. 5).

3 Feb. 1200. Charter of king John granting church of Bakewell to the church of St Mary and St Chad of Lichfield and to Geoffrey bishop of Coventry. (Jeayes, *Derbyshire Charters*, no. 171 (Lichfield A5)).

12 Nov. 1282. Quitclaim to bishop, dean and chapter of Coventry and Lichfield of the king's right in the advowson of the church of Bakewell whereof the king impleaded them before the justices last in eyre in co. Derby, the said defendants having come to the king in person during the pleadings and petitioned him to inspect the charters of John and Henry III touching the said advowson and to give them the benefit thereof. (*Cal.Pat.R. 1281–91*, p. 50).

13 June 1283. Acquittance to dean and chapter of Lichfield for payment to the king's clerk William de Perton by the hands of Master John de Craven at Chester on Monday the morrow of St Mark the Evangelist 11 Edward I of 500 marks in part payment of the 1,000 marks fine for his quitclaim of the advowson of the church of Bakewell. (ibid., p. 67).

248 An assize to recognise if Hugh del Hull, father of Edmund del Hull of Aston, died seised of three tofts, a bovate and 17 acres of land in Aston of which Agatha, daughter of Richard del Hyll of Aston, holds two tofts and 17 acres and Emma daughter of the same Richard a toft and a bovate.

They come and say that the assize ought not to be taken because a certain Sarra, grandmother of Edmund whose heir he is, enfeoffed them of those tenements, binding them and their heirs to warranty by their charters, which they proffer attesting this. They say that Edmund is the heir of Sarra, so if they are to be impleaded by any other, Edmund is bound to warrant them.

Afterwards Edmund did not prosecute, so he and his sureties are in *mercy*. The names of the sureties are to be enquired. The amercement is pardoned by the justices because he is under age.

Afterwards Agatha and Emma came and granted Edmund the aforesaid bovate of land to hold to him and his heirs and they surrendered, remised and quitclaimed it to him for them and their heirs forever. <*recognizance*>

249 William de Maysam appeared on the fourth day against Joan de Monte Alto in a plea that she warrant him a third of 3½ bovates of land in Meysam which Joan, widow of Nicholas de Wermundesworth, claims in dower against him.

She has not come and the sheriff was ordered to summon her to be here on this day and did nothing. So as before he is ordered to summon her to be at *Lincoln* at the quindene of Trinity [*22 June 1281*], when he is to be there to hear judgment on himself.

[refs. 316, 376]

250 Philip de Stonnesby and Isabella his wife appeared on the fourth day against Roger bishop of Coventre and Lichesfeld in a plea concerning a messuage and 2 bovates of land in Stanton near Sandiacre which they claim as their right against the bishop and against Julia widow of William Tornepeny.

He has not come and was summoned. Judgment: the tenements are to be taken into the king's hand by default of the bishop and he is to be summoned to be at *Lincoln* at the quindene of St John the Baptist [*8 July 1281*]. The same day was given Julia in the Bench. <*process mark*> Isabella appoints her husband Philip as her attorney.[1]

[ref. A24]

251 William Hayron claims against the prior of Tuttebyr' the manor of Osmundeston near Esseburn except six messuages and 10 bovates of land in that manor which Odenellus de Forde, William's grandfather whose heir he is, gave to Henry de Ryhill and the heirs of his body and which after Henry's death should revert to William according to the terms of the grant because Henry died without such heirs.

The prior comes, defends his right and says that he cannot answer him on this writ since Roger, brother of the chaplain, holds a messuage and 2 bovates, John Golyn a messuage, Ralph de Knyveton rector of the church of Breylesford 26 acres and Henry FitzHerbert 30s. rent, and they held them on the day of the sueing out of William's writ.

William says that the messuages, rent and land, except the 26 acres held by the rector, are part of the six messuages and 10 bovates which are held of a certain John de Aytrop whom he omitted in his writ and were held at the time when Odenellus made the grant to Henry de Ryhill, so they were exempted. As to 14 acres held by the rector, he says that the prior holds them in alms, which he is ready to prove as the court may decide.

The prior says that the messuages and land, the rent and 26 acres excepted, are not and never were part of the 10 bovates, and he asks that it be inquired by the country whether he should lose his seisin or William his action. William, asked if he wishes to concede, says such a trial is not indeed fitting.

Afterwards William says that he is ready to verify that the prior holds the manor in entirety but for the tenements excepted in his writ, both in demesne and service in alms as claimed, and did hold on the day of the sueing out of the writ.

The prior says that William cannot return to this since he accorded with the prior's non-tenure, the messuages, 2 bovates and rent being incorporated in the 10 bovates. On this he had offered proof, the prior likewise. On this they were admitted whence they seek judgment.

---

[1] 11 July 1281. William de Louseby came before the king on Monday the eve of Midsummer and sought to replevy to Roger bishop of Coventry and Lichfield and to Julia, late the wife of William Turnepeny, their land in Staunton near Sandiacre which was taken into the king's hands for their default before the justices in eyre at Derby against Philip de Stonesby and Isabella his wife. This is signified to the justices in eyre in co. Lincoln. See **A24**. (*Cal.Cl.R. 1279–88*, p. 128).

A day was given them on the morrow of St John the Baptist at *Lincoln* [*25 June 1281*]. The prior appoints Peter Savary or Henry Page as his attorney.
[ref. A35]

252 Robert son of Geoffrey de Devek was summoned to answer William le Herberur of Chaddesdenn in a plea that he warrant him 26s. rent in Lokhawe which he holds and claims to hold of him, whereof he has a charter of Geoffrey de Devek, Robert's father whose heir he is. He says that a certain Hubert de Freschenvill brought an assize of novel disseisin against him in this eyre concerning the rent and he asks that Robert warrant him whatever pertains to that assize. He proffers Geoffrey's charter which attests that Geoffrey gave and granted to William and his heirs etc. and bound himself and them to warranty.

Robert comes and readily acknowledges the charter and its contents and that he ought to warrant him and he does so.
[ref. 128]

253 Henry le Burgulun gives *a mark* for leave to concord with Thomas le Curzun and Emma his wife in a plea of warranty of charter by surety of Thomas and they have a chirograph.[1]

254 Richard de Glapwell and Avice his wife appeared on the fourth day against William Ball in a plea concerning a third of a messuage in Cestrefeld which they claim as dower of Avice. He has not come and was summoned. Judgment: the aforesaid third is to be taken into the king's hand and he is to be summoned to be at *Lincoln* at the quindene of Trinity [*22 June 1281*]. <process mark>

---

[1] At Derby, within a month of Easter. Acknowledgment and grant by plaintiff Henry le Burguylun to deforciants, Thomas de Curzun of Keteleston and Emma his wife, of two tofts and 59 acres of land in Chaddesden, to hold of the plaintiff and heirs of his body during the life of Emma at yearly rent of 20s. payable at Michaelmas and Easter. After the decease of Emma, the premises to revert to the plaintiff and heirs of his body to hold of the chief lords of that fee. If Robert should die without heirs of his body, premises to remain to the right heirs of Emma to hold of the chief lord of that fee for ever. (*DAJ*, xii. 40).

255 Henry de Irton, Philippa his wife and Isabella her sister claim against Henry de Curzun and Joan his wife 1½ carucates in Braydesal which Robert de Duyn, great-grandfather of Philippa and Isabella whose heirs they are, gave to Hugh de Dun and the heirs of his body and which after Hugh's death ought to revert to Philippa and Isabella according to the form of the grant because Hugh died without direct heir.[1] They say that Robert was seised thereof and gave the tenements to Hugh and his heirs. On Hugh's death without direct heir, the right reverted to the aforesaid feoffee through the form of the grant. From Robert the right of reversion descended to his son and heir Roger and from Roger to his son and heir Roger, from that Roger to a certain Margery his daughter, and from her to Philippa and Isabella who now claim as daughters and heirs. On this they bring suit.

Henry and Joan come, deny their right and say that whereas Henry, Philippa and Isabella claim through reversion because Hugh died without direct heir, he did indeed have a daughter, namely Joan herself, who succeeded him in those tenements as daughter and heir. Thus they seek judgment.

Henry, Philippa and Isabella say that Hugh did die without direct heir because Joan, being a bastard born of a certain Maud a long time before Hugh married her, cannot be his heir. On this they seek inquiry by the country.

Henry and Joan say that she is legitimately born of lawful wedlock, is Hugh's daughter and succeeded him as heir. This they are ready to prove wherever and whenever they ought.

A day was given them to hear their judgment at the octave of St John the Baptist [*1 July*]. <Lincoln>
[refs. 300, 329, 360, 361, A48]

256 Henry de Brailesford in the county court claimed Richard son of Ralph Wygot as his fugitive villein who fled his land after the coronation of king Henry, so this action was put before the justices here by writ of the king.

Now Henry and Richard have come. Richard acknowledges himself to be Henry's villein so as such, is released to him.
[ref. 375]

---

[1] The descent from Robert de Dun given here differs from that given in **129** by the inclusion of an extra generation.

257 Roger Baudry claims against Ralph de Dalby and Agnes his wife a messuage and 3½ bovates in Weston on Trent as his right by writ of aiel.

Ralph and Agnes come and vouch John de Dalby and Agnes his wife to warranty. They are to have them at *Lincoln* on the morrow of St John the Baptist [*25 June 1281*] and they are to be summoned in the county of *Leycestre*. Roger appoints Simon Pakeman and Hugh de Kibworth as his attorneys.

[ref. A8]

258 Ralph le Breton and Emma his wife appeared on the fourth day against William Brun of Derby in a plea that he render them the custom and right services which he ought for his free tenement held of them in Derby. He was summoned. Judgment: he is to be attached to be at *Lincoln* at the octave of St John the Baptist [*1 July 1281*].[1]

[refs. 382, A60]

259 Richard de Morley and Walter his brother were summoned to answer Robert de Notingham and Simon his brother in a plea that they allow them common of pasture in 3 acres of moor in Derby belonging to their free tenement there and of which Hugh de Morley, father of Richard and Walter, unjustly disseised Walter de Notingham, father of Robert and Simon.

Richard and Walter have come and claim a view. They are to come to Lincoln at the octave of St John the Baptist [*1 July 1281*]. Meanwhile etc. <Lincoln>

[refs. 391, 397, 398, A61]

260 Thomas de Mapelton appoints John de Brokton as his attorney against Matthew de Kneveton and Roger de Mercinton whom Matthew vouches to warranty in a plea of assize of mort d'ancestor.

[refs. 206, A28]

261 The jury between Henry de Holm demandant, and Henry de Wayngrif tenant, concerning 8 bovates in Wayngrif and between Henry de Holm plaintiff, and Henry de Wayngrif warrantor of Philip son of Payne de Codenovere and Maud his wife, concerning 4 bovates in the same vill, is put in respite until the octave of St John the Baptist at Lincoln for default of a jury because none came. The sheriff is to have them in person at that time.

---

[1] Presumably the defendant defaulted. The text omits this.

[*1 July 1281*]

The same Henry claims against Robert de Eswheyt and Emma his wife a bovate in the same vill as his right by writ of cosinage. Robert and Emma come and vouch Nicholas le Parker. They are to have him at the aforesaid term and he is to be summoned in this county.
    [ref. A57]

[*rot. 13*]   Still Juries and Assizes   Vaux

262 Robert le Venur of Wytokeshather gives *half a mark* for leave to concord with William de Adderlegh and Amice his wife in a plea of warranty of charter by surety of William. They have a chirograph.
    [ref. 881]

263 Oliver de Langeford is in *mercy* for many defaults.

He was attached to answer Roger Durdent in a plea that he keep the fine made in the court of king Henry, the present king's father, before the justices in eyre at Derby between the aforesaid Roger, querent, and Nigel de Langeford father of Oliver whose heir he is, deforciant, concerning reasonable estovers which Roger demanded in Nigel's woods in Langeford whereof [they had] a chirograph. In the king's court at Derby before John, abbot of Burgo St Peter, and Roger de Thirkelby and their fellows in eyre there, (at the quindene of Hilary) in the 40th year of king Henry [*recte* 42nd year, *1258*], it was agreed between Oliver's father Nigel and Roger that Nigel granted for himself and his heirs that Roger and his heirs should have and take reasonable estovers everywhere in the woods, moors and alder groves of Nigel and his heirs in Langeford and Bubelden without view of his foresters, for building, fuel and fencing, without let or hindrance of Nigel or his heirs for ever, except in Nigel's park and in a certain place called le Parrock in which his fowling glades were situated. In those places it should not be lawful for Roger or his heirs to fell or take estovers near them by which they might be destroyed, nor should it be lawful for Nigel or his heirs henceforth to exploit the moors, woods and alder groves nor to make waste, sale or destruction in them so that Roger and his heirs might have and take reasonable estovers according to the terms of the fine.[1] Thus he says that he has loss and damage to the value of £100. On this he brings suit and

---

[1] For the fine see *DAJ*, ix. 93.

produces part of the fine which attests this.

Oliver comes, denies force and injury, readily acknowledges the fine and its contents and firmly maintains that the waste, if such there be in the woods and alder groves, was not made by him but by Ralph de Crescy and Roger de Mersinton, his co-parceners, who felled in the woods at their will. Roger Durdent likewise felled around 200 oaks in the woods. Any waste has definitely not been by him but by Ralph, Roger and Roger Durdent.

Roger Durdent says that all the waste in the woods and alder groves was made by Oliver and by no other and on this he puts himself on the country. So let there be a jury. <*Friday next after Easter 3 weeks*> [*9 May 1281*]

Afterwards Roger did not prosecute so he and his sureties, whose names are to be enquired, are in mercy.

[ref. 279]

264 Alice widow of Roger de Deincurt claims against the abbot of Wellebek a third of a messuage, 47 acres of land, 6s. rent and of a water mill, 6 acres of wood and 7 bovates of land in villein tenure in Hallewine-feld as her dower.

The abbot comes by his attorney and elsewhere vouched John de Ayncurt, who now comes by summons, warrants him and says that Alice ought not to have her dower because, touching that, she has all the tenements which were her husband's in Morton and half of his lands in Boythorpe. Therewith she had held herself content.

Alice says that John assigned as dower to her the aforesaid tenements in the vills of Morton and Boythorp, of which she was merely feoffee, and not the other lands which were her husband Roger's, which tenements others held. On this she puts herself on the country.

John repeats that he assigned to her those tenements in Morton and Boythorpe which were her husband's wherever and in whosoever hands they were. On this he puts himself on the country, so let there be a jury. The sheriff is ordered to cause the 12 to come to Lincoln on the morrow of St John the Baptist [*25 June 1281*] by whom the truth can best be known and who have no affinity with the parties for judgment on the aforesaid terms because both parties put themselves on the country.

[refs. 311, 315, A16]

265 Geoffrey de Boyhawe and Richard de Sauney were summoned to answer Ralph de Crumwelle in a plea concerning the right by which they demand to have common of pasture in 160 acres of wood for all kinds of beasts throughout the year and with pigs from Michaelmas to Martinmas in

Ralph's land in West Halum, for which they do not render him the service they ought, whereas he has no common in their land. He complains of loss and damage to the value of £100 and thus brings suit.

Geoffrey and Richard come and (elsewhere) vouched the abbot of Dale who now comes by summons, warrants them and says that he demands common of pasture in Ralph's land in West Halum by right because the abbot is lord of the vill of Stanley. Ralph has common in his land in Stanley by reason of which he warranted the aforesaid commons to Ralph and Richard.

A day was given them at Lincoln at the octave of St John the Baptist [*1 July 1281.*]

[refs. 383, A38]

266 Thomas le Curzun was summoned to answer Ralph de Shirle in a plea that he permit him to grind his demesne corn at Thomas's mill in Shirlegh quit of multure as he ought and is accustomed to do there.

Thomas comes and seeks a view of the mill at which Ralph claims that he should grind. He is to have it. A day was given them at Lincoln on the morrow of St John the Baptist [*25 June 1281*] and meanwhile etc.

Afterwards Thomas freely answered the writ, denied force and injury, strongly maintaining that Ralph had never been accustomed to grind freely but rather on his authority. On this he puts himself on the country, likewise Ralph. So let there be a jury.

The jurors elected by consent of the parties say that Ralph and his ancestors were accustomed to grind there free of multure, so it was adjudged that Ralph henceforth should have multure there for his demesne corn. Thomas is to satisfy him for his damages assessed at 4s. and is to be in *mercy.*

267 John de Morley, chaplain, was summoned to answer William son of Avice de Stanlegh in a plea that he permit him to have common of pasture in Morlegh which belongs to his free tenement in Stanley of which Master Richard de Morlegh, John's brother whose heir he is, unjustly disseised William. John comes and seeks a view. He is to have it. A day was given them at *Lincoln* at the quindene of St John the Baptist [*8 July 1281*]. Meanwhile etc.

[ref. A59]

268 Robert son of Hervey de Wirkesworth claims as his right against William son of Henry de Cromford half a bovate of land in Wirkesworth, also against Hugh de Benteley and Clemence his wife a toft and half an acre of land in the same vill.

By summons William and Hugh come and their warrantors, Henry de Cromford, who warrants William, and the abbot of Darley, who warrants Hugh and Clemence. Henry and the abbot further vouch Roger son of Henry de Esseburn. They are to have him at *Lincoln* on the morrow of St John the Baptist [*25 June 1281*] by aid of the court. He is to be summoned in this county.

[refs. 356, 388, A46]

269   Nicholas de Breideston was summoned to answer Eudes de Henovere in a plea that he warrant him (a third of) a messuage and of 2 bovates of land in Ilkeston which he holds and whereof he has his charter.

Nicholas comes, they are agreed by licence and have a chirograph.[1]

[*rot. 13d*]   Still Juries and Assizes

270   Geoffrey son of Nicholas le Carectarius claims against Agnes widow of Nicholas de Henovere and William his son a toft and 3 acres of land in Milnehagh, against Philip de Milnhagh half a bovate and against the same Philip and Isabella widow of John de Milnehagh half a bovate in the same vill, of which Maud widow of Thomas de Hilton, Geoffrey's grandmother whose heir he is, died seised.

Agnes and the others come and she says that she claims nothing in the tenements except as dower from the inheritance of William her son. Isabella says that she claims nothing in the land claimed against her and Philip, but that he holds it all. Philip acknowledges this and both he and Agnes vouch William. He comes by summons, warrants them and denies Geoffrey's right, readily maintaining that Maud, grandmother of Geoffrey, did not die seised of the tenements. On this he puts himself on the country, likewise Geoffrey. So let there be a jury.

The sheriff is ordered to cause the 12 to come to *Lincoln* at the quindene

---

[1] At Derby, within a month of Easter 1281. Grant etc. and in consideration of a soar hawk by the defendant Nicholas de Breydeston to the plaintiff and his heirs for ever, of a third part of a messuage and two bovates in Ilkesdon. To hold of the defendant and his heirs at yearly rent of a rose at the feast of St John the Baptist and performing all other services to the chief lords of that fee for the defendant and his heirs. Acknowledgment by defendant that remaining two parts of the same messuage and land are the right of the plaintiff. (*DAJ*, xii. 41).

of Michaelmas [*13 October 1281*] by whom the truth can best be known etc. because both parties put themselves on the country.

　　[refs. 321, 349, 362, 364, A45]

271　William son of Adam de Blida appeared on the fourth day against John and Roger, sons of Beatrice de Cestrefeld, and against Margery, John's sister, in a plea concerning 12 acres of land in Magna Tapton and Neubold which he claims as his right against them and against Roger son of Beatrice.

　　They have not come and were summoned. Judgment: the tenements are to be taken into the king's hand. They are to be summoned to be at *Lincoln* at the octave of St John the Baptist [*1 July 1281*]. <*process mark*: Lincoln>

　　The same day was given Roger son of Beatrice in the Bench.

　　[refs. 312, A13]

272　Agnes widow of William de Chaddesden claims against William son of Richard Kempeknave a messuage in Derby as her right, in which he has no entry except by Richard Kempeknave to whom William de Chaddesden, her former husband whom she was not able to gainsay in his lifetime, demised it.

　　William comes and elsewhere vouched Ralph and John, sons of William de Chaddesden who come by summons and warrant him. By licence he returns the messuage to her, so she is to have her seisin and William is to have land to the value from Ralph and John.

　　[ref. 140]

273　Thomas de Caducis appeared on the fourth day against Eleanor the king's mother in a plea that she be here to hear the jury on which she put herself before the justices of the Bench, that she should return custody to him of two parts of the manor of Normanton. She has not come and had a day here by common summons, so the sheriff is ordered to distrain her by all her lands and chattels and have her in person at the octave of St John the Baptist at *Lincoln* [*1 July 1281*].

　　[ref. A22]

274　William abbot of Croxton claims against William le Fraunceys of Tybschelf 15 acres of land, and against John de Heriz 5 acres in Tybeschelf as the right of his church, by writ of entry. William and John have come and claim a view. A day was given them at the quindene of St John the Baptist at *Lincoln* [*8 July 1281*]. Meantime etc. <*process mark*>

　　[refs. 384, A23]

275 The same abbot appeared on the fourth day against William de Herdewyk in a plea that he permit him to have common of pasture in Oulecotes in Steynesby pertaining to his free tenement in le Lund, of which Jocelin de Steynesby, William's father whose heir he is, unjustly disseised Geoffrey the former abbot of Croxton. He has not come and was summoned. Judgment: he is to be attached to be at *Lincoln* at the quindene of St John the Baptist. [*8 July 1281*] <*process mark*>
[refs. 385, A62]

276 The same abbot appeared on the fourth day against Roger Bret in a plea that he should permit him to have common of pasture in Wylmethorp pertaining to his free tenement in Lund and le Heth of which William de Heriz, Roger's grandfather whose heir he is, unjustly disseised Geoffrey the former abbot.

He has not come and was summoned. Judgment: he is to be summoned to be at *Lincoln* at the aforesaid term.
[refs. 385, A62]

277 The same abbot appeared on the fourth day against John de Heriz in a plea that he permit him to have common of pasture in Tybeschelf which he ought to have. He has not come and was summoned. Judgment: he is to be attached to be at *Lincoln* at the aforesaid term.
[refs. 385, A62]

278 A day was given William son of William Ingeram, demandant, and Richard de Grey, tenant, in a plea of land at the octave of St John the Baptist at Lincoln [*1 July 1281*].
[refs. 381, A29]

279 Roger Durdent and Oliver de Langeford came to the king's court here and acknowledged agreement between them in a plea instituted before John de Vallibus and his fellow justices in eyre at Derby concerning reasonable estovers which Roger demanded to have in two of Oliver's woods called le Brandewod and le Parrok. It was finally agreed that Roger remised and wholly quitclaimed for himself and his heirs to Oliver and his heirs or assigns, all estovers in the aforesaid woods. Likewise for himself and his heirs he granted that Oliver and his heirs might exploit however and whenever they wish as seems expedient to them, both on the site of the woods and of Oliver's park in Langeford and in the standing wood, without let or hindrance of Roger or his heirs, saving to them common of pasture for

all kinds of beasts in the woods or in le Brentewode and le Parrok after the hay and corn have been carried. Roger also quitclaimed a mark of annual rent which he received out of Oliver's mill at Bubbedon through a certain final concord made between lord Nigel, Oliver's father, and Roger, saving however, to himself and his heirs, all liberties in all moors and alder groves except in le Brentewode, le Park and le Parrok, as is more fully contained in the aforesaid fine. For this remise and quitclaim Oliver has given and granted to Roger 30 acres by the perch of 18½ feet, in the wood or ground of le Brentewode with free ingress and egress, as is more fully contained in a charter of feoffment which Oliver made to Roger, namely that Roger and his heirs may do whatever they wish in those 30 acres, saving to Oliver and his heirs and his men, both free and villein, common of pasture in that land after the hay and corn has been carried. Moreover Oliver granted that Roger, his heirs or assigns may dig turf and peat in the entire common of Langeford and Bubbedon wherever and as often as they wish. In testimony of which the parties have interchangeably affixed their seals to this chirograph.
    [ref. 263]

280   Henry Macy of Derby has come before the justices bearing 24 charters and writings which belonged to Thomas son of Henry de Derby which were handed to him by a certain Ralph le Parmenter to whom Thomas had entrusted them when he took his journey to Jerusalem. Ralph on his deathbed gave them to Henry to be returned to Thomas or his next heir. A certain Henry son of that Thomas comes and says that he is next heir and Henry Macy acknowledges this. So the charters and writings are handed over to Ralph de Parva Cestria for the use of Henry or his surviving brothers if they return to hold them.

281   Peter Rouland claims against John de Brimington a messuage and a carucate of land in Basselewe of which Peter de Rouland, Peter's grandfather whose heir he is, died seised.
    John comes and they concorded. Peter gives *half a mark* for leave to concord. The agreement is this: John acknowledges the tenements to be Peter's by right and he returns them to him, so he is to have seisin.

282   Robert de Meynwarin and Athelina his wife give *half a mark* for leave to concord with James son of Robert de Meynwarin in a plea of warranty of charter and they have a chirograph.[1]

283 The same Robert and Athelina give *half a mark* for leave to concord with Roger son of Robert de Menwarin in a plea of warranty of charter. They have a chirograph[2] and Robert and Athelina appoint Robert de Boxton as their attorney.

284 Sarra widow of William de Thurleston claims against Natalia daughter of Michael de Breideston a messuage and 2 bovates in Ailwaston as her right, in which Natalia has no entry except by Michael de Breidaston and Elizabeth his wife, to whom Sarra's former husband William, whom she was not able to gainsay in his lifetime, demised them.

Natalia comes and vouches to warranty Michael de Breidaston. She is to have him at *Lincoln* at the quindene of Trinity by aid of the court and he is to be summoned in this county [*22 June 1281*]. The justices grant that Richard de Marnham should sue for Natalia because she is under age. Sarra likewise appoints Richard de Stapilford or John de Bramton as her attorney.
[refs. 123, 301, A31]

285 Sibyl widow of William de Saundeby (by her attorney) claims against Richard de Grey a third of a watermill in Sandiacre as her dower. Richard comes by his attorney and claims a view. A day was given them at *Lincoln* at the quindene of Trinity [*22 June 1281*] and meanwhile etc.
[refs. 343, 380, A44]

286 Robert Fox and Beatrice his wife and William de Breideston and Cecilia his wife claim against Laurence, abbot of Dale, 3 acres of land and half an acre of meadow in Stanton near Sandiacre as their right and inheritance, in which the abbot has no entry except after a demise which William le Waterlodere father of Beatrice and Cecilia whose heirs they are, made outwith the law for a term now expired.

---

[1] At Derby, within a month of Easter 1281. Grant and in consideration of a soar hawk by the defendants Robert de Meynwarin and Athelina his wife to the plaintiff and his heirs for ever of a bovate of land in Netherhurst. To hold of the defendants and the heirs of Athelina at yearly rent of one penny payable at Easter for all services. (*DAJ*, xii. 40).

[2] At Derby, within a month of Easter 1281. Grant and in consideration of a soar hawk by the defendants Robert de Meynwarin and Athelina his wife to the plaintiff and his heirs for ever of a bovate of land in Overhurst. To hold of the defendants and heirs of Athelina at yearly rent of 1d. payable at Easter. (*DAJ*, xii. 41).

The abbot comes and seeks judgment on their writ inasmuch as they claim to hold the land as their right in common, whereas William and Robert can only claim through Beatrice and Cecilia. Robert and the others cannot deny this and seek leave to withdraw. They have it.[1]

[ref. A1]

287 [*rot. 15d*] The abbot of Wellebeck by his attorney appeared on the fourth day against John de Mentham in a plea that he acquit him of the service which William de Stotevyle demands of him for his free tenement which John holds in Dukmanton, which John, who is mesne lord, ought to do. John has not come and was summoned. Judgment: he is to be attached to be at *Lincoln* at the quindene of Trinity [*22 June 1281*]. <*process mark*>

[refs. 10, A15]

288 [*rot. 16d*] John son of Ralph de Knyveton, Henry de Horyngham, Nicholas le Fiz la Persone and Henry de Sancto Mauro appeared on the fourth day against John son of John de Knyveton in a plea that he acquit them of the service which the abbot of Wellebeck demands of them for the free tenement which they hold of John son of John in Knyveton, which John, who is mesne lord, ought to do.

He has not come and has made many defaults. The sheriff, ordered to distrain him by all his lands and to have him here in person on this day, did nothing, nor did he send a writ. So as before he is ordered to distrain and to have John in person at *Lincoln* at the quindene of Trinity [*22 June 1281*]. The sheriff is to be there to hear judgment on himself. <*process mark*>

[ref. A43]

289 [*rot. 18d*] Richard de Trowell appeared on the fourth day against Robert Stredley and Elizabeth his wife in a plea that he be here on this day to warrant him 2 bovates of land in Trowell which Hugh son of Geoffrey claims as his right against him. He has not come and was summoned. Judgment: land of Robert's to the value is to be taken into the king's hand and he is to be summoned to be at *Lincoln* at the quindene of Trinity [*22 June 1281*]. The same day was given Hugh by his attorney in the Bench.

---

[1] At Lincoln, within a month of Easter 1281. Acknowledgment in consideration of a soar hawk by plaintiffs Robert Fox and and Beatrice his wife and William de Breydeston and Cicely his wife, that the premises named are the right of the tenant and his church of St Mary de la Dale. (*DAJ*, xii. 41).

<Derby: process mark>

290 [rot. 18d] Ellis de Staunton appeared on the fourth day against Thomas de Meverell and Agnes his wife, Roger de Mercinton and Eleanor his wife, Ralph de Mungoie and Isolda his wife, Henry de Knyveton and Isabella his wife, John de Grendon and Joan his wife, Richard de Dreycote and Agnes his wife and Thomas de Lokesleye in a plea that they, along with Roger le Boteler and Margery his wife, should acquit him of the service which Edmund the king's brother demands of him for his free tenement which he holds in Esterlek of the aforesaid Thomas, Agnes, Roger and the others. The sheriff, ordered to distrain them and to have them here on this day, did nothing. So as before he is ordered to distrain them and to have them at *Lincoln* at the quindene of Trinity [*22 June 1281*]. The sheriff is to be present to hear judgment on himself. Ellis appoints Henry Buntyng or Richard de Hampton as his attorney. <*process mark*>
  [ref. A50]

291 [rot. 22] Geoffrey de Quapelode acknowledges that he owes Ralph de Crumwell 20s. which he will pay him at the feast of St John the Baptist next [*24 June 1281*]. If he defaults, he grants that the sheriff may levy it of his lands and chattels. <*Derby: Recognizance*>

292 [rot. 30] A day was given Adam de Tapton, plaintiff, and Ralph de Hanley, defendant, by his attorney at the quindene of Trinity at *Lincoln* at request of the parties [*22 June 1281*].
  [refs. 223, A36]

ROLL OF ATTORNEYS AND PLEDGES

[rot. 44]

293 Alice de Staunton attorns William de Bredon against Ralph de Saucheverel in a plea of warranty of charter. [ref. 85]

294 Agnes de Percy attorns Nicholas del Holm or Robert de Raby against Richard le Meillur and Petronilla in a plea of land. [refs. 114, A5]

295 The abbot of Cestre attorns Nicholas de Clifton or Richard de Bentel' against Robert de Blundel; and against William son of Walter de Wilne in a plea of land. [refs. 8, A51]

296 Joan widow of Simon Bard attorns Thomas Nesebit against Thomas de Chatisden and Alice his wife; and against William de Spondon and Maud his wife in a plea of dower. *<per Wm de Saham>*

297 Margery de Deneston attorns Robert Dacovere or William de Deneston against the abbot of Roucestre in a plea of land. [ref. 108]

298 The abbot of Roucestre attorns brother Robert de Lenton or Walter le Sumpter against Robert de Denston and Margery his wife in a plea of land. [ref. 108]

299 William son of John Roscelin attorns Nicholas de Horstede or William de Felethorp against Robert de Stafford in a plea of land. [refs. 233, A2]

300 Joan wife of Henry de Custon attorns Henry her husband or Hugh her son against Henry de Irton and others in a plea of land. [refs. 129, 255, A48]

301 Elizabeth wife of Michael de Braydeston attorns Michael her husband against Sarra widow of William de Thurleston in a plea of land. [refs. 284, A31]

302 Julia wife of Geoffrey Dethek attorns Geoffrey her husband or Robert

Dethek against Henry de Irton and others in a plea of land. [ref. 130]

303 Letitia widow of Alexander le Mercer attorns Robert son of Alexander or Hugh Payn against Sewall le Foun in a plea of land; and against Richard de Morley and Joan his wife in a plea of land. [refs. 87, A7, 169, A10]

304 The abbot of Crokesden attorns brother Thomas de Leycestre or Robert de Gernedon against the prior of Gresley in a plea of land; and against Robert le Taillur of Quenybur' and Agnes in a plea of land; and against Richard de Pres in a plea of customs and services and a plea of covenant; and against William Russel in a plea of land. [refs. 100, 107, 106, A11]

305 Matthew de Knyveton attorns Henry de Knyveton, William de Benteley or William Puncham against Thomas de Mapilton in a plea of assize of mort d'ancestor. [refs. 206, A28]

306 Margery wife of Stephen de Irton attorns Stephen her husband against Robert Hildebrand in a plea of assize of mort d'ancestor. [ref. 90]

307 Thomas de Chaworth attorns Richard de Stapelford or Hugh de Normanton against the lord king in a plea of quo warranto. [ref. 466]

308 Joan wife of Richard de Morley attorns Richard her husband or Walter de Morley or John de Oulegreve against Letitia de Esseburn in a plea of land; and against Nicholas de Herigaud and Margery his wife in a plea of land and a plea of trespass. [refs. 169, A10, 168]

309 Alice wife of Robert de Halleys attorns Robert her husband or William de Pontefract against Adam de Tapton in a plea of land. [refs. 223, A36]

310 Robert de Bakepuz attorns Richard de Stapelford or Nicholas de Clifton against John de Lovetot in a plea of assize of mort d'ancestor. [refs. 239, A37]

311 The abbot of Wellebeck attorns Hugh de Grenley or William Burgoys against Alice de Eyncurt in a plea of dower; and against Walter le Bret in a plea of land. [refs. 264, A16]

312 Roger son of Beate of Cestrefeld and John and Roger his sons attorn Adam son of Roger de Cestrefeld or William de Pontefract against William de Blida in a plea of land. [refs. 271, A13]

313 Sarra wife of Henry son of Robert de Breydeston and Ellen, Sarra's sister attorn Sarra's husband Henry against Sarra widow of William de Thurliston in a plea of dower.

314 Nicholas de Segrave attorns Simon de Diseworth or William de Somervill against Adam Herlewin in a plea of assize of mort d'ancestor; and against the abbot of Burton in a plea of land. [refs. 105, 134]

315 Alice de Eyncurt attorns Hugh de Peton against the abbot of Wellebeck in a plea of dower. [refs. 264, A16]

316 Joan de Wermondisworthe attorns Martin de Wermondisworthe or Richard de Marnham against Adam de Mouhaut and others in a plea of dower. [ref. 249]

317 Letitia widow of Alexander le Mercer attorns Robert son of Alexander or Hugh Payn against William son of Simon de Schirleye in a plea of land. [ref. 191]

318 Richard son of Richard Bogge attorns Richard de Stapelford or John Rossel against Adam Basset in a plea of land. [refs. 64, A12]

319 Henry Broun attorns Ralph de Seleby against John de Lec of Chadisden in a plea of land.

320 Adam Basset attorns Peter Axstel before Walter de Wymborn against Richard de Bingham in a plea of land. [refs. 64, A12]

[*rot. 44d*]

321 Agnes widow of Nicholas de Henover attorns John de Oulegreve against Henry de Balthesweyt and others in a plea of dower; and against Ralph son of Reynold and Philip de Melnehaue in a plea of land.

322 Ellen widow of Serlo de Moungoye attorns Hugh de Akore or Roger le Breton against Richard Hervi of Esseburne in a plea of dower.

323 Aline wife of Robert Sireke attorns Robert her husband against Robert de Crekton in a plea of return of charter; and against Henry de Portejoye in a plea of land. [ref. 58]

324 Amice wife of Robert de Saperton attorns Robert de Saperton against Robert de Crekton in a plea of detinue of charter. [ref. ?89]

325 Ralph son of Roger de Shefdon attorns Richard Huberd against John Martin and Henry Hyne in a plea of assize of mort d'ancestor. [refs. 96, A47]

326 Margery widow of Robert de Ore attorns Richard de Marneham or William de Calton against Robert le Wyne in a plea of customs and services.

327 Richard de Cattesworth attorns Nicholas Martel against Ralph le Wyne in a plea of customs and services. [ref. 201]

328 The abbot of Derley attorns brother Robert de Denston or brother Geoffrey de Stokes or Walter de Hokerton against John de Bentlay in a plea of land. [ref. 99]

329 Henry de Irton, Philippa his wife and Isabella her sister attorn William de Wauburn or Robert de Cauland against Henry de Curzon and Joan his wife and others in a plea of land; against Henry son of Gilbert de Chaddisdene and others in a plea of land; and against John Morel and others in a plea of land. [refs. 255, A48, 71, 241]

330 Joan wife of Henry de Cursun attorns Hugh her son or Geoffrey Dethec against Richard de Dune in a plea of land.

331 The abbot of Burton attorns William de Thurleston or William de Tunstall against Nicholas de Segrave in a plea of land. [ref. 134]

332 Robert de Acovere attorns William de Hekyton against Joan widow of Nicholas de Wermondesworthe in a plea of dower; and against Roger, parson of the church of Nortbury, in a plea of land. [ref. 194]

333 William de Bernak attorns Richard de Stapelford or Geoffrey de Archis against Peter de Roland in a plea of land. [refs. 221, A30]

334 Avice de Calvofre attorns Richard Hubert against Peter de Rouland in a plea of land; and against Hicholas de Heryngeud and Margery his wife in a plea of land. [ref. 152]

335 Roger, vicar of the church of Tyddeswell, attorns Richard Huberd against Thomas son of Adam de Herdewykwell in a plea of land. [refs. 65, 209]

336 Agnes widow of William de Aldewerk attorns Ranulph de Aldewerk or William de Wendesley against Robert le Wyne and Ralph his brother in a plea of land. [ref. 197]

337 Roger Gode of Bawell attorns Richard Huberd against Roger de Esceburn in a plea of assize of mort d'ancestor.

338 John le Paumer of Notingham, Roger Crophull and Robert son of Levik attorn Richard de Stapilford against Richard le Meillor and Petronilla his wife in a plea of land. [refs. 179, A5]

339 Richard, abbot of Cumbermere, attorns brother Walter de la Grave or Nicholas de Mirival against Walter de Ridware in a plea of land. <per Wm de Saham> [refs. 151, A32]

340 Avice de Sutton attorns Jordan de Sutton or William de Bondesale against Nicholas le Gaunter, Hawise his wife and Avice her sister in a plea of mort d'ancestor.

341 William de Stotevill attorns William Loveday or Geoffrey de Wyleby against William Tyrpel of Ekinton in a plea of land.

342 Margery wife of Nicholas Herigaud attorns Nicholas her husband ... [*unfinished*] [ref. 152]

343 Sibyl widow of William de Saundeby attorns William Fraunceys or Ralph de Marneham against Richard de Grey in a plea of dower. [refs. 285, A44]

344 Lecia Attewall attorns Richard de Stapelford against Richard Melier and Petronilla his wife in a plea of land. [ref. 113]

345 Joan wife of Henry de Curcun, whom Stephen de Dunesmor, Geoffrey Dethek, Agnes de Cravene, Robert le Pape and Alice his wife vouch to warranty, attorns Hugh her son against Henry de Irton, Philippa and Isabella in a plea of land. [refs. 129, A48]

346 Ralph de Crombewell attorns William de Daneby against the prior of the Hospital of St John of Jerusalem in England in a plea of waste. It is a plea before the justices at Westminster.

347 Maria widow of Ralph de Stratton attorns Thomas her son against Hugh de Bingham and others in a plea of land.

[*rot. 45*]   Still Attorneys and Pledges

348 Margery wife of Roger de Bradeburn attorns Roger her husband against Ralph le Yape of Assheburne in a plea of land.

349 Geoffrey le Karter of Kyddesley attorns Eudes de Henovere or Richard de Stapelford or William de Codenovere against Agnes widow of Nicholas de Henovere, Philip de Milnehawe and Isabella widow of John de Milne-hawe in a plea of land. [refs. 270, A45]

350 Geoffrey de Gresele attorns John Hervy against Ranulph le Mercer in a plea of trespass; and against John de Norton in a plea of wardship.

351 Agnes wife of Richard de Draycote attorns Richard her husband against Henry FitzHerbert in a plea of land by two writs. [refs. 226, A40, 227, A41]

352 Elizabeth wife of Hugh de Stredleye attorns Robert le Archer or Henry Bullok against Richard de Trowell in a plea of land; and against Richard son of Richard Bugge in a plea of *quod permittat*. [ref. 289]

353 Maria wife of Robert de Ossemundesthorp attorns her husband against Roger son of John de Aldewerk in a plea of customs and services.

354 Robert de Saucheverel attorns Robert de Franceys against William de Morteyn in a plea of mort d'ancestor; and against the abbot of Derley for the taking of his chirograph. [refs. 170, A21, 225]

355 The abbot of Roucestre attorns brother Robert de Lenton or James de Grenehull against Adam Lyngell and Roger Wyldegos in a plea of land. [refs. 200, 165]

356 Clemence wife of Hugh de Bentley attorns Hugh her husband against Robert Hervy of Wyrkysworthe in a plea of land. [refs. 268, A46]

357 Alice wife of Nicholas de Killburne attorns Nicholas her husband against Roger son of Henry de Marketon in a plea of assize of mort d'ancestor. [ref. 164]

358 Maud daughter of Nicholas le Surreys attorns Richard Hubert against Margery daughter of William Kynne in a plea of land. [refs. 242, A53]

359 Richard de Byngham attorns John Rosel or Richard de Stapelford against Robert son of Robert de Roulislee in a plea of land. [ref. 13]

360 Henry de Corcoun of Breydeshal attorns Richard le Corcoun against Henry de Irton, Philippa and Isabella in a plea of land. [refs. 129, 255, A48]

361 Joan wife of the same Henry attorns Hugh her son or Geoffrey de Dethek against Henry de Irton, Philippa and Isabella in a plea of land. [refs. 129, 255, A48]

362 Agnes widow of Nicholas de Henover attorns John de Oulegrave or Philip de Milnehawe against Geoffrey le Charter in a plea of land. [refs. 270, A45]

363 The same Agnes attorns the same John or Philip against Henry le Columb' in a plea of pasture.

364 Philip de Mulehag and Isabella widow of John de Mulehag attorn Hugh de Normanton or Ralph son of Roger de Henovere against Geoffrey le Charter in a plea of land. [refs. 270, A45]

365 William de Kaweryswell and Joan his wife attorn Robert de Kaverswell or William Pare of the same against Geoffrey son of Nicholas de Blechele in a plea of land. [ref. 230]

366 Lucy wife of Alan Walteshef attorns Richard de Moreley or Richard

Rohole against Letitia widow of Alexander le Mercer in a plea of warranty. [refs. 169, A10]

367 Robert de Stafford attorns Robert Cayteweyt or Stephen son of Thomas de Hegkinton against William Roscelin in a plea of land. [refs. 233, A2]

368 Aline wife of Robert Schyret attorns her husband against Henry Portejoye of Schropton in a plea of land. [ref. 58]

369 Elizabeth wife of Matthew de Quyveton attorns William de Bentelegh or Henry de Quyveton against John Morel in a plea of land. [ref. 241]

[*rot. 45d*]   Still Attorneys and Pledges

370 Stephen Burge attorns Mazelina his wife against Ralph Sparewater in a plea of assize of novel disseisin. [ref. 35]

371 The dean of Lincoln attorns William le Porter or John de Manfeld against the lord king in a plea of advowson. [refs. 723, A3]

372 William de Catteclive and Agnes his wife attorn William Grymet or Richard de Cnapton against Richard de Glapwelle and Avice his wife in a plea of warranty of charter.

373 The chapter of Lichfeld attorn William de Colton or John Sampson against the lord king in a plea of darrein presentment. [refs. 247, A52]

374 Thomas Tuchet attorns Henry de Prestone or Richard Coles against Thomas de Curzun in a plea of *quod permittat.*

375 Henry de Breylesford attorns John le Blund or William Tappinger against Richard son of Ralph Wygot in a plea of naifty. [ref. 256]

376 William de Meisham attorns Thomas de Meisham or William de Appelby against Joan widow of Nicholas de Wermundeswurth in a plea of dower. [ref. 249]

377 John Leck attorns Hugh and John his sons against William de Scardeclyf in a plea of land.

378 Walter de Ridewar attorns William de Appelby or Simon Pakeman against the abbot of Combermere for hearing his judgment. [refs. 151, A32]

379 Maud widow of William de Asseburn attorns Roger her son against Richard son of Henry de Middelton in a plea of land. [ref. 91]

380 Richard de Grey attorns Richard de Stapelford against Sibyl de Saundeby in a plea of dower. [refs. 285, A44]

381 The same Richard attorns the same Richard against William son of William Inghram in a plea of land. [refs. 278, A29]

382 Emma wife of Ralph le Bretton attorns Ralph her husband against William Brun in a plea of customs and services. [refs. 258, A60]

383 The abbot of Dale, whom Richard Sauney and Geoffrey Boyhaw vouch and who warrants them, attorns Richard de Stapilford or William Ponger against Ralph de Crumwell in a plea of right. [refs. 265, A38]

384 The abbot of Croxton attorns John le Usser or Richard de Croxton against William le Fraunceys and John le Heriz in a plea of land. [refs. 274, A23]

385 The same abbot appoints the same attorneys against John le Heriz in a plea of *quod permittat*; and against William de Herdwyk and Roger Bret in the same plea. [refs. 277, 275, 276, A62]

386 John Daniell attorns Richard de Bischopton against Stephen de Mersington in a plea of debt.

387 John le Foune attorns Thomas le Foune against Sewall le Foune in a plea of land. [refs. 87, A7]

388 The abbot of Derley, whom Hugh de Benteley and Clemence his wife vouch and who vouches them, attorns Walter de Hokerton or Roger de Waut against Robert Hervi of Wyrkesworth in a plea of land. The same abbot appoints the same attorneys against Roger son of Henry de Esscheburn whom the abbot vouches. [refs. 268, A46]

389 The prior of Tuttebur' attorns Peter Savary or Thomas de Folkeshull against William de Codinton in a plea concerning a grand assize of 24 to attaint 12. [ref. 143]

390 Richard Walkeling attorns William de Bredun or Hugh Prestewald against Rose Borard in a plea of mort d'ancestor. [refs. 149, A17]

391 Simon de Notingham and Robert his brother attorn Richard de Stapelford and John their groom against Richard de Morley in a plea of *quod permittat.* [refs. 259, A61]

392 Goda widow of Herbert de Neubaud attorns Richard de Stapelford and John her groom against Nicholas le Lorimer in a plea of land.

393 Hubert de Frechevill attorns John de Brampton against William de Scaddesdene and others in a writ concerning a plea of novel disseisin. [refs. 128, A34]

394 Robert de Dethek attorns Henry de Dethek against Robert Beck in a plea of land.

395 The same Robert, whom Walter de Cotes vouches against Joan Clarall attorns Henry de Dethek against her in a plea of land.

396 Peter de Roland attorns Richard Hubert against William de Bernak in a plea of land. [refs. 221, A30]

397 Simon de Notingham attorns Robert his brother against Richard de Morley and Walter his brother in a plea of common of pasture. [refs. 259, A61]

398 Robert de Notingham and Simon his brother attorn William de Malton or Thomas his brother against Richard de Morley and Walter his brother in a plea of *quod permittat* concerning pasture. [refs. 259, A61]

399 Roger de Marcinton attorns Hugh de Normanton or Richard de Marnham against Henry de Mapelton in a plea of land; and against Thomas de Mapelton in a plea of mort d'ancestor. [refs. 142, A9, 206, A28]

400 Ralph le Wyne, whom Maud daughter of Nicholas le Surreys vouches, attorns Robert Mirival or Hugh de Calveton against Margery Kynne in a plea of land. [refs. 242, A53]

CROWN PLEAS OF THE COUNTY OF DERBY BEFORE JOHN DE VAUX AND HIS FELLOWS, JUSTICES IN EYRE, AT DERBY ON THE MORROW OF THE CLOSE OF EASTER IN THE NINTH YEAR OF THE REIGN OF KING EDWARD [*21 April 1281*]

401   These were the sheriffs since the last eyre of the justices, Gerard de Hedon, Hugh de Stapelford, Hugh de Babinton, Walter de Stirthele and Gervase de Clyfton who is now sheriff and answers.[1]

402   These were the coroners since the last eyre of the justices, Ralph de Reresby and Henry de Baggepuz who have died, William de Langeford, Henry FitzHerbert, John Grym and Walter de Rybuf who survive and answer.

403   Englishry is presented in this county as in the county of Nottingham by one on the father's side, the other on the mother's side, and this by males only and not by females.[2]

---

[1] Gerard de Hedon, as deputy to his father Simon, was sheriff 1268–9; Hugh de Stapleford [de Babington] served in 1270, then as deputy to Walter de Grey Archbishop of York until 1274; Walter de Strichesley was sheriff 1275–8; Gervase de Clifton was sheriff 1279–86.

[2] Englishry: when the slayer was unknown the coroner at his inquest might cause one or more of the deceased's kinsmen on the side of either parent to appear before him to prove Englishry. If not proved, the hundred had to pay the murder fine, 'murdrum'. This fine was abolished in cases of death by misadventure during Henry III's reign and totally abolished by statute in 1340. The two cases where Englishry was presented must be **410** and **538** as no judgment of murder was given in these homicides by unknown killers.

HIGH PEAK WAPENTAKE COMES BY 12 JURORS

404 The jurors present that Robert son of Geoffrey de Bradewell killed William son of William Hally of Schackton in the vill of Schacton, fled at once and is suspected, so *he is to be exacted and outlawed.* He had no chattels. The first finder has died. No Englishry. Judgment: *murder* on the wapentake. The jurors did not mention the first finder in their presentment, so they are in *mercy.* Robert son of Geoffrey was in the frankpledge of Robert Pole of Schacton which does not have him now, so it is in *mercy.* The vills of Schacton, Bradewell, Hope and Aston did not pursue him, so they are in *mercy.*
    [ref. 758]

405 Roger Smith of Moniasse killed Walter son of Adam de Moniasse with a knife in the vill of Moniasse, fled at once and is suspected, so *he is to be exacted and outlawed.* His chattels *2s. 6d.,* for which G. de Clifton the sheriff is to answer. He was in the frankpledge of William Ely of Moniasse which does not have him now, so it is in *mercy.* The vills of Moniasse, Cheilmerdon, Tadington with Presteclyve and Overaddon valued the chattels falsely before the coroner, so are in *mercy.* The first finder has come and is not suspected, so she is quit. No Englishry presented. Judgment: *murder* on the wapentake.
    [ref. 759]

406 Hugh Weaver of Derleye put himself in Derleye church, admitted having killed Thomas Quenild and *abjured* the realm before the coroner. His chattels *4s.,* for which the sheriff is to answer. He was in the frankpledge of Nicholas de Wakebrigg in Derleye which does not have him now, so is in *mercy.* The jurors concealed part of the chattels, so are in *mercy.* The vills of Derleye, Netherhaddon with Roulesley, Yolgreve and Wynster valued the chattels falsely before the coroner, so they are in *mercy.*
    [ref. 760]

407 Adam, former sergeant of Richard le Ragged, wounded Henry son of Henry de Stanton Leghes in the shin with a sword in the vill of Stanton, so that he died three weeks later. Adam was immediately arrested by Llewellyn, constable of Peak Castle under Roger le Estrange, and imprisoned in that castle, from which he later *escaped.* So to judgment on Roger le Estrange, keeper of the castle for the king. [ref. 761]

408 Walter, son of Petronilla de Basselowe, killed Eustace de Basselowe, fled at once and is suspected, so *he is to be exacted and outlawed.* His chattels *3d.*, for which the sheriff is to answer. He was in the frankpledge of Laurence de Basselowe in Basselowe which does not have him now, so it is in mercy. The vills of Edeneshowre, Beleye, Basselowe and Haddon did not pursue him, so they are in *mercy.*
[ref. 761]

409 William de Middelton put himself in Herthull church, admitted to being a thief (and to having harboured John Bulax and John son of the chaplain of Tadington), and he *abjured* the realm before the coroner. His chattels *12s. 4d.*, for which the sheriff is to answer. The vill of Herthull is in *mercy* for not arresting him. There is to be further inquiry about the chattels in Werkesworth wapentake. He was in the frankpledge of Middelton in Werkesworth wapentake which does not have him now, so it is in mercy. Because the jurors suspect John Bulax and John son of the chaplain of Tadington (of other felonies), *they are to be exacted and outlawed.* Neither their chattels nor frankpledge is known because they were strangers from Staffordshire. Afterwards it was attested that William had chattels in Wyrkesworth worth *11s. 4d.* which Adam de Herthil received and for which the sheriff is to answer. Because he took the chattels without warrant, he is in *mercy.*
[ref. 762]

410 Unknown evil-doers lodged at the house of Emma de Conkesbur', rose by night, killed Alice her daughter and fled at once. It is not known where they went. Because the vill of Conkesbur' did not pursue them, it is in *mercy.*
[ref. 762]

411 John son of William Cook of Nerthaddon freely hanged himself in Nerthhaddon wood. No other is suspected. Judgment: *suicide.* His chattels *5s. 1d.*, for which the sheriff is to answer. The vill of Netherhaddon valued the chattels falsely, so it is in *mercy.*
[ref. 763]

412 Alan le Seriant of Hope killed Richard son of Abusa with a knife and immediately after put himself in Hope church, admitted the deed and *abjured* the realm before the coroner. His chattels *10s.*, for which the sheriff is to answer. He was in the frankpledge of Geoffrey son of Brun de Hope which

does not have him now, so it is in *mercy*. Agnes widow of Richard, the first finder, has not come, nor is she suspected. She was attached by Simon de Hokelowe and Geoffrey son of Brun who do not have her now, so they are in *mercy*. The vills of Asseford, Schacton, Hope and Bradewell valued the chattels falsely before the coroner, so they are in *mercy*.
[ref. 763]

413 Two unknown men were found killed on Haversegg moor, killer unknown. The first finder has died. No Englishry. Judgment: *murder* on the wapentake. The vills of Haversegg, Eyom, Nether Padley, Over Paddelei and Over Offerton did not attend the inquest before the coroner, so they are in *mercy*.
[ref. 764]

414 Llewellyn de Seeg killed Henry del Hext at Horderne, fled at once and is suspected, so *he is to be exacted and outlawed*. He had no chattels nor is his frankpledge known as he was a stranger from Wales. Because this happened by day and the vills of Kombbes, Boudon, Qwithalgh and Litlebyrckes did not pursue him, they are in *mercy*.
[ref. 765]

415 William de Astanesfeld was found killed in Addon wood, killer unknown. No Englishry. Judgment: *murder* on the wapentake. The vills of Asseford and Mores did not attend the inquest, so they are in *mercy*.
[ref. 765]

416 Richard son of Nicholas de Padeleye killed Ralph de Calwovere between the vills of Eyum and Calowre, fled at once and is suspected, so *he is to be exacted and outlawed*. His chattels 4s. 6d., for which the sheriff is to answer. He was in the frankpledge of Nicholas de Padleye in Paddeleye which does not have him now, so it is in mercy. The vills of Magna Longesdon, Parva Longesdon, Over Padleye and Midelton valued the chattels falsely, so are in *mercy*.[1] [ref. 765]

---

[1] The Ragman inquest reporting on the trespasses in office of Henry Clerk of Bakewell gave details of this case. The younger son of Nicholas de Padley had struck Ralph de Calver on the head with an axe. Henry the clerk, along with William Hally the bailiff of Roger Estrange, attached Nicholas and his two sons and let them go in peace for a mark because they hoped Ralph would live. However he died on the 8th day, whereupon Henry and William attached Nicholas and his older son, took 10 marks from them for the use of Roger Estrange,

417 Thomas de Stanleye killed Robert de Norbyr' with an axe in the field of Lodeswrth, fled at once and is suspected, so *he is to be exacted and outlawed*. His chattels *9s. 2d.*, for which the sheriff is to answer. He was in the frankpledge of Peter de Lodewrth which does not have him now, so it is in *mercy*. The vills of Melvere, Lodewrth, Chisseworth and Chaweleswrth valued the chattels falsely, so they are in *mercy*.[1]
    [ref. 766]

418 Richard, sergeant of William de Hamelton, fell from a horse into the Derwent and was drowned.[2] The first finder has come and is not suspected, nor is any other. Judgment: *misadventure*. Price of the horse *10s.*, for which the sheriff is to answer. *<deodand>* The vill of Haversegg valued the deodand falsely, so it is in *mercy*.

419 William Pluckerose fell from a horse into the water called Bradelepte and was drowned. The first finder has died. No one is suspected. Judgment: *misadventure*. Price of the horse *half a mark*, for which the sheriff is to answer. *<deodand>* The 12 jurors concealed part of the chattels in their presentment, so they are in *mercy*.

420 Hugh de Manenecestre killed Richard Miller in the vill of Tiddeswell, fled at once and is suspected, so *he is to be exacted and outlawed*. His chattels *2s. 5d.*, for which the sheriff is to answer. He was in the frankpledge of Roger son of Roger Wolvet of Tideswell which does not have him now, so it is in *mercy*. The vills of Tiddeswell with members, Wyrmonhull, Tatindton and Litton valued the chattels falsely, so are in *mercy*.
    [ref. 767]

421 Lambert de Worth fell from a horse outside the vill of Worth so that he died instantly. The first finder has died. No one is suspected. Judgment: *misadventure*. Price of the horse *half a mark*, for which the sheriff is to answer. *<deodand>* Because Robert de Buckstones, former bailiff, took the

---

and the younger son secretly fled the country. (*Rot. Hun.*, ii. 289a).

[1] The clerk wrote Malvern and Cheddewrth, underlined them for correction, and superscribed Melvere and Chisseworth.

[2] William de Hamelton had a distinguished career both in Chancery and the Church. The presence of his sergeant in High Peak may have been connected with the fact that William was guardian of the lands of Robert, the under-age heir of Robert de Darley, in Nether Haddon with rents at Haddon and Rowsley and at Wysall (Notts.) (*Cal. Inq. p.m.*, ii. 101, 502).

deodand without warrant, he is in *mercy*.
[ref. 768]

422 Ellis le Cupere, miller of Castelton, killed Roger Colt of Castelton, fled at once and is suspected, so *he is to be exacted and outlawed*. His chattels *8d.*, for which the sheriff is to answer. He was in the frankpledge of William Hall of Castelton which does not have him, so it is in *mercy*. The vills of Aston and Thornovere did not attend the inquest, so they are in mercy. The vill of Castelton is in *mercy* because it did not arrest him.
[ref. 768]

423 Robert son of Robert de Langesdon, a boy three years old, was killed by a boar in the vill of Langesdon. No one is suspected. Judgment: *misadventure*. Price of the boar *2s. 6d.*, for which the sheriff is to answer. <*deodand*> The vills of Roulesley, Langesdon, Roland and Tonstedes valued the deodand falsely, so they are in *mercy*.
[ref. 768]

424 Robert son of Richard de Tadington killed Robert Lombard, was immediately arrested and taken to prison at Notingham. Later, by order of the king, he was released on bail to await the coming of the justices here. His bailors, Thomas atte Lidgat, Hugh Woods, Robert Townhead, John Woods, Thomas son of Ralph, all of Presteclyve, Ives de Tadington, John son of Robert son of Gilbert, John son of Robert Brun, Robert le Eyr, William son of Ralph, John Super le Clif and Thomas de la Hese of Tadington, do not have him here, so they are in *mercy*. Because Robert absconded on account of the deed and is suspected, *he is to be exacted and outlawed*. His chattels *17d.*, for which the sheriff is to answer. He was in the frankpledge of the vill of Tatindton which does not have him now, so it is in *mercy*.
[ref. 769]

[*rot. 1d*]   Still High Peak Wapentake   Vaux

425 Thomas le Cupere of Cluneslund put himself in Boudon chapel, admitted to being a thief and *abjured* the realm. His chattels *6s. 2d.*, for which the sheriff is to answer. His frankpledge is not known because he was a stranger. And ... [*unfinished*]
[ref. 770]

426 Athelina, daughter of Robert Schild of Gratton, was crushed by a ruinous house falling on her, causing her death. The first finder has died. No one is suspected. Judgment: *misadventure.* Price of the house *15d.*, for which the sheriff is to answer. *<deodand>* The vill of Gratton valued the deodand falsely, so it is in *mercy.*

427 Ralph son of William de Tydeswelle killed Adam de Litton, the miller at Litton, by day, fled at once and is suspected. So *he is to be exacted and outlawed.* His chattels *19s.* He had freehold land from which *7s. 4d.* year and waste. Issues of the intervening period *4s. 8d.*, for all of which the sheriff is to answer. Later John Daniel, the chief lord of the fee, came and made fine by *10s.* for year and waste of the land.
 [ref. 770]

428 Concerning defaults, they say that William de Stafford in Langedenne-dale, Richard de Knythwich, Adam le Hore of Bucstones, Richard de Clif, Nicholas le Moner, Richard Sibelye, all of Bucstones, Gilbert de Schirbrock, Robert de Alstede (he has a warrant through Ragman), Henry son of Adam de Calfowre, William de Aselford, William de Calton, Thomas son of Gilbert de Langesdon, William Gyn of Chattesworth, Thomas de Kendale, Robert son of Robert de Yolgreve, William son of Henry le Blund, Nicholas Champeneys, Ellis de Foulawe, William de Asseburn in Staunton, Nicholas son of Ralph de Schelmerdon, Geoffrey de Picheford, John son of Roger Blundi and Hugh de Albeney did not come on the first day, so all are in *mercy.*[1]
 [ref. 771]

429 Concerning bailiffs who take money to remove recognitors from juries and assizes, they say that Robert de Bucstones, bailiff of High Peak, took a gift of this kind after the king's statute. So he is in *mercy.*

430 Ralph le Coupere, arrested for the death of William de Wardelowe, has come, denies the death and all, and for good and ill puts himself on the country. The jurors say on oath that William and Ralph, coming drunk out of a certain tavern in the vill of Haselbach, were arguing together with the

---

[1] Of those noted as defaulters on the first day, two had quittance of common summons, namely Robert de Alstede and Geoffrey de Picheford, who was then keeper of Windsor Castle. (*Cal.Cl.R. 1279–88*, p. 117).

result that William struck Ralph on the head with a staff, so that he fell to the ground. William drew his knife, twice struck Ralph on the head as he fell on him and held him to the ground, wishing to kill him. Ralph, in self-defence, drew his knife inflicting a wound in William's left breast from which he died the following day. The jurors, asked if Ralph could have escaped otherwise than by killing William, say that they cannot definitely say that if he had not killed William, William would have killed him. So there is to be *discussion with the king*. Meanwhile Ralph is to be taken into *custody*. He had no chattels.

431 Richard de Sparch in Schaleswrth and Herbert de Lodwrth, arrested for harbouring Richard de Brodbiri outlawed in the county of York, Richard son of Magge de Holm, William Seman of Hope, Roysia la Coiffere, arrested on suspicion of larceny, Thomas Wlvet arrested for the death of Adam le Mouner of Litton and William de Hindesleye, arrested on suspicion of larceny, come and deny all and for good and ill put themselves on the country. The jurors say that none of them is guilty except Roysia, so all except Roysia are *quit*. Roysia <*is to be hanged*> She had no chattels.

432 Concerning those indicted, they say that William de Qwytefeld, Richard his brother, Geoffrey former shepherd of the countess de Ferrars, Thomas son of Robert Cote of Hendesovere, William de Combrigge in Endesovere, Michael de Assope. Richard de Fairfeld, John Mansel of Gratton, Hugh Cut of Baukwell, John Arnald, Nicholas de Normanwod, Robert de Sotil, accused of the death of John son of Sarra, Henry de Walleye in Baukwell and Thomas Scot of Roulesley, absconded on account of many larcenies and they are suspected. So *they are to be exacted and outlawed.* Chattels of the aforesaid William de Cumbrigge *2s.*, for which the sheriff is to answer. William de Qwytefeld and the others had no chattels nor are their frankpledges known.

    [ref. 772]

433 From Thomas de Furnivall concerning a fine for having respite until the quindene of St John the Baptist at Lincoln, *£20*, by surety of Thomas Folegaumbe and William de Ryther.

    [ref. 772]

SCKARWESDALE WAPENTAKE COMES BY 12 JURORS

434 The jurors present that Henry son of Gilbert de Essovere wounded Richard son of Emma de Stretton in the stomach with an arrow in the vill of Essovere so that he died on the fourth day after. Henry fled at once and is suspected, so *he is to be exacted and outlawed.* His chattels *71s. 10d.*, for which the sheriff is to answer. Agnes daughter of Richard, attached because she was present, has not come, nor is she suspected. She was attached by Henry Notekop of Wodethorp and Ralph le Bayllyf of Beckton who do not have her now, so they are in *mercy.* The vills of Essover, Wingerwrth, Brakenthweyt and Stretton valued the chattels falsely, so they are in *mercy.* The 12 jurors concealed part of the chattels in their presentment, so they are in mercy. The aforesaid Henry was in the frankpledge of the vill of Essovere which does not have him, so it is in *mercy.*
  [ref. 773]

435 William le Westreys of Pilesley killed William son of Robert de Morton with an axe in the vill of Pilesley, fled at once and is suspected, so *he is to be exacted and outlawed.* His chattels *6s. 2½d.*, He had freehold land whereof year and waste *7s.* Issues of the intervening period *5s.*, for all of which the sheriff is to answer. William was in the frankpledge of the vill of Pilesley which does not have him now, so it is in *mercy.* Roger son of Goda de Pillesleye, Roger son of Hawise of the same, Thomas son of Robert de Morton, Geoffrey his brother and Alice wife of Thomas le Westreys, attached because they were present, have come and are not suspected, so they are quit. But because they did not arrest William, they are in *mercy.* The jurors did not mention Roger and the others, so are in mercy. The vills of Morton, Steynesby, Tipschelf and Sckirlond valued the chattels falsely, so they are in *mercy.*
  Later it was attested by the coroner's rolls that William le Westreys had put himself in Wynesfeld church, admitted the deed and abjured the realm, (so nothing concerning the outlawry). Because the village of Winesfeld did not arrest him, it is in mercy. Later John le Westereye, chief lord of the fee, came and made fine by *10s.* for year and waste of the land, by surety of Walter de Ribof and Thomas Clerk of Morton.
  [ref. 774]

436 Thomas de Langwath killed Geoffrey de Stoke with a knife in the vill of Langwath, fled at once and is suspected, so *he is to be exacted and* *outlawed.* His chattels *6s.*, for which the sheriff is to answer. He was in the mainpast of Henry de Perpont who does not have him now to stand to right, so he is in *mercy.* The vills of Basset Langwat, Schardeclyve, (Heselond) and Glapwell valued the chattels falsely, so are in *mercy.* No Englishry. Judgment: *murder* on the wapentake.

[ref. 775]

437 Maria daughter of Lilla de Barley freely hanged herself in a pigsty in the vill of Barley. No other is suspected. Judgment: *suicide.* She had no chattels. The first finder has come and is not suspected, so she is quit. The vills of Barley, Holmesfeld, Brampton and Neubaud did not attend the inquest, so they are in *mercy.*

[ref. 776]

438 Lecia daughter of Adam de Kynewaldemers fell into a well in the field of Kinewaldemers and was drowned. No one is suspected. Judgment: *misadventure.* The vills of Kinewaldemers, Barleburg, Becton amd Ekington did not attend the inquest, so they are in *mercy.*

[ref. 777]

439 William de Gippesmere fell from a beam in the vill of Elmton so that he died instantly. The first finder has come and is not suspected, nor is any other. Judgment: *misadventure.* Price of the beam *6d.*, for which the sheriff is to answer. <*deodand*> The vills of Elmeton, Quytewell, Bolesovere, (Wytington) and Oxecroft valued the deodand falsely, so they are in *mercy.*

[ref. 778]

440 Hugh de Somerkote, smith, put himself in Alfriton church, admitted killing Gilbert de Riddinges and *abjured* the realm. He had no chattels. The vills of Alfreton, Wynefeld and Penkeston did not come to the abjuration, so are in *mercy.* Later the jury attested that Hugh was put in exigent at the last eyre [*April–May 1269*] and outlawed in the county court for the aforesaid death at the king's suit because of his contumacy. It was often discussed in the county court after the outlawry had been declared. So *to judgment on the whole county* because it did not arrest him.

[ref. 778]

441 Alexander de Foderingeye and Isabella his wife put themselves in Ekynton church, admitted to being thieves and *abjured* the realm. They had no chattels. Alexander's frankpledge is not known because he was a stranger.

The vills of Holmesfeld and Staveley did not attend the abjuration, so are in *mercy*.

[ref. 779]

442 William son of John de Colley wounded Hugh de Horseley with a knife in the market place of Cestrefeld so that he died at Holmesfeld on the fourth day after. William fled at once and is suspected, so *he is to be exacted and outlawed*. His chattels *11s. 8d.*, for which the sheriff is to answer. The vills of Dranefeld, Dore and Norton did not attend the inquest, so are in *mercy*.

[ref. 779]

443 Geoffrey de Horseleye, harper, fell into a vat full of hot water and was scalded to death. The first finder has come and is not suspected, nor is any other. Judgment: misadventure. Price of the vat *12d.*, for which the sheriff is to answer. <*deodand*> The vill of Walton valued the deodand falsely, so it is in *mercy*.

[ref. 780]

444 From G. the sheriff for the chattels of John Wysman and his fellows, thieves beheaded, *3s.*

[ref. 780]

445 Roger de Gaham killed Roger Nodger with a knife in the vill of Norton, fled at once and is suspected, so *he is to be exacted and outlawed*. His chattels *3s. 3d.*, for which the sheriff is to answer. The vills of Norton and Wittenton valued the chattels falsely, so are in *mercy*. No Englishry. Judgment: *murder* on the wapentake. Later the jurors attested that the same Roger had a certain house in fee, whereof year and waste *half a mark*, for which the abbot of Beauchief is to answer. Because Walter de Ribuf did not value the house nor waste in his inquest, he is in mercy.

[ref. 780]

[*rot. 2*]　　　　　　Still Skarwesdal Wapentake　　　　J. de Vaux

446 Richard, carter of Alice de Ayncurt, fell from a cart in Morton so that he died. The first finder has come and is not suspected, nor is any other. Judgment: *misadventure*. Price of the cart and horse *8s. 8d.*, for which the sheriff is to answer. <*deodand*> The vills of Morton, (Wynefeld, Normanton)

and Steinesby valued the deodand falsely, so they are in *mercy*.
    [ref. 780]

447 Nicholas Cowherd fell to the ground from an oak tree in Wynefeld so that he died instantly. The first finder has died. No one is suspected. Judgment: *misadventure*. Price of the oak *18d.*, for which the sheriff is to answer. *<deodand>* The vills of Alfreton and Suth Normanton valued the deodand falsely so they are in *mercy*.

448 William son of Robert de Birchewode killed Roger Brun of Normanton with an axe in the vill of Penkeston, fled at once and is suspected. So *he is to be exacted and outlawed.* His chattels *18d.*, for which the sheriff is to answer. The vills of Penkiston and Blacwell valued the chattels falsely so they are in *mercy*.
    [ref. 781]

449 Nicholas son of Robert Miller of Brakentwayt struck Richard le King with an axe in the vill of Brakentwayt so that he died instantly. The first finder has died. Nicholas fled at once and is suspected so *he is to be exacted and outlawed.* His chattels *3s.*, for which the sheriff is to answer. The vills of Brakentwayt, Stretton and Wingelworth valued the chattels falsely so they are in *mercy*.

450 Agnes daughter of Roger de Coventre put herself in Staveley church, admitted larceny and *abjured* the realm. Her chattels *4d.*, for which the sheriff is to answer. The vills of Quitenton and Dugmanton did not attend the abjuration so they are in *mercy*.
    [ref. 781]

451 Robert de London put himself in Alferton church, admitted killing WIlliam Hayward of Bothorp and *abjured* the realm. His chattels *12d.*, for which the sheriff is to answer. The vills of ... [*unfinished*]
    [ref. 781]

452 Edusa widow of William le Grubbere was crushed to death by a ruinous kitchen. The first finder has come, is not suspected, nor is any other. Judgment: *misadventure*. Price of the kitchen *2s. 4d.*, for which the sheriff is to answer. *<deodand>* The vills of Wyllyamthorp and Somerkote valued the deodand falsely, so they are in *mercy*.

453 Thomas son of the parson of Normanton and Ranulph Slencke killed Ranulph le Poer in the field of Bentleye, fled at once, put themselves in Blackwell church, admitted the deed and *abjured* the realm. Their chattels *37s. 7d.*, for which the sheriff is to answer. Their frankpledge is unknown because they were strangers.

At another time a certain William Bate and Edusa his wife were arrested for the death and *hanged* before the justices for gaol delivery. They had no chattels. Later it was found from the coroner's rolls that in the county court Joan, widow of Ranulph le Poer, had appealed Syward de Normanton and William Curebyhinde of her husband's death. She has now come and appeals them that wickedly and feloniously they hired and sent the aforesaid Thomas and Ranulph to kill her husband.

Syward and William have come, deny the death and all, and for good and ill put themselves on the country. The jurors say that they are guilty of the death, so <*they are to be hanged*>. Chattels of Syward *75s. 5d.*, and of William *45s. 5d.*, for which the sheriff is to answer. She also appealed of the death in the county court, Walter son of Ralph de Normanton, Robert Glide, Adam son of Geoffrey, Roger son of Ralph, Henry Wisning, Thomas son of Ralph, Simon Glyde, Roger son of Ranulph, Adam Sweng, Geoffrey Sweng and Simon de Birches. It was found from the coroner's rolls that in the county court she had prosecuted up to the fourth court at which they appeared and were freed by Hugh de Babington, then sheriff. Afterwards, by order of the king, they were put on bail until the coming of the justices. They have not come now, so they and their sureties are in mercy. Joan is told that she may prosecute against Walter son of Ralph and the others in the county court if she wishes. Hugh de Babington is to answer for their bail.

Afterwards Simon de Birches comes and Joan who appeals him. Simon denies the death and for good and ill puts himself on the country. The jurors say he is not guilty, so he is *quit*. Joan is to be committed and waived for a false appeal. <*gaol*> Later she is pardoned by the justices.

Afterwards Robert Glide comes and all the others except Walter son of Ralph de Normanton. Adam son of Geoffrey and Thomas son of Ralph now come and deny all and for good and ill put themselves on the country. The jurors say that they are not guilty, so they are quit but their chattels are to be confiscated because they absconded. Their chattels are in full on this roll. <*chattels on dorse of this roll*>

[refs. 455, 468, 782]

454 John Scot lodged at the house of John Wenge in Ekynton, rose by night wishing to do away with John Wenge, who seeing this, raised the hue.

John Scot fled at once. Richard, former groom of Hugh de Cantilupo, hearing the hue, joined in and together they pursued John Scot whom they beheaded as a thief in flight. Afterwards a certain Ralph de Ecleshall of county Yorks., the master of John Scot, came and attached himself to sue against John Wenge and Richard, so that by his suit John Wenge was arrested and imprisoned in the village of Ekynton to be taken to Notingham prison. That vill freely allowed him to go, so it is to answer for the *escape*.

Afterwards the jurors attested that Hugh de Babington, former sheriff of this county, (without warrant) levied for the escape from the vill, so he is in *mercy*. He is to answer for the escape. Because John Wenge is not suspected, *he may return* if he wishes.[1]

    [ref. 782]

455 Walter son of Ralph de Normanton, Adam son of Geoffrey and Thomas son of Ralph absconded on account of the death of the aforesaid Ranulph and are suspected, so they are to be exacted and outlawed. <*process mark*> Their chattels are elsewhere on the dorse of this roll.

    [ref. 453]

456 Robert, former groom of Robert de Rumley, rose by night and killed Robert his master, whose goods and chattels he carried away. He fled at once and is suspected, so *he is to be exacted and outlawed*. Neither his chattels nor his frankpledge is known because he was a stranger. The vill of

---

[1] Beheading of thief in flight. Manifest grand larceny was a capital crime. The sentence was often pronounced in local courts and was frequently executed by the pursuer or sakeber who struck off the thief's head. (Pollock and Maitland, *History of English Law*, ii, 496). Interesting light is shed on this case by three entries on the Close Roll.

9 July 1271. The king to the sheriff of Derby etc. Know that we have given and granted to our beloved squire [*valettus*] William de Staynesby 100s. which is ours for the escape of John Weng from prison at Eckington where he was held for us. And we order you that if you establish this, then you levy the 100s. and cause William to have them. (*Cal.Cl.R. 1268–72*, 360).

27 July 1271. The king etc. When we gave to our beloved squire William de Staynesby 100s. etc., we afterwards learned that 12 marks are payable for each escape etc. and desiring to show more abundant favour to William, we order you that 12 marks be levied for the escape and that William should have them of our gift without delay. (ibid. p. 364)

25 Sept. 1284 To the Treasurer and Barons of the Exchequer. Order to cause Hugh de Babington the late king's sheriff of Notts. and Derbys. to be acquitted of 12 marks that he levied from the township of Eckington for the escape from custody of John Weng as he paid this money to William de Staynesby of the late king's gift, as appears to the king by the late king's writ to him and by William's letters patent testifying receipt, which are in Chancery. (*Cal.Cl.R. 1279–88*, p. 278).

Rumley did not pursue him, so it is in *mercy*.

457 From G. the sheriff for the chattels of Geoffrey le Heis, a thief beheaded, *14d.*
[ref. 782]

458 In the county court Roger le Combere of Hanley appealed William de Langeford of making Cecilia de la Forde appeal him of the death of her father Ralph. Roger now comes to prosecute his appeal and William has not come. It is found from the coroner's rolls that Roger had proceeded against William at two county courts, so that by his suit William was attached to come before the justices here by Richard le Dun of Breydesale and John Fowayn jun., who do not have him now. So they are in *mercy*. Because the county court accepted that suit might be made against William in this appeal as for a felony, where no felony for which a man could be put to law surrendering life or members could be adjudged, so *to judgment on the whole county* concerning the coroner.
[ref. 783]

459 In the county court William de Langeford appealed William de Bingham of robbery and breach of the king's peace. William de Langeford has not come nor does he prosecute his appeal, so *he is to be arrested*. His sureties for prosecution, Roger brother of Robert Stowenn of Stretton and John his brother, are in *mercy*. William de Bingham has not come. He was attached by William the brother and Richard the son of Alkerus de Essovere who do not have him now, so they are in *mercy*. The jurors say that they have not come to an agreement and that William de Bingham is not guilty, so he is *quit*.
[ref. 783]

460 In the county court the same William de Langeford (and Robert son of Alexander de la Lee who has died) appealed Walter de Ribof, Richard de Ribof, Walter son of the said Walter, William de Huffeton and Hugh son of Henry de Stratton, of wounding, battery and breach of the king's peace. William has not come now, so *he is to be arrested*. His sureties for prosecution, William de Langeford del Hales and William, reeve of Thomas de Eddenesovere in Tyschington, are in *mercy*.

Walter, Richard, Walter and Hugh have now come and the jurors say that they have not come to an agreement, so they are *quit* as to William's appeal. But so that the king's peace may be maintained, the truth is to be inquired

of the country. The jurors say that none of them is guilty, so all are *quit*.
[ref. 783]

461 In the county court Richard de Sancto Georgio, living in Barleburg, appealed Walter le Chamberlain of Thorp of wounding, battery and breach of the king's peace. Richard has not come and does not prosecute his appeal, so *he is to be arrested*. His sureties, William Hening and Robert Huan, both of Barleye, are in *mercy*. Walter has not come and was not attached because Richard had proceeded against him at only two county courts. The jurors say that Walter is guilty, so he is to be arrested. They also say that they have not come to an agreement.

462 In the county court Simon de Byrches appealed Robert Carpenter of Alfreton of burning his houses and of breach of the king's peace. Simon has not come and does not prosecute his appeal, so *he is to be arrested*. His sureties, Roger le Neucomen of Pinkeston and John le Seingnur of Normanton, are in *mercy*. Robert Carpenter has not come nor was he attached because Simon had proceeded against him at only one county court. The jurors say they have not come to an agreement and that Robert is not guilty of arson, so he is *quit*
[ref. 783]

[*rot. 2d*]   Still Scharwedale Wapentake   J. de Vaux

463 They say that William Dureherre and William Colte of Alfreton sold wines against the assize, so they are in *mercy*.
[ref. 784]

464 Concerning defaults, they say that William de Stutewyll, Thomas Beck bishop of St David's, Robert bishop of Dunblane, Peter de Cestria prior of Thurgerton, Philip le Marscal of Ekynton, Robert de Cressy of Stennesby and William de Reinaldesschawe did not come on the first day, so they are in *mercy*. John le Paumer of Notingham and Robert son of Levike did not come on the first day, so they are in mercy.
[ref. 784]

465 Concerning squires, they say that Roger le Bret (he has a warrant), John de Ayncurt (he still does not have his lands), and ... [*erased*] have a whole knight's fee, are of full age and not yet knights. So they are in *mercy*.

Afterwards Roger came and produced a letter patent from the king granting him respite of knighthood for seven years from production of the letter whereof five years still remain to come. So nothing of him.[1]

466 Concerning warrens, they say that Thomas Beck bishop of St David's at Plesey, Henry de Perpont at Langwath, dame Annora de Haversheg at Barleburg, Anquerus de Frechevill at Schardeclyve, Ralph de Reresby at Essovere, Reynold de Grey at Schirlond, Thomas de Chawrth at Alfreton and Norton, William de Steinesby at Steinesby, Edmund de Eyncurt at Elmeton and Holmesfeld, have set up warrens in their lands, by what warrant unknown. So the sheriff is ordered to make them come to show [their warrants].[2]

Afterwards Reynold de Grey and Edmund de Aynekurth came and showed their warrants, so they are quit.

467 From G. the sheriff for chattels of John de Plauestowe, hanged, *8s.* From Roger de Cropphil for chattels of Henry de Oxecroft, hanged, *31s.* From the same sheriff for chattels of William Paris, hanged, *17d.*, of Henry Gale, hanged, *17d.*, of William Bate, hanged, *7s. 8d.* From Nicholas Wake for chattels of Robert de Wyteby, hanged, *2s. 1d.*, of Thomas Cisse, hanged, *9d.*, of John de Reinaldestorp, hanged, *5d.*, of Adam de Normanville, *2s. 6d.* From Roger de la Bache for chattels of William de Ikeling, hanged, *2s.* Because the aforesaid Nicholas and Roger took the chattels without warrant, they are in *mercy*.

[ref. 785]

468 From G. the sheriff for chattels of Walter son of Walter de Normanton, fugitive, *34s. 2d.*, of Robert Glide, fugitive, *48s. 8d.*, of Adam son of Geoffrey Gomme, fugitive, *53s. 11d.*, of Roger son of Ralph, fugitive, *40s. 3d.*, of Thomas son of Ralph, fugitive, *20s. 2d.*, of Adam Sweng, fugitive, *38s.*, of Geoffrey Sweng, fugitive, *40s. 3d.*, of Simon Glide, fugitive, *20s.*

---

[1] An inquisition taken on 24 June 1279 after the death of Robert le Breton found his heir Roger to be 19 on the Michaelmas preceding. He would therefore have been 21 at Michaelmas 1280. (*Cal. Inq. p.m.*, ii. no. 317).

[2] Free warren at Barlborough had been granted to Matthew de Hathersage and his heirs in Oct. 1249 (*Cal.Ch.R. 1226–57*, i. 345), to Ralph de Frecheville and his heirs at Scarcliffe on 1 Dec. 1251 (ibid., 371), to Thomas de Chaworth at Alfreton etc. on 13 Sept. 1257 (ibid. 472), to John de Aincurt and his heirs at Holmesfield and Elmton on 28 Apr. 1252 (ibid., 389), and to William de Steinesby at Herdewyk etc. on 20 Mar. 1271 (*Cal.Ch.R. 1257–1300*, ii. 115).

4d., of Roger son of Ranulph, fugitive, *53s. 6d.*, of Henry Wysning, fugitive, *£7 5s. 3d.*

[ref. 453, 786, 787]

469 Roger de Motrom and Margery de Brampton arrested for harbouring William Lether, an approver from Cheshire, come and deny all, and for good and ill put themselves on the country. The jurors say that they are not guilty so they are *quit.*

470 William Lether, approver of Cheshire, comes and withdraws himself so *<he is to be hanged.>* He had no chattels.

471 William son of Agnes de Wytynton, arrested on suspicion of larceny, comes, denies all, and for good and ill puts himself on the country. The jurors say that he is guilty, so *<he is to be hanged>.*

472 Concerning those indicted, they say that Thomas son of Hugh de Penkiston, Hugh Spinck of that place, Richard son of Hugh de Penkeston, Walter Falke, William de Langeford, Richard son of Nicholas le Keu of Essovere, Serlo son of Gilbert, Reynold his brother and Geoffrey Cassion of Wingerwrth, have absconded on suspicion of larceny and are suspected. So *they are to be exacted and outlawed.* They had no chattels.[1]

WERKESWRTH WAPENTAKE COMES BY 12 JURORS

473 Two unknown men were found killed in lord Edmund's sheepfold in Wirkeswrth park, killers unknown. No Englishry. Judgment: *murder* on the wapentake. William son of Gilbert de Wyrkeswrth, the first finder, has not come, nor is he suspected. He was attached by Hugh son of Brun de Wirkeswrth and Ralph de Matlock in Wirkeswrth who do not have him now, so they are in *mercy.* The 12 jurors who did not mention the first finder in their presentment are in *mercy.* The vills of Hopton, Crumford and Caldelowe did not attend the inquest, so they are in *mercy.*

[ref. 788]

---

[1] 26 June 1282. Pardon at the instance of Eleanor the king's consort to William de Langeford kt. of his outlawry for larceny whereof he was indicted before the justices last in eyre in the county of Derby. (*Cal.Pat.R. 1281–91*, p. 29)

474 Ralph son of Richard de Middelton wounded Robert son of Robert de Middelton in the stomach with a knife so that he died four days later. Ralph fled at once and is suspected, so *he is to be exacted and outlawed.* His chattels 27s. 8d., for which the sheriff is to answer. The vills of Wirkeswrth, Middelton, Hertindon, Bracenton and Elton valued the chattels falsely, so are in *mercy.* Because Adam de Herthil took the chattels without warrant, he is in *mercy.*
  [ref. 789]

475 Reynold de Crudecote fell from a weak horse into the water of Bradeburn and drowned. The first finder has died. No one is suspected. Judgment: *misadventure.* Price of the horse 5s., for which the sheriff is to answer. *<deodand>* The vills of Mappelton, Thorp, Bentley and Offedecote valued the deodand falsely, so they are in *mercy.*
  [ref. 790]

476 John le Venur fell from a mare into the Dove and was drowned. The first finder has died. No one is suspected. Judgment: *misadventure.* Price of the mare 5s., for which the sheriff is to answer. *<deodand>* And [*unfinished*]

477 Robert son of Aylward de Alsop wounded Roger Hayward of Alsop in the head with an axe so that he died the third day after. Robert fled at once and is suspected, so *he is to be exacted and outlawed.* His chattels 7s., for which the sheriff is to answer. The 12 jurors are in *mercy* for concealing part of the chattels in their presentment. The vill of Knyveton is in *mercy* for not attending the inquest.
  [ref. 790]

478 Unknown evil-doers by night burgled the sheepfold of Cronkendon and killed William Shepherd whom they found there. They fled at once. The first finder has died. No Englishry. Judgment: *murder* on the wapentake. The jurors later attested that a certain Gotte de Crudecote and Roger son of Adam de Crudecote absconded on account of the death and are suspected, so *they are to be exacted and outlawed.* Roger's chattels 5s., for which the sheriff is to answer. Gotte had no chattels. The vills of Irton, Bondesale, Alsope and Crudecote are in *mercy* for valuing the chattels falsely.
  [ref. 791]

479 From G. the sheriff for the chattels of Sweyn de Yrton, hanged, 7s. 10d. The vills of Hokenaston, (Lee, Matlok) and Kersington are in *mercy* for

valuing the chattels falsely. From the same sheriff for the chattels of William Godale, hanged, *half a mark*. The vills of Milnefeld and Underwode are in *mercy* for valuing the chattels falsely.
[ref. 792]

480 Ralph Bonbel killed Richard, Geoffrey Bunbel's man in the vill of Peverwych, fled at once and is suspected, so *he is to be exacted and outlawed*. He had no chattels and was in the frankpledge of the vill of Peverwych which does not have him now, so is in *mercy*. The vills of Tanesley, Ybule and Elton are in *mercy* for not attending the inquest.
[ref. 793]

481 Adam Fox and Richard son of Geoffrey wounded Henry Bonde of Wendesley in the vill of Vendesley so that he died the fifth day after. Adam and Richard fled at once and are suspected, so *they are to be exacted and outlawed*. They had no chattels and were in the frankpledge of the vill of Wendesleye which does not have them now, so it is in *mercy*.
[ref. 793]

482 Richard Lyngell put himself in Hokenaston church, admitted to being a thief and *abjured* the realm. His chattels *10s*. He had free land whereof year and waste *8s*. Mid time of that land *11s.*, for all of which the sheriff is to answer. He was in the frankpledge of the vill of Hokenaston which does not have him now, so it is in *mercy*.
[ref. 793]

483 Budens le Hirdman killed Margery daughter of John de Middelton in the vill of Middelton, fled at once and is suspected, so *he is to be exacted and outlawed*. He had no chattels and was in the frankpledge of the vill of Middelton which does not have him now, so it is in *mercy*.

[*rot. 3*]   Still Werkewrth Wapentake   J. de Vaux

484 Henry son of Richard de Bondesal killed Ralph son of Osbert with a knife in the vill of Bontesal, fled at once and is suspected. So *he is to be exacted and outlawed*. His chattels *2s. 8d.*, for which the sheriff is to answer. He was in the frankpledge of Bontesal which does not have him now, so it is in *mercy*. William son of Richard de Bondesal, brother of Henry, absconded on account of the death, so his chattels are to be confiscated for the flight. His chattels *5s. 4d.*, for which the sheriff is to answer. William has come now and asked how he would acquit himself, denies the death and all and for good and ill puts himself on the country.

The jurors say that he is not guilty, so he is *quit*. But because he was present and did not arrest or pursue, he is in *mercy*. Walter de Ribuf the coroner did not attach Walter Bate who took part in the aforesaid death, so *to judgment* on him.

[ref. 793]

485 William de Morcanston killed Nicholas de Hokenaston his master in a certain mill in the vill of Hokenaston, fled at once and is suspected, so *he is to be exacted and outlawed.* He had no chattels and was in the frankpledge of the vill of Hokenaston which does not have him now, so it is in *mercy*.

486 From G. the sheriff for the chattels of Robert Shepherd, thief beheaded, *12d.*, of John Curlu, thief beheaded, *6d.*, of Simon de la Grene, thief hanged, *2d.*, of Robert le Halte, hanged, *6d.*, of Thomas de Gouleswrth, thief beheaded, *15d.*, of Henry Hole, thief beheaded, *3s.*, of Nicholas Baker, hanged, *8s.*, of Peter Scot and Robert Saltman, thieves beheaded, *3s. 5d.*

[ref. 794]

487 Concerning defaults, they say that Robert Tipetot, William de Audeleye, the prior of Felleye, Henry le Pescur and John le Marchant both of Matlock, John de Hurste, Roger son of Laurence de Matlock, John son of Gilbert de Bedeford in Mapelton, Henry de Tyssington, Ralph de Swynesco in Thorpe, Thomas de Weston, John de Aldewerck, William son of Cecilia de Peverwyg, John de Kestewenn in Peverwy, John son of Maud of the same, Adam de Stopel in Werkewrth, William son of Gilbert of the same, Geoffrey de Bello Monte [*struck through;* per Roger Loveday *written over*], did not come on the first day, so they are in *mercy*.[1]

[ref. 795]

488 Concerning squires, they say that Robert de Dethec and Roger de Bradeborn have a whole knight's fee, are of full age and are not yet knights, so they are in *mercy*.

---

[1] William de Audley had quittance of common summons, 3 Mar. 1281. (*Cal.Cl.R. 1279–88*, p. 117).

489 In the county court Avice sister of Master Simon de Underwode appealed Adam de Gretewych, Gilbert son of William, Cecilia daughter of Eva de Bentley and William son of Gilbert, clerk, of the death of her brother Master Simon. She has not come, nor prosecutes her appeal, so *she is to be arrested.* Her sureties for prosecution are in *mercy,* William de Hulton, clerk, who has died and William de Cubele. Gilbert, Cecilia and the others have come. So that the king's peace may be maintained, the truth of the matter is to be inquired of the country. The jurors say that none of them is guilty of the death, so all are *quit.*

490 In the county court Julia daughter of William le Hine of Braylesford appealed Hugh son of Roger de Mappelton in Esseburn of the death of her husband. She has not come, so *she is to be arrested.* Her sureties for prosecution are in *mercy,* Henry le Chirchemon of Knyveton and Thomas son of Thomas of the same. Hugh has now come. So that the king's peace may be maintained, the truth of the matter is to be inquired of the country. The jurors say that Hugh is not guilty and that they have not come to an agreement, so he is *quit.*
[ref. 796]

491 From William de Parco concerning a fine for trespass, *20s.* by surety of Henry Rosel and William de Addridele.
[ref. 796]

GAOL DELIVERY

492 Ammoria widow of John de Allerwasseleye, arrested on suspicion of stealing lead from the chapel of Allerwasseleye, Simon son of Julia, similarly arrested on suspicion of larceny, and Richard Wildegos, arrested for harbouring Simon, have come, deny all and for good and ill put themselves on the country. The jurors say that Richard Wildegos and Ammoria are not guilty so they are *quit.* They say that Simon is guilty of many larcenies, so *<he is to be hanged>.* He had no chattels.

493 Concerning those indicted, they say that Henry son of William Kryche, Adam le Archer, Matthew son of William de Milnefeld, William de Milnefeld, Maud daughter of Ammoria, Adam Kok, Ralph Pycolet, William son of William de Langbone, Robert de Pecco, Roger Cay, William son of

William Smith of Bassington, Nel Fytun, Walter Fytun, William son of Henry de Perture, Henry his brother and Robert son of William de Bredelowe absconded on suspicion of larceny. All except Maud are suspected, so *they are to be exacted and outlawed.* If Maud wishes *she may return,* but her chattels are to be confiscated for the flight. She had no chattels. William de Milnefeld's chattels, *12d.* for which the sheriff is to answer.

[ref. 796]

REPPINDON WAPENTAKE COMES BY 12 JURORS

494 The jurors present that Robert Hodeke of Fornewerk freely hanged himself from an oak tree in the park of Reppindon. The first finder, his brother William, has come and is not suspected, nor is any other. Judgment: *suicide.* His chattels £6 6s. 6d. for which the sheriff is to answer. The vills of Reppindon, Fornewerck, Bretteby and Neuton valued the chattels falsely so are in *mercy.* The 12 jurors did not mention the price of the oak in their presentment, so are in *mercy.*

[ref. 797]

495 Richard son of Swein struck Robert de Lee on the head with an axe so that he died four days later. Richard fled at once and is suspected, so *he is to be exacted and outlawed.* He had no chattels and was in the frankpledge of the vill of Neuton on Trent which does not have him now, so is in *mercy.*

[ref. 798]

496 John Levedybodi of Potelock, Elota de Wylington and Felicity de Hockwell fell from a boat into the river Trent and were drowned. The first finder has died. No one is suspected. Judgment: *misadventure.* There is to be *inquiry in Luthchirch* about the price of the boat. Price of the boat 2s., for which the sheriff is to answer. <deodand>

497 Ralph son of Richard de Reppindon killed Walter Hayward of Reppindon with a staff in the field of Reppindon, fled at once and is suspected. So *he is to be exacted and outlawed.* He had no chattels and was in the frankpledge of the vill of Reppindon which does not have him now, so it is in *mercy.* No Englishry. Judgment: *murder* on the wapentake. Alice widow of Walter, the first finder, has not come and is not suspected. She was attached by William Mone and William le Gathird both of Reppindon who do not have her now, so they are in *mercy*.

498   Unknown evil-doers came by night to the house of Robert de Andesakre in Reppindon, entered and killed Robert and led away his two horses. No Englishry. Judgment: *murder* on the wapentake.

499   John Buchon fell from a boat into the Trent and was drowned. The first finder comes and is not suspected, nor is any other. Judgment: *misadventure*. Price of the boat *12d.*, for which the sheriff is to answer. *<deodand>*

500   Gilbert Gerard killed Alice his wife in the field of Lollington, was immediately arrested and taken to Notingham *gaol* where he was hanged before the justices for gaol delivery. His chattels *a mark*, of which the sheriff answers for *5s. 8d.* and Walter de Stirthesle for *7s. 8d.* The vills of Catton, Lollinton, Crokesal and Kotonne valued the chattels falsely so are in *mercy*.
   [ref. 799]

501   Ralph de Roslaston, greasing the wheel of Catton water mill, was crushed between the wheel and the spindle so that he died four days later. No one is suspected. Judgment: *misadventure*. Price of the wheel and spindle, *12d.* for which the sheriff is to answer. *<deodand>* The vills of Walton, Wineshill, Roslaston and Stapenhill valued the chattels falsely, so are in *mercy*.
   [ref. 799]

502   Thomas le Stedeman, former groom of William la Suche, killed Simon Porter of Swinesby with a sword in the vill of Stapenhill. He fled at once and is suspected, so *he is to be exacted and outlawed*. He had no chattels. Henry Porter the first finder has not come, nor is he suspected. His sureties, Geoffrey Porter of Pipewell and Robert son of Amice of the same, do not have him now, so they are in *mercy*. The vills of Ethcote, Gresele with Wineshill, Stanton and Drakelowe did not pursue him, so are in *mercy*.
   [ref. 800]

503   Robert Charles struck Thomas Arnald in the stomach with a knife so that he died instantly. Robert fled at once and is suspected. so *he is to be exacted and outlawed*. His chattels *7s. 2d.*, for which the sheriff is to answer.

He was in the frankpledge of Stapenhill which does not have him now, so it is in *mercy*. The 12 jurors concealed part of the chattels, so are in *mercy*.
[ref. 800]

[*rot. 3d*]   Still Reppindon Wapentake   J. de Vaux

504 William Martin of Lynton killed his brother Robert in the vill of Lynton, fled at once and is suspected. So *he is to be exacted and outlawed*. His chattels *10s.*, for which the sheriff is to answer. He was in the frankpledge of the vill of Lenton which does not have him now, so it is in *mercy*.
[ref. 800]

505 Robert de Haventon and Alan son of Robert Pers, crossing a plank beside Lollington mill, fell into the water under the wheel and were so lacerated that they died. Robert son of Thomas Auger, the first finder, has come and is not suspected, nor is any other. Judgment: *misadventure*. Price of the wheel and plank *2s.*, for which the sheriff is to answer. <*deodand*>

506 Robert Stacey of Childecote killed John son of Adam of the same with an axe in Robert's croft in the vill of Childecote. He fled at once and is suspected, so *he is to be exacted and outlawed*. His chattels *18s.*, for which the sheriff is to answer. The vills of Childecote, Appelby, Stretton and Meissam valued the chattels falsely, so are in *mercy*.

Afterwards the jurors attested that Robert had free land whereof year and waste *20s.*, for which the sheriff is to answer. Mid time of that land *4 marks*, for which Nicholas de Finderne is to answer. Because he took it without warrant he is in *mercy*.
[ref. 801]

507 Thomas, sergeant of the abbot of Lylleshull, killed John Abbelot of Hesseby in the field of Wyvelesle, fled at once and is suspected, so *he is to be exacted and outlawed*. He had no chattels. He was in the mainpast of the abbot of Lellushill who does not have him now, so he is in *mercy*.

Wyvelesle, Melburn, Ockthorp and Greseleye did not pursue him, so are in *mercy*.
[ref. 801]

508 Adam son of William Miller of Esseby la Suche put himself in the church of Wyvelesley, admitted to being a thief and *abjured* the realm. His chattels and frankpledge are unknown as he was a stranger from the county of *Leycestre,* so inquiry there concerning his chattels.

509 Adam, a boy three years old, son of Swein de Stoni Stanton, fell into a well in the vill of Stoni Stanton and was drowned. The first finder has come and is not suspected, nor is any other. Judgment: *misadventure.* The vills of Stoni Stanton, Colde Stanton, Pakenton, Caldewell and Engelby did not attend the inquest, so are in *mercy.*
[ref. 802]

510 Nicholas de Stoni Stanton wounded Geoffrey son of Reynold de Bretteby in the head with an axe so that he died three weeks later. Nicholas fled at once and is suspected, so *he is to be exacted and outlawed.* His chattels *12d.,* for which the sheriff is to answer. He was in the frankpledge of the vill of Bretteby which does not have him now, so it is in *mercy.*
[ref. 802]

511 Walter Litlegod killed John de Leghes in the field of Bretteby, fled at once and is suspected. So *he is to be exacted and outlawed.* His chattels *12s.,* for which the sheriff is to answer.
[ref. 802]

512 Hugh son of Geoffrey de Bretteby killed Ranulph son of Robert of the same, fled at once and is suspected, so *he is to be exacted and outlawed.* His chattels *3s.,* for which the sheriff is to answer. Because this happened by day the vill of Bretteby is in mercy for not arresting him. The first finder has died. No Englishry. Judgment: *murder* on the wapentake. The vills of Cotes, Smythby, Herteshorn and Tykenal did not attend the inquest, so are in *mercy.*
[ref. 803]

513 John Baret of Bretteby killed Robert son of Emma with a knife in the vill of Bretteby, fled at once and is suspected, so *he is to be exacted and outlawed.* His chattels *12d.,* for which the sheriff is to answer. The first finder has died. John was in the frankpledge of the vill of Neuton which does not have him now, so it is in *mercy.*
[ref. 803]

514 In the county court William Carter of Fornwerck appealed Robert de Stanton and Robert de Venables of wounding, battery and breach of the king's peace. He has not come nor prosecutes his appeal, so *he is to be arrested*. His sureties for prosecution are in *mercy*, William Reeve of Fornewerk and Geoffrey Townhead. Robert and Robert have now come. The jurors say that they have not come to an agreement and that they are not guilty, so they are *quit*.

[ref. 803]

515 In the county court John le Wens of Reppindon appealed Hervey de Akle of mayhem, wounding and breach of the king's peace. John has not come nor does he prosecute his appeal, so *he is to be arrested*. His sureties are in *mercy*, John le Moner and William le Mercer, both of Reppindon. Hervey has not come and was attached by William de Appelby and Hugh de Haregreve, so they are in mercy. The jurors say that Hervey is not guilty of mayhem and that they have come to an agreement, but they say that he did indeed wound John against the peace, so he is in *mercy*.

[ref. 804]

516 Concerning churches, they say that the church of Melleburn used to be in the king's gift. Now the bishop of Karliol' holds it, by what warrant unknown. So the sheriff is ordered to cause the bishop to come to show his warrant.[1]

517 Concerning ladies, they say that Joan de Monte Alto is in the king's gift and is marriageable. Her lands in this county are worth 20 marks, so there is to be *discussion*.

518 Concerning defaults, they say that Bernard de Brus of Reppindon, Henry le Bercher of Melton, the vill of Edeinghal, William le Blund of Wyvelesleye, Imbert de Monte Ferardi, Reynold de Tykennale and Robert Fisher of Steyneston in Huntebothe (cancelled because he appeared in Luthchirch), did not come on the first day, so they are in *mercy*.

[ref. 805]

519 The jurors present that at another time Reynold de Tykenale was

---

[1] Master Simon de Waltham holds the church of Meleburn by gift of king John who had given it at another time. King Henry father of king John likewise gave it, but the jurors do not know whether they gave it by reason of the custody which they had of the bishopric of Carlisle or by another means. (*Book of Fees*, i. 288).

indicted on suspicion of larceny, was arrested and imprisoned. Later, by order of the king, he was bailed to be before the justices here by Adam son of John de Tikenhal, Geoffrey Wymond, Richard de Fornewerck, Henry de Barew, all in Tikenhal, John son of Ralph de Engelby, Simon Cook and Robert Townsend both in Reppindon, Robert Barue in Melton, William Wodeward in Reppindon, William Douceamur, Henry son of William, Henry Lomb, Robert son of William and Richard de Melton all in Reppindon and Robert Reeve of Melton, who do not have him. So all are in *mercy*.

Afterwards Reynold comes. Questioned as to how he wishes to acquit himself, he says that he is trustworthy and on this he puts himself on the country. The jurors say that he is not guilty of any wrong doing, so he is *quit*.

[ref. 806]

520   The jurors present that William le Brevetur was arrested by the vill of Reppindon on suspicion of larceny. As he was led to prison at Nottingham he escaped and fled to the church at Schardelowe where he admitted to being a thief and *abjured* the realm. He had no chattels in this wapentake, but inquiry is to be made in Luthchirch concerning his chattels and frankpledge. The vill of Reppindon is to answer for the *escape*.

[ref. 806]

521   Concerning squires, they say that John de Bailliolo has a full knight's fee, is of full age and not yet a knight. So he is in *mercy*.[1]

[ref. 807]

522   Concerning warrens, they say that Roger de Monte Alto has warren in Walton and Geoffrey de Greseley in Drakelowe, by what warrant is unknown. So the sheriff is ordered to make them come to show [their warrants.]

523   From G. the sheriff for the chattels of beheaded thieves, Richard Leveson, *10d.*, Roger de Foderingeye, *4s. 6d.*, Richard de London, *12d.*, and of Hugh son of Kenne de Kettegston, *2s. 6d.* [ref. 807]

---

[1] The inquisition taken at Newcastle on 15 Dec. 1278 after the death of Alexander de Balliol found that his brother John, aged 30 and more, was his next heir. (*Cal. Inq. p.m.*, ii. no. 249).

524   Concerning those indicted, they say that Peter son of Robert Heyolf of Meleburn, Walter son of Roger Barunt of Meleburn park, Adam son of Ellis Carter, Robert son of William le Tailleur and Richard Elyis all of Meleburn, Richard de Tibshelf, Robert son of John de Stapenhill, William Cobbe, Agnes de Totesbyr', ... Matinel and Goda his sister, absconded on suspicion of larceny. So all are to be exacted and outlawed and the women waived. They had no chattels. Their frankpledge is not known because they were vagabonds.

[*rot. 4*]   Still Reppindon Wapentake   J. de Vaux

525   <*Gaol delivery*> Henry Asselot, William le Rede and Richard Bogge, all of Huntebothe, Richard Petit and Roger Los, both of Waleton, Richard de Brunne and Hugh Britwyne of Croxsale, arrested on suspicion of larceny, come, deny all and for good and ill put themselves on the country. The jurors say that Richard Petit, Roger Los, Richard de Brunne and Hugh Britwyne are not guilty of any ill deed, so they are *quit*. Concerning Henry Asselot, William Rede and Richard Bogge, they say that they are guilty of many larcenies so <*they are to be hanged*>. Chattels of Richard Bogges *8s. 8d.*, of Henry Hasselot *24s. 7d.*, of William le Rede *20s.*, for all of which the sheriff is to answer.
    [ref. 808]

526   Simon Dyot, accused of harbouring Robert Russel, a thief indicted in the county of Notingham by the wapentake of Bingham, comes, denies all and for good and ill puts himself on the country. The jurors say that he is not guilty so he is *quit*.

LUCHERCH WAPENTAKE COMES BY 12 JURORS

527   The jurors present that a certain unknown man was found killed in the field of Clifton, his killer unknown. The first finder has come and is not suspected. No Englishry. Judgment: *murder* on the wapentake. The vills of Clifton, Longesley, Mackwrth and Weston did not attend the inquest, so are in *mercy*. The 12 jurors did not mention the finder's sureties in their presentment, so are in *mercy*.
    [ref. 809]

528 William de Malmerton, former sergeant of Engelard de Curschon, wounded Viotus son of Hugh de Mackewrth in the head with a gimlet so that he died within a month. William fled at once and is suspected, so *he is to be exacted and outlawed.* He had no chattels. The vills of Grauntovere, Querendon and Marketon did not pursue him, so they are in *mercy.* He was in the mainpast of the aforesaid Engelard who does not have him now, so he is in *mercy.*
    [ref. 810]

529 Thomas Besing of Mackwrth killed Robert son of Maud de Trossele in Mackwrth, fled at once and is suspected. So *he is to be exacted and outlawed.* His chattels *10s.,* for which the sheriff is to answer. He was in the frankpledge of the vill of Mackwrth which does not have him, it is in *mercy.*
    [ref. 811]

530 William son of Roger de Egeton wounded Stephen Alwyne in the head with a staff so that he died the fourth day after. William fled at once and is suspected, so *he is to be exacted and outlawed.* His chattels *12d.,* for which the sheriff is to answer. He was in the frankpledge of Eginton which does not have him now, so it is in *mercy.* The vills of Hulton, Merston, Etewall and Amboldeston are in *mercy* for valuing the chattels falsely.
    [ref. 811]

531 Margery daughter of Bonde fell from a cart in Radburne so that she died. The first finder has died. No one is suspected. Judgment: *misadventure.* Price of the cart and horse *6s. 8d.,* for which the sheriff is to answer. <*deodand*> The vills of Radburne, Dalbir', Chelardeston and Boolton are in *mercy* for valuing the deodand falsely.
    [ref. 812]

532 William Shepherd of Lutchirche was found in the field of Luthchurch killed by unknown evil-doers. The first finder has died. No Englishry. Judgment: *murder* on the wapentake. Because this happened by day and they did not pursue them, the vills of Lutcherch, Normanton, Parva Overe and Aywaldeston are in *mercy.* [ref. 813]

533 Unknown evil-doers killed Henry Reeve of Finderne on Egenton moor and fled at once. No Englishry. Judgment: *murder* on the wapentake. The vills of Finderne and Wylington did not attend the inquest, so are in *mercy.*
    [ref. 813]

534[1] The jurors present that Robert de Meynill and Richard de Derleye, coming from the vill of Derby to Langeley, found John de Langeleye, chaplain and William de Derleye, clerk, disputing over a certain bounded acre with their swords drawn. At length Robert, in order to settle the fight, drew his sword to separate them without harm or injury to either. Richard, seeing this and fearing lest Robert de Meynill might either incur or cause injury, rushed towards him and falling into his arms, accidentally received a wound in the stomach from Robert's sword so that he died the fourth day after. Robert immediately absconded, was afterwards arrested and taken to Notingham where he was imprisoned and released before the justices for gaol delivery because this had happened by accident. Because it is not known who the justices were who might certify the release to the justices here, the sheriff is ordered to arrest Robert and confiscate his chattels for the flight. His chattels 8s., for which the sheriff is to answer.

[ref. 814]

535 William de Wauton, bailiff, in mercy for contempt, is amerced at 100s. Afterwards he is pardoned by the justices.

[ref. 814]

536 William Ambrose put himself in the church of Magna Overe, admitted to being a thief and *abjured* the realm. He had no chattels. His frankpledge is unknown because he was a stranger.

[*rot. 4d*]   Still Luthchurch Wapentake   J. de Vaux

537 Robert son of Ralph de Ketelleston freely struck himself in the stomach with a knife, dying instantly. No other is suspected. Judgment: *suicide.* His chattels 6d., for which the sheriff is to answer. The vill of Ketelleston is in *mercy* for burying him without coroner's view. The jurors attest that John Grim the coroner held an inquest into the death and does not answer now concerning the plea, so *to judgment* on him.

[ref. 814]

538 Unknown evil-doers came by night to the house of Henry Cabbel in Swerkeston, entered and killed his wife Isolda. They carried off goods and

---

[1] A long piece has been torn away with loss of marginations from **534–536**.

chattels found there and fled at once. The vills of Swerkeston, Osmudeston and Parva Marketon are in *mercy* because they did not pursue them.
[ref. 815]

539   Nicholas Burge of Alewaston and William his brother put themselves in the church of Alwaston, admitted to being thieves and *abjured* the realm. They had no chattels. They were in the frankpledge of the vill of Alwaston which does not have them, so it is in *mercy*.

540   Robert Meronde killed Ellis de Amboldeston with an axe in the vill of Alwaston, fled at once and is suspected. So *he is to be exacted and outlawed*. His chattels £8 *18s. 4d.*, for which the sheriff is to answer. He was not in a frankpledge, being a free man. The vills of Amboldeston, Boolton and Chillardton are in *mercy* for valuing the chattels falsely.

Afterwards it was attested by the coroner's rolls that Robert had put himself in the church of Okebrock, admitted the deed and *abjured* the realm. So nothing concerning the outlawry. Because the vill of Okethorp did not arrest him it is in *mercy*.
[ref. 815]

541   Simon, three-year-old son of Simon de Erleston, was found dead in the field of Ersleston as though strangled. The first finder has come and is not suspected. It is not known who killed him. No Englishry. Judgment: *murder* on the wapentake. The vills of Twyford, Barwe and Normanton are in *mercy* because they did not attend the inquest.
[ref. 815]

542   John Janne of Alwaston put himself in Alwaston church, admitted to being a thief and *abjured* the realm. His chattels *14s. 6d.*, for which the sheriff is to answer. He was in the frankpledge of the vill of Alwaston which does not have him. The 12 jurors are in *mercy* for concealing part of the chattels. The vills of Weston on Trent, Sydenfenn and Chellardeston are in *mercy* for not attending the abjuration.
[ref. 816]

543   Richard son of Geoffrey le Cannere killed Margery Rappock in the vill of Ambaldeston, fled at once and is suspected. So *he is to be exacted and outlawed*. His chattels *5s.*, for which the sheriff is to answer. He was in the frankpledge of the vill of Ambaldeston which does not have him now, so it is in *mercy*. [ref. 816]

544 Simon son of Henry de Luthchurche and William le Pesckur of Ambaldeston, arrested for the death of Roger son of Adam Wylne, come and deny all and for good and ill put themselves on the country. The jurors say that they are not guilty of the death, so they are *quit*. But they say that William Wastel absconded on account of the aforesaid death and is suspected, so *he is to be exacted and outlawed*. Neither his chattels nor frankpledge is known because he was a stranger.

545 Concerning defaults, they say that Henry de Lacy earl of Lincoln,[1] Master Henry Lowel, Ralph de Sancto Mauro, Bernard de Brus, Imbert de Monte Ferardi, Adam de Aldedeley and Adam de Burghes did not come on the first day, so are in *mercy*.
[ref. 817]

546 Concerning escapes of thieves, they say that a certain William Qwyting of Morlegh put himself in the church of Langel' and came out voluntarily. He was immediately arrested by the vill of Langel' and imprisoned in a house there from which he later escaped. So the village of Langel' is to answer for the *escape*. Because he is suspected of many larcenies, *he is to be exacted and outlawed*. Neither his chattels nor frankpledge is known because he was a vagabond.
[ref. 816]

547 In the county court Henry le Lorimer and Robert Tappe in Derby appealed William le Jovene of Mackworth of battery, wounding and breach of the king's peace. Henry and Robert have not come, nor do they prosecute their appeal, so *they are to be arrested*. Their sureties are in *mercy*, Laurence le Seller, William le Tyxtor, Henry le Lorimer and Henry Galion, all of Derby. William le Jovene has now come, so for the sake of maintaining the king's peace, the truth of the matter is to be inquired of the country. The jurors say that he is not guilty of robbery or battery, so he is *quit*.
[ref. 817]

548 From G. the sheriff for the chattels of Twete of Makewrth, thief

---

[1] Amercements of barons and prelates holding by barony could not be imposed in eyre as they could only be amerced by the peers or equals of those to be amerced. The Exchequer barons would in such a case assess a reasonable amount. Consequently no amount was entered in the roll of amercements and estreats, where 'Baro' was marginated.

hanged, *16s. 6d*, of William le Marscal of Wylne, thief hanged, *10s.*, of Stephen Buck, hanged, *6d.*, of Peter Black, fugitive, *2d.*, of Thomas Balle of Weston, thief hanged, *2s.* Hugh de Gurney took the chattels of Twett without warrant, so is in *mercy*. Afterwards he is pardoned by the justices.

[ref. 818]

549 Robert Atwell of Eginton appeals William son of Roger le Machon of mayhem and breach of the king's peace. William comes and denies mayhem and all and for good and ill puts himself on the country. The jurors say that William is not guilty so he is *quit*. Robert is to be committed to gaol for a false appeal. Afterwards he is pardoned by the justices.

550 From G. the sheriff for the chattels of Astin Barun of Aboldeston, a suicide, *52s.* The 12 jurors are in *mercy* for concealing part of the chattels.

[ref. 819]

551 Ralph le Brevetur, arrested on suspicion of larceny and for harbouring William le Brevetur and other thieves, comes, denies all and for good and ill puts himself on the country. The jurors say he is not guilty so he is *quit*.

552 Nicholas de Mackeworth, arrested for the death of Thomas de Warrewick, comes, denies the death and all and for good and ill puts himself on the jury of the vill of Derby. The jurors say that he is not guilty of the death, so he is *quit*. Because Nicholas was arrested at another time and released by the king's writ on bail to Robert alias le Qwite of Mackworth, Robert le Fox, William le Jovene, Hugh Freman, Hugh le Taillur, Hugh Godchild, Robert son of Henry, Thomas de Breitesal, William le Wlf, John de la More, Hugh son of Alan and Robert Shepherd, all of Breitesal, who did not have him here on the first day, they are all in *mercy*.

[ref. 819]

553 Concerning those indicted, they say that Thomas le Kidiere, Baldwin Forester of Mogginton, Robert Adekok of Egenton, Lewin son of Walkelin de Eginton and Ralph son of Peter de Murkaneston, Peter Black of Chillardeston, Robert de Grangia and Roger son of William de Meisham, absconded on account of many larcenies, so *they are to be exacted and outlawed*. They had no chattels. Their frankpledge is unknown because they were vagabonds.

554 Henry de Hachern put himself in the church of Potlock, admitted to being a thief and *abjured* the realm. He had no chattels. His frankpledge is unknown because he was a stranger.

[*rot. 5*] J. de Vaux

APPELTRE WAPENTAKE COMES BY 12 JURORS

555 The jurors present that Robert Oliver and Roger son of Geoffrey killed Robert de Etewell in the fields of Benteleye, fled at once and are suspected. So *they are to be exacted and outlawed*. Chattels of Roger *10s.*, for which G. the sheriff is to answer. Robert had no chattels. Agnes, widow of Robert de Etewell, the first finder, has not come nor is she suspected. She was attached by Peter son of Richard de Hatton and John son of William de Brouchon who do not have her, so they are in *mercy*. No Englishry. Judgment: *murder* on the wapentake. Roger son of Geoffrey was in the frankpledge of Hatton which does not have him, so it is in mercy. The 12 jurors are in mercy for concealing part of the chattels. The vills of Hatton, Brouchon, Sutton and Scropton did not attend the inquest, so they are in mercy.

Afterwards it was found from the coroner's rolls that Agnes widow of Robert de Etewell had appealed Robert Oliver and Roger son of Geoffrey in the county court of the death of her husband and by her suit they were outlawed. So nothing at present concerning the outlawry against them.[1]
[ref. 820]

556 Lecia de Underwode was found drowned in a stream in Trossel'. The first finder has died. No other is suspected. Judgment: *misadventure*. Dalbiry, Trossele and Hoslaston buried Lecia without coroner's view, so are in *mercy*.[2]
[ref. 820]

557 Unknown evildoers came by night to the house of Julia de Foleford, entered and killed a certain Hugh who was there. The first finder has come

---

[1] When coroner, Henry de Bagepuz took 2s. from Etwall for viewing the body of Robert de Etwall. (*Rot.Hun.*, ii. 293b).

[2] When coroner, Henry de Bagepuz took half a mark from Trusley for view of the body of a drowned boy. (ibid.).

and is not suspected. No Englishry. Judgment: *murder* on the wapentake. The 12 jurors presented a false finder in their presentment, so are in *mercy*. Julia de Fuleford, Avice her daughter and William de Holyton, attached because they were present, have not come, nor are they suspected. Julia was attached by William de Crofto in Holington and Gilbert son of Nicholas de Ednaston, Avice by Robert Miller and Henry Reeve both of Holington, William de Holington by William Wyldey and William Bars, both of Thurvaston, who do not have him now. So they are in *mercy*. The vills of Holington, Langeford, Schirle and Edenaston did not attend the inquest, so are in *mercy*.[1]

[ref. 821]

558 Henry Dancelevedi killed Serlo de Braylesford with a stick in Osmundeston, fled at once and is suspected. So *he is to be exacted and outlawed.* His chattels *30s.*, for which the sheriff is to answer. The 12 jurors concealed the chattels in their presentment, so are in *mercy*. He was in the frankpledge of Osmundeston which does not have him, so it is in *mercy*. The vills of Wyardeston and Snelleston valued the chattels falsely, so are in *mercy*.

Afterwards it was attested by the coroner's rolls that Hawise de Braylesford, who has died, appealed a certain Eytropus de Osmundeston, who has died, in the county court of the death of Serlo her son. In that court she appealed Henry Dancelevedi, Roger brother of Richard Chaplain of Osmundeston, Lucia sister of Hugh le Gardiner, Richard Gris and Eustace de Osmundeston of aiding and abetting. Because it was found from the coroner's rolls that she had proceeded against Aytropus and the others up to the fourth court, at which all except Henry appeared and found mainpernors, and according to the ruling in the king's Great Charter, which states that no one may be arrested or imprisoned by a woman's appeal for the death of a man other than her husband killed in her arms, and also on account of the contumacy which Henry showed at the fourth court, he was outlawed since he had been appealed of aiding and abetting as a partner in the execution of the deed as appears above, before Aytropus had been thus appealed. So *to judgment* on the whole county. The 12 jurors attest that Aytropus has died, so nothing at present concerning him nor Henry Dancelevedi because he is

---

[1] When coroner, Henry de Bagepuz took 4s. and a cow from Julia Fulford for view of William de Novo Castro killed at her house by thieves. This may refer to the same incident. (ibid.).

an outlaw.

Roger brother of Richard the chaplain, Eustace de Osmundeston, Lucia and Richard have now come. So that the king's peace may be maintained, although Aytropus has died, the truth of the matter is to be inquired into by the country. The jurors say that they are not guilty and that they had not come to an agreement before the death, so they are quit.[1]

[ref. 822]

559 Robert son of Ralph de Mersington, lying under a haystack, was crushed to death by part of the hay falling on him. The first finder has come and is not suspected, nor is any other. Judgment: *misadventure*. Price of the hay *2s.*, for which the sheriff is to answer. *<deodand>* Because the prior of Tuttebur' took the deodand without warrant he is in *mercy*. The vills of Merston, Howen, Hilton and Egginton valued the deodand falsely, so are in *mercy*. The 12 jurors concealed the deodand in their presentment so are in mercy.

[ref. 823]

560 Richard Carter of Schirle killed Robert son of John Cook of the same with a stake, fled at once and is suspected. So *he is to be exacted and outlawed*. His chattels *4s. 6d.*, for which the sheriff is to answer. He was in the frankpledge of Schirle which does not have him, so it is in *mercy*. The vills of Rodesle, (Boyleston, Barton and Alkmonton) valued the chattels falsely so are in *mercy*.[2]

[ref. 824]

561 Richard son of Gilbert de Claunham killed Hugh Spandi in the vill of Segeshal, was immediately arrested and taken to prison at Notingham where he died. So nothing concerning him. He had no chattels. The vills of Seggeshale, Subbir', Eyton, Yildrisle and Mersington Muntegomeri did not attend the inquest, so they are in *mercy*.[3]

[ref. 825]

---

[1] When coroner, Henry de Bagepuz took 2s. from the widow of Eytropus for view of his body. (ibid.).

[2] When coroner, Henry de Bagepuz took 2s. from Shirley for view of the body of Robert Cook. (ibid.).

[3] When coroner Henry de Bagepuz took 5s. from Sedsall for view of the body of Hugh Spandi. (ibid.).

562   Henry son of Walter de Yildesle was crushed in a marl pit in the field of Yildresle, dying instantly. The first finder has come and is not suspected. Judgment: *misadventure*. The vills of Bentley, Attelowe, Huland, Wifele and Cubeleye are in *mercy* for not attending the inquest.[1]
   [ref. 826]

563   Philip de Coleshull and Alice de Beaurepir put themselves in the church of Doubrigg, admitted to being thieves and *abjured* the realm. They had no chattels. The vill of Doubrigg is in *mercy* for not arresting them since it happened by day. Philip's frankpledge is not known because he was a stranger.
   Afterwards it was attested by the jurors that they had chattels worth 2s. for which the sheriff is to answer. The vill of Doubrigg is in *mercy* for concealing the chattels.
   [ref. 827]

564   Adam de Kent of Colbeleye was struck by a tame stag in the park of Cobele so that he died. The first finder has come and is not suspected nor is any other. Judgment: *misadventure*. Price of the stag 3s., for which the sheriff is to answer. <*deodand*> The vills of Northbire and Yeldrisle are in *mercy* for not attending the inquest. William de Montegomeri took the deodand without warrant so he is in *mercy*.
   [ref. 827]

565   Richard de Badinton killed Robert Ged of Malverton in Longeford, fled at once and is suspected. So *he is to be exacted and outlawed*. The vills of Langeford, Þormindesle[2] and Murcaston did not pursue him so are in *mercy*.
   Afterwards it was found from the coroner's rolls that Richard had chattels worth 25s. 5d., for which the sheriff is to answer. The 12 jurors are in *mercy* for concealing the chattels in their presentment.
   [ref. 827]

566   Geoffrey son of Nicholas le Carectarius killed William Wyldegos in

---

[1] The roll of amercements and estreats distinguishes the two parts of Yeaveley (see **826**). The hospital was that of the Hospitallers who had a preceptory at Stydd. Ralph le Foun during the reign of Richard I gave lands for the founding of the hospital.

[2] Thurmansley is Nuns' Clough: the prioress of King's Mead, Derby, had a grant of 1 acre of wood in 1236 (*P.N. Derbys.*, p. 613).

the vill of Somersale, fled at once to the church of Doubrigg, admitted the deed and *abjured* the realm. His chattels 2s., for which the sheriff is to answer. He was in the frankpledge of Somersale which does not have him, so it is in *mercy*. John Grim the coroner does not reply concerning this, so *to judgment* on him. The vill of Etewell did not attend the inquest.
[ref. 828]

567 Loneta de Mersington was found frozen to death in the field of Mersington. Robert son of Robert, the first finder, has not come and is not suspected, nor is any other. Judgment: *misadventure*. Robert was attached by Walter Blake of Mersington and Thomas son of Geoffrey of the same who do not have him, so are in *mercy*.
[ref. 828]

568 Robert Sewale killed Richard de Thorpesle in the vill of Eyton, fled at once and is suspected. So *he is to be exacted and outlawed.* He had no chattels. The first finder has come and is not suspected, so is quit. The vills of Eyton and Etewell are in *mercy* for not pursuing him. Hugh son of the reeve of Eyton and John Schethard absconded on account of the death, so they are suspected. *They are to be exacted and outlawed.* They had no chattels. Their frankpledge is not known but they were of the mainpast of Urian de Sancto Petro who does not have them, so is in *mercy*. Afterwards it was attested by the jurors that Hugh was harboured at the house of Robert the reeve his father in Eyton. So the sheriff is ordered to arrest Robert. Afterwards Robert the reeve came and made fine by *£10* for the trespass by surety of Adam le Venur, Richard de Kingelie, Robert de Seggeshale, Simon de Clyfton, Thomas de Dodeleye and Robert Schiret.
[ref. 828]

[*rot. 5d*]   Still Appeltre Wapentake   J. de Vaux

569 William Fallehus was found drowned in the water of Holebrock. Lecia daughter of Alice de Howen, the first finder, has not come. She is not suspected, nor is any other. Judgment: *misadventure*. Lecia was attached by Nicholas Judas of Howen and Henry son of Henry de Howen who do not have her, so are in *mercy*. The vill of Howen is in *mercy* for burying the dead man without coroner's view.
[ref. 829]

570 John Briddesmuth was found killed in the water of Douve, killer unknown. The first finder has died. No Englishry. Judgment: *murder* on the wapentake. The vill of Atton is in *mercy* for burying him without coroner's view.

[ref. 829]

571 Philip Swary of Osmundeston killed Robert Smith of the same, fled at once and is suspected. So *he is to be exacted and outlawed.* His chattels, *6s. 4d.*, for which the sheriff is to answer. The vills of Osmundeston, Attelowe, Schirle and Weyardeston valued the chattels falsely so are in *mercy.*

[ref. 829]

572 Richard Cook of Colbele, William Greydogge and Hugh Baghwel by night killed Robert the chaplain in the hall of the parson of Colbele church, fled at once and are suspected. So *they are to be exacted and outlawed.* Chattels of Hugh *9s. 4d.*, for which the sheriff is to answer.

Richard and William had no chattels. They were in the frankpledge of the vill of Cubeleye which does not have them, so it is in *mercy.* The first finder has come and is not suspected, so is *quit.* No Englishry. Judgment: *murder.* The vill of Rothington did not attend the inquest so is in *mercy.*

[ref. 829]

573 Hugh de Herdewickwell fell from a cart in Barton so that he died. The first finder has come and is not suspected nor is any other. Judgment: *misadventure.* Price of the cart *5s. 7d.*, for which the sheriff is to answer.

<deodand> The vills of Barton and West Broutton valued the deodand falsely so are in *mercy.*

[ref. 829]

574 Julia la Marscale fell from a cart in the vill of West Brouchton so that she died. Robert le Marscall the first finder has come and is not suspected, nor is any other. Judgment: *misadventure.* Price of the cart *9s. 8d.*, for which the sheriff is to answer. *<deodand>.*

575 Henry son of John le Gerneter of Doubrigge was crushed to death by a cart full of firewood. The first finder has come and is not suspected, nor is any other. Judgment: *misadventure.* Price of the cart and horses *11s.*, for which the sheriff is to answer. *<deodand>.* The vill of Mersington Montgomery valued the deodand falsely so is in *mercy.*

576 Richard son of Henry Reeve of Langeford killed John son of William de Sutton with a knife in the vill of Langeford, fled at once and is suspected. So *he is to be exacted and outlawed.* His chattels £9 4s., for which the sheriff is to answer. A certain Robert Judde absconded on account of the death. He is not suspected, so he may return if he wishes but his chattels are to be confiscated for the flight. His chattels 8s. 6d., for which the sheriff is to answer. Ralph son of William de Sutton, Adam Godladde and Ralph his brother, attached because they were present, have not come nor are they suspected. Ralph was attached by Ralph le Paumer and Henry Reeve, both of Sutton, Adam by Robert son of Ralph de Sutton and Henry Hardi of Sutton, and Ralph brother of Adam by Robert at le Doyt of Sutton and Henry son of Ralph de Sutton, who do not have them, so they are in *mercy.*
[ref. 830]

577 In the county court Sibyl de Perton and Sibyl daughter of Henry de Hokenaston appealed Nigel son of Richard Feton of Benteleye, who has died, and William Scharp of the deaths of Henry de Perton and William de Perton, brothers of that Sibyl. In that court she appealed John de Benteleye, brother of Nigel, of incitement and commission. Sibyl and Sibyl have not come, nor do they prosecute their appeals, so *they are to be arrested.* Their sureties for prosecution are in *mercy,* of Sibyl de Perton, Henry Morel of Hokenaston and Adam Attelowe, of Sibyl daughter of Henry, William de Esseburne, clerk, and Reynold son of William de Okenaston. William Scharp and John de Benteleye have now come. So that the king's peace may be maintained, the truth of the matter is to be inquired of the country. The jurors say that they have not come to an agreement, nor are they guilty, so they are *quit.*
[ref. 831]

578 In the county court Athelina widow of Aytropus de Osmundeston, Joan and Margery his sisters, and Agnes daughter of Joan appealed Jordan de Derleye, Richard son of Hugh de Doun, Jordan groom of Hugh de Doun, Robert son of Elena de Braylesford, Walter Prat and Ankyn Scherman of the death of Aytropus, husband of Athelina, father of Margery and Joan and grandfather of Agnes. They also appealed William son of the lady of Bradeleye, Nicholas brother of Robert de Derleye and Thomas Elene of aiding and abetting.

Athelina, Joan, Margery and Agnes have not come, so *they are to be arrested.* Their sureties for prosecution are in *mercy,* of Athelina, John Morel and Alan Shepherd of Osmundeston, of Margery, Ralph de la Sale and

Thomas Swet of Osmundeston, of Joan, Walter de Schirley and Henry le Mercer of Osmundeston, of Agnes, Stacy de Osmundeston and William Carpenter of the same.

Richard son of Hugh de Doun, William son of the lady of Bradeleye, Nicholas brother of Robert de Derleye and Thomas Elene have now come, deny all and for good and ill put themselves on the country. The jurors say that they have not come to an agreement and that they are not guilty, so they are *quit*.

It is found from the coroner's rolls that Jordan groom of Hugh de Doyn, Robert son of Elena and Ankyn Scherman are outlaws in the county by suit of Athelina, Joan, Margery and Agnes. So nothing concerning the outlawry. They had no chattels. Their frankpledge is not known as they were vagabonds. Jordan de Derleye has now absconded on account of the death and is suspected, so *he is to be exacted and outlawed*.

Afterwards it was attested that he lives at Cefton in the county of Lancs., so the sheriff of *Lancs.* is ordered to arrest him and to have him here on the Thursday next after Easter three weeks [*8 May*]. Because Jordan was at another time arrested through the appeal of Athelina and the others, imprisoned and later, by the king's writ, bailed until the coming of the justices here, *to judgment* on Hugh de Babington the sheriff at that time who does not answer now for Jordan's bail.

[ref. 831]

579 William son of John de Sutton and Richard son of Adam de Sutton put themselves in the church of Sutton, admitted to being thieves and *abjured* the realm. Chattels of William *12s.*, for which the sheriff is to answer. Richard had no chattels. They were in the frankpledge of the vill of Sutton which does not have them, so it is in *mercy*.

[ref. 831]

580 Alan Shepherd of Braylesford appealed John Penicod of mayhem, wounding and breach of the king's peace. John has come, denies all and whatever is against the peace, and for good and ill puts himself on the country.

The jurors say that he is not guilty of mayhem or of any act against the peace. But they say that a certain Richard son of Richard le Bole of Cobele, Richard son of Thomas Clerk, Richard son of John de Snelleston, Simon Shepherd of Clifton and Simon son of Henry de Rossinton, who were of John's mainpast, beat and wounded Alan, leaving him for dead. But they did not maim him. Because the jurors attest that John harboured them and does not have them here, *he is to be taken into custody.*

It is found from the coroner's rolls that John was at another time bailed to be here on the first day by Robert de Lee and Thomas Smith of Rossington. They have not come, so they are in *mercy.* Richard, Richard, Richard, Simon and Simon, similarly appealed of the deed, have not come. Richard son of Richard Bole was attached by his father and Henry son of Henry de Rossington, Richard son of Thomas Clerk by Simon le Moner and William Russel, Simon Shepherd of Clyfton by Adam le Forester and John Golyn, Richard son of John de Snelleston by William de Grendon and Thomas Smith of Norbir', who do not have them now. So they are in *mercy.* Because they beat Alan against the peace, the sheriff is ordered to arrest them.

Afterwards John Penicod came and made fine by *4 marks* for the trespass by surety of Alan le Bercher and Nicholas de Sancto Petro of Esse.

[ref. 832]

581 Richard Miller, arrested for the death of Richard de Ydolfeston, has come, denies the death and for good and ill puts himself on the country. The jurors say that he is guilty of the death, so <*he is to be hanged*> His chattels *35s.*, for which the sheriff is to answer.

[*rot. 6*]   Still Apeltre Wapentake   J. de Vaux

582 William son of Robert de Norburgh appeals Robert son of Ives de Braylesford of mayhem, wounding and breach of the king's peace. Robert has come now and William comes and withdraws, so he is to be committed to *gaol.* His sureties are in *mercy,* Hugh Reeve of Bradeleye and Thomas son of Lecia de Thorleston. But for the sake of maintaining the king's peace, let the truth of the matter be inquired of the country. The jurors say that Robert beat William, so *he is to be taken into custody* for the trespass. Afterwards he made fine by *a mark* for the trespass by surety of Henry de Braylesford.

[ref. 833]

583 The jurors present that Robert son of William Forester of Marketon, chaplain, absconded on suspicion of larceny and is suspected. He lives at Hambur' in the county of *Staffs.* So the sheriff is ordered to arrest him and to have him here at Easter three weeks [*4 May 1281*].

584   Richard de West Brouton, arrested on suspicion of larceny, has come, says that he is a clerk and thus not obliged to answer here. On this the dean of *Court Christian at Derby*, proctor of the bishop of Coventry, by his letters patent seeks him as a clerk. But that it might be known by what right he is to be handed over to him, the truth of the matter is to be inquired by the country. *<fuller inquiry in Morleystan>* The jurors say that he is guilty of many larcenies, so on that account *he is to be handed over to the bishop* of Coventry. His chattels, £13 0s. 2d., for which the sheriff is to answer.[1]
   [ref. 833]

585   Concerning squires, they say that Ralph de Schirle has a full knight's fee, is of full age and not yet a knight. So he is in *mercy*. Afterwards Ralph comes and shows certain letters patent which attest that the king has given him respite for five years from taking the arms of a knight.

586   Concerning those indicted, they say that Robert Trulle, Alan de Elkesdene, William de Waterfal, Roger Aldris of Schyrele, Nicholas de Cestreschyre, Robert le Parker of Douvebrigge, Roger de Meysham, William son of Richard Shyne, Richard Kriche of Eyton, Richard son of Hoyt and John Dyot absconded on suspicion of larceny and are suspected. So *they are to be exacted and outlawed.* They had no chattels. Richard de Knyveton in Peverwyc similarly absconded on suspicion of larceny and is not suspected, so *he may return* if he wishes, but his chattels are to be confiscated for his flight. He had no chattels.

---

[1] 12 July 1282. To the sheriff of Derby. Order to restore to Robert [*sic*] de Brocton, clerk, his goods and chattels which were taken into the king's hands upon his being indicted before the justices last in eyre in that county for larcenies, as he has purged his innocence before Roger bishop of Coventry and Lichfield to whom he was delivered in accordance with the privilege of clergy. (*Cal.Cl.R. 1279–88*, p. 162).

   5 Oct. 1283. To the treasurer and barons of the Exchequer. Whereas Gervase de Clyfton sheriff of Notts and Derby delivered by the king's writ to Richard de Brouchton, clerk who was indicted of larcenies before the justices last in eyre at Derby and who purged his innocence before the bishop of Lichfield, £13 0s. 2d. of the king's gift as appears by the letters of the said Richard in Gervase's possession, the king orders the treasurer and barons to cause Gervase to be acquitted of these sums. (ibid., p. 221)

MORLEYSTAN WAPENTAKE COMES BY 12

587 The jurors present that Hugh de Boneye, sergeant of Hugh de Gurney, killed Eustace de Thorp with a knife in the vill of Krych, fled at once and is suspected, so *he is to be exacted and outlawed.* His chattels *15d.*, for which the sheriff is to answer. He was in the mainpast of Hugh de Gurney who does not have him, so he is in *mercy.* The vills of Krych, Duffeld, Deneby, Rippelai and Pentrech are in *mercy* for valuing the chattels falsely.
  [ref. 835]

588 Robert le Bulur, Julia his wife and Nicholas their son by night burgled the house of Susanna de Roulegh and carried away goods which they found there. They were immediately arrested, taken to Nottingham prison and, before the justices for gaol delivery, *hanged* there. Chattels of Robert le Bulur *8d.*, for which the sheriff is to answer. The vills of Cruch and Codenhovere are in *mercy* for valuing the chattels falsely.
  [ref. 835]

589 William son of Serlo Fox of Duffeld struck Robert Miller of Duffeld on the head with a staff so that he died four days later. He fled at once and is suspected, so *he is to be exacted and outlawed.* His chattels, *5s.*, for which the sheriff is to answer. The 12 jurors are in *mercy* for concealing part of the chattels in their presentment.
  [ref. 835]

590 Thomas Clerk of Suthwell killed William vicar of Pentre' in the forest of Duffeld, fled at once and is suspected. So *he is to be exacted and outlawed.* He had no chattels. His frankpledge is unknown because he was a stranger.

591 Geoffrey Brun of Morton struck Henry son of William de Kilburne with a staff in the field of Duffeld, so that he died instantly. Geoffrey fled at once and is suspected, so *he is to be exacted and outlawed.* He had no chattels. The vills of Kilburn and Morley are in *mercy* for not attending the inquest.
  [ref. 835]

592 Roger Drocolf of Suthwode wounded John Duce with an axe in the field of Holebrock so that he died four days later. (Roger fled at once and

is suspected, so *he is to be exacted and outlawed.*) He was in the frank-pledge of the vill of Duffeld which does not have him, so it is in *mercy*. His chattels 9*s.*, for which the sheriff is to answer.
   [ref. 836]

593 Cadel de Hibernia beat Thomas Shepherd of Deneby in the vill of Deneby so that he died eight days later. Cadel fled at once and is suspected, so *he is to be exacted and outlawed.* He had no chattels. Payne, sergeant of William de Parko, accused of the death, is not suspected, so he is *quit.* The vills of Horseley and Rippeley are in *mercy* for not attending the inquest.

594 Reynold de Wilsford put himself in the church of Horseley, admitted to being a thief and *abjured* the realm. His chattels 6*d.*, for which the sheriff is to answer. The vills of Holebrock, Beaurepeyr and Horselewodehuses are in *mercy* for valuing the chattels falsely. [ref. 836]

595 Robert le Tornur [*struck through*] of Horselewodehuses, William his brother and Robert Godhale killed Stephen son of Geoffrey in the vill of Horseleghwodehuses, fled at once and are suspected. So *they are to be exacted and outlawed.* They had no chattels but were in the frankpledge of the vill of Horsele' which does not have them, so it is in *mercy.*

596 Unknown evil-doers by night killed Dilke le Pipere and Ralph Hayward in the vill of Spondon and fled at once. The first finder has come and is not suspected, so is *quit.* The vills of Spondon, Ockebrook, Staneleye, Chadesdenn and Breydesal are in *mercy* for not attending the inquest.
   [ref. 836]

597 An unknown man was found killed in the park of la Dale with his throat cut, killer unknown. The first finder has come and is not suspected, so is *quit.* No Englishry. Judgment: *murder* on the wapentake. Parva Cestria, Stanesley, Westhalom and Morley are in *mercy* for not attending the inquest.
   [ref. 837]

598 Henry Page and John, former sergeant of Thomas de Codenhovere, meeting in the field of Codenhovere and a dispute arising between them, Henry shot John in the leg with an arrow so that he died four days later. Henry fled at once and is suspected, so *he is to be exacted and outlawed.* Henry had no chattels. Codenhovere, Rippeley and Kydesleye are in *mercy* for not attending the inquest.

[*rot. 6d*]　　　　　Still Morleystan Wapentake　　　　J. de Vaux

599 Ralph Smith of Sippeley wounded John de Waterfal with an arrow in the vill of Maperley, fled at once and is suspected, so *he is to be exacted and outlawed*. His chattels *31s. 4d.*, for which the sheriff is to answer. Robert de Stredleye is in *mercy* because he took the chattels without warrant. Ralph was in the frankpledge of the vill of Schippley which does not have him, so it is in mercy. The vills of Maperley, Kirkehalom, Halom, Smalleye and Ilkesdoun are in *mercy* for valuing the chattels falsely.
　　[ref. 837]

600 James, former man of Geoffrey de Herdeby, killed Ralph, sergeant of Master Thomas de Luc in Mapperley, fled at once and is suspected. So *he is to be exacted and outlawed*. He had no chattels. His frankpledge is unknown because he was a stranger. The vill of Mapperley is in *mercy* for not arresting him.

601 Hugh son of Ralph Reeve of Sandiacre killed Herbert his brother in the vill of Sandiacre, fled at once and is suspected. So *he is to be exacted and outlawed*. His chattels *12d.*, for which the sheriff is to answer. He was not in a frankpledge as he was a clerk. The vills of Sandiacre, Riseley, Bredeston and Stanton are in *mercy* for valuing the chattels falsely.
　　[ref. 838]

602 Richard Frost, servant of Felicity de Sandiacre, going with her from Stanton to Sandiacre, when they had come into the field of Sandiacre, and wishing to lie with her by force, threw her to the ground and because she resisted him, strangled her. He fled at once, was later arrested and released before the justices for gaol delivery, wholly *acquitted* by the country of the death. The country imputed the felony to Robert son of Henry de Eyton who absconded on account of the accusation. The jurors do not suspect him, so *he may return* if he wishes. His chattels are to be confiscated for his flight. His chattels *7s. 6d.*, for which the sheriff is to answer. Because Richard fled before he was arrested, his chattels are also to be confiscated for his flight. His chattels *5s. 5d.*, for which the sheriff is to answer. Sallowe, Hopwell and Okebrok are in *mercy* for valuing the chattels falsely.
　　[ref. 839]

603 William Peny put himself in the church of Wivelesthorp, admitted to being a thief and *abjured* the realm. He had no chattels. The vills of

Sallowe, (Wilne, Henhovere) and Wivelesthorp are in *mercy* for not arresting him.

604 Thomas brother of Simon de Leylondeschire killed Robert son of Robert de Smalley with a knife in a place called Blackwellstock, fled and is suspected. So *he is to be exacted and outlawed.* His chattels *2s.*, for which the sheriff is to answer. He was in the frankpledge of the vill of Smalley which does not have him, so it is in *mercy.* The first finder has come and is not suspected, so he is quit. No Englishry. Judgment: *murder* on the wapentake.
[ref. 840]

605 William de Eyton, William son of Robert Trunket of Salleye, William son of William son of Ralph, Thomas son of Emma la Noreys, Bate le Peskur and William Barun, arrested through an appeal made in the county court by Thomas Harding, who has died, and concerning the death of William his brother, have come, deny the death and all, and for good and ill put themselves on the country. The jurors say they are not guilty of the death, so they are *quit.*

606 In the county court Isabella daughter of Thomas de West Halum appealed Richard de Wappeley of rape and breach of the king's peace. She has not come now, so *she is to be arrested.* Her sureties are in *mercy,* Thomas West and Richard le Rowr, both of West Halum. Richard has now come. So that the king's peace may be maintained, let the truth of the matter be inquired of the country. The jurors say that he is not guilty of the rape and that they have not come to an agreement, so he is *quit.*
[ref. 840]

607 Isabella daughter of Chiche de Westhalum appealed Geoffrey son of Baldewin in the county court of rape and breach of the king's peace. She has now come and prosecutes her appeal. Geoffrey has not come. She was attached by Richard del Wappelode del Bredes and Richard de Trowell in Mapperleg, so they are in *mercy.* Because it was found from the coroner's rolls that Isabella had proceeded against him up to the fourth county court, she is told that, having been allowed to sue at four courts, if she wishes *she may proceed* against him. Afterwards Geoffrey came. Isabella, solemnly summoned by proclamation and forewarned, did not appear to prosecute her appeal, so *she is to be arrested.* Her sureties are in mercy. Their names are to be inquired. Geoffrey, asked how he wished to acquit himself, for good and ill puts himself on the country.

The jurors say that he not guilty, so he is *quit*. Isabella is pardoned by the justices.

[ref. 840]

608 Lecia, daughter of William son of Renner de Lokington living in Spondon, appealed William son of Robert de Cardoil in Spondon in the county court of rape and breach of the king's peace. She has not come nor does she prosecute her appeal, so *she is to be arrested* and her sureties are in *mercy*, Robert de Cardoil of Spondon and John le Blund. William has now come. So that the king's peace may be maintained the truth of the matter is to be inquired of the country. The jurors say that they have not come to an agreement and that William is not guilty, so he is quit.

[ref. 840]

609 Alice daughter of Roger son of Gilbert de Breidesal appeals Gilbert Tute of Spondon of the death of Ralph her brother. Gilbert has come, denies the death and all and for good and ill puts himself on the country. The jurors say that he is not guilty, so he is *quit*. Alice is to be committed to gaol for a false appeal. Afterwards she is pardoned by the justices. William son of Alan de Breydesal, accused of the aforesaid death, has come, denies all and for good and ill puts himself on the country. The jurors say that William is not guilty of that death, so he is *quit,* but they say that a certain William le Messer, formerly hayward of William de Chaddesdenn, is guilty and has now absconded. So *he is to be exacted and outlawed.* He had no chattels. His frankpledge is unknown because he was a stranger from Yorkshire.

610[1] Robert de Lambeley appealed Henry Strolegg in the county court of mayhem and breach of the king's peace. Robert has not come nor does he prosecute his appeal, so *he is to be arrested.* His sureties are in *mercy,* Stephen at Church of Halom and Robert son of Goda of the same. Henry has now come. So that the king's peace may be maintained the truth of the matter is to be inquired of the country. The jurors say that he is not guilty nor have they come to an agreement, so he is quit.

[ref. 840]

---

[1] A long piece has been torn from the left-hand margin with consequent loss of marginations from **610–617**.

611 Cecilia daughter of Richard son of Bate de Bol appealed Robert son of Benne Pachet in the county court of rape and breach of the king's peace. She has not come so, she is to be arrested. Her sureties are in mercy, Geoffrey son of Bate de Bol and William son of Richard de Bole. Robert son of Benne has not come and was not attached because Cecilia had not proceeded against him in the county court as far as etc. The jurors say that he is not guilty, so he is quit.   *suretes amerced 3/4d*
   [ref. 841]

612 Peter son of William Reynbaud of Boneye appealed Richard Chaplain brother of Hugh son of Richard de Notingham in the county court of mayhem and breach of the king's peace. Peter has not come, so he is to be arrested and his sureties for prosecution are in mercy, Peter Reeve of Sandiacre and Geoffrey his brother. Richard Chaplain has not come and was attached by Collard de Breideston and Henry de la Grene of the same, who are in mercy. The jurors say that they have not come to an agreement and that Richard Chaplain is not guilty, so he is quit.
   [ref. 841]

613 Edusa widow of William le Coilliere appealed John son of Richard de Stapelford and Annora his wife in the county court of the death of William her husband. Edusa has not come, so she is to be arrested and her sureties are in mercy, Geoffrey son of Richard de Halom and Henry son of John of the same. John and Annora have not come and were not attached because Edusa had proceeded against them at only two courts. The jurors say that they have not come to an agreement and are not guilty, so they are quit.
   [ref. 841]

614 Concerning warrens, they say that Richard de Grey at Crych, Kirkehalom and Sandiacre, Robert de Stredley jun. at Sippeleg, William de Ros of Hilkeston, the bishop of Chester at Sallowe and Henry de Grey at Codenovere have set up warrens in their lands, it is not known by what warrant. So the sheriff is ordered to cause them to come to show their warrants.
   And [*unfinished*]

615 Ralph Jolyf, arrested for the death of Ralph le Seriant, has come, denies the death and all and for good and ill puts himself on the country. The jurors say on oath that he is not guilty, so he is quit.

616 It is presented that Robert Gaderys of Schadesdene, Richard Hasard of Alrewassele, Ralph Byhoke, William Jordan, John son of William Jordan of Sallowe, Ralph son of Juliana of the same, John Ravenis of Hegge, Robert Attelawe of Peverwick, Geoffrey Dammessone of Hokenhull, and Gilla wife of William de Arderne in Breidaston absconded on account of many larcenies and all are suspected. So all are to be exacted, the men outlawed and Gilla waived. They had no chattels.

617 [*illegible*] ... Ralph de Mungoye and Walter de Rybuf.

[*rot. 7*]   Vaux

THE VILL OF ESSEBURN COMES BY 12 JURORS

618 The jurors present that two unknown thieves came to Esseburn with seven stolen oxen, which they later abandoned, and fled. The vill of Esseburn is in *mercy* for not arresting them. Price of the oxen, which were their chattels, *46s. 8d.*, for which Gervase de Clifton the sheriff is to answer.
    [ref. 842]

619 Robert Torkard put himself in the church of Esseburn, admitted to being a thief and *abjured* the realm. His chattels 25s., for which the sheriff answers for *22s.* and Ralph de Baggepuz, son and heir of Henry de Baggepuz, for *3s.* The vill of Esseburn is in mercy because it did not arrest him. The 12 jurors concealed part of the chattels in their presentment, so are in *mercy*. Robert's frankpledge is not known because he was a stranger.[1]
    [ref. 842]

620 Mabel de Addon fell into the water of Scolebrock[2] in Esseburn and was drowned. Simon son of John Tanner of Esseburn, the first finder, has not come. He is not suspected nor is any other. Judgment: *misadventure*. He was

---

[1] The Ragman inquiry reported that Henry de Bagepuz as coroner took ½ mark to come to the abjuration of Robert Thorcard who had fled to Ashbourne church in the time of the present king, but noted 'nothing of this because he has died' (*Rot. Hun.*, ii. 299a).

[2] In addition to their ecclesiastical duties chantry priests in certain cases followed the profession of schoolmasters. Scolebroke and Scolebridge, applied in certain documents to the Henmore Brook and the bridge across it leading to the school, show that a school existed in connection with the chantry of St Mary. (*DAJ*, xiv. 141).

attached by Robert Alybon and Richard le Tanur, both of Esseburn, who do not have him, so are in *mercy*.
[ref. 842]

621 A certain unknown thief was arrested in the vill of Esseburn by Ralph Sperwater and Adam brother of Alexander, former bailiffs of Esseburn. He was imprisoned and later escaped from their custody. Ralph and Adam are to answer for the *escape*. He had no chattels.
[ref. 842]

622 The jurors present that Roger le Ogghirde, an outlaw, was arrested in Esseburn by Simon de Clifton the king's bailiff and afterwards handed over to the four vills, Hertingdton, Hethcote, Neubinging and Crudecote, to be taken to prison at Notingham. They freely allowed him to escape. So the said vills are to answer for the *escape*. The names of those who took him to prison are to be *inquired*. His frankpledge is unknown because he was a stranger from Staffs. His chattels *105s.*, for which the sheriff is to answer. Simon de Clyfton, the bailiff, took part of the chattels without warrant, so is in *mercy*. Afterwards it was attested that Thomas le Wodeward and Richard son of Thomas, both of Crudecote, Peter de Longenowre, William le Hogghirde and Robert de Tissington escorted Roger and allowed the escape, so they are in *mercy*.
[ref. 843]

623 The jurors present that Richard Gamel of Esseburn, merchant, had a false weight by which he sold wool and other merchandise against the assize. So he is in *mercy*. The sheriff is ordered to cause the aforesaid weight to be brought for smelting down.
[ref. 843]

624 Two men and two women, all unknown, lodged at the house of Robert le Dissere in Esseburn with wax and other merchandise worth 10s. Nicholas de Merchington and Laurence Clerk of Esseburn came upon them and sought pledges that they had come by the merchandise honestly. Since they had no pledges they abandoned the merchandise and fled. Their chattels *10s.*, for which the sheriff is to answer. Because Nicholas and Laurence allowed them to go away thus, *to judgment* on them.
[ref. 844]

625 Concerning the king's exchange, they say that Richard Bralynde, Ralph

Duffeld, Robert Somer and Robert de Burton, merchants, sold their merchandise for old coin after the king had prohibited anyone in the realm of England from buying or selling with such coin. So they are in *mercy*.[1]

626 From Richard son and heir of Henry de Benteley, bailiff, for the escape of John Ploutstou a runaway thief, *£8*. Because John is suspected *he is to be exacted and outlawed*. He had no chattels.

[ref. 844]

627 Robert de Hoby appealed Adam brother of Alexander de Esseburn in the county court of robbery and breach of the king's peace. Adam has not come and was not attached because Robert had proceeded against him at only two courts. So *he is to be arrested*. His sureties are in *mercy*, Peter de Hilton in Esseburn and William son of William Brayn of the same.

[ref. 844]

628 John Hobelay appealed John de Kestewenn in the county court of wounding, mayhem and breach of the king's peace. John de Kestewenn has not come and was not attached because John Hobelay had proceeded against him at only three courts. So *he is to be arrested*. His sureties are in *mercy*, Roger de la Dale of Peverwyk and Nicholas de la Dale in Peverwyk. The jurors attest that John Hobelay absconded and is suspected of many larcenies, so *he is to be exacted and outlawed*. Neither his frankpledge nor his chattels are known because he was a stranger. Because the jurors attest that John de Kestewen wounded John Hobelay against the peace, he is in *mercy*.

[ref. 844]

629 From John son of Hugh le Carpenter of Esseburn, fine for a trespass, *half a mark* by surety of Robert de Tiddeswell and Robert de Ver.

[ref. 844]

---

[1] June 1278. On this day the king commanded the sheriffs of England that counterfeit or clipped money be no longer given. And he sent from his own treasury whole unclipped coin to 10 cities of England that there might be exchange while the new coinage was being made. Later on the 4th day after the kalends of August there was the first exchange of the new coinage, namely of pence and round farthings and the old coinage was still current with the new for the whole of the following year. The old coinage is now generally prohibited. Meanwhile whole halfpence were coined and began to be current on the day on which the old coinage was prohibited. (*Annales Monastici*, iii. 280).

630 Concerning cloth sold against the assize, they say that Richard Coutheved and Andrew de London, both in Esseburn, and Richard son of Gamel sold cloths against the assize, so they are in *mercy*.
[ref. 844]

631 Concerning wines sold against the assize, they say that Thomas de Tiddeswell and Adam son of Alexander de Esseburn sold wines against the assize, so they are in *mercy*.
[ref. 844]

632 Concerning those indicted, they say that Thomas de Duffeld, Emma Black, Henry de Beyleston, Richard son of Richard le Clerk and Roger Hakkesmal absconded and are suspected of many larcenies, so *they are to be exacted and outlawed*: *she is to be exacted and waived*. They had no chattels. Roger Hakkesmal was in the tithing of Robert le Teler who does not have him, so he is in *mercy*. The tithings of the others are not known because they were vagabonds. The jurors attest that Richard son of Richard le Clerck was at some time a lay clerk in the king's chancery and that he stole 30s. from Robert de Thorp of Clifton, so etc.

THE VILL OF BAUKWELL COMES BY 12 JURORS

633 The jurors present that Thomas son of Maud de Baukwell put himself in the church of Baukwell, admitted to being a thief and *abjured* the realm. His chattels 7d., for which G. de Clifton the sheriff is to answer. The vill of Baukwell is in *mercy* because it did not arrest him. The 12 jurors attest that Thomas was harboured as a servant at the house of Hubert de Baukwell, who was afterwards arrested, taken to Notingham and there hanged before William de Meynill and his fellows, justices for gaol delivery. The 12 jurors are in mercy because they concealed this in their presentment. Thomas was not in a tithing because he was a clerk. Chattels of Hubert 3s. 6d., which Robert Buckston received, so the sheriff is ordered to cause him to come etc.
[ref. 845]

634 Hugh son of Avice killed Henry Springald in the vill of Baukwell, was at once arrested and taken to Notingham prison where he was hanged before William de Meynill and his fellows, justices for gaol delivery. So nothing at present of him, nor of his chattels (because the said justices have sent their estreats to the Exchequer.) Mariota wife of Henry, attached because she was present, has come and is not suspected so she is *quit*.

635 Ranulph de Overhaddon by day killed Robert de Cressevill with an axe in Baukwell, fled at once and is suspected. So *he is to be exacted and outlawed*. He had no chattels and was in the frankpledge of Robert son of Ranulph in Overaddon which does not have him, so is in *mercy*. The vill of Baukwell is in *mercy* because this happened by day and it did not arrest him. Afterwards it was attested that he had chattels at Overaddon worth *6d.*, for which for which the sheriff is to answer.
[ref. 845]

636 John de Norton put himself in the church of Baukwell, admitted to being a thief and *abjured* the realm. His chattels *18d.*, for which etc. His frankpledge is not known because he was a stranger. The 12 jurors are in *mercy* for valuing the chattels falsely.
[ref. 846]

[*rot. 7d*]   Still Vill of Baukwell

637 Avice de Calowre put herself in the church of Baukwell, admitted that she had killed Simon son of William de Calton and *abjured* the realm. Her chattels *2s. 4d.*, for which the sheriff is to answer. She was not in a frankpledge, being a woman.
[ref. 846]

638 Robert le Franceys was struck by a horse in Baukwell so that he died instantly. The first finder has come and is not suspected nor is any other. Judgment: *misadventure*. Price of the horse and saddle *40s.*, for which the sheriff is to answer. <deodand> The 12 jurors are in *mercy* for valuing the horse falsely.

639 In the county court Hubert de Lenton appealed John de Hethinton, former bailiff of Baukwell, who has died, and Robert Bissope of Baukwell of burning houses which were in his keeping. Robert Bissope has not come and was not attached because Hubert had proceeded against him at only one court, so *he is to be arrested*. His sureties, Ralph son of Ralph de Moniasse and Robert Ely of Moniasse, are in *mercy*. The jurors say that they have not come to an agreement and that Robert is not guilty. The jurors are in *mercy* because they concealed this appeal.

640   Concerning purprestures, they say that Henry de Langedon, who has died, erected twenty shops on the king's highway in Baukwell, Robert de Revidon one, Matthew Drapel another and John de Shelhadon two, to the detriment of the whole vill. All except Henry, who has died, are in *mercy*. The sheriff is ordered to cause whatever is to the detriment of the vill to be demolished at their costs by view of the jurors.
     [ref. 646]

641   Concerning the selling of cloths made against the assize, they say that Agnes de Blida, Hugh Hering, Reynold le Brun and Robert le Crudere sold cloths made against the assize, so they are in *mercy*.
     [ref. 846]

642   Concerning wines sold against the assize, they say that Ralph Sparwater, William Foleiambe, Robert de Reverdon, Matthew Drabel, Nicholas Clerk, Henry Bertram and Alan de Lenn' sold wines against the assize, so they are in *mercy*.
     [ref. 846]

643   The jurors present that Walter de Cantia, the queen's bailiff at Baukwell, every year on the day of the fair impounds the oxen of merchants coming there until they have paid a ransom to him, so that they should not be taken for the queen's use when the queen has not been accustomed to have, nor ought by law to have, any prise. So he is in *mercy*. <*Kant'*>
     [ref. 846]

644   From John de Hecham, former bailiff of the queen in Baukwell, for escape of Julia la Wallesck, £8.
     [ref. 847]

645   Concerning those indicted, they say that Richard de Chelmardon, Emma his wife, Robert son of Richard de Magna Longesdon, Thomas de Agenhal, William le Carter, Robert le Hirdman, Richard son of Richard and William Hering absconded on suspicion of larceny and are suspected. So all are to be exacted, the men outlawed and the woman waived. <*they are to be exacted and outlawed*>; <*she is to be exacted and waived*> Chattels of Richard de Chelmardon 2d. The same man had a house in fee, whereof year and waste *4s. 6d.* Chattels of Richard son of Richard *12d.* Chattels of William Hering *4d.* The same man had free land whereof year and waste *7s.* for all of which the sheriff is to answer. Thomas de Dakenale and the others had no chattels. Their frankpledges are unknown because they were vagabonds.

[ref. 847]

THE VILL OF CESTREFELD COMES BY 12 JURORS

646 Thomas de Sandiakre put himself in the church of Cestrefeld, admitted to being a thief and *abjured* the realm. His chattels *3s.*, for which etc. His tithing is unknown because he was a stranger. The vill of Cestrefeud is in *mercy* because it did not arrest him. The 12 jurors are in *mercy* for concealing part of the chattels in their presentment.

[ref. 848]

647 Robert de Kynewaldmers wounded John son of Matthew de Cestrefeud in the head with a spade in the fields of Barleburg so that he died at Cestrefeld 30 days later. Robert fled at once and is suspected so *he is to be exacted and outlawed.* His chattels *4d.*, for which the sheriff is to answer. A certain Oliver le Brun absconded on account of the death and is not suspected, nor is any other. So *he may return* if he wishes but his chattels are to be confiscated for the flight. He had no chattels. They were in the frankpledge of John son of the reeve of Barleburg which does not have them now, so is in *mercy.* The 12 jurors are in *mercy* because they did not mention Oliver in their presentment.

[ref. 848]

648 William son of Simon de Brimington killed Geoffrey son of Maria de Cestrefeld in Cestrefeld, fled at once and is suspected, so *he is to be exacted and outlawed.* He had no chattels but was in the tithing of William de Yslep which does not have him now, so is in *mercy.* The vill of Cestrefeld is in *mercy* because it did not arrest him. [ref. 848]

649 Concerning wines sold against the assize, they say that Alan de Lenn', Roger de Saltergate, Geoffrey de Becton, William son of William de Cateclif and Robert de Lenn' sold wines against the assize, so they are in *mercy.*

[ref. 849]

650 Concerning cloths sold against the assize, they say that Simon de Hospicio, Peter de Tappeton and Ralph de Hibernia, all of Cestrefeud, sold cloths against the assize, so they are in *mercy*.
[ref. 849]

651 Concerning purprestures, they say that Henry Clerk of Cestrefeud obstructed a certain lane which used to lead to the water of Hipir, so he is in *mercy*. The sheriff is ordered to cause the aforesaid lane to be freed of obstruction at Henry's costs by view of the jurors.
[ref. 849]

652 Concerning those indicted, they say that Henry son of John le Brune, Alan son of John le Combere and Hugh Horelock absconded on suspicion of larceny and are suspected. So *they are to be exacted and outlawed.* They had no chattels, but Alan and Hugh were in the tithing of Hugh Scutard who does not have them now, so he is in *mercy*. Henry son of John was not in a tithing because he was a clerk.
[ref. 849]

[*rot. 8*]   J. de Vaux

THE BOROUGH OF DERBY COMES BY 12 JURORS

653 Robert de Stratton put himself in the church of All Saints in Derby, admitted to being a thief and *abjured* the realm. His chattels *3s. 5d.*, for which the sheriff is to answer. The 12 jurors are in mercy for concealing part of the chattels in their presentment. The borough of Derby is in *mercy* for valuing the chattels falsely.
[ref. 850]

654 Ralph de Beaurepeyr by day killed John le Mey with an axe in the market place of Derby, fled at once and is suspected. So *he is to be exacted and outlawed.* His chattels *32s.*, for which the sheriff is to answer. Because this happened by day and the borough of Derby did not arrest him, it is in *mercy*. He was in the tithing of Simon Eadel who does not have him now, so it is in *mercy*.
Afterwards it was found from the coroners' rolls that Emma widow of John had appealed Ralph of the death in the county court. Because she had

proceeded against him at only two courts, *she is to be arrested* and her sureties are in *mercy*, Roger de Feri and Clement le Coner of Derby.

[ref. 850]

655   Walter de Oxon' shot Richard de Charleton with an arrow, wounding him in the stomach. Richard died instantly. Walter fled at once and is suspected, so *he is to be exacted and outlawed*. His chattels *36s. 9d.*, for which William de Steynesby is to answer. Walter was in the tithing of Richard de Breidesal who does not have him now, so it is in *mercy*.

[ref. 850]

656   Henry son of Hubert Smith of Stokes put himself in the church of St Alkmund in Derby, admitted to being a thief and *abjured* the realm. His chattels *8d.*, for which the sheriff is to answer. His tithing is unknown because he was a stranger.

[ref. 851]

657   Cecilia daughter of Peter de Leghes put herself in the church of the nuns of Derby,[1] admitted to being a thief and *abjured* the realm. Her chattels *6d.*, for which the sheriff is to answer.

[ref. 851]

658   Roger de Neuton killed Maud widow of Henry de Spondon, fled at once and is suspected, so *he is to be exacted and outlawed*. He had no chattels. He was in the tithing of Roger Dodding who does not have him now, so it is in *mercy*.

[ref. 851]

659   John de Frecheby, accused of the death of William son of Geoffrey, absconded on account of the death and is not suspected because William was killed by misadventure and not by any felonious intent. So *he may return* if he wishes, but his chattels are to be confiscated for the flight. He had no chattels. He was in the tithing of Richard Dedowe who does not have him now, so it is in *mercy*.

[ref. 851]

---

[1] The Benedictine nunnery of King's Mead, Derby, usually styled St Mary de Pratis, was founded *c.* 1160 by the abbot of Darley. The site was later known as Nuns' Green.

660 John de la Alwe of Ovre fell from a boat into the Derwent and was drowned. The first finder has died. No one is suspected. Judgment: *misadventure.* Price of the boat *2s.*, for which the sheriff is to answer. *<deodand>*

661 Alice de Waynflet put herself in the church of St Peter in Derby, admitted to being a thief and *abjured* the realm. Her chattels *9d.*, for which the sheriff is to answer.
    [ref. 852]

662 Hugh son of William de Derby by night killed Simon Baker with a knife in the vill of Derby, fled at once and is suspected. So *he is to be exacted and outlawed.* He had no chattels.

663 John Chubbock killed William son of Robert de Aneston with an axe in the vill of Derby, fled at once and is suspected. So *he is to be exacted and outlawed.* He had no chattels but he was in the tithing of Alan Schoute who does not have him now, so it is in *mercy.* [ref. 852]

664 Henry Horhod struck Ralph de Stannford on the head with an axe so that he died instantly. He fled at once and is suspected, so *he is to be exacted and outlawed.* His chattels *11s. 3d.*, for which the sheriff is to answer. He was in the tithing of Roger Hogelin who does not have him now, so it is in *mercy.*
    [ref. 852]

665 William de Rossington, Thomas his brother and Henry le Hoppere by night burgled the house of Thomas de Warrewyck, carried off his goods and killed him. They fled at once and are suspected, so *they are to be exacted and outlawed.* They had no chattels but were in the tithing of Roger Kaym who does not have them now, so it is in *mercy.*
    [ref. 852]

666 William de Neuport put himself in the church of St Alkmund in Derby, admitted to being a thief and *abjured* the realm. His chattels and frankpledge are unknown because he was a stranger.

667 From G. the sheriff for chattels of Roger Geri of Derby, hanged, *23s. 8d.*, of Roger Trillock, hanged, *6s.*, of William Chiry, fugitive, *40s.* The same William had a certain house in fee, whereof year and waste *half a*

mark and mid time of the house 5*s.*, for which the sheriff is to answer.
   [ref. 853]

668   In the county court Richard son of William Talenar of Neuton appealed Richard Floke of mayhem and breach of the king's peace. Richard son of William has not come, so *he is to be arrested.* His sureties are in *mercy,* William de Neuton and Robert his brother. Richard Floke has come now. So that the king's peace may be maintained, the truth of the matter is to be inquired of the country. The jurors say that he is not guilty, so he is quit.
   [ref. 853]

669   In the county court Hugh son of Richard le Carpenter of Morley appealed Ralph le Taillur of Neuton and Roger his brother of wounding, battery and breach of the king's peace. He has not come, so *he is to be arrested.* His sureties are in *mercy,* Roger de Morley and Nicholas Cuttefys. The aforesaid Ralph and Roger have not come and the jurors say that they are not guilty, so they are *quit.*
   [ref. 854]

670   In the county court Alice widow of Henry de Ulegreve appealed Robert Colle of the death of Margery her daughter. Alice has not come, so *she is to be arrested.* Her sureties are in *mercy,* Michael le Furbur and Simon le Lorimer. Robert has now come and questioned as to how he wishes to acquit himself of the death, denies it and all, and for good and ill puts himself on the 12 jurors of the borough of Derby. They say that he is not guilty of the death, so he is *quit.*
   [ref. 854]

671   Concerning purprestures, they say that Gilbert le Tailleur made an embankment on the king's highway at Baggelane 24 feet long and in breadth at one head 6 feet and at the other 10 feet. They also say that he raised the wall of a house on the king's highway, 4 feet broad at one head, 6 feet broad at the other and 40 feet long. They also say that Robert Tappe raised a wall on the king's highway 16 feet long and 2 feet broad. Also Roger Thagou made a step 2 feet broad and 6 feet long. Also John de Chaddesdenn, who has died, made a step 2 feet long and 6 feet broad to the nuisance of the whole borough and of all passers-by. So all are in *mercy.* The sheriff is ordered to cause whatever is to the nuisance of the borough to be demolished at their costs by view of the jurors.
   [ref. 854]

672   Richard de Capella in le Frith and Alan de Cestrefeld, arrested on suspicion of forging the king's coinage, and John de Bracington, arrested on suspicion of larceny, have come, deny all and for good and ill put themselves on the country. The jurors say that none of them is guilty so all are *quit.*

673   Thomas le Barber, arrested for harbouring Richard de London, William le Marchant, arrested on suspicion of stealing 20 ewes, Maud wife of William Diry, arrested for harbouring Richard de London and John Truchet brother of the said Maud, John Shepherd, John le Glovere, Isabella his wife, Nigel le Moner, Henry Roscel, Hugh Colle with Robert Colle and Maud his wife for harbouring the aforesaid Hugh, arrested on suspicion of larceny, have come, deny all and for good and ill put themselves on the country. The jurors say that none except Hugh Colle is guilty. So all except Hugh are *quit.* And Hugh *is to be hanged.* He had no chattels.

674   Concerning wines sold against the assize, they say that Roger de Cropphil, Henry Dod, John Scoyle, Richard le Taverner, John dc Cestrefeld, Roger son of Simon, William le Oyller and Richard de Ettewell sold wines against the assize, so all are in *mercy.*
     [ref. 855]

675   Concerning those indicted, they say that Henry son of Geoffrey le Somenur, John Truchet, Robert groom of Henry le Tanur, John son of Ralph son of Ranulph, Richard le Taillur of Neuton, William de Kersington, Thomas his brother, Thomas le Oiller and Alexander son of Walter le Machon, absconded on suspicion of larceny and are suspected. So *they are to be exacted and outlawed.* They had no chattels.

[*rot. 9*]   J. de Vaux

PLEAS OF PLAINTS AND TRESPASSES

676   John de Calton chaplain and Ela widow of William de Handesacre, executors of his will, by their attorney bring an action against Gervase de Wilford the sheriff and Milo de Melton, that they on the Saturday next after the quindene of Michaelmas in the king's 8th year [*19 Oct. 1280*], wrongfully took two of William's oxen from their seisin, drove them to Notingham outside this county against the king's statute and detained them there against gage and pledge, wherefore he says they suffer damage and loss to the value of 20s. Thus they bring suit.

Gervase and Milo have come, deny force and injury, saying that, on the day and year which the executors state, William was alive. They seek judgment on John and Ela's allegation that they took the oxen from their seisin on that day when, William being alive, they could not have had administration or seisin of his goods. John and Ela cannot deny this, so it is adjudged that Gervase and Milo are without day and John and Ela are to receive nothing by this action but are to be in *mercy* for a false plaint.

677 It is established by the jury on which Robert Abel, plaintiff, and Geoffrey de Gresele put themselves, that Geoffrey wrongfully detains from Robert a certain mare which by judgment of the county court was to be released to him. His damage was adjudged to be 4s. Judgment: Geoffrey is to cause the mare to be released to Robert, is to satisfy him concerning damages and is to be amerced for wrongful detention.

678 <*Recognizance*> Ralph Ferebraz acknowledges that he owes Henry Chaplain 2½ marks and 20d. of which he will pay him a mark on the Friday next after the third week of Easter this year, and the remainder at Michaelmas next following [*9 May, 29 Sept. 1281*]. If he does not, he grants that the sheriff may cause it to be levied of his lands and chattels.

679 <*Recognizance*> Richard de Stapelford acknowledges that he owes Geoffrey son of Ralph Bugge £20 of silver of which he will pay him at Notingham at the quindene of Michaelmas in the king's 9th year 10 marks, at the quindene of Easter next following 10 marks, and at the quindene of Michaelmas next following 10 marks [*13 Oct. 1281, 27 April, 13 Oct. 1282*]. For this Richard finds these sureties who have jointly appointed themselves principal debtors of the entire amount, namely Robert de Deteck and Richard son of Richard Bugge. If the aforesaid Richard does not do so, then Robert and Richard son of Richard grant that the sheriff may cause it to be levied of their lands and chattels.

680 <*Recognizance*> William de Menil acknowledges that he owes Richard de Kynton 40s. of silver which he will pay him on the Friday in Pentecost week in the king's 9th year [*6 June 1281*]. If he does not, he grants that the sheriff may cause it to be levied of his lands and chattels. Moreover, he finds Henry FitzHerbert and Ralph Montjoye as sureties for payment, who grant that the sheriff may cause it to be levied of their lands and chattels if William defaults.

681 John de Morley complains of Thomas le Gretesmyth of Rydinges, Robert Rosseleyn of Hakenhale, and Bate de la More that he lent £4 10s. to Thomas, viz. 20s. at Pentecost in the king's 8th year, 50s. at Christmas next following and 20s. on Easter eve next following [*9 June, 25 Dec. 1280, 12 April 1281*], which ought to have been paid within the quindene of Easter of the same year [*27 April 1281*]. He also lent to Robert 39s. on the Monday next after the Circumcision in the king's 7th year [*3 Jan. 1279*] which ought to have been paid at Pentecost next following [*21 May 1279*]. He also lent to Bate 37s. which ought to have been paid him at Pentecost in the king's 8th year [*9 June 1280*]. Thomas, Robert and Bate withheld from him the aforeaid debts and still refuse to pay. He says that he has suffered damage and loss to the value of 100s. and thus brings suit.

Thomas, Robert and Bate have come, deny force and injury and readily admit that at some time they did owe to John, but they say that they later paid him, so are by no means obliged to him. Concerning this they put themselves on the country, likewise John. So the sheriff is ordered to cause 12 impartial jurors of the vill of Notingham to come before him in full court by whom the truth can best be known and the inquest is to inform the justices by their letters at *Lincoln* at the octave of Trinity because both the parties put themselves on that inquest. [*5 June 1281*]

ROLLS OF RAGMAN
AND OF QUO WARRANTO
IN THE COUNTY OF DERBY
BEFORE THE JUSTICES IN EYRE
THERE IN THE NINTH YEAR OF THE
REIGN OF KING EDWARD

682 <*Wapentake of High Peak*> It was presented in the Ragman Pleas by the 12 of High Peak that the wapentake is in the king's hand, that its bailiffs hold pleas of *vee de naam* and of fresh force and that they have return of writs. As to return of writs, the sheriff of Derb' says that he himself writes to the bailiff of High Peak when necessary so that the bailiff may make summons and attachments in his bailiwick without mentioning the king's writ in his return. If the bailiff does not make summons or attachment in this way within eight days of the sheriff's order, the sheriff enters the wapentake to distrain the bailiff without the king's order by the writ called *non omittas*. He carries out these actions as formerly he used to do. The bailiff says that in return of a writ of this kind, for the past seven years the sheriffs of Derby used to mention the king's writ and that they were not accustomed to enter the wapentake for distraint of any bailiff unless by the king's writ of *non omittas propter libertatem.*[1]

Because such distraint belongs to the king, a day is given at the *next parliament.*

683 <*High Peak*> It was presented in the Ragman Pleas by the 12 of High Peak that John Daniel claims to have amends of breach of assize of bread and ale at Tyddeswell. John summoned has come and says that he claims that franchise by a charter of the present king's father given at Westminster on 24 February in the 25th year of his reign [*1241*]. By it the king granted to Master Paulinus de Brampton that he and his heirs should have a market

---

[1] The franchises named were held by High Peak wapentake from king to king after William Peverel's time. (*Rot. Hun.*, ii. 288b).

and fair in his manor of Tyddeswell for ever. Because it was found that John is not the heir of Paulinus but rather the assignee, so to judgment. It is to be discussed with the king and his council.[1]

A day was given at Lincoln at the quindene of Trinity. [*22 June 1281*]

684 *<High Peak>* It was established by the jury of High Peak on which Michael de Hartla, guardian of the son and heir of Gilbert Fraunceys, put himself, that Gilbert died seised of amends of breach of assize of bread and ale at Netheraddon in that part of the vill belonging to him. So this action is to stand over until the heir is of *age*. Then the king may have his writ if he wishes.[2]

685 *<High Peak>* Henry de Bykerton, Henry Clerk of Baucwell and Thomas de Ros, former bailiffs of Peak, in *mercy* for trespasses.[3]

---

[1] 30 Jan. 1232. Grant to Paulinus son of John, Joan his wife and their heirs with remainder to her heirs, of the manor of Tideswell which king John gave to Thomas father of Joan whose heir she is, rendering therefor the old farm of 60s., the said manor having rendered £4 owing to an increment imposed upon it. (*Cal.Ch.R. 1226–57*, p. 148).

24 Feb. 1251 (i.e. 35 Hen. III, not 25 Hen. III as in Eyre Roll). Grant to Master Paulinus de Bampton and his heirs of a weekly market on Wednesday at his manor of Tideswell also a yearly fair there on the vigil, feast and morrow of St John the Baptist [23–25 June] (ibid., p. 353).

King John gave Tideswell to Thomas de Lameley for 40s. payable at Peak Castle. It descended to his son Monekinus and from him to his two daughters. One died without heir and Paulinus de Pauntone (Bampton) who married the other, held it. He sold it to Richard Danyel in king Henry's time and after Richard's death it descended to John Danyel his son, who now holds it. (*Rot. Hun.*, ii. 287a).

[2] The Ragman inquiry reported that half of Nether Haddon was held of the king in chief, the heir being a minor in the king's wardship. Service, finding two sergeants in time of war. (*Rot. Hun.*, ii. 287b).

An inquisition of 3 March 1278 found that the lands of Gilbert le Fraunceys in Derbyshire included Haddon manor with hamlets of Rowsley, Baslow and Bubnell held of the earl of Derby by service unknown. Richard the heir, 15 on St Dunstan's day next [19 May], had with his father's consent affianced the daughter of Michael de Hartla and after his father's death married her. A writ of 28 March 1278 to Thomas de Normanville the king's steward commanded him to take the lands of Michael de Hartla into the king's hands and attach him to appear to answer for having caused Gilbert's heir to marry his daughter, to the king's prejudice. (*Cal. Inq. p.m.*, ii. no. 246).

On 17 Aug. 1283 Richard le Fraunceys, aged 21, paid homage and had seisin of his lands in Derbyshire held of Edmund the king's brother in chief of the honor of Tutbury for half a knight's fee (ibid., no. 455).

[3] The trespasses committed by Henry de Bykerton while under-bailiff, along with Richard his brother, were the taking of 35s. from Thomas de Lyndeseye in Alport for concealing theft and with Arnald his fellow, of taking 5s. from Nicholas Pole for concealing theft. The trespasses of Henry Clerk of Bakewell acting with William Hally bailiff of Roger Extraneus keeper of

686 *<High Peak>* It was presented by the 12 of High Peak that Ralph le Wyne encroached on the king's ground in Tadinton and Presteclyve in making a lead mine from which the king was used to receive *le lot minere*, that is, the 13th dish. Ralph has come and readily says that he never made mines in the king's ground and that he and his ancestors had always been used to make mines in his own ground at Monyas. He himself had made no other. Thus he puts himself on the country. The jurors, William Folejambe, Adam de Herthill, Robert de Melvere, Thomas le Raggede, Hugh de Stredeley, Thomas de Langedon, Peter de Rouland, Adam Rounesle, Robert Bozun, Simon de Gousell, Thomas de Gratton and William de Langedon, say on oath that Ralph never encroached on the king's ground at Tatindon and Presteclyve in making a lead mine, but did so only on his own ground at Monyas. So it is adjudged that Ralph is without day and the king is to take nothing from this jury.[1]

687 *<High Peak>* It was presented by the 12 of High Peak that Thomas le Archer took 6s. rent from 2 bovates of land with appurtenances of the forest in Okelawe which used to be paid at Peak Castle. Thomas has come and readily acknowledges the rent. Because the jurors find that he has taken the rent for the past 18 years, the king may therefore recover it along with arrears for that time, namely £5 8s. Thomas is in *mercy*.[2]

688 *<High Peak>* The king by his attorneys Gilbert de Thornton and William de Beverlaco presented himself against Geoffrey de Pickeford in a plea as to the warranty by which Geoffrey holds the vill of Selmidon which is a member of the manor of Esseford and 18 marks rent which he received

---

Peak Castle, concerned the taking of 2 marks from Adam Baskin a felon, for his escape from the country; also with Hally of taking 1 mark and 10 marks from Nicholas de Padley and his sons of Eyam in a case between Ralph de Calver and Nicholas de Padley (see **416**).

As bailiff he also took money to remove recognitors from assizes (*Rot. Hun.*, ii. 289a). He also took from John de Nedham while in prison 1 acre of meadow worth 40s. to aid his release (ibid., i. 60b). Thomas de Ros was reported as having taken money for removing recognitors from assizes (ibid., ii. 289a).

[1] The Ragman inquiry stated that there was a moor in Taddington from which 'le lot Minere' used to be paid to king Henry the king's father, but that it was withdrawn from the time Ralph Bugge was bailiff until now. Warrant unknown. Note added: Explained as appears in the pleas. (*Rot. Hun.*, ii. 288b).

[2] The Ragman inquiry stated that Robert le Archer gave 2 bovates of his forest land held of the king in Hucklow to his daughter Alota. After his death she exchanged them with her brother Thomas le Archer but he paid nothing to the king. Note added: The matter is explained as appears in the pleas. (*Rot Hun.*, ii. 288a).

from the mills of Esseford, which used to be held of king Henry father of the king by Griffin son of Wenunwen who gave the vill to Geoffrey, as the jurors of High Peak present.[1]

Geoffrey has not come. He was attached by Geoffrey Reeve and William le Mercer both of Esseburn. So the sheriff is ordered to distrain him by all his lands and chattels and to have him in person at *Lincoln* at the quindene of Trinity [*22 June 1281*].

689 <*Lytelchirch : Morleyston*> It was presented by the 12 of Lytelchirch and Morleyston that Hugh de Gurney, while king's bailiff, made many extortions in his bailiwick. Hugh has now come and made fine by *40s.* for his trespass, by surety of Michael de Breydeston and Henry Clerk of Chaddesden.[2]

690 <*High Peak*> William Hally, former bailiff of High Peak, made *fine by 100s.* for certain trespasses charged to him before judgment, by surety of Hugh de Stratleye, Robert Bozun and Thomas le Ragged.[3]

---

[1] King John gave his daughter Joan in marriage to Llewellyn younger son of Wenunwen. Griffin was the elder son. The king 'bought over' Wenunwen by grants over England including the manor of Ashford (grant of 6 April 1200). On Wenunwen's death Henry III instructed the constable of the Peak that the widow Margaret, daughter of Lord Rhys ap Tudor, was entitled to a third of the manor as dower and Griffin seems to have had no difficulty in asserting his right to the whole manor. On Griffin's death Henry bestowed the manor of Ashford on Eleanor wife of his eldest son Edward afterwards Edward I. (Cox, *Derbyshire Churches*, ii. 47–8).

8 April 1281. Confirmation of charter whereby Queen Eleanor gave to Geoffrey de Pichford kt. of her household and Alice his wife, the manor of Dreyton (Sussex) to be held etc. For this gift Geoffrey has given all the land which he had in Ashford and Sheldon (Derbys.). (*Cal.Ch.R. 1257–1300*, p. 261).

[2] The Ragman inquiry stated that when he was bailiff of Hugh de Babinton he took half a mark from William son of Gilbert de Chaddesden for having aid and also took 40s. from Henry de Chaddesden and William his brother who burned the house of William son of Peter. Acting with Hugh de Babinton he took from various people large sums, making approvers appeal honest and innocent persons. (*Rot. Hun.*, i. 58b). When bailiff of Litchurch he took from John Horsekanne of Mackworth 40s. for not arresting his son Henry convicted of larceny (ibid., 59a).

[3] See note to **685** for trespasses committed along with Henry Clerk of Bakewell. He also, when bailiff, allowed his brother John guilty of homicide to go in peace and also took half a mark from Henry de Kersinton for concealing theft (*Rot. Hun.*, ii. 289a). He also took 20s. from Bowden because it did not attend where he summoned in a place where they had not been wont to attend (ibid., 289b).

[*rot. 10d*]   Still Pleas of Ragman for County Derby   J. de Vaux

691 <*High Peak*> Thomas Foleiambe made fine by *40s.* for many trespasses charged to him, by surety of William Foleiambe and Thomas de Gratton.[1] It is received.

692 Roger Asser in *mercy* for many trespasses.[2]

693 <*High Peak*> It was presented in the Ragman Pleas that Roger le Estrange by Richard le Ragged his bailiff took £6 3s. 4d. from Henry de Bucston for concealment of treasure found at Wyneshull.[3] The sheriff attests that he has no lands or tenements in his bailiwick by which he may be distrained, but that he has lands and tenements in Bedfordshire, so the sheriff of *Beds.* is ordered to cause Roger to come to *Lincoln* at the quindene of Trinity [*22 June 1281*].

694 <*High Peak*> It was presented by the 12 of High Peak that Richard de Puelasdon, when a bailiff in the county of Derby, made many illegal extortions and exactions from various people in his bailiwick.[4] The sheriff attests that he has no land or tenements in his bailiwick by which he may be

---

[1] He took from Michael de Hathersage a mark for concealing his felony; also half a mark from Nicholas Pole for concealing theft (ibid., ii. 289a). He took from Monyash 40s. because they did not arrest Ranulph de Overhaddon after he wounded Robert Cressevyle, no hue having been raised; he also took 20s. from Bowden because they did not come before him in the place where they were summoned where they were not wont to come; he also took 2 marks from Overhaddon for not keeping Ranulph as above (ibid., 289b). He took from Edensor and Baslow 8s. for default before the coroner; also as bailiff of Roger Estrange once went to Hubert Tarun's house in Bakewell, defamed and attached him for larceny by his goods there and took him to Nottingham jail where he was hanged; he also found a certain Ranulph and his groom, beheaded the groom and Ranulph and others of the same society fled the country (ibid., 290a). Robert de Lyndop, receiver of the society, was attached and imprisoned. He paid 2½ marks fine to Thomas Foljambe to remain in the country, He also took 4s. for licence to bury the corpse of Brun in Hathersage. Noted: Nothing concerning the beheading as it pertains to the Crown and nothing concerning Thomas because he has made fine as shown in the pleas (ibid., 290b).

[2] When custodian of Peak Castle he maliciously troubled the poor men of Castleton, extorting half a mark on no authority but his own will (ibid., ii. 289b).

[3] Noted that Roger, who was to be distrained in Beds., had been given a day in Parliament and that Richard le Ragged his bailiff had died (ibid., ii. 289b).

[4] He took 20s. from Bowden because he forbade carriage of the goods of Richard le Ragged to Peak Castle; he also took 8 oxen, 7 sheep, 18 cows and 20 bullocks, 21 quarters of oats, 2 quarters of rye, one mazer cup and 5 marks from Philota de Kinder for having her goods in peace (ibid., ii. 289b).

distrained, but that he has lands and tenements in Staffordshire, so the sheriff of *Staffs.* is ordered to cause him to come to *Lincoln* at the quindene of Trinity [*22 June 1281*].

695 <*High Peak*> It was presented by the 12 of High Peak that Richard de Morleye and Joan his wife hold 2 bovates of land in Tatindon and Presteclyve which Michael de Ockele formerly used to hold of the king, paying 10s. yearly. This was withdrawn nine years ago.

Richard and Joan have come and readily acknowledge that they hold that land of the king, nor can they deny the arrears. So it is adjudged that the king is to recover the rent as well as the arrears, namely *£4 10s.* Richard and Joan are in *mercy.*[1]

696 <*Apeltre*> Henry Ouweyn, former bailiff of Lord Edmund the king's brother in the county of Derby, made fine by *5 marks* for certain trespasses charged to him in the Ragman inquests by the 12 of Apeltre and elsewhere in the same county, by surety of Ralph de Burgh and Robert Champion.[2]

---

[1] The Ragman inquiry stated that Michael de Hockeleye holds the entire land that was William de Horsindene's in Peak and the land of Henry de Calvore in Taddington and Priestcliffe and one forest that was Ranulph Talebot's in Hope, escheat to the king and that he renders 6 barbed arrows and has it of the gift of king Edward. The jurors and Thomas de Leukenovere, inquisitor for the king, attest that Richard de Morley and Joan, widow of Michael, hold the land in Taddington and Priestcliffe of the king. (*Rot. Hun.*, ii. 287b).

[2] As former bailiff of Appletree in king Henry's time he released the oxen of Henry Fitzherbert by order of the king, took them a second time and would not release them until Henry had made security to him that he would not implead him at London or elsewhere for them (ibid., ii. 292a). He ejected Thomas Morel from his free tenement and carried off 24 thraves of oats. Thomas later recovered seisin but Henry Oweyn kept the grain. Noted that he had made fine. He also took 100s. from the executors of Hawise de Bradel' appealed for the death of Eytropus de Osmundeston by Aline his wife. Hawise was released by the inquest but he did not allow her ingress to her lands and chattels, demanding 40 marks and took 100s. for ingress though she had the king's writ. She later died and Henry levied 100s. from her executors (ibid., 292b). He also took John Gelyn and imputed larceny to him because he had recovered seisin of 1 acre by writ of novel disseisin at Derby from Ralph son of William de Rossinton (tenant of Roger de Wardinton who acted with Henry Oweyn) and stole four thraves of corn from his barn. He also took 40s. from John Trucock who stole grain from the prior of Trentham's barn at Sutton, was arrested with it and was released because of the payment. He also took 20s. from Stephen Miller for handing over Thomas de Burton who stole Stephen's cloths, was arrested with them and released because of the payment. He also arrested Robert, parson of Boyleston, imprisoned him in Tutbury Castle, did not allow him to thresh his grain and kept him in prison until he paid 40s. He also arrested Robert le Parker and Robert de Brailsford, imputed larceny to them (by Wiliam Saveney an approver in prison), kept them in Tutbury Castle and when they came before the approver he did not know them and Henry Oweyn took a mark from them for heir release. He also took a mark from Richard de Aula

697 *<High Peak>* James de Pockelington, former clerk of Hugh de Babington, sheriff of Notingham and Derby, made fine by *a mark* for certain petty trespasses charged to him, by surety of Hugh de Babington.[1]

698 Hugh de Babington, former sheriff of Notingham and Derby, made fine by *2 marks* for certain trespasses charged to him in the aforesaid counties, by surety of Thomas de Babington.[2]

699 *<Scarvedale>* It was presented in the Ragman Pleas by the 12 jurors of Scarvedale that Ralph de Reresby held the manor of Pleseley with its appurtenances of king Henry father of the king in chief by service of a knight's fee as of the honor of Tykehull. Now the manor is in the hands of Master Thomas Beck, bishop of St David's, by the alienation of Robert de Wyleby, to whom Ralph demised it. So the bishop is to come to Lincoln at the quindene of Trinity [*22 June 1281*]. Meanwhile there is to be discussion with the king. The bishop is also to answer as to whether he claims warren in the aforesaid manor.[3]

700 *<Scarvedale>* Peter de Rolaund and John de Wodehusses, former

---

because he refused to take his sons to prison at Tutbury Castle for a fight between them and John son of Nicholas le Chaloner (ibid., 293a). As bailiff of lord Edmund in Ashbourne he released Thomas de Gouleswick arrested and imprisoned, for 40s. in king Henry's time (ibid., 298a).

[1] As sheriff's clerk he took 5 marks from Chellaston and 7s. 4½d. from the total for the Exchequer unaccounted for (ibid., 290a). With the sheriff Hugh de Babinton he amerced John and Robert de Sutton and Philip de St Quentin in Appletree and took 2s. from each. Noted that Babinton and his clerk had made fine (ibid.. 292b). He also amerced four burgesses of Derby 4s. each, William Chiry, Henry de Mackworth, William Bernard and Henry son of Adelyne (ibid., 295b). He also levied 18d. on the sale of 18 oxen belonging to the king's farm of the burgh of Derby and extorted 20s. from the bailiff of Derby at the feast of St James in the king's 1st year (25 July 1273). He extorted from Agnes de Croftes in Derby 2 marks for letting her out on bail and took £10 from Wirksworth for allowing felons in prison to go free (ibid., 296a).

[2] As sheriff he took 40s. from William son of Gilbert de Chaddesden a felon for his release, from John le Turner of Crowdicote a felon, 5 marks for his escape and from Ralph de Kylburn 20s. for discharge from prison (*Rot. Hun.*, i. 58b). He also took 2s. each from John and Robert de Sutton and Philip de St Quentin along with his clerk (ibid., ii. 292b). He also took half a mark from Nether Haddon without warrant for default before the coroner (ibid., ii. 290a). Also with Hugh de Gurney he took money from various people for making approvers in prison appeal innocent persons (ibid., i. 58b). He also took 40 marks from Robert rector of Boyleston church and Nicholas son of Roger de Kersinton for replevy as well as from many others for respite of imprisonment (ibid., 59a).

[3] The Ragman inquest stated that Robert de Wyleby had appropriated to himself warren in Pleasley (ibid., 60a).

clerks of Henry de Bakepuz, and William, former clerk of Robert de Herthull the coroner, in *mercy* for petty trespasses committed in the office of coroner.[1]

701 Andrew de Alvaston in *mercy* for a petty trespass. Nothing here because he has made fine.

702 Nicholas le Breton in mercy for a serious trespass.[2]

703 <*Scarvedale : Cestrefeld*> Walter de Reppinghale, former bailiff of Scarvesdale, made fine by *2½ marks* for himself and John le Tollere his sub-bailiff for trespasses charged to him. It is received by surety of Geoffrey de Beton and William de Steynnesby.

704 <*Scarvedale*> Geoffrey de Beton made fine by *half a mark* for a trespass by surety of Walter de Reppinghale. It is received.

705 <*Repindon*> It was presented in the Ragman Pleas by the 12 of Repindon that the lords of Repindon have gallows and amends of breach of assize of bread and ale, from what time and by what warrant they do not know. They found that Lord Edmund the king's brother holds a fourth part of the said manor through the Ferrars inheritance in purparty with Devorgilla de Balliol, Robert de Brus and his other parceners, who hold the remainder. They say that John de Hastinges, son and heir of Henry de Hastinges, is one

---

[1] The Ragman inquest stated that all coroners took gifts and money. The clerks said they knew nothing of it (*Rot. Hun.*, ii. 290b). Of Henry de Bagepuz who was dead by 1281, trespasses reported included 2s. taken from Shirley for view of Robert Cook, killed; 2s. from the widow of Eytropus de Osmundeston for view of her husband; 4s. and a cow from Julia Fulford for view of William de Novo Castro killed at her house by thieves; 2s. from Snelston for view of Thomas Gill, drowned; 5s. from Sedsall and Eaton for view of Hugh Spandi, killed; 2s. from Etwall for view of Robert de Etewall, killed; half a mark from Trusley for view of boy drowned; and half a mark from Doveridge for Agnes who fled to the church there; all in the time of king Henry (ibid., 293b). He also took half a mark to come to the abjuration of Robert Torkard who fled to Ashbourne church (ibid., 299a). Of the clerks of Robert de Herthull only two specific trespasses were reported: 8s. taken from Baslow for the death of Ralph Rafur and half a mark from 4 vills near *Jactisworth* for the same (ibid., 290b). Robert de Herthull also took 2s. from Henry de Kersinton for concealing his larceny (ibid., 289a).

[2] Nicholas le Breton is probably Nicholas de Sussex, escheator, accused of extorting £8 from Derby seven years before (*c.* 1267) (ibid., 296a) and of making waste and destruction to the amount of £13 in the woods of Horston while sub-escheator in the time of king Henry (*Rot. Hun.*, i. 58b).

of the heirs of that inheritance, is under *age* and in the king's wardship.[1]

706 *<Repindon>* Milo de Melton, bailiff of Repindon, made fine by *half a mark* for certain petty trespasses by surety of William de Harteshorn.[2]

707 *<Repindon>* It was presented by the 12 of Repindon that, from the 30th year of king Henry father of the king [*1245–6*], the prior of Repindon has 3 virgates of land with appurtenances in Hertishorn and half of the park called Denewellehay, of the gift of Richard Bertram, who held that land and park of Theobald de Verdun and Theobald of Earl Ferrars, who held of the king in chief. It was presented that the same prior, from the 44th year of king Henry [*1259–60*], holds a sixteenth part of the manor of Repindon which Robert de Tateshal, father of the present Robert, held of king Henry in chief of the gift and feoffment of the aforesaid Robert.[3]

So a day was given the prior at *Lincoln* at the quindene of Trinity. Meanwhile there is to be *discussion with the king.*

708 *<Lutchirch>* It was presented in the Ragman Pleas by the 12 of Lutchirch that Robert de Dethek holds 13 bovates of land with appurtenances in Lutelchirch which Peter de Sandiacre held in chief of king John, the present king's grandfather. Robert has come and says that Peter de Sandiacre held the castle of Hareston from the ancestors of Baldewin Wake and that king John exchanged the 13 bovates in Lutchirch with Peter for the castle, so Peter and his heirs were then holding the said tenements from the ancestors of Baldewin in allowance for the demands and services which they had received for the castle.[4] So there is to be *discussion with the king* and

---

[1] After his defeat in 1266 at Chesterfield the earldom and possessions of Robert de Ferrars III passed to the house of Lancaster. On 26 Feb. 1281 custody of the lands of John de Hastings, a minor in the king's custody, and his castle of Abergavenny were given to William de Valence the king's uncle. (*Cal.Pat.R. 1272–81*, p. 426).

[2] As former bailiff he took from Drakelow for his own use 40s. from the amercements of the eyre of the Abbot of Peterborough and his fellows at Derby (1258), and from the eyre of John de Preston (1269) 2½ marks. (*Rot. Hun.*, i. 59b).

[3] The Ragman inquest stated that Robert de Tateshal had held from 50 Hen. III (ibid.).

[4] The Ragman inquest stated that Chelmorton was in king John's hand and he exchanged it with Peter de Sandiacre for Horeston Castle and Horsley which were in king Edward's hand (*Rot. Hun.*, ii. 287a). It was also stated that the king's ancestors formerly had in Litchurch 2 carucates for geld and 9 villeins who had 2 carucates and 12 acres of meadow until the time of king John who exchanged that vill for the manor of Horsley and its sokes with Peter de Sandiacre, value 100s. After Peter's death his son and heir Richard held the vill and sold it in

Baldewin Wake.

A day was given at Lincoln at the octave of St John Baptist [*1 July 1281*].

[*rot. 11*]   Still Pleas of Ragman for the County of Derby   J. de Vaux

709 <*High Peak*> It was presented by the jurors of High Peak that Simon de Gousel and Oliver de Langeford have free chase in their lands at Haversegge. Simon and Oliver have come and say that they claim free chase in Haversegge from time out of mind. Moreover Oliver says that king Henry father of the present king granted to Matthew de Haversegge, his ancestor whose heir he is, that he and his heirs should have free warren in all his demesne lands there and elsewhere in the county of Derby. He proffers his charter attesting this.[1] William de Beverlaco for the king seeks judgment, since inasmuch as free chase is a more important franchise than free warren, in accepting the charter concerning warren, Oliver had tacitly renounced the right which he had in chase, and since Simon claims to have the franchise from the enfeoffment of Maud his mother, who was the sister and one of the heirs of Matthew, so *to judgment.*

A day was given them for a hearing at Lincoln at the quindene of Trinity [*22 June 1281*].

[ref. A57]

710 <*Cestrefeld*> It was presented by the 12 of Cestrefeld that Richard de Bingham holds the vill of Boythorp which William Brewer held in chief of king John grandfather of the king. Richard has come and says that he need not answer the king because there are four moieties between the king and himself, from which it seems to him that since he has entry into the land through the third moiety, no injury should be charged to him.

William de Beverlaco for the king says that even if there are many moieties and Richard enters through the last one, yet nevertheless the king loses wardship and escheat from the demesne. Thus he seeks *judgment* for

portions viz. to William de Dicheforde 3 bovates which his heirs now hold, to John de Henovere 13 bovates which Geoffrey de Dethek now holds except for 15 acres of land and 3 acres of meadow and 3 acres of pasture which the abbot of Darley now holds. Warrant unknown. (ibid., 294b; *DAJ*, x. 19).

[1] The grant of free warren was by a charter to Matthew de Hathersage of 25 Oct. 1249 (*Cal.Ch. R. 1226–57*, 345).

the king.

A day was given at Lincoln at the quindene of Trinity. [*22 June 1281*]

711 *<Lutchirche>* Walter de Stirthesleye, former sheriff of Derby, in *mercy* for a petty trespass.[1]

712 *<Scarvedale>* It was presented by the 12 of Scarvedale that the abbot of Beauchief holds the vill of Haneley which Ralph Musard held in chief of king John grandfather of the king.[2]

The abbot has come and shows a charter of Ralph Musard which attests that he gave the vill of Haneleye with appurtenances to God and the Blessed Mary and to the church of St Thomas the Martyr of Beauchief and the canons there serving God, with his body, in free, pure and perpetual alms, along with the men in the aforesaid vill, saving to himself the services of Richard son of Herbert de Haneleye, Alexander Berkun, Ingelram and William Parker with their land. Gilbert de Thornton for the king seeks judgment as to whether the charter in itself should be valid without the king's confirmation or that of his ancestors.

A day was given him at Lincoln at the quindene of Trinity [*22 June 1281*] and meanwhile there is to be *discussion with the king*.

713 *<Lutchirche>* All matters concerning Edmund the king's brother in the Ragman Pleas in the county of Derby are adjourned until the octave of St John the Baptist at Lincoln [*1 July 1281*]. Then Edmund is to come and show his charters. The same day was given him by his attorney concerning his franchises in the county of Notingham and concerning the Honour of Lancaster.

714 *<Lutchirche>* It was presented that the abbot of Cestre has a market and fair at his manor of Aston, view of frankpledge of his own men there, gallows in the same manor with its members and he pleads suits where blood is shed and the hue raised, unless concerned with homicide or mayhem.

---

[1] The Ragman inquest reported his taking money from many men for respite of imprisonment (*Rot. Hun.*, i. 59a).

[2] 1 July 1230. Order to the sheriff of Notingham that not withstanding the king's command that the lands which were Ralph Musard's be taken into the king's hands, the abbot of Beauchief is permitted to hold in peace the land which Ralph in his lifetime gave to the abbot in Wadshelf and Handley with the goods and chattels of the abbot in that land. (*Close R. 1227–37*, 357).

The abbot has come and as to the market, fair and assize of bread and ale, shows a charter of king Henry the king's father which he proffers attesting this. So as for this, he is without day at present. As for view of frankpledge and hearing of plaints where blood is shed, the hue raised and prosecuted, he says that king John grandfather of the present king, by his charter granted to the abbey of St Werburg of Cestre and the monks there serving God that they and all their men of the soke of Weston in Derbyshire should be quit of view of frankpledge and that the abbot and monks should have their charter free of all pleas and plaints which pertain to the sheriff, arising in their lands in the aforeaid soke.[1]

Gilbert de Thornton for the king says that plaints arising where blood is shed, the hue raised and prosecuted, belong purely to the king and he seeks *judgment* for him.

A day was given at *Lincoln* for hearing him at the octave of St John the Baptist. [*1 July 1281*]

[*rot. 11d*]   Still Pleas of Ragman for the County of Derby

715 <*Wyrkeswrth*> It was presented by the 12 of Wirkeswrth that Robert de Akovere made an encroachment of half an acre on the present king in the vill of Akovere. Robert has come and says that elsewhere it was found by inquest before Thomas de Normanville, the king's steward, that the ground was Robert's own. Concerning this he puts himself on Thomas's record.[2]

A day was given him at Lincoln at the quindene of St John the Baptist and meanwhile the record is to be followed up [*8 July 1281*].

716 <*Wirkeswrth*> It was presented in the Ragman Pleas by the 12 of

---

[1] 15 Sept. 1257. The king has granted to the abbot and convent of St Werburg a weekly market on Tuesday at Aston in their manor of Weston and a yearly fair there on the vigil, feast and morrow of St Peter's Chains (31 July–2 Aug.) (*Cal.Ch.R. 1226–57*, 473).

11 Jan. 1215. Grant by king John that the momks of Chester and their men of the soke of Weston shall be free of suits to county and hundreds and to ridings and wapentakes and from view of frankpledge and from aids, mercies and all demands, pleas and complaints pertaining to the sheriff or his bailliffs and from carriage and from all works in castles, fishponds, stanks, walls, bridges, roads, parks and all other enclosures and that they shall have their free court for all pleas etc. arising in their land which belong to the sheriff with soke and sake etc. and that none shall trouble them in these matters on pain of forfeiting £10. (*Cartulary of Chester Abbey Pt. I* (Chetham Soc. lxxix), 142).

[2] The purpresture was at Bredlowe two years before (*c.* 1273). (*Rot. Hun.*, i. 59a).

Wirkeswrth that the abbot of Cumbermere, the abbot of Derleye and many others, religious and lay, were feoffees of earl de Ferrars and his ancestors in the county of Derby which the earl held in chief of king Henry. Because the lands and tenements of earl de Ferrars came by forfeiture into the hands of king Henry who enfeoffed his son lord Edmund of them, the justices have therefore stayed proceedings.[1] There is to be *discussion with the king.*

717 <*Wirkeswrth*> Simon de Clyfton, former bailiff of Wirkeswrth, in mercy because he took a certain ox for exercising his office. He is amerced at *40s.*

718 Robert Waldeshef and Clement de Stanford, former bailiffs of lord Edmund, in *mercy* for many trespasses. Amercement aggravated concerning Robert Waldeshef who took 26s. from Matthew de Knyveton for having respite from taking arms.

719 <*Wirkeswrth*> Roger de Wardington, former bailiff of lord Edmund, made fine by *5 marks* for trespasses charged to him before the inquest. It is accepted by surety of Robert de Akovere and William de Menill.[2]

720 In the county of Derby Edmund the king's brother has the wapentake of Wirkeswrth, the hundred of Apeltre, the hundred of Greseley, half the wapentake of Repindon and a quarter of the other half, namely five of the eight parts and also almost half the wapentake of Lutilchirche. The other half of the wapentake of Repindon is in the hands of the heirs of Cestre. So there remain in the king's hands the wapentake of High Peak, the wapentake of Morleyston and half the wapentake of Lutilchirche.[3]

---

[1] 17 Aug. 1285. Inspeximus and confirmation of charter whereby king Henry gave to Edmund his son the castles and lands late of Robert de Ferrars late earl of Derby. King Henry's charter was dated 28 June 50 Hen. 1266 (*Cal.Ch.R. 1257–1300*, 321).

[2] The Ragman inquest stated that as bailiff of lord Edmund in Wirksworth he had taken half a mark from both Richard Priket of Ashbourne and Henry de Tideswell in king Henry's time and still took. (*Rot. Hun.*, ii. 298b).

[3] 10 Nov. 1279. Gift to Edmund earl of Lancaster the king's brother for his homage and service of the manors of Wirksworth and Ashbourne and of the wapentake of Wirksworth to be held by Edmund and his heirs with all appurtenances in exchange for the counties and castles of Carmarthen and Cardigan and the lands which Edmund had there and which he has quitclaimed to the king; to be held by performing for the said manors and wapentake the service of two knight's fees, provided that if any shall deraign the said manors and wapentake against the said Edmund or his heirs or against the king or his heirs according to the law or custom of

721 *<Scarvesdale>* It was presented in the Ragman Pleas that Margery widow of Ralph de Reresby appropriated warren at Essovere.

Margery has come and says that she does not claim warren there. It is found that she did not appropriate warren in Essovere after the death of Ralph her husband. The sheriff is ordered not to allow her to use warren in that vill henceforth.

722 *<Scarvesdale>* It was presented in the Ragman Pleas by the 12 of Scarvesdale that the abbot of Wellebek holds the vill of Neubaud, which is a member of the manor of Cestrefeld, which William Bruere held in chief of the father of the present king.[1]

The abbot by his attorney has come and shows his feoffment but does not show the king's confirmation. So a day was given him at *Lincoln* at the octave of St John the Baptist [*1 July 1281*]. Meanwhile there is to be *discussion with the king.*

723 A day was given the king and the dean and chapter of Lincoln concerning the advowson of the church of Derlegh in the Peak at Lincoln at the quindene of Trinity [*22 June 1281*].[2]

[ref. 371]

724 *<Apeltre>* It was presented by the 12 of Apeltre that William de Boyvill, the king's escheator, and Roger Duredent under him, seized the manor of Langeford which they held of the bishop of Cestre by reason of the death of Nigel de Langeford who had held of the king in chief. They levied

England or shall in any other way oblige the king to restore those lands, Edmund and his heirs shall not be disseised until the king have made them a reasonable exchange. (*Cal.Ch.R. 1257–1300*, 215). The Ragman inquest stated that Wirksworth with Ashbourne used to render in king John's time £80 and were now worth £260; pleas and perquisites in Appletree were worth £10, sheriff's aid £9 8s. 8d. with a palfrey worth 40s.; the hundred of Gresley was worth 100s.; Repton was worth 40s., the sheriff's palfrey 40s.; Litchurch and Morleyston used to render 10 marks per year, now 14 marks over and above 8 marks at Michaelmas and £7 0s. 6½d. sheriff's aid. (*Rot. Hun.*, ii. 288a).

[1] 4 Apr. 1230. Grant to William Basset of the gift which William Briwer son of William Briwer made to him and his heirs of the holdings and men in Neubold and Berlegh with all that goes with the said men and of 65 acres in Chesterfield. (*Cal.Ch. R. 1226–57*, 116).

[2] Easter 13 Edw. I (1285). The king claims against the dean and chapter of Lincoln advowson of the church of Darley of the seisin of king Henry senior (i.e. Henry II). They say it does not seem to them that they ought to reply to the king concerning the seisin of his ancestor so long ago and thus they reply and so to the country. (*Abbreviatio Placitorum: Coram Rege*, Easter rot. 3).

100s. from the issues of the manor from Ascension in the 2nd year of the present king [*10 May 1274*].

Roger Duredent, charged with this, says that he never took nor levied that money, but he says that William de Boyvill his master took the money. On this he puts himself on the country.

Afterwards indeed, Roger made fine by *a mark* which is received by surety of Robert de Akovere and Stephen de Irton. The sheriff of *Leycestre* is ordered to cause William de Boyville to come to *Lincoln* at the quindene of Trinity to answer the king for the aforesaid 100s.

725 <*High Peak*> It was presented in the Ragman Pleas by the 12 of High Peak that William Gernun has warren in his manor of Baukwelle which by demise of William's ancestors is in the hands of the queen, the king's consort, as a life interest. Because it is not known whether the queen wishes to claim life interest or fee in the manor, so nothing at present.

[*rot. 12*]   Still Pleas of Ragman for the County of Derby

726 <*Morleyston*> It was presented in the Ragman Pleas by the 12 of Morleyston that William son of Thomas Bardolf holds half the vill of Ockebrok which William Bardolf held in chief of the father of the present king for half a knight's fee, by what warrant is unknown.[1] A day was given him at *Lincoln* at the octave of St John the Baptist [*1 July*] and meanwhile there is to be *discussion with the king*.

727 <*Morleyston*> It was presented by the 12 of Morleyston that the manor of Maperle, which Master Thomas de Luda holds, has gallows and amends of the assize of bread and ale and that he claims warren there, by what warrant is unknown.[2] So a day was given him up to the next *parliament*.

---

[1] In 49 Hen. III (1264–5) Thomas Bardolf's land in Ockbrook was seized by the king (*Cal. Misc. Inq.*, i. 195). The Ragman inquest stated that suit at county and wapentake for the Ockbrook fee was withdrawn by Thomas Bardolf in king Henry's time. (*Rot. Hun.*, i. 58a).

[2] William de Louth was Keeper of the Wardrobe from Nov. 1280 until Nov. 1290, Walter de Langton acting for him in that office from May 1290. He was consecrated bishop of Ely in Oct. 1290 and died in March 1298. He served for 16 years in the Wardrobe, service there under Thomas Bek who was later bishop of St Davids preceding his own term at the Wardrobe. (Tout, *Chapters in Med. Admin. History*, ii. 14–16).

728 <*Morleyston*> William de Alta Ripa, former constable of Donington, and Geoffrey de Herdeby, former bailiff in the county of Derby, are in *mercy* for many and various extortions and trespasses charged to them by the 12 of Morleyston.

729 <*Morleyston*> Andrew de Alvaston, former bailiff of Morleyston, made fine by *half a mark* for trespasses charged to him by surety of John de Oulegreve and Robert de Carlio.

730 William Ponger, former bailiff of Morleyston, made fine by *40d.* for petty trespasses charged to him and it is received by surety of Michael de Breydeston. He is pardoned at the request of John de Metingham and William de Beverlaco.

731 <*Morleyston*> It was presented by the 12 of Morleyston that Nicholas le Breton, sub-escheator, has made waste and destruction for the past 11 years in the woods of king Henry father of the present king at Hareston, to the value of £13. He has not come and it is attested that he has lands and tenements in the county of Leycestre. So the sheriff of *Leycestre* is ordered to cause Nicholas to come to *Lincoln* at the octave of St John the Baptist [*1 July 1281*].

732 The dean and chapter of Lychefeld have various regalian franchises in this county and they were not shown in this eyre, so the sheriff is ordered to take them into the king's hands and to keep them safely. He is to answer concerning the issues if they ought to pertain to the king.

733 <*Scarvesdale*> The sheriff was ordered to summon the prior of Felleye to be here at Easter three weeks to answer the king concerning the warrant by which he holds 18 bovates of land with appurtenances in Tybeself, also that he summon Symon Basset for the same day to answer on his claim to have warren at Langwath, also that he summon William de Stotevill for the same day to answer on the plea of his entering the manor of Hekynton which used to be held in chief of king Henry father of the king.[1]

---

[1] An inquest taken on 4 Sept. 1282 after the death of William de Stuteville found that he held the manor of Eckington of his brother Robert by one knight's fee. (*Cal. Inq. p.m.*, ii. no. 423). In 54 Hen. III (1269–70) he had grant of free warren in Eckington. (*Cal. Rot. Ch. et Inq. ad quod damnum*, 100b).

They have not come and the sheriff attests that he had summoned them. So he is ordered to attach them to be at *Lincoln* at the octave of St John the Baptist [*1 July 1281*].

734 *<Scarvesdale>* It was presented by the 12 of Scarvesdale that Roger le Sauvage claims to have warren in his manor of Steynesby. Roger has come and says that he claims warren, amends of breach of assize of ale, gallows and waif in his manor and that he and his ancestors had those franchises from ancient time. He also says that he need not answer without the king's writ. Gilbert de Thornton for the king says that Roger seized the aforesaid franchises and asks that this be inquired into.

The 12 jurors say that in the time of king Henry, father of the present king, the vill of Steynesby was under forest law and that the king gave the vill with all its appurtenances and franchises to a certain Robert le Sauvage, grandfather of Roger. It was at that time that the vill was put in the status of warren by reason of being within forest law. They say that Roger and all his ancestors used the franchises after the aforesaid grant. So Roger is quit as to amends of the assize of ale, gallows and waif. The king is to have a writ of *quo warranto* concerning warren against Roger.

735 *<Derby>* It was presented by the 12 of Derby that in the time of king John, grandfather of the present king, the water of Derewent was open so that ships and boats used to come up to Derby conveying wood, foodstuffs and other merchandise. The abbot of Dale keeps the water blocked by his weirs at Burgh so that no ships can go through to the borough of Derby. Similarly the bishop of Cestre keeps the water blocked by his weirs at Wylne so that ships cannot go through to Derby. Because it is found by the jurors that the burgesses of Derby held the borough in fee-farm of the king from ancient time, they may purchase the king's writ against the abbot of Dale and the bishop of Cestre.[1]

---

[1] The Ragman inquest stated that the obstructions caused by the dams were against the meaning of the charters which king John and king Henry gave to the burgesses of Derby. (*Rot. Hun.*, i. 60b).

15 May 1229. Grant to the burgesses of Derby of all the free customs which the king's burgesses of Nottingham have and had in the time of Henry I and Henry II etc. And the Derwent shall be open to navigation by the length of a pole on each side of mid-stream. (*Cal.Ch.R. 1226–57,.* 96).

29 Apr. 1269. Quitclaim by Thomas Bardolf to the canons of Dale in consideration of 45 marks of all his right in the new mills built by them at Borrowash on the Derwent together with the site of the mills, an acre by the garden of the canons at Ockbrook and 4 acres between the

736 *<Morleyston>* It was presented in the Ragman Pleas by the 12 of Morleyston that the bishop of Cestre claims to have regalian franchises except crown pleas, gallows from ancient time and amends of the assize of bread and ale in his manor of Sallauwe. He has not come and was attached to be here at Easter three weeks by Walter son of Roger de Sallauwe and Hugh King of the same, so they are in *mercy*. The sheriff is ordered to distrain him by all his lands and as for the issues etc. He is to have him in person at *Lincoln* at the octave of St John the Baptist. [*1 July*] Because the bishop does not show his charters concerning the franchises in this eyre, the sheriff is ordered to take them into the king's hands and keep them safely.[1]

737 *<Derby>* It was presented by the 12 of Derby that William de Adderdeleye and Amice his wife hold as her dower a certain house in Derby near the king's highway, and that Henry le Gaunter holds another house too near the king's highway so that they take up part of it. A certain Richard de Morley, guardian of the dower, and Henry and others offered the king *40d.* for the trespass. On account of the small size of the tenements, the assessment was 2s. from Richard de Morley and 16d. from Henry, by surety of John de Ulegreve and Henry le Gaunter of Sallauwe.

738 *<Derby>* William de Alta Ripa of the county of *Leycestre*, former constable of the castle of Donington, and Nicholas of the county of *Sussex*, former escheator in the county of Derby, are in mercy for great extortions made by them, as was found by the 12 of the Ragman inquests for Derby.[2]

739 *<Derby>* It was presented by the 12 of Derby that Jordan le Fullere, to the nuisance of all passers-by, built a drain on the king's highway by which the course of a certain water was diverted from its proper course.

Jordan has come and says that it has been set right and this is attested by the jurors. He is in mercy for the trespass and the sheriff is ordered to cause

---

abbey and Boyah [Grange] as decided at Derby before the justices of assize on 29 Apr. 1269. (*Cartulary of Dale Abbey* (DAS Record Series), 69).

[1] Easter 1283. John de Kyrkeby sends word on behalf of the lord king that the suit which the king has against Roger bishop of Coventry and Lichfield with respect to the manor of Sawley with its soke and appurtenances in Derbyshire should be put in respite for various reasons until a fortnight after next Michaelmas (*Select Cases in Court of King's Bench* (Selden Soc. lv), i. 115).

[2] The Ragman inquest stated that he had extorted 20s. from the bailiffs of Derby in 56 Henry III (1271–2) while he was constable of Castle Donington. Nicholas de Sussex (*alias* le Breton) had extorted £8 from Derby seven years previously (i.e. *c.* 1268) (*Rot. Hun.* ii. 296a).

the watercourse to be restored to its proper channel at Jordan's costs.[1]

[*rot. 12d*]   Still Pleas of Ragman for the County of Derby

740   *<Derby>* It was presented by the 12 of Derby that Jordan le Fullere, Henry de Bylhauwe, Andrew de Normanton and John le Marchaunt, who are men and tenants in chief of the king, let their tenements to the master of the Hospital of St John of Jerusalem in England and they give annual levies to him by which he appropriates lordship of their tenements. Similarly they present that Nicholas le Lorymer holds a certain messuage in Derby in burgage tenure of the king in chief over which 10 years ago the master of the Hospital of St John of Jerusalem put the hospital's sign, by which he appropriates lordship of that tenement.

Nicholas has come and, questioned as to how he claims to hold the messuage, says that he holds it of the king in chief by service of 2½d.

The jurors, questioned as to whether the master or his predecessors used to receive anything from that messuage, say that a certain Nicholas son of Andrew de Derbie, who held it of the king in chief, 20 years ago granted to the hospital an annual rent of 12d. from that tenement. Because it is found that the master by reason of that rent takes and appropriates lordship of the aforesaid tenement, which is held of the king in chief, to the great disherison of the king, the sheriff is ordered to cause the master to come to *Lincoln* at the quindene of Trinity. [*22 June 1281*]

The same day was given Nicholas in the Bench.

741   *<Derby>* It was presented by the 12 of Derby that Walter, vicar of the church of Werburg, built a privy over the water of Oddebrok by which the water is putrified, to the nuisance of the whole borough. Because it is attested that the house in which the privy was made is not a nuisance but rather the privy, the sheriff is ordered to cause it to be removed at Walter's costs. Because he built the privy three years ago, he is therefore in *mercy*. Nothing concerning amercement because he does not have a lay fee.

742   *<Lutelchirch>* The sheriff was ordered to attach Roysia Doyly to be here at Easter three weeks to answer the king in a plea of entering 8 bovates

---

[1] The Ragman inquest stated that the sewer had been made five years previously (i.e. *c.* 1269–70) (*Rot. Hun.*, i. 61b).

of land in Lutelchirch which used to be held in chief of king John. She has not come and was attached by William in le Wro and William le Mareschal both of Stanton, so they are in *mercy*. The sheriff is ordered to distrain her by all her lands and as for the issues etc. and have her at *Lincoln* at the quindene of Trinity. [*22 June 1281*]

743 <*Derby*> It was presented by the 12 of Derbie that Jordan le Fullere, Henry de Bylhauwe, Andrew de Normanton and John le Marchaunt, who are men and tenants in chief of the king, let their tenements to the master of the Hospital of St John of Jerusalem in England and give annual levies to him so that he, by reason of the letting, appropriates lordship of those tenements.

Jordan and the others have come and say that they paid the master annual levies as alms and not in the name of protection and avowry.[1] Concerning this they put themselves on the country.

Gilbert de Thornton for the king says that up to this time they have paid chevage[2] and levies that they might be under the protection of the master and not as alms, so that Jordan and the others sued their neighbours, tenants of the king, before the Conservators of Privilege, the masters of the Hospital of St John of Jerusalem in England, in London and elsewhere in the realm. He asks that this be inquired into.

Afterwards Jordan and the others came and could not deny that they had given certain levies as chevage, so they are to be detained.

Afterwards Jordan made fine by *half a mark* and it is received by surety of Richard de Cardel. Henry de Bilhauwe, Andrew de Normanton and John le Marchaund came and made fine by *10s.* (whereof John le Marchaund 5s.) and it is received by surety of Gervase de la Cornere. They are prohibited by the justices from encumbering their tenements which they hold in chief of the king so that he loses lordship.

[*rot. 13d*]   Close of Easter 9th Year of King Edward

744 The abbot of Crockesden appoints as his attorney brother Thomas de Leyc' or Robert de Gerndon against the king in a plea of Ragman and *quo warranto*.

---

[1] Avowry: a payment for warranty or protection made to a feudal lord.

[2] Chevage: head money paid by unfree tenants in recognition of their lord's rights (Pollock and Maitland, *History of English Law*, i. 418).

745 Matthew de Knyveton appoints as his attorney Henry de Knyveton, William de Benteleye or William Peyncham against the king in a plea of Ragman and *quo warranto*.

746 Geoffrey de Greseley appoints as his attorney Richard de Kingesley or John Hervy against the king in a plea of Ragman and *quo warranto*.

[KALENDAR OF PRESENTING JURIES]

747   WAPENTAKE OF HIGH PEAK

Richard Lucas,
  bailiff – sworn
William Folegaumbe - sworn
Thomas de Gratton - sworn
Thomas de Langesdon - sworn
Henry de Derley - sworn
Adam de Stonesleye - sworn

Electors, Robert Bozun - sworn
  Adam de Herthull - sworn
William de Yolgreve - sworn
Peter de Roland - sworn
William Hally - sworn
Robert de Melvere - sworn
Hugh de Stredleye - sworn

748   WAPENTAKE OF WYRKEWORTHE

Symon de Clifton,
  bailiff - sworn
Richard le Porter - sworn
Roger de Wendesley - sworn
Jordan de Sniterton - sworn
Ranulph de Sniterton - sworn
Nicholas de Smerehull - sworn

Electors, Henry de Cromford -
  sworn
  Henry son of Thomas de Hopton
  - sworn
Henry son of Thomas de Alsop -
  sworn
Robert de Alsop - sworn
Henry son of Henry de Hoperton -
  sworn
Thomas de Nedham - sworn
John de Lee - sworn

749   WAPENTAKE OF APPELTRE

The same Symon [de Clifton]
  bailiff - sworn
Roger de Mersinton - sworn
John Saule - sworn
Thomas de Mapelton - sworn
Roger de Wardinton - sworn
Hamo de Saperton - sworn

Electors, William de Meynil -
  sworn
Henry FitzHerbert - sworn
Richard Rundel - sworn
John son of Symon - sworn
Robert Shyret - sworn
John Wase - sworn
Roger Durdent - sworn

750   WAPENTAKE OF SCHARWEDALE

Adam de Catteclywe,
  bailiff - sworn
Robert le Eraunt
Henry de Scharlethorp - sworn
John de Brymneton - sworn
Peter de Dunston - sworn
Henry de Thathayt - sworn

Electors, William de Steynesby -
  sworn
Roger de Somerville - sworn
Hugh de Canonicis - sworn
Simon de Glapwelle - sworn
Ralph de Heton - sworn
Richard de la Graunge - sworn
William le Mareschal - sworn

751   WAPENTAKE OF MORLEYSTAN

William de Waleton,
  bailiff - sworn
William Makerel - sworn
Thomas de Codenhowre - sworn
Nicholas de Wakebrigg - sworn
Henry de Burleye - sworn
Collard de Breidaston - sworn

Electors, Ralph de Chaddesden -
  sworn
William de Tynereye - sworn
Henry de Skon - sworn
William Nurri - sworn
Simon Puther - sworn
Payn de Ridinges - sworn
William de Abierne - sworn

752 WAPENTAKE OF LUTHCHIRCH

The same William [de Walton]
   bailiff - sworn
William de Musckham - sworn
Roger de Tuck - sworn
William de Ekenton - sworn
William Burgullum - sworn
Robert Campion - sworn

Electors, Giles de Meynill - sworn
John Fanwell - sworn
Thomas de Curchon - sworn
Richard Busson - sworn
Ralph Ferbraz - sworn
Robert de Morkaneston - sworn
Nicholas de Finderne - sworn

753 WAPENTAKE OF REPPENDON

Milo de Meuton, bailiff - sworn
William de Meissham - sworn
Ingelard de Curzon - sworn
Robert son of Adam de Waleton –
   sworn
William de Herteshorn - sworn
William Pinchard - sworn

Electors, Nicholas de Werdon -
   sworn
   Nicholas de Ingwardeby - sworn
William de Stepenhill - sworn
Adam le On - sworn
Stephen de Wyneshill - sworn
Geoffrey Walram - sworn
Hugh son of Matthew - sworn

754 VILL OF BAUKWELL

Richard Lucas,
   bailiff - sworn
Roger de Esseburne - sworn
Richard his brother - sworn
Ellis Clerk - sworn
Henry Hyne - sworn
Philip de Esseburne - sworn

Electors, Ralph le Wyne - sworn
   William Clerk - sworn
Matthew son of Ralph - sworn
Robert Parson - sworn
Henry le Roter
Robert Cruder - sworn
Roger de Flyry - sworn

755 VILL OF ESSEBURNE

Simon de Clyfton,
  bailiff - sworn
Thomas Hervy - sworn
John Baker - sworn
Hugh Carpenter - sworn
Thomas de Tyddeswelle - sworn
Nicholas de Aula - sworn

Electors, Robert s. of Alexander -
  sworn
John le Mercer - sworn
John de Offedecote - sworn
Peter de Offedecote – sworn
Ralph Sperewater - sworn
John Lylye - sworn
Walter le Veer - sworn

756 VILL OF CESTREFELD

Adam de Catteclyve,
  bailiff - sworn
John de Peck - sworn
Philip de Len - sworn
Ralph de Beston - sworn
John de Staunford - sworn
Hugh Dorant - sworn

Electors, Nicholas de Thorp -
  sworn
William de Neubold - sworn
William son of Thomas - sworn
John son of Inge - sworn
John Dorant - sworn
Robert son of William - sworn
Richard Scotard - sworn

757 BOROUGH OF DERBY

Robert de Notingham,
  bailiff - sworn –
Simon de Notingham - sworn –
Ranulph de Mabeneye - sworn –
Henry de Trussele - sworn –
Henry Swift - sworn –
Payn Smith - sworn

Electors, Robert de Dyninton -
  sworn
Gervase de la Cornere - sworn –
John Lafful - sworn –
William le Ferur - sworn –
Roger Gery - sworn –
William Swift - sworn –
Henry de Berde - sworn –

ESTREATS OF FINES AND AMERCEMENTS OF CROWN PLEAS FOR THE COUNTY OF DERBY

JUST 1/148 [Rex Roll]

WAPENTAKE OF HIGH PEAK

758 [ref. 404]	£	s.	d.
That wapentake the liberties excepted, for murder	10	0	0
Frankpledge of Robert Pole of Shatton for flight of Robert son of Geoffrey de Bradewell		6	8
Vill of Schatton for not making pursuit		13	4
Vill of Bradewell for the same	1	0	0
Vill of Hope for the same	1	6	8
Vill of Aston for the same		13	4

759 [ref. 405]	£	s.	d.
G. the sheriff for chattels of Roger Smith of Moniasse, fugitive		2	6
Frankpledge of William Ely for flight of Roger		6	8
Vill of Moniasse for false valuation	1	0	0
Vill of Cheylmerdon for the same	1	0	0
Vill of Tadington with Presteclyf for the same	1	0	0
Vill of Overhaddon for the same		13	4

760 [ref. 406]	£	s.	d.
The sheriff for chattels of Hugh Weaver of Derley who abjured the realm		4	0
Frankpledge of Nicholas de Waggebrigge for flight of that Hugh		6	8
Vill of Derley for false valuation	1	6	8
Vill of Netherhaddon with Roulesley for the same	1	0	0
Vill of Ylegreve for the same	1	0	0
Vill of Winster for the same		13	4

	£	s.	d.
761 [refs. 407–8]			
Roger Le Estrange former keeper of Peak Castle for escape			
of Adam former sergeant of Richard le Ragged	8	0	0
G. the sheriff for chattels of Walter son of Petronilla			
de Basselowe, fugitive			3
Laurence de Basselowe for flight of Walter		6	8
Vill of Hedenesovere for not making pursuit	1	0	0
Vill of Beley for the same		10	0
Vill of Basselowe for the same	1	6	8

	£	s.	d.
762 [refs. 409–10]			
G. the sheriff for chattels of William de Middelton who			
abjured the realm		12	4
The same sheriff for chattels of that William in the			
wapentake of Wyrkesworth		11	4
Adam de Herthull for taking chattels without warrant		3	4
Vill of Herthull for not arresting that William		6	8
Vill of Middelton near Eyam for false valuation		13	4
Vill of Conkesbyr' for the same		10	0

	£	s.	d.
763 [refs. 411–12]			
G. the sheriff for chattels of John son of William Cook,			
suicide		5	1
The same sheriff for chattels of Alan le Seriant who			
abjured the realm		10	0
Frankpledge of Geoffrey son of Brun de Hope for flight			
of Alan		6	8
Simon de Hokelowe and Geoffrey Brun, sureties for			
Agnes, widow of Richard son of Abusa		6	8
Vill of Asseford for false valuation	1	6	8

	£	s.	d.
764 [ref. 413]			
Vill of Haversegges for not attending inquest	1	6	8
Vill of Eyom for the same		13	4
Vill of Nether Paddeley for the same		6	8
Vill of Over Paddeley for the same		6	8
Vill of Over Offerton for the same, with vill of Nether			
Offerton		10	0

	£	s.	d.
765 [refs 414–16]			
Vill of Boudon with members for not pursuing	1	6	8
Vill of Mores with members for the same		13	4
G. the sheriff for chattels of Richard son of Nicholas de Paddeley, fugitive		4	6
Frankpledge of Nicholas de Paddeley for flight of Richard		6	8
Vill of Magna Longesdon for false valuation	1	0	0
Vill of Parva Longesdon for the same		10	0

	£	s.	d.
766 [ref. 417]			
G. the sheriff for chattels of Thomas de Stanley		9	2
Frankpledge of Peter Loddeswirth for flight of Thomas		6	8
Vill of Melvere for false valuation		6	8
Vill of Chysseworth for the same		6	8
Vill of Loddesworth for the same		6	8
Vill of Chauelesworth for the same		6	8

	£	s.	d.
767 [ref. 420]			
G. the sheriff for chattels of Hugh de Mamechestre, fugitive		2	5
Frankpledge of Roger son of Roger de Tyddeswell for flight of Hugh		6	8
Vill of Tyddeswelle for false valuation		6	8
Vill of Wyrmonhill for the same		6	8
Vill of Litton for the same		13	4

	£	s.	d.
768 [refs. 421–3]			
Robert de Buxestones for taking a deodand without warrant		13	4
G. the sheriff for chattels of Ellis le Cupere, fugitive			8
Frankpledge of William de Aula of Castleton for flight of Ellis		6	8
Vill of Castleton for false valuation	2	0	0
Vill of Thornovere for the same		10	0
Vill of Rolaund for false valuation		10	0

	£	s.	d.
769 [ref. 424]			
Hugh Woods of Presteclyfe, surety, for not having Robert son of Richard de Tadington		6	8

Robert Townhead, John Woods and Thomas son of		
Ralph, all of Presteclyfe for the same	10	0
Ives de Tadington for the same	3	4
John son of Robert son of Gilbert in Tadington for the same	6	8
John son of Robert Brun for the same	6	8
Robert le Eyr in Tadington for the same by surety of		
Robert de Buxstones	6	8
William son of Ralph for the same	6	8
John super le Hull and Thomas de la Heuse of Tadington,		
for the same, whereof 3s. 4d. from John	10	0
G. the sheriff for chattels of Robert son of Richard		
de Tadington, fugitive	1	5
Frankpledge of village of Tadington for flight of		
Robert	6	8

770 [refs. 425, 427]

	£	s.	d.
G, the sheriff for chattels of Thomas le Cupere of			
Clunesland who abjured the realm		7	2
G. the sheriff for chattels of Ralph son of William			
de Tyddeswell, fugitive		19	0
John Danyell, fine for year and waste of Ralph's land		10	0
G. the sheriff for mid time of Ralph's land		4	8

771 [ref. 428]

	£	s.	d.
William de Stafford in Langedendale and Richard			
de Knythewyt, default		6	8
Adam le Hore, Richard de Clif, Nicholas le Moner and			
Richard Sibylle, all of Buxstones for the same		13	4
Gilbert de Schyrebrok and Henry son of Adam			
de Calfovere, the same		6	8
William de Haselford, William de Calton, Thomas son of			
Gilbert de Langedon and William Gyn of Chattesworth			
for the same		6	8
Thomas de Kendale, Robert son of Robert de Ylegreve,			
William son Henry le Blund and Nicholas le Champenys			
for the same		6	8
William de Asseburne in Staunton and Nicholas son of			
Ralph de Cheylmerdon for the same		6	8
Geoffrey de Pichford for the same < + >		-	-
John son of Roger le Blund for the same		3	4

	£	s.	d.
772 [refs. 432–3]			
Richard Lucas, bailiff, for several trespasses		6	8
Adam de Herthull and Hugh de Stredley with their 12			
fellow jurors for concealment and other trespasses	4	0	0
G. the sheriff for chattels of William de Cumbrigg,			
fugitive		2	0
Thomas de Furnyvall, fine for having respite until the			
quindene of St John the Baptist at Lincoln, by surety			
of Thomas Folejam and William de Ryther	20	0	0

WAPENTAKE OF SKARVEDALE

	£	s.	d.
773 [ref. 434]			
That wapentake, the liberties excepted, for murder	4	0	0
G. the sheriff for chattels of Henry son of Gilbert de			
Essovere, fugitive	3	11	10
Henry Notelok of Wodethorp and Ralph le Bayllyf of			
Becington for not having Agnes daughter of Richard		6	8
Vill of Essovere for false valuation		13	4
Vill of Wingerworth for the same		10	0
Vill of Brakenwayt for the same		6	8
Vill of Stretton for the same		13	4
Frankpledge of the vill of Essovere for flight of Henry		6	8

	£	s.	d.
774 [ref. 435]			
G. the sheriff for chattels of William le Westerneys,			
fugitive		6	2½
The same sheriff for mid time of William's land		5	0
John le Westereys, fine for year and waste of that land			
by surety of Richard de Morton		10	0

	£	s.	d.
[rot. 39d]			
Vill of Morton with members for false valuation	1	0	0
Roger son of Goda de Pillesley, Roger son of Awisia,			
Thomas son of Robert de Morton and Geoffrey his			
brother, for not arresting William le Westreys	1	0	0
Vill of Staynisby for false valuation	1	0	0
Vill of Tybechelf for the same	1	6	8

	£	s.	d.
775 [ref. 436]			
G. the sheriff for chattels of Thomas de Langwath, fugitive		6	0
Henry de Perepont for flight of Thomas and fine from			
the same Henry's mainpast	1	0	0
Vill of Langwath for false valuation		6	8
Vills of Schardeclif and Langwath for the same		3	4
Vill of Eselund for the same		6	8
Vills of Glappwell and Routhorn for the same		10	0

	£	s.	d.
776 [ref. 437]			
Vill of Barley for not attending inquest		6	8
Vill of Holmesfeud for the same		13	4
Vill of Brampton for the same	1	0	0
Vill of Neubaud for the same		6	8

	£	s.	d.
777 [ref. 438]			
Vill of Kynewaldemersch for the same		6	8
Vill of Barleburgh with Whytewell for the same	1	0	0
Vill of Beckton for the same		13	4
Vill of Eykington for the same		13	4

	£	s.	d.
778 [refs. 439–40]			
Vill of Elmeton for the same		13	4
Vill of Bollesovere for the same	3	6	8
Vill of Whytington for the same	1	0	0
Vill of Alferton for the same	2	0	0
Vill of Suth Wynefeud for the same		13	4
Vill of Penkeston with Normanton for the same		10	0

	£	s.	d.
779 [refs. 441–2]			
Vill of Stavely for the same		13	4
G. the sheriff for chattels of William son of John			
de Colney who abjured the realm		11	8
Vill of Dranefeud for false valuation	1	6	8
Vill of Dore for the same		6	8
Vill of Norton for the same	1	0	0

	£	s.	d.
780 [refs. 443–6]			
Vill of Walton for the same		10	0
G. the sheriff for chattels of John Wysman, beheaded thief		3	0

	£	s.	d.
The same sheriff for chattels of Roger de Gahram, fugitive		3	3
Abbot of Beauchief for year and waste of Roger's land		6	8
Vill of Temple Normanton for not attending inquest		13	4

781 [refs. 448, 450–1]

	£	s.	d.
G. the sheriff for chattels of William son of Robert de Byrchewode		1	6
Vill of Blakwell for false valuation		13	4
G. the sheriff for chattels of Agnes daughter of Roger de Coventre who abjured the realm			4
Vill of Dukmanton for not attending inquest		10	0
G. the sheriff for chattels of Robert de London who abjured the realm		1	0

782 [refs. 453–4, 457]

	£	s.	d.
G. the sheriff for chattels of Thomas son of the parson of Normanton and his fellows who abjured the realm	1	18	6
The same sheriff for chattels of Siward de Normanton, hanged	3	15	5
The same sheriff for chattels of William Curebyhinde	2	5	5
Hugh de Babengton, former sheriff, levied by him from the vill of Eykengton for escape of John Wenge	8	0	0
G. the sheriff for chattels of Geoffrey le Heys, beheaded thief		1	2

783 [refs. 458–60, 462]

	£	s.	d.
Richard le Doun of Breydesale and John Foun jun., sureties, for not having William de Langeford		6	8
Roger de Stretton and John his brother, sureties, for that William		6	8
William de Langeford of Hales and William reeve of Thomas de Edenesovere in Tyssington, sureties for the same William		6	8
Simon de Byrches of Normanton for not prosecuting his appeal, sureties, Roger le Neucomen and John le Seingur of Normanton		6	8

784 [refs. 463–4]

Innkeepers' pence in Alfreton for wine sold against

	£	s.	d.
the assize		6	8
William de Stotevill for default		6	8
Master Thomas Beck for the same, < + >		-	-
Peter de Cestria for the same		-	-
Philip le Marschal for the same [*deleted*]		3	4
Robert de Cressy of Steinsby for the same		3	4
John le Paumer of Notingham and Robert Levik for the same		6	8

785 [ref. 467]

	£	s.	d.
G. the sheriff for chattels of John de Plaghstowe, hanged [*deleted*]		8	0
Roger de Crophull for chattels of Henry de Oxcroft, hanged	1	11	0
G. the sheriff for chattels of William Parys, hanged		1	5
The same sheriff for chattels of Henry Gale, hanged		1	5
The same sheriff for chattels of William Bate, hanged		7	8
Nicholas Wake for chattels of Robert de Wyteby, hanged		2	1
The same Nicholas for chattels of Thomas Cysse, hanged			9
The same Nicholas for chattels of John de Raynaldthorp, hanged			5
The same Nicholas for chattels of Adam de Normanville, hanged		2	6
Roger de la Bache for chattels of William de Hykling, hanged		2	0
Nicholas Wake for taking chattels without warrant	1	0	0
Roger de la Bache for taking chattels without warrant		3	4

786 [ref. 468]

	£	s.	d.
G. the sheriff for chattels of Walter son of Walter de Normanton, fugitive	1	14	2
The same sheriff for chattels of Robert Glide, fugitive [*deleted*]	2	8	8
The same sheriff for chattels of Adam son of Geoffrey Gumme, fugitive	2	13	11
The same sheriff for chattels of Roger son of Ralph, fugitive [*deleted*]	2	0	3
The same sheriff for chattels of Thomas son of Ralph, fugitive	1	0	2

	£	s.	d.
The same sheriff for chattels of Adam Sweng, fugitive [*deleted*]	1	18	0
The same sheriff for chattels of Geoffrey Sweng, fugitive [*deleted*]	2	0	3
The same sheriff for chattels of Simon Glyde, fugitive [*deleted*]	1	0	4
The same sheriff for chattels of Roger son of Ranulph, fugitive [*deleted*]	2	13	6
The same sheriff for chattels of Henry Wysening, fugitive [*deleted*]	7	5	3

787 [ref. 468]

	£	s.	d.
William de Steynesby and Roger de Somerville, fine for them and their 12 fellow-jurors (except Henry de Sarlesthorp) for concealment and other trespasses	2	0	0
Robert le Wyne, fine for chattels of Robert Glyde, Roger son of Ralph, Adam Sweng, Geoffrey Sweng, Simon Glyde, Roger son of Ranulph and Henry Wysening, to be recovered, of which he is to pay half at Michaelmas in the 9th year and the remainder at Easter next following, by surety of Ralph le Wyne	13	6	8

[rot. 40]   WAPENTAKE OF WYRKESWORTH

788 [ref. 473]

	£	s.	d.
That wapentake for murder	4	0	0
Ralph de Matlok, surety, for not having William son of Gilbert de Wyrkesworth		1	8
Vill of Hopton for not attending inquest		10	0
Vill of Cromford for the same		10	0
Vill of Caldelowe for the same		3	4

789 [ref. 474]

	£	s.	d.
G. the sheriff for chattels of Ralph son of Richard de Middelton, fugitive	1	7	8
Vill of Wyrkesworth for false valuation	1	0	0
Vill of Jolgreve for the same		13	4
Vill of Hertington for the same	1	0	0

	£	s.	d.
Vill of Bracington for the same		13	4
Vill of Elton for the same		13	4
790 [refs. 475, 477]	£	s.	d.
Vill of Mapelton for the same		6	8
Vill of Thorp for the same		10	0
Vill of Benteley for the same		10	0
Vill of Offedecote for the same		6	8
G. the sheriff for chattels of Robert son of Ayleward, fugitive		7	0
Vill of Knyveton for false valuation	2	0	0
791 [ref. 478]	£	s.	d.
G. the sheriff for chattels of Roger son of Adam, fugitive		5	0
Vill of Hyrton for false valuation	1	6	8
Vill of Bondesale for the same	1	0	0
Vill of Alsop for the same		13	4
Vill of Crudecote for the same		6	8
792 [ref. 479]	£	s.	d.
G. the sheriff for chattels of Sweyn de Hyrton, hanged		7	10
Vill of Hokenaston for false valuation		6	8
Vills of Lee and Devek for the same		6	8
Vill of Tanesley on the hospital side, for the same		6	8
Vill of Matloke for the same		13	4
Vill of Kersington for the same		10	0
G. the sheriff for chattels of William Godal, hanged		6	8
793 [refs. 480-482, 484]	£	s.	d.
Vill of Peverwich for flight of Robert Bumboll	1	6	8
Vill of Ibule for not attending inquest		3	4
Vill of Wendesley for flight of Adam Fox and Richard son of Geoffrey		10	0
G. the sheriff for chattels of Richard Lyngell who abjured the realm		10	0
The same sheriff for year and waste of Richard's land		8	0
The same sheriff for mid time of that land		11	0
The same sheriff for chattels of Henry son of Richard de Bondesale, fugitive		2	8

			£	s.	d.
The same sheriff for chattels of William son of Richard de Bondesale, fugitive				5	4

794 [ref. 486]

			£	s.	d.
The same sheriff for chattels of Robert Shepherd, beheaded thief				1	0
The same sheriff for chattels of John Corlu, beheaded thief					6
The same sheriff for chattels of Symon de la Grene, hanged thief					2
The same sheriff for chattels of Robert le Halt, hanged					6
The same sheriff for chattels of Thomas Gouseworth				1	3
The same sheriff for chattels of Henry Hole, beheaded thief				3	0
The same sheriff for chattels of Nicholas Baker, hanged				8	0
The same sheriff for chattels of Peter Scot and Robert Saltman, beheaded				3	5

795 [ref. 487]

			£	s.	d.
Henry Baker of Matlok, John le Merchaunt of the same and John de Hurst for default, whereof John le Marchaunt 5s.				6	8
John son of Gilbert de Bedeford in Mapelton and Henry de Tyssington for the same				3	4
Ralph de Swynescowe in Thorp and Thomas de Weston for the same				6	8
John de Aldewark and William son of Cecilia de Peverwych, the same				3	4
John de Kestevene in Peverwych and John son of Maud for the same				3	4
Adam de Stophull in Wyrkesworth for the same				3	4

796 [refs. 490–1, 493]

			£	s.	d.
Julia daughter of William le Hyne for not prosecuting, sureties, Henry le Chyrcheman and Thomas son of Thomas, both of Knyveton				3	4
William de Parco, fine for trespass by surety of Henry Rosell and William de Addrydeley			1	0	0
G. the sheriff for chattels of William de Milnefeud, fugitive				1	0
Jordan de Sutton, Henry de Cromford and their fellow jurors, fine for themselves and their fellows for concealment and other trespasses			2	0	0

WAPENTAKE OF REPINGDON

797 [ref. 494]	£	s.	d.
That wapentake the liberties excepted, for murder	3	6	8
G. the sheriff for chattels of Robert Hodeke of Fornewerk, suicide	6	6	6
Vill of Repinghdon for false valuation	1	0	0
Vill of Fornewerk for the same		10	0
Vill of Engelby for the same		10	0
Vill of Bretteby for the same		13	4
Vill of Neuton Sulny for the same		13	4

798 [refs. 495, 500]	£	s.	d.
Vill of Kynges Neuton for the same	1	0	0
G. the sheriff for chattels of Gilbert Gerard, hanged		5	4
Walter de Styrthesley former sheriff, for chattels of Gilbert		7	9
Vill of Lollington for false valuation		13	4
Vill of Catton for the same		13	4
Vill of Crokesale for the same		13	4
Vill of Cotene for the same		13	4

799 [ref. 501]	£	s.	d.
Vill of Walton for the same	1	0	0
Vill of Wynshull for the same		13	4
Vill of Roslaston for the same		6	8
Vill of Stapenhill for the same		13	4

800 [refs. 502–4]	£	s.	d.
Vill of Greseley with members for the same	1	0	0
Vill of Stony Staunton for the same		10	0
Vill of Cold Staunton for the same		6	8
Vill of Draklowe for the same		6	8
G. the sheriff for chattels of Robert Charles, fugitive		7	2
The same sheriff for chattels of William Martyn, fugitive		10	0

801 [ref. 506]	£	s.	d.
The same sheriff for chattels of Robert Stacy, fugitive		18	0
Nicholas de Fynderne, fine for year and waste of Robert's land, by surety of Ralph de Burgh	1	0	0

Nicholas de Findern for mid time of that land	2	13	4
The same Nicholas for taking chattels without warrant		6	8
Vill of Chyldecote for false valuation		10	0
Vill of Appelby for the same		10	0
Vill of Stretton with Wyvesley and Pakinton for the same		13	4

802 [refs. 507, 509–11]

	£	s.	d.
Vill of Melburn for the same	2	0	0
Vill of Caldewell for the same		6	8
G. the sheriff for chattels of Nicholas de Stony Stanton, fugitive		1	0
The same sheriff for chattels of Walter Lyttelgod, fugitive		12	0

[rot. 40d] STILL WAPENTAKE OF REPINGDON

803 [refs. 512–14]

	£	s.	d.
G. the sheriff for chattels of Hugh de Bretteby, fugitive		3	0
Vill of Smetheby for not attending inquest		6	8
Vill of Herteshorn for the same		13	4
Vill of Tykenal for the same		13	4
G. the sheriff for chattels of John Baret, fugitive		1	0
William Carter of Fornewerk for not prosecuting his appeal by surety of William Reeve of Fornewerk		3	4

804 [ref. 515]

	£	s.	d.
John le Wenys for not prosecuting his appeal, by surety of John le Mouner of Repindon		1	8
Hervey de Ackle <Staffs> for not coming and for trespass concerning suit of John le Wenys of Repindon	2	0	0
William de Appleby, surety for Hervey		6	8
Hugh de Hergrave for the same		3	4

805 [ref. 518]

	£	s.	d.
Bernard de Brus for default		3	4
Henry le Bercher for the same		1	8
Vill of Edeninghale for the same		6	8
Reynold de Tykenale for the same		1	8

806 [refs. 519–20]

	£	s.	d.
Adam son of John de Tykenal, Geoffrey Wymond, Richard de Fornewerk and Henry de Barowe, sureties for Reynold de Tykenal, for not having him		6	8
John son of Ralph de Engelby, Simon le Keu of Reppindon, Robert Townsend and Robert de Barowe for the same		6	8
William Wodeward of Repingdon, William Duceamur, Henry son of William and Henry Lomb all of Repindon, for the same		6	8
Robert son of William de Repindon and Robert Reeve of Melton for the same		3	4
Vill of Repingdon for escape of William le Brevetur	8	0	0

807 [refs. 521, 523]

	£	s.	d.
John de Ballyolo who is not yet a knight <Ebor>	5	0	0
G. the sheriff for chattels of Richard Levesone, beheaded			10
The same sheriff for chattels of Roger de Foderingeye, beheaded		4	6
The same sheriff for chattels of Richard de London, beheaded		1	0
The same sheriff for chattels of Hugh son of Henry de Quingeston, beheaded		2	6

808 [ref. 525]

	£	s.	d.
The same sheriff for chattels of Richard Bogges, hanged		8	8
The same sheriff for chattels of Henry Basselot, hanged	1	4	7
The same sheriff for chattels of William le Rede, hanged	1	0	0
Nicholas de Verdenn and Nicholas de Inwardeby and their fellow-jurors, fine for concealment and other trespasses	2	0	0

WAPENTAKE OF LUCHYRCHE

809 [ref. 527]

	£	s.	d.
That wapentake, the liberties excepted, for murder	3	6	8
Vill of Clifton for not attending inquest		6	8
Vill of Langley for the same	1	10	0
Vill of Makworth for the same	1	10	0
Vill of Weston for the same		6	8

810 [ref. 528]	£	s.	d.
Vill of Magna Overe for not pursuing	2	0	0
Vill of Querendon for the same		13	4
Vill of Marketon for the same		10	0
Ingelard de Corcon for flight of William de Malverton who was of his mainpast		6	8

811 [refs. 529–30]	£	s.	d.
G. the sheriff for chattels of Thomas Besyng, fugitive		10	0
The same sheriff for chattels of William son of Roger de Egeton, fugitive		1	0
Vill of Egeton for false valuation	1	0	0
Vill of Etewell for the same	1	6	8
Vill of Amboldeston for the same		6	8

812 [ref. 531]	£	s.	d.
Vill of Radburn for the same		13	4
Vill of Dalbyr' for not attending inquest		6	8
Vill of Boulton for the same		6	8
Vill of Chelardeston for the same		13	4

813 [refs. 532–3]	£	s.	d.
Vill of Luchyrchem with members for the same	1	6	8
Vill of Parva Overe for the same		6	8
Vill of Aylewaston for the same	1	0	0
Vill of Alewaston for the same		13	4
Vill of Finderne for the same		6	8
Vill of Wylington for the same		6	8

814 [refs. 534, 535, 537]	£	s.	d.
G. the sheriff for chattels of Robert de Meynill, fugitive		8	0
William de Wauton, bailiff, for trespass	-	-	-
G. the sheriff for chattels of Robert son of Ralph de Kedelston, suicide			6
Vill of Keteleston for burying without coroners' view		10	0
John Grym, coroner, for trespass		6	8

815 [refs. 538, 540–1]	£	s.	d.
Vill of Swerkeston for not pursuing		6	8
G. the sheriff for chattels of Robert Merond, fugitive	8	18	4

	£	s.	d.
Vill of Erleson for not attending inquest		6	8
Vill of Twyford for the same	1	0	0
Vill of Barowe for the same	1	6	8

816 [refs. 542–3, 546]

	£	s.	d.
G. the sheriff for chattels of John Janne of Alwaston who abjured the realm		14	6
Vill of Weston on Trent for false valuation	2	0	0
Vill of Schardelowe for the same		6	8
Vill of Sydenfen for the same		6	8
G. the sheriff for chattels of Richard son of Geoffrey le Canner, fugitive		5	0
Vill of Wylne for false valuation		6	8
Vill of Langeley for escape of William Whyting	8	0	0

817 [refs. 545, 547]

	£	s.	d.
Henry de Lacy Earl of Lincoln, for default. <*baron*>	-	-	-
Master Henry Lovell for the same		13	4
Ralph de Sancto Mauro for the same		13	4
Adam de Audydelay for the same		3	4
Adam de Burghes for the same		3	4
Laurence le Seler, William le Tyxtor and Henry Galyon, all of Derby, sureties for Henry le Lorymer and Robert Tappe, both of Derby who did not prosecute their appeal		6	8

818 [ref. 548]

	£	s.	d.
G. the sheriff for chattels of Twete de Makworth, hanged		16	6
The same sheriff for chattels of William le Marchall of Wylne hanged		10	0
The same sheriff for chattels of Stephen Buk, hanged			6
The same sheriff for chattels of Peter Black, fugitive			2
The same sheriff for chattels of Thomas Balle, hanged		2	0

819 [refs. 550, 552]

	£	s.	d.
Giles de Meynill and John Fannell, for themselves and their 12 fellow jurors, fine for concealment and other trespasses	1	6	8
G. the sheriff for chattels of Astyn Barun of Amboldeston, suicide	2	12	0

Ralph le Wyte, Robert Fox, William le Jovene, Hugh Freman,
all of Makworth, Hugh le Tayllur, Hugh Godchild, Robert
son of Henry, Thomas de Brettesel, William le Wolf,
John de la Grene, Hugh son of Alan and Robert Shepherd
of Bretteshull, sureties for Nicholas de Makworth, for
not having him   2   0   0

WAPENTAKE OF APPELTRE

820 [refs. 555–6]	£	s.	d.
That wapentake for murder	4	0	0
G. the sheriff for chattels of Roger son of Geoffrey, fugitive		10	0
Peter son of Richard de Hatton and John son of William de Brunchton, sureties for not having Agnes wife of Robert de Etewell		-	-
Vill of Hatton for flight of Roger		6	8
Vill of Trosell' for burial without coroner's view		6	8
Vill of Oselaston for the same		6	8

821 [ref. 557]	£	s.	d.
Vill of Crofton in Holington and Geoffrey son of Nicholas de Ednaston, sureties for one they did not have		3	4
Robert Miller of Holington and Henry Reeve for the same		3	4
William Wyldy and William Bars both of Thurvaston, for the same		3	4
Vill of Holington for not attending inquest		6	8
Vill of Langeford for the same		13	4
Vill of Schyrley for the same		10	0
Vill of Edeneston for the same		10	0

[rot. 41]   STILL WAPENTAKE OF APPELTRE

822 [ref. 558]	£	s.	d.
G. the sheriff for chattels of Henry Dauncelevedy, outlaw	1	10	0
Vill of Osmundeston for his flight		6	8
Vill of Schardeston for the same		6	8

	£	s.	d.
Vill of Snelleston for the same		13	4

823 [ref. 559]

	£	s.	d.
Prior of Tuttebyr' for keeping a deodand without warrant	2	0	0
Vill of Merston for false valuation		13	4
Vill of Howen for the same		13	4
Vill of Hylton for the same		13	4

824 [ref. 560]

	£	s.	d.
Vill of Roddeley for the same		6	8
Vill of Boyleston for the same		13	4
Vill of Barton for the same		13	4
Vill of Alkemanton for the same		10	0
G. the sheriff for chattels of Richard Carter, fugitive		4	3

825 [ref. 561]

	£	s.	d.
Vill of Seggessell for not attending inquest		6	8
Vill of Eyton for the same		6	8
Vill of Sudbyr' for the same		13	4
Vill of Mersington Montgomery for the same	1	0	0

826 [ref. 562]

	£	s.	d.
Vill of Benteley for the same		10	0
Vill of Attelowe for the same		13	4
Vill of Yffeley outwith the hospital part, for the same		6	8
The same vill for the hospital part, for the same		6	8
Vill of Cubeley for the same		13	4

827 [refs. 563–5]

	£	s.	d.
Vill of Doubrigge for the same	1	10	0
G. the sheriff for chattels of Philip de Coleshull and Alice de Beurepayr who abjured the realm		2	0
Vill of Northbyr' with Eston for false valuation	1	0	0
Vill of Morkaston for the same		13	4
G. the sheriff for chattels of Richard de Badington	1	5	5

828 [refs. 566–8]

	£	s.	d.
The same sheriff for chattels of Geoffrey son of Nicholas Carter who abjured the realm		2	0
Vill of Somersalle for flight of Geoffrey		6	8

	£	s.	d.
Walter le Blake and Thomas son of Geoffrey, both of Mersington, sureties, for not having Robert son of Robert		3	4
Urian de Sancto Petro for flight of Hugh son of the reeve of Eyton who was of his mainpast	1	0	0
Robert, reeve of Eyton, fine for trespass by surety of Adam le Venur, Richard Kyngeley of Seggesale, Simon de Clifton, Thomas de Audeley and Robert de Schyret	10	0	0

829 [refs. 569-573]

	£	s.	d.
Nicholas Judas of Howen and Henry son of Adam, sureties, for not having Lecia daughter of Alice	-	-	-
Vill of Hatton for burial without coroner's view		6	8
G. the sheriff for chattels of Philip Swary of Osmundeston, fugitive		6	4
The same sheriff for chattels of Hugh Baghwell, fugitive		9	4
Vill of North Brochton for false valuation		6	8

830 [ref. 576]

	£	s.	d.
The same sheriff for chattels of Richard son of Henry Reeve,	10	4	0
The same sheriff for chattels of Robert Joddes, fugitive		8	6
Ralph le Paumer and Henry Reeve of Sutton, sureties for Ralph son of William de Sutton who did not come		6	8
Robert son of Ralph de Sutton and Henry Hardy, sureties for Adam Godladde for the same		6	8
Robert at le Doyt of Sutton and Robert son of Ralph, sureties for Ralph Godladde who did not come		6	8

831 [refs. 577–9]

	£	s.	d.
Reynold son of William de Hokenaston, surety for Sibyl de Perton and Sibyl daughter of Henry de Hokenaston, for not having them		6	8
Alan Shepherd of Breylesford, surety for Athelina widow of Aytropus de Osmundeston		6	8
Joan sister of Aytropus for not prosecuting her appeal		3	4
Eustace de Osmundeston and William le Carpenter of the same, sureties for Agnes daughter of Joan		3	4
G. the sheriff for chattels of William son of John de Sutton who abjured the realm		12	0
Vill of Sutton for flight of William	1	0	0

	£	s.	d.
832 [ref. 580]			
Thomas Smith of Rossington, surety for not having			
John Penicod		3	4
Richard Bule and Henry son of Henry de Rossington, sureties			
for Richard son of Richard Bule who did not come		6	8
Simon le Mouner and William Russell, sureties for Richard			
son of Thomas Clerk who did not come		6	8
Adam Forester and John Golyn, sureties for Simon Shepherd			
of Clifton who did not come		3	4
William de Grendon, surety for Richard son of John de			
Snelleston		3	4
John Penicod, fine for trespass by surety of Alan le			
Bercher of Breylesford and Nicholas de Sancto Petro	2	13	4

	£	s.	d.
833 [refs. 582, 584]			
Robert son of Ives de Bralesford, fine for trespass by			
surety of Henry de Braylesford		13	4
G. the sheriff for chattels of Richard de West Brochton,			
thief	13	0	2
William de Meynill and Henry FitzHerbert, fine for			
themselves and their 12 fellow-jurors for concealment			
and other trespasses	2	0	0

WAPENTAKE OF MORLEYSTON

	£	s.	d.
834 [ref. 587]			
That wapentake, the liberties excepted, for murder	4	0	0
G. the sheriff for chattels of Hugh de Boneye		1	3
Vill of Crych for false valuation		6	8
Vill of Duffeud for the same	2	0	0
Vill of Deneby for the same		10	0
Vill of Rippeley for the same		13	4

	£	s.	d.
835 [refs. 588–9, 591]			
G. the sheriff for chattels of Robert le Bulur, hanged			8
Vill of Codenovere for false valuation	1	0	0
G. the sheriff for chattels of William son of Serlo,			
fugitive		5	0
Vill of Horseley with Kylburn for false valuation		13	4

Vill of Morley for the same   13   4

	£	s.	d.
836 [refs. 592, 594, 596]			
G. the sheriff for chattels of Roger Brokolf, fugitive		9	0
The same sheriff for chattels of Reynold de Wyleford who abjured the realm			6
Vill of Spondon for not attending inquest	1	0	0
Vill of Chaddesden outwith William de Chaddesden's part		13	4
Vill of Stanleye for the same	1	0	0
Vill of Breydesale for the same		13	4

	£	s.	d.
837 [refs. 597, 599]			
Vill of Parva Cestre with Eyton for the same		6	8
G. the sheriff for chattels of Ralph Smith of Schippeley, fugitive	1	11	4
Vill of Schyppeley for his flight	1	0	0
Robert de Stredley sen. for taking the aforesaid chattels without warrant	1	0	0
Vill of Maperley with Kyrkhalom for false valuation		6	8
Vill of Ilkesdon with members for the same	1	0	0

	£	s.	d.
838 [ref. 601]			
G. the sheriff for chattels of Hugh son of Ralph Reeve of Sandyacre, fugitive		1	0
Vill of Sandyacre for his flight	1	0	0
Vill of Ryseley for the same		13	4
Vill of Braydeston for the same	1	0	0
Vill of Staunton for the same	1	0	0

	£	s.	d.
839 [ref. 602]			
Vill of Sallowe for the same	5	0	0
G. the sheriff for chattels of Robert son of Henry de Eyton, fugitive		7	6
The same sheriff for chattels of Richard Frost, fugitive		5	5
Vill of Hoppewell for false valuation		6	8
Vill of Okebroke for the same		13	4

	£	s.	d.
840 [refs. 604, 606–8, 610]			
G. the sheriff for chattels of Thomas de Leylondschyre, fugitive		2	0

Thomas West and Richard le Rower both of West Halom,
  sureties for Isabella daughter of Thomas West de
  West Halom who did not prosecute her appeal   6   8
Richard de Quappelode del Bredes and Richard de Trowell,
  sureties, for not having Geoffrey son of Baldewyn   6   8
Robert de Karl' in Spondon and John de Blount of the same,
  sureties for Lecia daughter of Reyner de Lokington who
  did not prosecute her appeal   6   8
Stephen at Church of Halom and Robert son of Goda, sureties
  for Robert de Lambley who did not prosecute his appeal   3   4

841 [refs. 611–13]   £   s.   d.
Godfrey son of Bate and William son of Richard, sureties
  for Cecilia daughter of Richard Bate of Bole who
  did not prosecute her appeal   3   4
Peter Reeve of Sandiacre and Geoffrey his brother,
  sureties for Peter son of William Reynebaud of Boneye
  who did not prosecute his appeal   6   8
Geoffrey Collard and Henry de la Grene both of Breydeston,
  sureties for Richard Chaplain who did not come   6   8
Geoffrey son of Richard de Halom and Henry son of John
  of the same, sureties for Edusa widow of William Colyer
  who did not prosecute her appeal   6   8
William Norry, William Peverell, fine for themselves and
  their 12 fellow jurors for concealment and other
  trespasses   2   0   0

[rot. 41d.]   **VILL OF ESSEBURN**

842 [refs. 618–21]   £   s.   d.
G. the sheriff for chattels of certain unknown thieves   2   6   8
The same sheriff for chattels of Robert Torkard who abjured   10   0
Ralph son and heir of Henry de Bagepuz for Robert's
  chattels   3   0
Robert Alybon, surety for one he did not have   6   8
Richard le Tanur for the same   6   8
Ralph Sparewater and Adam brother of Alexander, former
  bailiff of Esseburn for escape of a certain unknown
  thief   8   0   0

843 [refs. 622–3]   £   s.   d.
Vills of Hertingdon, Hethcote, Neubigging and Crudecote
    for escape of Roger le Hoghyrd   8   0   0
G. the sheriff for Roger's chattels   5   5   0
Thomas le Wodeward and Richard son of Thomas, both of
    Crudecote, for trespass   3   4
Peter de Langenovere for the same <Staffs>   6   8
William le Hoggehyrd for the same   6   8
Richard Gamell of Esseburn, trespass concerning false
    weights   2   0   0

844 [refs. 624, 626–31]   £   s.   d.
G. the sheriff for chattels of 4 fugitive thieves   10   0
Richard son and heir of Henry de Benteley, former bailiff
    of Esseburn, for escape of John de Plawestowe   8   0   0
Robert de Houby for not prosecuting his appeal   1   8
Roger de la Dale of Peverwych and Nicholas de la Dale,
    sureties for John Obelay   6   8
John son of Hugh le Carpenter of Esseburn for trespass,
    by surety of Robert de Tyddeswelle and Robert de Ver   6   8
Vill of Esseburn for drapers, vintners and the 12 jurors,
    fine for trespass   5   0   0

VILL OF BATHEKWELL

845 [refs. 633, 635]   £   s.   d.
G. the sheriff for chattels of Thomas son of Maud who
    abjured the realm   7
The same sheriff for chattels of Hubert de Baukwell, hanged   3   6
Robert de Bukstones, former bailiff for taking chattels
    without warrant   6   8
Frankpledge of Robert son of Ranulph in Overhaddon,
    for flight of Ranulph de Overhaddon   6   8
G. the sheriff for chattels of the same Ranulph, fugitive   6

846 [refs. 636–7, 640–3]   £   s.   d.
The same sheriff for chattels of John de Norton who
    abjured the realm   1   6

	£	s.	d.
The same sheriff for chattels of Avice de Calfovere who abjured the realm		2	4
Robert de Reyvdon and Matthew Drapel for purpresture		3	4
Vill of Baukwell, fine for drapers, vintners and the 12 jurors for concealment and other trespasses	2	13	4
Walter de Kantia, former bailiff of the queen, for many trespasses there	5	0	0

847 [refs. 644–5]

	£	s.	d.
John de Hecham, former bailiff of Baukwell for escape of Julia la Walesck, thief	8	0	0
G. the sheriff for chattels of Richard de Cheylmerdon, fugitive			2
The same sheriff for year and waste of Richard's land		4	6
The same sheriff for chattels of Richard son of Richard, fugitive		1	0
The same sheriff for chattels of William Heryng, fugitive			4
The same sheriff for year and waste of William's land		7	0

VILL OF CESTREFEUD

848 [refs 646–8]

	£	s.	d.
G. the sheriff for chattels of Thomas de Sandyacre who abjured the realm		3	0
The same sheriff for chattels of Robert de Kynewaldesmersch, fugitive			4
Frankpledge of John son of the reeve of Barleburgh for flight of Oliver le Brun		6	8
Tithing of William de Yslep for flight of William son of Simon de Brimington		3	4

849 [refs. 649–52]

	£	s.	d.
Henry Clerk of Cestrefeud for purpresture		6	8
Tithing of Hugh Scutard for flight of Alan son of John le Komber and Hugh Horelok		6	8
Vill of Cestrefeud, fine for drapers, vintners and the 12 jurors for concealment and other trespasses and for the whole vill	3	6	8

BOROUGH OF DERBY

	£	s.	d.
850 [refs. 653–5]			
G. the sheriff for chattels of Robert de Stretton who abjured the realm		3	5
The same sheriff for chattels of Ralph de Beaurepayr, fugitive	1	12	0
Roger del Ferye and Clement le Cuner of Derby, sureties for Emma widow of John le Mey who did not prosecute her appeal		6	8
William de Staynesby for chattels of Walter de Oxon', fugitive	1	16	9
Tithing of Richard de Braydesale for flight of Walter		6	8
	£	s.	d.
851 [refs. 656–9]			
G. the sheriff for chattels of Henry son of Hubert Smith who abjured the realm			8
The same sheriff for chattels of Cecilia daughter of Peter de Leghes who abjured the realm			6
Tithing of Roger Dodding for flight of Roger de Neuton		6	8
Tithing of Richard Dedowe for flight of John de Frycheby		6	8
	£	s.	d.
852 [refs. 661, 663–5]			
G. the sheriff for chattels of Alice de Weynflet who abjured the realm			9
Tithing of Alan Schute for flight of John Chubbok		6	8
G. the sheriff for chattels of Henry Horhod, fugitive		11	3
Tithing of Roger Ogelyn for flight of the same Henry		6	8
Tithing of Roger Kaym for flight of William de Rössington, Thomas his brother and Henry le Hoppere		6	8
	£	s.	d.
853 [refs. 667–8]			
G. the sheriff for chattels of Roger Gery, hanged	1	3	8
The same sheriff for chattels of Roger Trellock, hanged		6	0
The same sheriff for chattels and year and waste of the land of William Chyrye, fugitive		6	8
The same sheriff for mid time of that land		6	0
William de Neuton and Robert his brother, sureties for Richard son of William Talenar of Neuton who did not prosecute his appeal		6	8

854 [refs. 669–71]	£	s.	d.
Roger de Morley and Nicholas Cutfichs, sureties for Hugh son of Richard le Carpenter of Morley who did not prosecute his appeal		6	8
Michael le Furbur and Nicholas le Lorymer, sureties for Alice widow of Henry de Ulegreve who did not prosecute her appeal		6	8
Gilbert le Tayllur for purpresture		6	8
Robert Tappe for the same		3	4
Roger Thagow for the same		3	4

855 [ref. 674]	£	s.	d.
Roger de Crophill for wine sold against the assize		6	8
Henry Dod for the same		6	8
John Scoyll at Derby for the same		6	8
John de Cestrefeud for the same		6	8
Burgh of Derby, fine for drapers, vintners and for trespasses of the 12 jurors	10	0	0

see p. lxi

[rot. 42]

ESTREATS OF FINES AND AMERCEMENTS OF CIVIL PLEAS

856 [refs. 2–6]	£	s.	d.
Henry de Aston and Alice his wife for disseisin		6	8
John Beck, fine for leave to concord		-	-
Thomas de Mapelton, fine for the same		6	8
Robert son of William de Barley for not prosecuting, by surety of Adam de Catteclyve of Holmesfeld		6	8
Nicholas Theobald for disseisin		6	8

857 [refs. 8–9, 11–13]	£	s.	d.
William son of Walter de Wylne for not prosecuting, by surety of John de Jaspervile and William de Kypsmere		6	8
John de Saynton and Petronilla his wife for the same, sureties		6	8

William son of Walter de Tonsteden, John Smith of
  Tonsteden, Agnes widow of William de Auderwyk for
  not prosecuting, by surety of William de Bondesale
  and Robert de Kettesteven 6 8
Reynold le Brun for unjust detention 3 4
Robert son of Robert Miller of Parva Roulesley for unjust
  detention 3 4

858 [refs. 14, 18–20]   £   s.   d.
William de Cateclyve and Alice his wife for not prosecuting,
  by surety of Henry de Goldington and John de
  Lyttelchirche 6 8
Walter le Mercer and Edith his wife, Roger de Cestria and
  Maud his wife, for false claim 3 4
Robert le Escreweyn, fine for leave to concord, by surety
  of the abbot of Derley 13 4
Hugh son of Simon de Twyford for not prosecuting 6 8
Fuchers de Marketon and Ralph Feyrbra, Hugh's sureties,
  whereof Fuchers pays 3s. 4d. 10 0

859 [refs. 22–4, 26, 28]   £   s.   d.
Roger le Wyte and Felicity his wife, fine for leave to
  concord by surety of Ranulph de Hassop 6 8
Matthew de Sancto Claro for unjust detention 1 0 0
Robert son of Robert de Wodenhow for not prosecuting,
  by surety of William Reeve of the same and Nicholas
  his brother 6 8
Robert son of Robert de Schelford for the same, by surety
  of Robert le Champion of Morkaston and William
  le Burgon 6 8
Emma daughter of Payne Smith of Derby for the same, by
  surety of Robert de Notingham and Walter le Roer of
  Derby 6 8

860 [refs. 30–32, 34, 37]   £   s.   d.
Robert son of Richard de Wystanton for the same, by surety
  of Hugh le Mariscall of Irton and Henry son of Richard
  de Weston 6 8
Giles son of Robert le Wys for the same, by surety of
  Robert son of Ives de Langeley and William his brother ... 6 8

Robert son of Henry de Wynley for false claim, by surety
of Gervase de Wyleford 6 8
William son of Peter de Bemigton, fine for leave to concord 13 4
William Swyft, fine for himself and sureties for not
prosecuting 6 8

861 [refs. 38–40, 43, 44]	£	s.	d.
John de Kynkeston, fine for leave to concord		6	8
Thomas de Tydeswelle for himself and his sureties for not prosecuting		6	8
Gregory son of William le Fevere of Allemanton, for not prosecuting by surety of John de Kynkeston and Peter de Hatton		6	8
Hugh son of Roger de Morley for unjust detention		1	8
Nicholas son of Ellis de Breydeston for false claim		3	4

862 [refs. 45, 49–50, 52–3]	£	s.	d.
Giles de Bobenhill for not prosecuting, by surety of Roger de Bugestanes and William son of William de Tonstedes		6	8
William de Meynill for not prosecuting		13	4
His sureties, Matthew de Yiveley and Richard son of Alan		6	8
Roger de Mechenton for disseisin		6	8
Robert de Estewayt for not prosecuting, by surety of Hugh de Neuthorp and Robert de Chisellwell		6	8
Thomas son of Ralph Attebridge, fine for leave to concord		6	8

863 [refs. 54, 59, 61–3]	£	s.	d.
Nicholas Martel, fine for the same		6	8
Henry Bergoylon, fine for the same		13	4
Norman de Bygham for not prosecuting, by surety of William Balle of Schirlegh		6	8
Gervase de la Corner, fine for leave to concord		10	0
Simon de Notingham for false claim		6	8

864 [refs. 66, 68, 70, 72–3]	£	s	d
John le Fevere for leave to concord		6	8
Abbot of Derley, fine for the same		6	8
Stephen de Irton, fine for the same	1	0	0
Henry de Irton, Philippa his wife and Isabella her sister fine for leave to concord by surety of Giles de Meynill		13	4

Adam son of Adam le Blund of Cesterfeud for not
prosecuting, by surety of William de Barleburgh and
Gilbert de Marcham   6   8

865 [refs. 78–80, 82, 83]   £   s.   d.
Hugh son of Simon de Barow for false claim   3   4
Thomas de Corzon for the same   6   8
Peter Pollard and William his brother for not prosecuting   6   8
Robert Sauncheverell for himself and sureties, for the same   6   8
Ralph son of Robert de Buterley for false claim   3   4

866 [refs. 84, 86, 90–92]   £   s.   d.
Simon de Notingham and Joan his wife for leave to concord   6   8
Robert son of Robert Payne for not prosecuting, by surety
    of William son of Walter de Tonstedes and William
    his son, surety for payment, Roger de Bradeburne   3   4
Robert son of Ellis Hildebrand fine for leave to concord,
    by surety of Roger de Brandburn   6   8
Richard son of Henry de Middelton for false claim   3   4
Adam de Staveley and Cassandra his wife, fine for leave to
    concord, by surety of Stephen de Jarom   13   4

867 [refs. 93, 95–6, 100, 108]   £   s.   d.
Joan widow of Walter de Scheyrley for not prosecuting, by
    surety of Thomas de Wytteclyf in Thornston and
    Henry Baret   6   8
John de Birsecute, fine for leave to concord   13   4
Ralph son of Roger de Schelandon for false claim   3   4
Robert de Quenesburch and Agnes his wife for leave to
    concord   6   8
Robert de Acovere of Denston and Margaret his wife for
    false claim   6   8

868 [refs. 109–11, 113–14]   £   s.   d.
Robert de Stafford, fine for leave to concord   6   8
Ranulph de Wendesley and Millicent his wife, fine for the
    same, by surety of John de Brommeley   6   8
Richard son of Richard de Litton fine for the same, by
    surety of Richard de Sancto Georgio   6   8
William Attewalle of Notingham for unjust detention   13   4

	£	s.	d.
Richard Meylur and Petronilla his wife for false claim		3	4

869 [refs. 119, 122, 124, 126, 132]

	£	s.	d.
Ralph le Breton and Emma his wife, fine for leave to concord		6	8
William de Batteley and Joan his wife for the same		6	8
Henry del Heth and Emma his wife for false claim		1	8
William de Bredon fine for leave to concord, by surety of Geoffrey de Burgo		6	8
Henry son of Richard de Normanton for false claim		1	8

870 [refs. 136–7, 139, 143, 152]

	£	s.	d.
William son of Matthew fine for leave to concord, by surety of Roger Balioyn		6	8
Oliver de Langeford for not prosecuting, by surety of Robert son of Henry de Langeford and Henry Reeve of the same		6	8
Ralph de Hanley for the same, by surety of William Trepell and Robert de Bromley		6	8
William de Goldington, fine for having jury of 24	1	0	0
Nicholas Herigold and Margery his wife for false claim	1	0	0

871 [refs. 153, 156–7, 160]

	£	s.	d.
Ralph de Bosco for himself and sureties for not prosecuting		6	8
Henry de Chadesden clerk, for not prosecuting, by surety of Richard de Mannefeld and Ralph son of Peter, both of Chadesden whereof Richard pays 1s. 8d.		6	8
Nicholas Keys for not prosecuting, by surety of John de Etton, surety for payment G. the sheriff		6	8
William Basket for the same, by surety of Robert de Yolegrave and Adam of the same, surety for payment, G. de Clifton		6	8
Emma de Narudale for the same, by surety of William de Langeton and Henry de Hotoft		6	8

872 [refs. 161, 162, 166–8]

	£	s.	d.
Richard le Taverner of Derby for false claim		6	8
John Gambon of Doubrigg and John Chaumberleyn, sureties for Ralph de Bosco		6	8
William Baret fine for leave to concord, by surety of Gilbert his brother		13	4

Margery widow of Hugh de Chadesden for not prosecuting,
  by surety of Henry le Macy of Derby and Hugh de
  Chadesden   6   8
Nicholas Herigaud fine for leave to concord, by surety
  of Richard de Morley   6   8

873 [refs. 171, 173–4, 176, 178]   £   s.   d.
Richard son of Amice de Whytindon, Roger son of Beatrice
  and Thomas de Wygeley for unjust detention   3   4
Robert de Estwayt for not prosecuting, by surety of Peter
  son of Thomas de Yssingden and Henry son of Myn   6   8
Orm son of Herbert de Burwes for not prosecuting, by
  surety of Thomas de Burwes and William of the same   3   4
Richard de Restwayt for false claim   3   4
Thomas del Heved for not prosecuting, by surety of Payne
  son of William and Matthew de Chaddesden   6   8

874 [refs. 180–2, 184, 190–1]   £   s.   d.
William le Wyte and Roger his brother for not prosecuting,
  by surety of Henry de Rosell and Nicholas de Killeburn   6   8
Henry son of Richard de Mapelton for not prosecuting, by
  surety of Henry de Wardington and Walter Ver   3   4
Peter son of William Swyft for the same, by surety of
  William Pollard and William Okys both of Derby   3   4
William de Calton for the same, by surety of Ralph del Hul
  and Ralph his son   3   4
Robert son of Philip for the same, by surety of Robert de
  Bokeston and Robert de Tyssington   3   4
William son of Simon de Skyrlegh for the same, by surety
  of Ralph Ferbraz   3   4

[rot. 42d.]

875 [refs. 192–6]   £   s.   d.
Richard son of Nicholas de Magworth for not prosecuting, by
  surety of Herbert de Mora of the same and Hugh Bugge   6   8
Robert de Wodecote for himself and his sureties for not
  prosecuting   3   4
Roger, parson of Snelleston chapel for not prosecuting, by
  surety of William Hert and John Galyn both of Northbur'   6   8

	£	s.	d.
Gervase the sheriff for the issues of Oliver Langeford's lands	2	0	0
Robert le Blake of Bronelveston for not prosecuting, by surety of Geoffrey de Staneley and Simon de Huppewell		3	4

876 [refs. 198–9, 201]

	£	s.	d.
John de Brommesley for unjust detention, by surety of William de Walton		6	8
Agnes widow of William de Sandiacre for the same, by surety of William de Walton		6	8
Hugh de Langeford for the same, by surety of William de Walton		6	8
William son of Alice de Kirkelangeley, fine for withdrawal for himself and his sureties		13	4
Ralph Wyne for many defaults	1	0	0
Richard de Chaddesworth fine for leave to concord	1	0	0

877 [refs. 202, 204–5, 209–10]

	£	s.	d.
Walter de Ridewar fine for the same		6	8
Ralph de Mounjoye fine for withdrawal for himself and his sureties		6	8
Henry de Chaundoys for not prosecuting		6	8
Thomas son of Adam de Herdewykwalle for not prosecuting, by surety of William son of William de Tonstedes and Robert de Lolynton		6	8
Thomas de Corzom of Keteleston fine for leave to concord		6	8

878 [refs. 211–15]

	£	s.	d.
Robert son of Philip for not prosecuting, by surety of William de Bukeston and Robert de Tissington		3	4
Henry de Chaddesden for the same, by surety of Richard de Mamfeud and Ralph son of Peter de Mamfeud		3	4
Roger son of Ralph de Weston for the same, by surety of Richard de Weston in Alewaynton and Walter Attegrene		6	8
Roger Lichtefote of Bucstanes and Richard son of Lucy del Frith, sureties for Thomas son of Adam de Herdewykwall who did not prosecute		6	8
Thomas Abbot and Alice his wife for not prosecuting, by surety of Simon Talbot of Wyvesflet and Thomas Abbot of Pakington		6	8

879 [refs. 216–18, 220, 222]   £   s.   d.

Robert son of Thomas Attekerkeyard for the same, by surety
    of Richard Donger of Eyton and William Attekerkeyard   6   8
Robert son of John de Gilford for the same, by surety of
    Thomas Cacehors and William Maunderell   6   8
Thomas son of Swayn de Litton fine for leave to concord   6   8
William Martyn and Isabella his wife fine for the same   6   8
William Fox fine for the same   6   8

880 [refs. 226, 229–32]   £   s.   d.

Richard de Draycote for false claim   3   4
Nicholas de Clifton fine for leave to concord   6   8
Geoffrey son of Nicholas de Blechell' for not prosecuting,
    by surety of Robert son of Robert de Staneley and
    William son of John Staneley   6   8
Reynold le Vicar of Derby fine for leave to concord   6   8
Walter de Rideware fine for trespass, by surety of
    William Rither   1   0   0

881 [refs. 235, 238, 246, 262]   £   s.   d.

Isabella widow of Ralph de la Rode for not prosecuting,
    by surety of Richard de Ridewath and John his brother   3   4
Richard son of Henry le Seriant fine for leave to concord   6   8
Robert son of Geoffrey Dewek fine for the same   6   8
Robert le Venur fine for the same, by surety of
    William de Auderley   6   8

APPENDIX A

DERBYSHIRE ACTIONS ADJOURNED FROM DERBY

Unless otherwise stated all references are from JUST 1/499, Foreign Pleas of the Lincolnshire Eyre, Trinity and Michaelmas 1281 and Hilary 1282. References to adjournments to Westminster and Shrewsbury are from CP 40/45–48.

A1 Ref. 286
Octave of Trinity. The parties concorded, Robert and the others giving half a mark for leave to concord by surety of the abbot. Chirograph. The tenements were acknowledged to be the right of the abbot and his church. [*rot. 1d*]

A2 Ref. 233
Octave of Trinity. Essoin for Robert le Megre, warrantor of Robert de Stafford. The parties concorded. William Rocelin gave half a mark for leave to concord by surety of Robert who acknowledged William's right and quitclaimed etc. for himself and his heirs to William and his heirs forever. William to have seisin. [*rot. 59d, rot. 2*]

A3 Ref. 723
Octave and Quindene of Trinity. William de Beverlaco, for the king, traced the right of advowson from Henry II, who presented his clerk, Henry le Normaund, in turn to the king's sons Henry, Richard and John, from John to his son Henry and thence to king Edward. The dean and chapter denied the king's right. Adjourned to St John the Baptist three weeks. [*rot. 3*]
   Quindene of St John the Baptist. Two essoins for the dean and chapter. To Michaelmas one month. [*rot. 63*]

A4 Ref. 740
Quindene of Trinity. The prior defaulted and was attached. Sheriff ordered to have him at the quindene of Michaelmas. [*rot. 3d*]
   Quindene of Michaelmas. The prior defaulted. His mainpernors, William Barent, William le King, John Gelyns and Richard Bishop, amerced. The sheriff, who had done nothing, again ordered to distrain and have him at the

octave of Hilary, along with half a mark received for the issues of the lands. [JUST 1/1250 rot. 3d]

Octave of Hilary 1282. The prior defaulted. The sheriff had done nothing but reported distraint and receipt of half a mark issues. The sheriff was mainperned by his sons Simon, Nicholas, Robert and Henry de Clifton and again ordered to have the prior at Easter one month wherever etc. with the issues received at the terms named. Later addition: to Michaelmas one month wherever. [JUST 1/1250 rot. 3d]

A5 Refs 114, 179
Octave of Trinity. Essoins for John, Roger and Robert in a plea of dower. To quindene of Michaelmas. [*rot. 57*]

Quindene of Trinity. Essoin for Agnes in a plea of land. [*rot. 59*]

The demandants claimed against Agnes the manor of Oxcroft, except 4 messuages, a toft and 4 bovates, with which Richard Ingram's son Robert, Petronilla's former husband, had dowered her at the church door etc. with his father's assent and whereof she has nothing. Agnes denied their claim since Robert had committed larceny, put himself in Neuton church in Kesteven and abjured the realm. The demandants acknowledged this but said it had been during the life of his father, who had assented to the dower, and sought judgment as to whether they should be debarred from action. [*rot. 4*]

Quindene of Michaelmas. Claim against Agnes as above and against each of the other tenants a messuage and a bovate. They alleged that the felony was committed before Robert Ingram had seisin of the tenements claimed. The demandants claimed that before taking the religious habit Robert's father gave his lands to Robert as son and heir and that the tenants had been enfeoffed from that seisin. The felony, if any, had been committed afterwards. Both parties sought judgment. [*rot. 38*]

Quindene of Hilary 1282. Adjournment to quindene of Easter at Westminster as judgment not yet made. [*rot. 55*]

Trinity three weeks 1282 Westminster. Agnes de Percy defaulted. The manor, with exceptions as above, to be taken into the king's hand. Agnes to be summoned to hear judgment, quindene of Michaelmas at Shrewsbury. [CP 40/46 rot. 46d]

Quindene of Michaelmas at Shrewsbury 1282. Richard and Petronilla held themselves to Agnes's default. She says her attorneys, John le Bry and Ralph de Rapy, summoned to the king's court on the Thursday in Pentecost week last past for defending this plea, were met in Lincolnshire by John de la More, the bailiff, and others unknown and taken to Old Lafford in the same county and kept in prison until the morrow of St James the Apostle. Summons for quindene of Hilary. [CP 40/47 rot. 5d]

Quindene of Michaelmas at Shrewsbury 1282. Roger and the others came, saying Richard and Petronilla could claim no dower, and cited the abjuration of her first husband. They said Robert died in the lifetime of his father and could not have forfeited by abjuration the tenements of others which had never been in his seisin. Judgment: Roger and the others without day. Richard and Petronilla to be amerced for false claim. [CP 40/47 rot. 30d.]

A6   Ref. 101

Quindene of Trinity. The parties concorded. William and Cecilia gave half a mark for leave to concord, surety William Danvers. Chirograph. [*rot. 5*]

A7   Ref. 87

Quindene of Trinity. Essoins for Letitia's attorneys, Robert son of Alexander and Hugh Payn. [*rot. 58d*]

John le Fowen's warrantor Richard defaulted. The sheriff had not summoned, so ordered to re-summon etc. for the quindene of Michaelmas and to be present to hear judgment on himself. Same day for Sewall. [*rot. 5*]

Quindene of Michaelmas. John le Fowen, warrantor of Letitia, defaulted. The tenements to be taken into the king's hand. Summons for the quindene of Hilary to hear judgment. [*rot. 34d.*]

Quindene of Hilary 1282. Essoins for Letitia's attorneys. [*rot. 73d*] John le Fowen again defaulted. The sheriff attested the confiscation and a summons. Judgment: Sewall to have seisin against Letitia who was to have land to the value from John who was to be amerced. [*rot. 53d*]

A8   Ref. 257

Quindene of Trinity. John de Dalby and Agnes, warrantors of Ralph de Dalby and Agnes, defaulted. The sheriff had not summoned nor sent the writ. Ordered to re-summon for the quindene of Michaelmas and be present to hear judgment on himself. [*rot. 5*]

Quindene of Michaelmas. Essoins for John de Dalby and Agnes. To quindene of Hilary. [*rot. 68*]

Octave of Hilary. Roger Baudry claimed as heir of his grandfather Roger Swarry who, the tenants' warrantors maintained, did not die after the time limited by writ of mort d'ancestor. Both parties put themselves on the country. Sheriff to summon 12 impartial jurors for quindene of Trinity at Westminster. [*rot. 50*]

A9 Ref. 142
Octave of Trinity. Essoin for Henry son of William de Stansop, warrantor of Roger de Merston. [*rot. 57*]

    Quindene of Trinity. Henry de Stansop defaulted. The sheriff of Staffs. had done nothing nor sent the writ. Ordered to re-summon him for quindene of Michaelmas and to be present to hear judgment on himself. [*rot. 5d*]

    Quindene of Hilary 1282. Essoins for attorneys of Roger de Mersington, Hugh son of Hugh and Richard son of Robert. [*rot. 73d*]

    Trinity three weeks 1282 Westminster. Both warrantors came. Henry de Stansop further vouched John Hylom's daughter and heir Joan, who was under age. She proffered a charter of her great-grandfather Henry, son of Turgis whose heir she was, testifying that Henry gave the tenements claimed to William son of William clerk of Alstonesfeld, his father whose heir he was, warranting for himself and his heirs. Henry son of Roger de Mappelton claimed that she was of age and should be summoned to warrant. Order that she be summoned in Staffs. to appear in person at Shrewsbury at the octave of Michaelmas for her age to be verified. Later that day Henry son of Roger acknowledged her nonage. Judgment: stay of action until she was of age. [CP 40/46 rot. 55]

A10 Ref. 169
Quindene of Trinity. Alan de Waldeschef and Lucy, warrantors of Richard de Morley and Joan, defaulted. Sheriff had done nothing nor sent the writ. Ordered to summon them for quindene of Michaelmas and be present to hear judgment on himself. John de la Plaunche and Elena did not come. Same day given to all parties. [*rot. 5d*]

    Essoins for Richard de Morley and Joan's attorneys against Letitia and for John de la Plaunche and Elena. Alan de Waldeschelf and Lucy, John and Elena, warrantors, to be exacted. To quindene of Michaelmas. It did not lie because no summons was attested. [*rot. 58*]

    Essoins for attorneys of Letitia against Alan and Lucy. [*rot. 58d*]

    Octave of St John the Baptist. Essoins for Richard de Morley and Joan against Letitia in a plea of dower. [*rot. 62d*]

A11 Refs 106, 107
Quindene of Trinity. Richard de Pres defaulted. Sheriff, ordered to distrain, had done nothing. Again ordered to distrain, have him at quindene of Michaelmas and be present to hear judgment on himself. [*rot. 5d*]

A12 Ref. 64

Quindene of Trinity. John Asser defaulted. The sheriff had done nothing. Again ordered to summon him for the quindene of Michaelmas and be present to hear judgment on himself. [*rot. 6*]

Essoin for Adam Basset's attorney. Exaction of John Asser, warrantor who did not come. To quindene of Michaelmas. [*rot. 57d*]

Quindene of Michaelmas. Essoin for John Asser. To quindene of Hilary. [*rot. 69*]

Quindene of Hilary 1282. Essoin for Peter Axstel, attorney of Adam Basset. [*rot. 73*]

Quindene of Trinity 1282 Westminster. Richard de Byngham claimed that Adam had no entry except after a demise made to Richard Asser by Ralph Bugge for a term which had expired and which ought to have reverted to him as heir of his father Ralph. John questioned Adam's right to vouch him, Adam claiming to hold of John by homage and service of 1d. yearly, which homage he paid on the Sunday next before the Purification in the present king's first year at Netherhaddon in Simon Basset's house in the presence of Simon, Robert de Estaunton, John le Turnur and Herbert le Peschur [*29 Jan. 1273*]. By that homage John ought to warrant him. John denied this and both parties put themselves on the country. Order to sheriff to have the four witnesses and 12 impartial jurors at Shrewsbury at the octave of Martinmas. Adam appointed John de Meleford as attorney. [CP 40/46 rot. 46]

Octave of Martinmas at Shrewsbury 1282. Respited till Easter one month because no-one came. Richard by his attorney. [CP 40/47 rot. 119d.]

A13 Ref. 271

Quindene of Trinity The defendants sought a view. To quindene of Michaelmas. [*rot. 6*]

Quindene of Michaelmas. After the view. Essoin for defendants' attorneys. To quindene of Hilary. [*rot. 68*]

Octave of Hilary 1282. William son of Adam claimed as heir of his grandfather Roger de Blida. The defendants denied this. Both parties put themselves on the country. Sheriff ordered to summon 12 for quindene of Trinity at Westminster. William's mother Agnes may sue for him. [*rot. 50*]

A14 Ref. 150

Quindene of Trinity. In the king's court at Westminster William de Morteyn complained that though he held of Robert de Pavely one knight's fee in Risseley by homage and scutage of 40s. for all services and Robert ought therefore to acquit him etc., through default of quittance, the bishop distrained him by homage and suit at his court at Salley every three weeks. Thus he had suffered damage of £100. Robert acknowledged that he ought to acquit John but denied William had been distrained for default of his quittance. William's case was upheld. Judgment: William to recover damages assessed at £20, half to the clerks. Robert to be amerced. [*rot. 6*]

A15 Refs 10, 287
Quindene of Trinity. The abbot of Wellebek came by his attorney. John de Mentham defaulted. Sheriff ordered to distrain and have him at quindene of Michaelmas. [*rot. 7*]

Easter four/five weeks 1282 Westminster. John defaulted. Sheriff reported distraint by lands and chattels, 40d. Mainpernors John, reeve of Wytenton, and William son of John de Wytenton amerced. Sheriff ordered to distrain and have him at Shrewsbury at Michaelmas one month. [CP 40/45 rot. 50]

Qindene of Hilary at Shrewsbury 1283. The sheriff had done nothing. John again defaulted. To quindene of Trinity. [CP 40/48 rot. 32d.]

A16 Ref. 264
Morrow of St John the Baptist. John d'Eyncurt defendant without day by default of Alice. Sureties to be amerced, names to be enquired. [*rot. 8*]

A17 Ref. 149
Morrow of St John the Baptist. Rose Borard demandant and Richard Walkelin warrantor of Robert le Chapelyn tenant, by their attorneys, to octave of Michaelmas as judgment not yet made. [*rot. 8*]

Quindene of St John the Baptist. Assize to be taken by default of defendant's warrantor, put in respite until octave of Michaelmas for default of recognitors. Order to sheriff etc. [*rot. 27*]

Quindene of Michaelmas. Defaults as before. Day given parties at quindene of Hilary to hear judgment and sheriff to hear judgment on himself. [*rot. 36*]

A18 Ref. 207
Quindene of Trinity. Day in Michaelmas three weeks to hear judgment. [*rot. 9*]

A19 Ref. 219
Octave of St John the Baptist. Day in Michaelmas three weeks given

Richard de Byngham and John son of Nicholas Staymore to hear judgment. [*rot. 10d*]

Quindene of Michaelmas at Shrewsbury 1282. Richard son of Ralph Bugge claims fourth part of manor of Repton, except one messuage, as his right. He says that John son of Nicholas de Sancto Mauro has no entry except after disseisin made by Robert de Ferrars on Ralph Bugge, his father whose heir he is. John claims a view. Day given them at quindene of Hilary. [CP 40/47 rot. 20]

A20 Ref. 245

Octave of St John the Baptist. Essoins for John de Skeftington and Ellis de Hibernia, attorneys of Geoffrey. [*rot. 62*]

Quindene/St John the Baptist three weeks. William de Audeley asked to be shown by what he ought to warrant. John de Skeftington proffered a charter of William's father James to Geoffrey de Skeftington his father attesting warranty and also confirmatory instruments containing a special clause of warranty from both William's brother Henry, whose heir he was, and from William himself. William questioned his need to answer until John held to the instrument with the special clause. John maintained that all the confirmations depended on the charter. A day was given to hear judgment at the octave of Martinmas. [*rot. 24*]

Octave of Martinmas. Essoins for Robert Chese and John del Holt, attorneys of William de Audeley. To Easter one month at Westminster. [*rot. 70*]

Quindene/Easter three weeks 1282 Westminster. Respited until Michaelmas three weeks at Shrewsbury. William de Audeley had the king's writ that all pleas touching him should be respited until then except those of dower 'unde nihil habet', 'quare impeditum', novel disseisin and darrein presentment. [CP 40/45 rot. 35]

A21 Ref. 170?

Octave of St John the Baptist. William de Morteyn, by attorney, against Robert de Sauncheverell in a plea of reasonable estovers, roadway across his land and common pasture in Risley, whereof his father Eustace died seised. Robert defaulted. Attached to be present at Michaelmas three weeks. [*rot. 12d*]

Quindene/Easter three weeks 1282 Westminster. Robert defaulted and was summoned by Thomas son of Walter de Hopwell and Ellis de Breydeston who were amerced. Sheriff ordered to distrain etc. and have him at Shrewsbury at quindene of Michaelmas. [CP 40/45 rot. 45]

Quindene of Michaelmas at Shrewsbury 1282. Robert Sacheverell defaulted. Distrained. His mainpernors amerced. Sheriff had done nothing. To be summoned again for quindene of Hilary. [CP 40/47 rot. 24d.]

Quindene of Hilary at Shrewsbury 1283. Robert Sacheverell defaulted. As above. To quindene of Trinity. [CP 40/48 rot. 32d.]

A22   Ref. 273

Octave of St John the Baptist. Thomas de Cadurcis came by attorney. Queen Eleanor defaulted. The sheriff had done nothing, reported that she had nothing in his bailliwick by which she could be distrained but attested that she could be distrained by her custody. Sheriff orderd to distrain and have her with jurors at Michaelmas one month. [*rot. 13d*]

A23   Ref. 274

Octave of St John the Baptist. William le Franceys could not answer, claimed nothing except by custody of Robert son of Philip who was under age. The abbot could not deny this and sought leave to withdraw. [*rot. 13d*]

A24   Ref. 250

Octave of St John the Baptist. The defendants came by the bishop's attorney. Julia could not answer because she held of the bishop in villeinage. The bishop sought a view. To Michaelmas three weeks. [*rot. 14*]

A25   Ref. 133

Octave/Quindene of St John the Baptist. The sheriff had not summoned Richard de Grey nor the jury of 24 to attaint the 12 who had held the inquisition at Derby. Ordered to re-summon them for octave of Michaelmas to enquire as to the inquisitors, to have them also and be present to hear judgment on himself. [*rot. 14d*]

New writ. Essoins for Richard and Walter de Morley, demandants. The defendants had not come and the sheriff had not returned the writ in the form which he ought. [*rot. 63*]

St James's Day. Essoin for John de Brampton attorney of Richard de Grey. [*rot. 66*]

Quindene of Michaelmas. Essoin for Richard de Grey. [*rot. 69*]

A26   Ref. 56

Octave of St John the Baptist. Robert de Milnehause and John de Laufol defaulted. Sheriff had not distrained. Again ordered to distrain, have them at Michaelmas three weeks and be present to hear judgment on himself. [*rot.*

16d]

Easter one month/five weeks 1282 Westminster. Sheriff had done nothing, but reported names of mainpernors, Richard de Clifton, Matthew Mareballock, Peter Swyft and John Leek who were amerced. To Shrewsbury for quindene of Michaelmas. [CP 40/45 rot. 49]

Quindene/three weeks of Michaelmas at Shrewsbury 1282. Robert de Milnehaus and John de Laffol did not come and had made many defaults. Sheriff to distrain them and have them at quindene of Hilary. [CP 40/47 rot. 50.]

A27 Ref. 243
Octave of St John the Baptist. Grand assize between Ralph de Crumwell and William son of Stephen de Stanleye put in respite until Michaelmas three weeks for default of 12 knights because no-one came. Re-summons for that term. Ralph appointed Hugh de Normanton as attorney. [*rot. 17*]

A28 Ref. 206
Octave of St John the Baptist. Jordan, warrantor of Roger, defaulted. Judgment: land of Jordan's to the value to be taken into the king's hand. To be re-summoned for Michaelmas three weeks. Same day to Thomas's attorney. [*rot. 17*]

Quindene of Trinity 1282 Westminster. Sheriff of Derby ordered to have recognitors at Shrewsbury for morrow of Martinmas. Jordan son of Robert to be summoned in Lancs. [CP 40/46 rot. 43]

Morrow of Martinmas at Shrewsbury 1282. Jordan son of Robert defaulted. Sheriff of Lancs. had done nothing. To summon him for Easter three weeks. The like to sheriff of Derby. [CP 40/47 rot. 101d.]

A29 Ref. 278
Octave of St John the Baptist. William son of William Ingram claimed against Richard de Grey two parts of a messuage, 11 bovates of land and 18s. rent in Long Eyton and Sandiacre in which Richard had no entry except by William de Grey, to whom William Ingram demised them while of unsound mind. Richard acknowledged this but maintained that William had been of sound mind. Order to sheriff to have 12 impartial jurors at Michaelmas three weeks. [*rot. 17*]

A30 Ref. 221
Quindene of Trinity. Essoins for Gervase and attorney of Peter de Rolaund. [*deleted*] It did not lie because no summons was attested. [*rot. 58d*]

Gervase de Bernak, warrantor of William, defaulted. Sheriff reported that the writ had arrived too late for execution. Ordered to summon for Michaelmas three weeks. [*rot. 18*]

A31   Ref. 284
Octave/Quindene of St John the Baptist. Essoin for Michael de Breydeston, warrantor of Natalia. [*rot. 62*]
   Michael defaulted. Sheriff had not summoned nor sent the writ. Ordered as before to summon etc. for Michaelmas one month and be present to hear judgment on himself. [*rot. 18*]
   Quindene of Michaelmas. Essoin for Michael de Breydeston. [*rot. 67d*]
   Michaelmas one month. Michael again defaulted. Sheriff had not summoned. Order as before to summon for Hilary three weeks. Same day given Sarra. [*rot. 41*]
   Morrow of Martinmas at Shrewsbury 1282. Michael de Breydeston defaulted. The tenements to be taken into the king's hand. Both parties to be summoned for Easter three weeks. [CP 40/47 rot. 100d.]

A32   Ref. 151
Octave of St John the Baptist. Essoin for both attorneys of abbot. To Michaelmas three weeks. [*rot. 61*]
   Walter de Rydware demandant defaulted. Judgment: the abbot was without day. Walter and his sureties to be amerced, their names to be enquired. [*rot. 18d*]

A33   Ref. 57
Octave of St John the Baptist. The defendants defaulted as several times before. Order to sheriff to distrain etc. and have them at Michaelmas one month. Roger Scott appointed John Puterel as attorney. [*rot. 21d*]
   Easter one month/five weeks 1282 Westminster. The defendants again defaulted. Sheriff had done nothing but reported mainprise by William son of Robert de Rependen and Richard Reeve of the same who were amerced. Order to distrain and have them at Shrewsbury at quindene of Michaelmas. [CP 40/45 rot. 49]

A34   Ref. 128
Octave of St John the Baptist. Hubert de Frechevill, by his attorney, and William de Chaddesden, by his bailiff, to hear judgment at Michaelmas three weeks. [*rot. 22d*]
   Quindene of Michaelmas at Shrewsbury 1282. Hubert came, Robert

and the others defaulted. It was not found by the assize with whom the rent ought to remain. A further assize to be taken but respited until morrow of Close of Easter at Sandyacre before Nicholas de Stapelton and Elia de Bek. Sheriff ordered to have recognitors there at that time. [CP 40/47 rot. 39.]

A35 Ref. 251

Morrow of St John the Baptist. Essoin for prior's attorney. To St John the Baptist one month. [*rot. 59d*]

Quindene/St John the Baptist three weeks. The parties by their attorneys to hear judgment at quindene of Hilary. [*rot. 24*]

Quindene of Michaelmas. Essoin for prior's attorneys. To quindene of Hilary. [*rot. 67d*]

Quindene of Hilary. The parties by their attorneys to hear judgment at Westminster Easter one month. [rot. 52]

Quindene/three weeks Michaelmas at Shrewsbury 1282. The prior came. Said Odenellus did not demise the manor as aforesaid but to Henry and his heirs. Both parties seek jury. To be summoned for Hilary three weeks. [CP 40/47 rot. 19d.]

Quindene of Hilary at Shrewsbury 1283. Respited until Easter one month for lack of jury. Attorneys for both parties. [CP 40/48 rot. 52d.]

A36 Refs. 223, 292

Quindene/St John the Baptist three weeks. Ralph de Hanley, warrantor of Robert Halewas, defaulted. Judgment: the messuage to be taken into the king's hand and Ralph summoned to hear judgment at Michaelmas one month. [*rot. 24d*]

Michaelmas one month. The sheriff had done nothing nor sent the writ. Ordered to take messuage into the king's hand, summon Ralph for Hilary three weeks and be present to hear judgment on himself. [*rot. 39*]

Easter one month/five weeks 1282 Westminster. Ralph defaulted. Adam de Tapton came. The messuage to be taken into the king's hand. Summons etc. for Michaelmas three weeks at Shrewsbury. [CP 40/45 rot. 64d]

A37 Ref. 239

Octave of St John the Baptist. Day given at quindene of Michaelmas at request of the parties, Robert de Bakepuz by attorney and John de Lovetoft. [*rot. 26*]

Quindene of Michaelmas. Day given at quindene of Hilary at request of the parties. [*rot. 37*]

A38   Ref. 265
Quindene of St John the Baptist. Day at quindene of Michaelmas given Ralph de Crumwell, by attorney, and abbot of Dale. Judgment not yet made. [rot. 26d]

   Quindene of Michaelmas. To quindene of Martinmas. [*rot. 33*]

   Quindene of Martinmas. To Easter five weeks at Westminster. [*rot. 46d.*]

   Easter one month/five weeks 1282 Westminster. To Michaelmas one month at Shrewsbury. [CP 40/45 rot. 53]

A39   Ref. 244
Quindene of St John the Baptist. Ralph de Crumwelle came. All three defendants defaulted. Sheriff had not distrained, summoned or sent the writ. Again ordered to distrain etc. and have them at Michaelmas one month and be present to hear judgment on himself. [*rot. 27d*]

   Michaelmas one month. Sheriff had again done nothing. Ordered as before for Hilary three weeks. [*rot. 40*]

   Easter one month/five weeks 1282 Westminster. The defendants defaulted. Sheriff had done nothing but reported that they had nothing in his bailiwick but sufficient in West Halum. Ordered to have them at Shrewsbury for Michaelmas one month. [CP 40/45 rot. 50]

   Michaelmas three weeks and one month at Shrewsbury 1282. The defendants defaulted. Sheriff had not distrained, said they had no lands etc. in his bailiwick but it was testified that they had. As before, to have them at quindene of Hilary. [CP 40/47 rot. 56]

   Quindene of Hilary at Shrewsbury 1283. The defendants again defaulted. To be distrained. Sheriff to resummon for quindene of Trinity. [CP 40/48 rot. 37.]

A40   Ref. 226
Octave of Trinity. Essoins for Henry FitzHerbert and Godfrey le Mouner, tenants. New plea by two writs. To octave of Michaelmas. [*rot. 57*]

   Octave of Michaelmas. Richard de Draycote and Agnes came. Godfrey defaulted. Judgment: The tenements to be taken into the king's hand. Summons etc. for octave of Hilary. [*rot. 28*]

   Octave of Hilary. Godfrey claimed a view. To Westminster for quindene of Easter. [*rot. 48*]

A41   Ref. 227
   Octave of Trinity. Essoin for Henry FitzHerbert. To octave of Michael-

mas. A new plea. [*rot. 57*]

Morrow of Michaelmas. Richard de Draycote and Agnes claimed a messuage, a carucate, 10 bovates, 4 acres of meadow, a third of 24 acres of wood and two-thirds of a mill with appurtenances in Northburgh and Rossington. The defendant claimed a view. To octave of Martinmas. [*rot. 28*]

Octave of Martinmas. After the view. Essoin for defendant. To quindene of Easter at Westminster. [*rot. 70*]

Quindene of Easter 1282 Westminster. The demandants traced descent of the tenements claimed, saying that John FitzHerbert, dying without direct heir, the right descended to his brother William, from him to his son John and from John, dying without heir, to his brother Roger, who also dying without direct heir, the right passed to Agnes his sister and heir. Henry denied their right, saying that William succeeded John, dowered John's widow Margery and afterwards enfeoffed Henry of two parts of the tenements along with those held in dower by Margery. She acknowledged Henry as tenant by homage and service, so he was in seisin by her hand. Thus he entered not by intrusion but by William's enfeoffment. The demandants proffered a fine made at Derby in 53 Henry III before the justices in eyre (Apr.–May 1269), in which William acknowledged the manor to be the right of Henry by William's gift. They said that Margery then held the tenements in dower and the fine made no mention of Henry's tenements descending after her death by William's gift. Henry said that William had enfeoffed him of the manor as well as the tenements claimed and which Margery held in dower. Before the fine he was in seisin, by William's assignment, of Margery's homage and service and 13s. 11d. yearly. The demandants said that Margery did not acknowledge Henry as tenant by homage and service, nor was he in seisin by her hand before the fine. Both parties put themselves on the country.

Sheriff ordered to have 12 impartial jurors at the octave of Michaelmas. Henry appointed William de Benteleye or Adam de Northbury as his attorney.

Afterwards, Morrow of All Souls in the king's 13th year (3 Nov. 1285). A jury found that by William's assignment, Henry was in seisin of Margery's homage and service for one year before the fine was levied. Judgment: Henry went without day and Richard and Agnes were amerced for a false claim. [CP 40/45 rot. 7]

Octave of Hilary at Shrewsbury 1283. Put in respite for default of jury until Octave of Trinity 1283. [CP 40/48 rot. 10]

See Postea above enrolled on CP 40/45 rot.7

A42   Ref. 159
Octave of Michaelmas. The defendant Maud defaulted and had been summoned. Land to be taken into the king's hand. Re-summons for octave of Hilary. [*rot. 28*]

A43   Ref. 288
Octave of Michaelmas. John son of Ralph de Knyveton and the others came. John son of John defaulted. Order to distrain etc. and have him at quindene of Hilary. [*rot. 29*]
   Quindene of Hilary. Sheriff again ordered to distrain and have him at Westminster at quindene of Trinity and be present to hear judgment on himself. [*rot. 54*]

A44   Ref. 285
Quindene of Trinity. After the view. Essoin for Richard son of Geoffrey, attorney of Richard de Grey. To quindene of Michaelmas. [*rot. 58d*]
   Quindene of Michaelmas. Richard de Grey, tenant, by attorney said that William de Saundeby had right in only a third of the mill, which he surrendered to Sibyl. As to the remainder he claimed that William was not seised of the mill as of fee etc. on the day of marriage, so that Sibyl could claim no dower. Both parties put themselves on the country. Order to sheriff to have 12 impartial jurors at quindene of Martinmas. [*rot. 33*]
   Quindene of Martinmas. Put in respite until quindene of Purification at Westminster for default of jury which is to be re-summoned. [*rot. 47*]
   Easter one month/five weeks 1282 Westminster. To Shrewsbury for quindene of Michaelmas at request of the parties. [CP 40/45 rot. 53]
   Michaelmas quindene and three weeks at Shrewsbury 1282. Day given at request of both parties. To quindene of Hilary. [CP 40/47 rot. 45d.]
   Quindene of Hilary at Shrewsbury 1283. Respited until Easter three weeks. No-one came. [CP 40/48 rot. 35d.]

A45   Ref. 270
Octave of Trinity. Essoins for attorneys of Geoffrey le Carectarius. [*rot. 57*]
   Quindene of Michaelmas. To quindene of Hilary at request of the parties. [*rot. 33*]

A46   Ref. 268
Quindene of Trinity. Essoins for Roger son of Henry, warrantor of William son of Henry de Cromford, and for abbot of Darley. To quindene of Michaelmas. [*rot. 59d*]

Quindene of Michaelmas. Robert son of Hervey claimed that the tenants had no entry except after a demise made to Robert de Asseburne by Henry de Brond, his guardian, who had the tenements only by wardship while he was under age. William's warrantors and their warrantor, Roger son of Henry de Asseburne, came. Roger denied that Henry de Brond had wardship in Robert's name because the tenements were the right and inheritance of Alice mother of Robert, the son of her first husband Hervey, after whose death she allowed herself to be married to Henry Brond. Thus Henry had nothing in the tenements except in her name. Both parties put themselves on the country. Order to sheriff to have 12 jurors at quindene of Hilary. [*rot. 33d*]

Quindene of Hilary. Essoins for William son of Henry and Henry de Cromford. [*rot. 73d*]

Respited until quindene of Trinity at Westminster for default of jury. Sheriff to have them at that term. [*rot. 52d*]

A47 Ref. 96

Quindene of Trinity. New plea. Essoin for John son of Hugh de Tiddeswell and Ralph de Scheladon. To quindene of Michaelmas. [*rot. 58d*]

Quindene of Michaelmas. To quindene of Hilary at request of the parties. [*rot. 34d*]

Quindene of Hilary 1282. The demandant defaulted. Amercement for non-prosecution. Names of sureties to be enquired. [*rot. 55*]

A48 Refs. 129, 255

Morrow/Octave of St John the Baptist. Essoins for Hugh and Geoffrey, attorneys of Joan wife of Henry de Curzon. To quindene of Michaelmas. [*rot. 59, 61d, 62*]

Quindene of Michaelmas. Essoin for Richard, attorney of Henry Curzon. [*rot. 67d*]

Day given Henry de Irton, Philippa and Isabella at quindene of Hilary. [*rot. 35*]

Quindene of Hilary 1282. To Westminster for Easter one month because Judgment not yet made. [*rot. 53*]

Quindene of Michaelmas at Shrewsbury 1282. Respited until Octave of Hilary. Henry de Curzon has gone to Wales. [CP 40/47 rot. 30d.]

A49 Ref. 76

Quindene of Michaelmas. Robert de Bradesal, warrantor, defaulted. Sheriff had not summoned nor sent the writ. Ordered to summon and have recognitors at quindene of Hilary. [*rot. 37d*]

Quindene of Hilary 1282. John de Leyk and his warrantor further vouched the prioress of de Pratis, Derby. William de Leyk said that voucher should not stay the assize because the prioress did not have the tenements in demesne so that she could have demised them. Both parties sought inquiry by assize rather than by jury. Order to sheriff to have recognitors at Westminster at quindene of Trinity. Robert de Breydesale appointed John son of John de Lek as his attorney. [*rot. 52*]

Quindene of Trinity 1282 Westminster. Respited until morrow of Martinmas at Shrewsbury for lack of recognitors. None came. Sheriff ordered to summon them for that term. [CP 40/46 rot. 43]

Morrow of All Souls at Shrewsbury 1282. Respited until Quindene of Easter for default of recognitors. No-one came. [CP 40/47 rot. 91d.]

A50 Ref. 290

Quindene of Michaelmas. The defendants defaulted. Sheriff reported that they had nothing in his bailiwick etc. but attested that they had sufficient in Staffs. Sheriff of Staffs. to distrain them and have them at quindene of Hilary. [*rot. 37d*]

Octave of Hilary 1282. Day at quindene of Trinity at Westminster given at request of the parties, Ellis de Staunton and Roger le Botiller and Margery. [*rot. 49*]

Quindene of Hilary 1282. The defendants defaulted. Sheriff had not distrained. Sampson de Ruyding and Adam le May of Cayton, mainpernors of Richard de Draycote and Agnes to be amerced. Order as before to sheriff to distrain and have them at Westminster at quindene of Trinity. [*rot. 49*]

A51 Ref. 8

Quindene of Trinity. New plea. Essoin for abbot of Chester. To quindene of Michaelmas. [*rot. 59*]

Quindene of Michaelmas. William son of Walter de Wylne, who claimed two parts of a messuage and 4 bovates in Great Wylne near Schardlowe, came by his attorney and claimed a view. To quindene of Hilary. [*rot. 38d*]

Quindene of Hilary 1282. After the view. Essoins for the abbot's attorney, Henry de Stanton, and Peter de Perfit. To quindene of Trinity at Westminster by surety of Richard de Stapelford. [*rot. 73*]

Quindene of Trinity 1282 Westminster. William claimed that the abbot had no entry except by William de Hautrive, to whom his father Walter de Wylne had demised them and who had unjustly disseised him. The abbot acknowledged entry but denied disseisin since the demandant had never been in seisin. Both parties put themselves on the country. Order to sheriff to have 12 jurors at Shrewsbury on the morrow of Martinmas. [CP 40/46 rot. 37d] **Morrow of Martinmas at Shrewsbury 1282.** Respited until Easter three weeks for default of jury. No-one came. [CP 40/47 rot. 101.]

A52 Ref. 247
Quindene of Trinity. Essoin for dean and chapter of Lychefeld. [*rot. 59*]

Quindene of St John the Baptist. Essoins for Ellis de Grendon and Richard Du, attorneys of dean and chapter. To octave of Michaelmas. [*rot. 63*]

The assize was to be exacted because no-one came. Sheriff to have them etc. [*rot. 64*]

Quindene of Michaelmas. By their attorney the dean and chapter said that the assize ought not to be taken since the church was not vacant and was occupied before the sueing out of the king's writ. Asked by whose presentation this was done, they replied that it was their right and asked for judgment on the writ. Gilbert de Thornton for the king denied their right and sought enquiry by assize, the charter of feoffment granting them advowson to be produced as evidence. He also questioned whether or not the church could be said to be filled. The dean and chapter said that Levenot was the last parson presented by a true patron and that after his death his son had held the church and so from father to son until six weeks before the king's writ. They declared themselves ready to verify their claim and sought judgment on the writ. [*rot. 38d*]

Octave of Hilary 1282. Essoin for Richard, attorney of the dean and chapter. [*rot. 72*]

12 Nov. 1282 at Rhuddlan. Quitclaim to the bishop, dean and chapter of Coventry and Lichefeld of the king's right of advowson, the defendants having come to the king in person during the pleadings, petitioning him to inspect the charters of John and Henry touching the advowson and to give them the benefit thereof. [*Cal.Pat.R. 1281–92, 50*]

13 June 1283 at Conwy. Acquittance to dean and chapter of Lychefeld for payment to king's clerk, William de Perton, by the hand of master John de Cravene at Chester on the morrow of St Mark 11 Edw. I of 500 marks in part payment of 1,000 marks fine for his quitclaim of the advowson. [*Cal.Pat.R. 1281–91, 67*]

A53 Ref. 242
Octave of St John the Baptist. Essoin for Richard Huberd, attorney of Maud le Surreys. Ralph le Wyne, warrantor of Margery Kynne, to be

exacted. To Michaelmas three weeks. [*rot. 62d*]

Quindene/three weeks Easter 1282 Westminster. Ralph le Wyne again vouched by Maud. To have him at Shrewsbury at Michaelmas three weeks. [CP 40/45 rot. 34d]

Morrow of All Souls at Shrewsbury 1282. Ralph Wynne did not come. Sheriff had done nothing etc. To be summoned for Hilary three weeks when sheriff to hear judgment on himself. [CP 40/47 rot. 82.]

A54   Ref. 709

Quindene of Trinity. Simon de Gousil said he claimed free chase in lands the hereditary right of the ancestors of Maud de Gousil who enfeoffed him. He was seised of free chase and thus of free warren since chase included warren. That he had used such a liberty after he was enfeoffed, he put himself on the country. Gilbert de Thornton for the king sought enquiry as to Maud's ancestors, her use of the liberty and continuity of their seisin. Sheriff to have 12 impartial jurors at the quindene of Michaelmas. [JUST 1/500A rot. 8d]

A55   Ref. 713

Quindene of Trinity. It was presented elsewhere before the justices in eyre in Derby in the Ragman Pleas for Morleyston that Spondon was the king's manor in ancient time and that Edmund the king's brother now held it. By attorney he said that he held nothing in demesne in that vill but in fee and service of freemen, also liberties, namely view of frankpledge, assize of bread and ale, gallows, waif, infangenthief and blood-shedding. It was likewise presented by that wapentake that the hundred of Gresley was in the hands of the heirs of the earl of Chester. Edmund said that the hundred was in his hand because he had the estate of Robert de Ferrars earl of Derby and that Ranulph, former earl of Chester, gave that hundred in free marriage with Agnes his sister to William de Ferrars, grandfather of Robert, and that he, Edmund, had not encroached on the king nor any of his ancestors. This he was ready to prove by the country or in whatever way the court decided. He also sought judgment as to whether he need answer without the king's writ.

It was also presented that the wapentakes of Ludcherch, Wyrkesworth, Apeltre and Repindon were in Edmund's hands. By attorney he said that he held only half of Ludcherche, a fourth part of Reppindon and the whole of Apeltre. He never encroached in those wapentakes on the king nor any of his ancestors. Gilbert de Thornton could not deny this, so it was adjudged that Edmund was without day and the king should take nothing by this presentment but might take action by writ.

As to the wapentake of Wyrkesworth, he said that he held it by warrant of the present king who gave him the wapentake, and the manors of Wirkesworth and Esseburn and confirmed by his charter to have and to hold to Edmund and his heirs of the king and his heirs with knights' fees, advowsons of churches, all liberties, free customs and all other things pertaining to those manors and wapentake forever, in exchange for the county and castle of Kermerdyn and Cardygan and the lands and tenements which Edmund held in that county and that he rendered and quitclaimed them to the king for himself and his heirs forever, doing service of two knights' fees to the king for those manors and wapentake. He proffered the king's charter attesting these gifts and grants and sought judgment as to whether he need answer the king. So Edmund was without day. [JUST 1/500A m. 8d; *C.Ch.R. 1257–1300*, 215].

A56 Ref. 736

Octave of St John the Baptist. Essoin for attorneys of Roger bishop of Coventry and Lichefeld, Nicholas de Wyvlegh and Norman le Usser against the king in a plea of *quo warranto*. [*rot. 61*]

Easter 1283 John de Kirby sends word on behalf of the lord king that the suit which the king has against Roger bishop of Coventry and Lichfield with respect to the manor of Sawley with its soke and appurtenances in Derbyshire, should be put in respite for various reasons until a fortnight after next Michaelmas. [KB 27/75, rot. 2, printed in *Select Cases in Court of King's Bench* (Selden Soc. lv), 115]

Essoins only were recorded at Lincoln for the following cases adjourned from Derby

A57 Ref. 261

Octave of St John the Baptist. Essoins for attorneys of both parties. Jury to be exacted because no-one came. To Michaelmas three weeks. [*rot. 61*]

A58 Ref. 118

Octave of St John the Baptist. Essoin for John le Fowen. To hear judgment at Michaelmas three weeks. [*rot. 61*]

Michaelmas quindene/three weeks at Shrewsbury 1282. Because John le Fowen could show nothing of the remise or quitclaim, nor could he say anything whereby Oliver ought not to have his seisin, it was adjudged that

Oliver should recover seisin and Roger have land from John to the value. John was to be in mercy. [CP 40/47 rot. 35.]

A59   Ref. 267
Octave of St John the Baptist. Essoin for John de Morley. [*rot. 62*]

A60   Ref. 258
Octave of St John the Baptist. Essoin for William Brun. To Michaelmas three weeks. [*rot. 62*]

A61   Ref. 259
Octave of St John the Baptist. After the view. Essoin for Richard and Walter de Morley. To Michaelmas three weeks. [*rot. 62d*]

A62   Refs. 275–7
Trinity three weeks. Essoin for Roger le Bret. [*rot. 59d*]
   Octave of St John the Baptist. Essoins for Roger and William de Staynesby. [*rot. 62d*]
   Quindene of St John the Baptist. Essoins for Roger, William and John de Heriz. To Michaelmas three weeks. [*rot. 63*]

A63   Ref. 714
Octave of St John the Baptist. Essoins for Nicholas de Clifton and Ralph Saucheverel, attorneys of the abbot of Chester against the king. [*rot. 61*]

APPENDIX B

ESTREATS OF FINES AND AMERCEMENTS

Crown Pleas	No. of items	£	s.	d.
High Peak	89	86	16	6
Scarsdale	90	[a]82	2	5½
Wirksworth	55	30	8	4
Repton	63	57	2	2
Litchurch	55	54	5	2
Appletree	70	73	7	4
Morleyston	43	34	0	4
Ashbourne	18	41	19	8
Bakewell	16	17	11	5
Chesterfield	7	4	13	4
Derby	29	21	13	4
Totals	535	£504	0	0½

[a] Takes account of seven deletions, total £19 6s. 3d., for chattels of felons which bailiff was to recover and pay at two named terms (**786**).

Civil Pleas	No. of items	£	s.	d.
Withdrawal/non-prosecution	60	18	16	8
Licence to concord	39	16	10	0
False claim	17	4	6	8
Unjust detention	9	3	5	0
Disseisin	3	1	0	0
Attaint	1	1	0	0
Default	1	1	0	0
Trespass	1	1	0	0
Issues of Land	1	2	0	0
Totals	132	£48	18	4

Total items in Estreats Roll	667			
Total issues		£552	18	4½

NUMBERS AND TYPES OF ACTIONS

	Enrol-ments	Actions		Enrol-ments	Actions
Rights to land			**Personal liberty**		
entry	54	49	**and status**		
novel disseisin	37	35	naifty	3	3
warranty	31	31	proof of liberty	1	1
right	28	26			
			The person and		
Dower and formedon			**chattels**		
dower	16	16	debt	9	9
formedon	1	1	covenant	8	7
			detinue	5	5
Services and incidents			trespass	3	3
customs and services	5	5	replevin	1	1
mesne, quittance	8	7			
			Advowson: utrum		
Rights over land			advowson	2	1
common pasture	8	8	darrein presentment	1	1
estovers	3	3	utrum	1	1
multure	1	1			
			Miscellaneous		
Custody of land			attachment	1	1
custody of part of manor	1	1	sheriff's payment of		
			issues	1	1
Torts to land			memo	1	1
nuisance	3	3	acknowledgment of grant	1	1
waste	1	1	handing over of charters	1	1
			escheat	1	1
Limited descents			royal writ re attorney	1	1
mort d'ancestor	37	37	appointment of attorney	1	1
aiel	14	13			
cosinage	3	3			

Total: 292 enrolments (278 cases)

Linked Enrolments: Entry 67/75: 69/100: 123/284: 140/272: 223/292:
Covenant 263/279: Aiel 65/209: Novel disseisin 143/147/148, 128/252:
Advowson 68/225: Right 71/130, 92/120: Mesne 10/287

Numbers of enrolments in order of frequency: entry 54, novel disseisin 39, mort d'ancestor 37, warranty 31, right 28, dower 16, aiel 14, debt 9, covenant, mesne, common pasture 8 each, customs and services 6, detinue, personal freedom 4 each, trespass, estovers, nuisance, cosinage 3 each, advowson 2, formedon, replevin, multure, waste, utrum, darrein presentment, attachment, note of sheriff's payment, memo, acknowledgment of grant, handing over of charters, escheat, writ re royal servant, appointment of attorney, custody of part of manor 1 each.

APPENDIX D

NON-PROSECUTIONS AND WITHDRAWALS

Non prosecutions	66
novel disseisin	16
mort d'ancestor (1 later quitclaimed, **248**)	14
entry (1 cancelled then later concorded, **69**, **100**)	12
aiel	4
2 each of cosinage, covenant, detinue, dower, trespass, warranty (1 covenant later concorded, **263**, **279**)	12
1 each of attachment, customs and services, escheat, formedon, proof of liberty, naifty, replevin, *utrum*	8
Withdrawals	18
novel disseisin (1 later quitclaimed, **199**)	7
entry	4
right (1 in suit with several claims, **72**)	2
1 each of covenant, dower, mort d'ancestor, naifty, nuisance	5

After adjournment within the eyre at Derby, 2 withdrawn (**35**, **153**).
Later concorded: **67** [**75?**], **286** [A1]; quitclaimed, **199**.

Reasons given for withdrawal	10
defendant's co-feoffee (wife) not named in writ	2
defendant says tenement was wife's at time of marriage	1
defendant cannot answer as does not hold in entirety	1
defendant says nuisance, if any, by other	1
defendant questions plaintiff's account of demise of tenement	1
defendant jointly seised with wife not named in writ	1
defendant cannot answer without the king	1
defendant denies entry by person named in writ	1
defendant says writ does not run as tenement is within ancient demesne of the crown	1
Amercement of non-prosecutors	
amercements of selves/sureties enrolled in estreats of fines etc.	53
not thus recorded though stated to be amerced	8

pardoned amercements by justices   2
pledged faith (1 pardoned)   2

Issues of non-prosecution amercements
44 @ 6s. 8d., 12 @ 3s. 4d., 1 @ 10s., 1 @ 13s. 4d., total £17 16s. 8d.

Issues of withdrawal amercements
1 @ 13s. 4d., 1 @ 6s. 8d., total £1

Total issues of non-prosecutions and withdrawals   £18 16s. 8d.

DEATHS BY MISADVENTURE AND DEODANDS

Entry	Cause of death	Deodand	s.	d.
418	Drowning: fall from horse	horse	10	0
419	Drowning: fall from horse	horse	6	8
421	Falling from horse	horse	6	8
423	Killing by boar [child]	boar	2	6
426	Crushing: fall of ruinous house	house	1	3
438	Drowning in well	–	-	-
439	Falling from beam	beam		6
443	Scalding: fall into vat	vat	1	0
446	Falling from cart	cart & horse	8	8
447	Falling from oak tree	oak tree	1	6
452	Crushing: fall of ruinous kitchen	kitchen	2	4
475	Drowning: fall from weak horse	horse	5	0
476	Drowning: fall from mare	mare	5	0
496	Drowning: fall from boat	boat	2	0
499	Drowning: fall from boat	boat	1	0
501	Crushing by mill wheel	wheel & spindle	1	0
505	Drowning: fall from plank at mill	wheel & plank	2	0
509	Drowning in well [child]	–	-	-
531	Falling from cart	cart & horse	6	8
556	Drowning in stream	–	-	-
559	Crushing: fall of haystack	haystack	2	0
562	Crushing in marl pit	–	-	-
564	Striking by tame stag	stag	3	0
567	Freezing to death	–	-	-
569	Drowning	–	-	-
573	Falling from cart	cart	5	7
574	Falling from cart	cart	9	8
575	Crushing by cart of firewood	cart & horses	11	0
620	Drowning	–	-	-
638	Striking by horse	horse & saddle	40	0
660	Drowning: fall from boat	boat	2	0

31 deaths by misadventure involving 35 persons   £6 17 0

12 by drowning, 7 by falls, 5 by crushing, 3 by animals, 2 at mills, 1 by freezing, 1 by scalding.

24 deodands.

APPENDIX F

CHATTELS OF FELONS INCLUDING SUICIDES

Entry	£	s.	d.	Entry	£	s.	d.
405		2	6	467			5
406		4	0	467		2	6
408			3	467		2	0
409		12	4	467		2	0
409		11	4	468	1	14	2
411s		5	1	468d	2	8	8
412		10	0	468	2	13	11
416		4	6	468d	2	0	3
417		9	2	468	1	0	2
420		2	5	468d	1	18	0
422			8	468d	2	0	3
424		1	5	468d	1	0	4
425		6	2	468d	2	13	6
427w	1	6	4	468d	7	5	3
432		2	0	474	1	7	8
434	3	11	10	477		7	0
435w		13	2½	478		5	0
436		6	0	479		7	10
442		11	8	479		6	8
444		3	0	482w		18	0
445w		9	11	484		2	8
448		1	6	484		5	4
449		3	0	486		1	0
450			4	486			6
451		1	0	486			2
453	1	17	7	486			6
453	3	15	5	486		1	3
453	2	5	5	486		3	0
457		1	2	486		8	0
467		8	0	486		3	5
467	1	11	0	493		1	0
467		1	5	494s	6	6	6
467		1	5	500		13	4
467		7	8	503		7	2
467		2	1	504		10	0
467			9	506w	1	18	0

Entry	£	s.	d.	Entry	£	s.	d.
510		1	0	584	13	0	2
511		12	0	587		1	3
512		3	0	588			8
513		1	0	589		5	0
523			10	592		9	0
523		4	6	594			6
523		1	0	599	1	11	4
523		2	6	601		1	0
525		8	8	602		7	6
525	1	4	7	602		5	5
525	1	0	0	604		2	0
529		10	0	618	2	6	8
530		1	0	619	1	5	0
534		8	0	622	5	5	0
537s			6	624		10	0
540	8	18	4	633			7
542		14	6	633		3	6
543		5	0	635			6
548		16	6	636		1	6
548		10	0	637		2	4
548			6	645w		4	8
548			2	645		1	0
548		2	0	645w		7	4
550s	2	12	0	646		3	0
555	1	10	0	647			4
558	1	10	0	653		3	5
560		4	6	654	1	12	0
563		2	0	655	1	16	9
565	1	5	5	656			8
566		2	0	657			6
571		6	4	661			9
572		9	4	664		11	3
576	9	4	0	667	1	3	8
576		8	6	667		6	0
579		12	0	667w	2	6	8
581	1	15	0				

Abbreviations: d deleted; *s* suicides; *w* year, day and waste included.

INDEX OF PERSONS AND PLACES

Places in Derbyshire are arranged under civil parishes as given in K. Cameron, *The place-names of Derbyshire* (English Place-Name Society, 1959). County suffixes are given only for places outside Derbyshire. All place-name variants in the text are indexed and are cross-referenced to the modern spelling. Where the Ordnance Survey spelling differs from that in Cameron, the former is given. The abbreviation 'h.w.' means 'his wife'.

Auderwyk, Audewerk: *see* Aldwark
Audley (Aldedeley, Aud(e)deley, Audele,
  Audeley(e), Audydelay, Dodeleye),
  Adam de 545, 817
  Thomas de 568, 828; and Agnes h.w. 162
  William de 228, 245, 487, A20
  Henry, brother of 228, A20
  James, father of A20
Auferton: *see* Alfreton
Auger, Robert son of Thomas 505
Aula, de: *see* Hall
Ault Hucknall, Astwith (Estewayt, Est(th)-
  wayt, Estweit, Eswheyt) in, Robert de
  52, 146, 173, 862, 873; and Emma h.w.
  261
  Hardwick (Herdewyk) in, William de, *al.*
    Stainsby 275, 385
  Rowthorn (Routhorn) in 775
  Stainsby (Staynes-, Staynis-, Steines-,
    Stennes-, Steyne(s)-, Steynis-, Steyn-
    nesby) in 275, 435, 446, 464, 466,
    734, 774, 784
  manor of 734
  Jocelin de 275
  William de, *al.* de Hardwick 243, 466,
    655, 703, 750, 787, 850, A62
Avice, Hugh son of 634
Avota, William son of 243
Axstel, Peter 320, A12
Ayl(e)waston: *see* Elvaston
Ayncurt, Aynekurth: *see* Deincourt
Aytrop', John de 251
Aywaldeston: *see* Elvaston
Azelford: *see* Eyam, Hazelford in

Babington (Babengton), Hugh de, former
  sheriff 401, 453, 454, 578, 697, 698,
  782
  Thomas de 698
Bache, Roger de la 467, 785
Badington (Badinton), Richard de 565, 827
Bag(g)epuz: *see* Bakepus
Baggelane, in Derby 671
Baghwel: *see* Bakewell
Bailiff (Bayllyf), Ralph le, of Beighton 434,
  773
Bailliolo: *see* Balliol
Bakepus (Bag(g)epuz, Bakepuz), Henry de,
  402, 619, 700
  Ralph son of 619, 842
  John son of Peter de 48
  Robert de 239, 310, A37
Baker (Pestur, Pistor, Pystor), Henry le, of

Matlock 487, 795
  John 755
  Nicholas 486, 794
  Simon 662
Bakewell (Baghwel, Bathec- Batheke-well,
  Bauc- Bauke-well(e), Bauk(es)well(e),
  Bawell), 12, 36, 41, 91, 96, 337, 432,
  634, 635, 638, 639, 643, 685, 846
  bailiffs of, Cantia (Kantia), Walter de 643
  Hecham (Hethinton), John de 639, 644,
    847
  Lucas, Richard 747, 754, 772
  Wyne, Ralph le 91
  church of 633, 636, 637
  advowson of 247
  jury of 754
  manor of 725
  Crown pleas of 633–45
  amercements from 845–7
  shops in 124, 640
  Catcliffe (Cateclif, Catteclyve, Catteclive)
    in, Adam de 5, 750, 756, 856
  William de, and Alice h.w. 14, 372;
    Agnes 858
  William, son of William de 649
  Dagnall (Agenhal, Dakenale), in,
    Thomas de 645
Bakewell, Hubert de 633, 845
  Hugh de 572, 829
  John de, and Cecilia h.w. (former wife of
    Roger Theobaud, q.v.) 203
  Robert son of Richard de 36
  Thomas son of Maud de, clerk 633, 845
Baldwin (Baldewin, -wyne), Geoffrey son of
  607, 840
Balioyn: *see* Balon
Ball (Balle), Thomas 548, 818
  William, 254; of Shirley 61, 863
Balliol (Bailliolo, Ballyolo), Devorgilla de
  705
  John de 521, 807
  William de 135
Ballyolo: *see* Balliol
Balon (Balioyn), Geoffrey 136
  Roger 136, 870
Balthesweyt, Henry de 321
Barber, Thomas le 673
Bard, Joan widow of Simon 296
Bardolf, Thomas and William his son 726
Barent, William A4
Baret, Henry 93, 867
  John 513, 803
  Simon 166

Walter, 493

Gadereys, Robert 616
Gaham, Roger de 445, 780
Gale, Henry 467, 785
Galion (Galyon), Henry 547, 817
Galyn, John 194, 875
Gambon (Gaumbon), John 162, 183, 872
Gamel (Gamell), Richard 623, 843
   Richard son of 630
Garendon (Gern(e)don), Leics., Robert de
   304, 744
Gardiner, Lecia sister of Hugh le 558
Gathird, William le, of Repton 497
Gaumbon: see Gambon
Gaunter, Avice daughter of Emmma le 231
   Henry le, in Derby 80, 737; and Eustacia
     his wife 62, 203
   Henry le, of Sawley 737
   Nicholas le, Hawise h.w. and Avice her
     sister 340
Ged, Robert 565
Gelyns, John A4
Geoffrey, Adam son of 453, 455
   Hugh son of 289
   Richard son of 481, 793, A44
   Roger son of 555, 820
   Stephen son of 595
   William son of 659
Gerard, Gilbert 798; and Alice h.w. 500
Geri: see Gery
Gern(e)don: see Garendon
Gerneter, Henry son of John le 575
Gernun, William 725
Gery (Geri), Roger 116, 667, 757, 853
Gilbert, John son of Robert son of 424, 769
   Reynold and Serlo, sons of 472
   William, 144
Gildeford (Gilford), Robert son of John de
   217, 879
Gippesmere (Gyppesmere, Kypsmere),
   William de 8, 857
   William de, in Elmton 439
Glapwell (Glappwell, Glapwell(e)) 436, 775
   Richard de, and Avice h.w. 254, 372
   Simon de 750
Glide (Glyde), Robert and Simon 453, 468,
   786, 787
Glossop, Whitfield (Qwytefeld), in, William
   de, and Richard his brother 432
Glovere, John le, and Isabella h.w. 673
Glyde: see Glide
Goda, a felon 524

Robert son of 610, 840
Godale (Godal, Godhale), Roger 240
   Robert 595
   William 479, 792
Gode, Roger 337
Godechild (Godchild), Hugh 552, 819
Godladde, Adam and Ralph his brother 576,
   830
Golde, Litholf and Roger 176
Goldington: see Coddington
Golyn, John 251, 580, 832
Gomme (Gumme), Adam son of Geoffrey,
   453, 455, 468, 786
Gos, Alan and Hawise h.w. 84
Goulesworth (Gouseworth), Thomas de 486,
   794
Goushill (Gousel(l), Gousil, Gousyl), Simon
   de 3, 243, 686, 709, A54
   Maud mother of 709, A54
Grace Dieu, Leics., prioress of 224
Grange (de Grangia, Graunge), Richard de la
   750
   Robert de 553
   Roger de, of Chesterfield 33
   Roger de la, and Alice h.w. 103
Gratton 426, 432
   Thomas de 686, 691, 747
Graunge: see Grange
Grauntovere: see Mickleover
Grave, Brother Walter de la, 339, A32
Great Clifton (Magna Clifton) [near Ash-
   bourne] 143, 147, 148
Great Ireton (Magna Irton) 136
Great Longstone (Magna Longesdon) 416,
   765
   Robert son of Richard de 645
Great Rowsley (Roulesley, Roulislee, Roun-
   esle, Roysle) 406, 423, 432, 760
   Adam 686
   Adam son of Peter de 13
   Robert son of Robert de 359
Great Tapton (Magna Tapton) 223, 271
   see also Tapton
Great Wilne (Magna Wilne) 126, A51
Grendon, Ellis de A52
   John de, and Joan h.w. 290, A50
   William de 580, 832
Grene [near Buxton?] 45
Grene, John de la 819; (de la More) 552
   Simon de la 486, 794
Grenehull, James de 355
Grenley, Hugh de 10, 311
Gresley (Gresele, Greseley(e)) 502, 507, 800

William le, juror in Scarsdale 750
William le, of Stanton 742
William le, of Wilne 548, 818
Marston (Marchenton, Marc(h)inton, Mech-
    inton, Merchin-, Merchington, Merch-
    yngton, Mercinton, Mersin(g)ton) 48,
    567, 828
  Loneta de 567
  Nicholas de 624
  Roger de 3, 48, 50, 118, 142, 206, 243,
    260, 263, 399, 749, 862; and Eleanor
    h.w. 48, 290
  Stephen de 386
  Thomas son of Geoffrey de 567, 828
Marston on Dove (Merston, Mersington)
    530, 559, 823
  Robert son of Ralph de 559
Marston Montgomery (Mersington Mongom-
    ery, - Mungomery, Muntegomeri) 561,
    575, 825
Martel, Nicholas 54, 228, 327, 863
Martyn, John 325
  John son of Hugh 96, A47
  William, and Isabella h.w. 220, 879
  William, of Linton 504, 800
    Robert brother of 504
Maskary, Simon 165
Matinel, — 524
  Goda sister of 524
Matlock (Matlok(e)) 479, 487, 792, 795
  Ralph de 473, 788
  Roger son of Laurence de 487
Matthew, Hugh son of 753
  William son of 136, 870
Matton, Henry son of Richard de 240
Maunderell: see Manderell
Maunefeld: see Mansfield
Maunnecestre: see Manchester
May, Adam le A50
Measham (Maiseam, Maysam, Meisham,
    Meiss(h)am, Meys(h)am) 172, 249, 506
  Roger de 586
  Thomas de 376
  William de 249, 376, 753
    Roger son of 553
Mechinton: see Marston
Medewe, Reynold del, and Emma h.w. 16
Megre, Robert le 233, A2
Meillor (Meillur, Melier, Meyl(l)ur), Richard
    le, and Petronilla h.w. 113, 114, 179,
    294, 338, 344, 868, (formerly wife of
    Robert Ingram) A5
Meisham, Meiss(h)am, Meissam: see Meas-

ham
Melbourne (Melburn(e), Mel(l)eburn) 144,
    507, 524, 802
  church of 516
  park of 524
  King's Newton (Kynges Neuton) in 798
Meleford, John de A12
Melier: see Meillor
Melleburn: see Melbourne
Mellor (Melvere) 417, 766
  Robert de 686, 747
Melnhaue: see Heanor, Milnhay in
Melton: see Milton
Melvere: see Mellor
Menil: see Meynell
Mentham, John de 10, 287, A15
Mercaston (Morcanston, Morka(ne)ston,
    Mourstaldiston, Munkarston, Murcas-
    ton, Murdiston, Murka(ne)ston, Mur-
    keston) 26, 67, 75, 186, 565, 827, 859
  John son of Walter de 26
  Ralph son of Peter de 553
  Robert de 752
    Robert son of 67
  Walter son of Henry de 186
  William de 485
Mercer, Alexander le, of Ashbourne, Letitia
    widow of 87, 169, 191, 303, 317,
    366
    Robert son of 303, 317
  Henry le, of Osmaston 578
  John le 755
  Ranulph le 350
  Walter le, and Edith h.w. 18, 858
  William le, of Ashbourne 688
  William le, of Repton 515
Merchants 623, 625, 643; of Society of
    Scotti 46, 47
Merchin(g)ton, Merchyn(g)ton, Mercinton:
    see Marston
Merlache: see Darley, Morledge in
Merond (Meronde), Robert 540, 815
Mersin(g)ton: see Marston
Merston: see Marston on Dove
Messer, Hugh le 163
  William le 609
Mettingham, John de, justice 730
Meuton: see Milton
Meverel (Meverell), Thomas, 66; and Agnes
    h.w. 290
Mey, John le 654
  Emma widow of 654, 850
Meyl(l)ur: see Meillor

SUBJECT INDEX